Voices
from
Under _____

Contributions in Afro-American and African Studies
Series Advisers: John W. Blassingame and Henry Louis Gates, Jr.

Voices from Under

BLACK NARRATIVE IN LATIN AMERICA AND THE CARIBBEAN

Edited by William Luis

CONTRIBUTIONS IN AFRO-AMERICAN AND
AFRICAN STUDIES, NUMBER 76

GREENWOOD PRESS
WESTPORT, CONNECTICUT · LONDON, ENGLAND

Library of Congress Cataloging in Publication Data

Main entry under title:

Voices from under.

(Contributions in Afro-American and African studies,
ISSN 0069-9624 ; no. 76)
Bibliography: p.
Includes index.
1. Blacks in literature—Addresses, essays, lectures.
2. Latin American literature—Black authors—History and
criticism—Addresses, essays, lectures. 3. Caribbean
literature—Black authors—History and criticism—Ad-
dresses, essays, lectures. I. Luis, William. II. Series.
III. Title: Black narrative in Latin America and the
Caribbean.
PN56.3.B55V64   1984   809.3′9352039608   83-22792
ISBN 0-313-23826-X (lib. bdg.)

Library of Congress Catalog Card Number: 83-22792
ISBN: 0-313-23826-X
ISSN: 0069-9624

First published in 1984

Greenwood Press
A division of Congressional Information Service, Inc.
88 Post Road West
Westport, Connecticut 06881

Printed in the United States of America

10 9 8 7 6 5 4 3 2 1

Copyright Acknowledgments

Grateful acknowledgment is given for permission to reprint the following:

Lines from "Negus" in *The Arrivants: A New World Trilogy* by Edward Brathwaite. © 1978.
Oxford University Press. Reprinted with permission.

Excerpts from *The Autobiography of a Runaway Slave* by Esteban Montejo, edited by Miguel Barnet, translated by Jocasta Innes. © 1968. Pantheon Books, a Division of Random House, Inc.

Lyrics from "Babylon System" by Bob Marley. © 1979 Bob Marley Music Ltd. (ASCAP). All
rights administered by Almo Music Corp. (ASCAP) for the world. All rights reserved.

Brief extracts from Derek Walcott's poems, "Crusoe's Journal" and "Crusoe's Island" from *The
Castaway* and "Ruins of A Great House" from *In a Green Light* published by Jonathan Cape Ltd.

From John Milton's *Complete Poems and Major Prose,* ed. Merritt Y. Hughes. © 1957 Odyssey
Press. Permission given by Bobbs-Merrill Educational Publishing.

From "Song of Rising" published in *Dread Beat and Blood* by Linton Johnson. © 1975. Reprinted
by permission of Bogle-L'ouverture Publications Ltd.

In memory of all slaves and freed Blacks who died fighting for their freedom and in memory of Haitians who died on the seas escaping political persecution from their homeland.

For Sister Mary Edward, in memoriam.

I come to speak for your dead mouths.
Throughout the earth
let dead lips congregate,
out of the depths spin this long night to me
as if I rode at anchor here with you.
And tell me everything, tell chain by chain,
and link by link, and step by step;
sharpen the knives you kept hidden away,
thrust them into my breast, into my hands,
like a torrent of sunbursts,
and Amazon of buried jaguars,
and leave me cry: hours, days and years,
blind ages, stellar centuries.

And give me silence, give me water, hope.

Give me the struggle, the iron, the volcanoes.

Let bodies cling like magnets to my body.

Come quickly to my veins and to my mouth.

Speak through my speech, and through my blood.

> Pablo Neruda, *The Heights of Macchu Picchu*

And I would say more:
"My lips shall speak for miseries that have no mouths,
my voice shall be the liberty of those who languish in the
dungeon of despair."

Aimé Césaire, Return to My Native Land

Contents

Acknowledgments

This collection was conceived at Cornell University while writing on the Cuban author César Leante. As I sought diversion from my own work, I became acquainted with Richard Jackson's *The Black Image in Latin American Literature* and Miriam DeCosta's anthology *Blacks in Hispanic Literature*. While reading other related works, I noticed that there was a vacuum in and a need to bring unity to the field of black narrative in Latin America and the Caribbean. Not understanding the full implication of my ideas, I set out to commission essays from both established and aspiring scholars to compose the present volume. It was only after a few years, much reading and rereading, writing and rewriting that I became aware of the importance, complexity and demand of my task. My optimism in search of a meaningful dialogue with the academic profession provided the enthusiasm to continue my work.

As I approach the completion of this collection, I would like to thank my professors at Cornell for providing me with a thirst for knowledge. Of these, I owe special gratitude to my advisor, Roberto González Echevarría, and to Professors Ciriaco Morón Arroyo, John Kronik, Enrico Mario Santí and Arthur Paris. Colleagues at Dartmouth College also contributed immensely. Of these, I would like to thank those in the Department of Spanish and Portuguese and in particular those in the African and Afro-American Studies Program for allowing me to coteach, with Professor Richard Joseph, an interdisciplinary course on Africa and the Caribbean.

I would also like to thank Professors Henry Louis Gates and Robert Márquez for having faith in my project and supporting my ideas. I owe a special debt to Lemuel Johnson and Robert Márquez and Roberto González Echevarría for their valuable suggestions. Finally, I would like to thank Dianne Ladd for her help in typing the manuscript, my mother Petra, and Stephanie Garceau for their moral support and Linda Garceau for her assistance with the manuscript.

Voices from Under

1

History and Fiction: Black Narrative in Latin America and the Caribbean

William Luis

I

The study of Blacks as a unifying force in Latin American and Caribbean literatures is a recent venture in literary criticism. Only in the last twenty-five years have critics seriously analyzed narratives of and about Blacks not as a manifestation of a particular country's national literature but as a basis for a comparative approach to Western literary studies.[1] An analysis of Blacks outside the context of a national literature or a region provides insights into the lives of a people whose destiny was altered and determined by others. The enslavement, oppression and marginality of Blacks in Africa and in the New World are what brings their history and literatures together.

The literature of and about Blacks allows for another reading of history. If the history of America was conceived as a European invention[2] and dramatized by the search for El Dorado, black narrative in Latin America and the Caribbean offers an alternative to a European understanding of America. Blacks as a people have experienced history according to different circumstances, not as the initiators and recorders of events, but as the victims of actions imposed upon them by others. The black concept of history is different. Their view of events is a product not of a dominant but of a marginal position in society. And the literature of and about Blacks reflects this reality. The present study attempts to rescue black narrative in Latin America and the Caribbean from the fringe and bring it to the foreground of Western literature. As a marginal part of Western culture, the black experience is at odds with the dominant one. The tension between the two, one attempting to subvert the other, provides an understanding of Blacks in literature and, at the same time, allows for another perspective on the white dominant view. What may have been an objective perception of history is now seen as a writing clouded by European language and culture. Black literature exists as a historical continuum in Western literature but also in opposition to it. An understanding of some important events helps us to come to terms with current developments in black literary criticism.

Narrative of and about Blacks in Latin America and the Caribbean is not a recent phenomenon. Present-day readers may be familiar with Alejo Carpentier's *The Kingdom of This World* (1949), Miguel Barnet's *The Autobiography of a Runaway Slave* (1966), V. S. Naipaul's *Guerrillas* (1975) and Michael Thelwell's *The Harder They Come* (1980). However, few are acquainted with early accounts of and about Blacks. The presence of Blacks in Latin American and Caribbean literatures is as early as the "discovery" and conquest of America and can be traced to book 3 of Bartolomé de las Casas' *History of the Indies*, written between 1511 and 1520. A known supporter of the native inhabitants of the New World, Las Casas was convinced by some residents that if permission were granted to import black slaves from Castile, the rapidly dying Amerindians would be spared. In the interest of the Amerindians, Las Casas, who enjoyed the king's favor, asked Ferdinand to sanction the transport of some slaves to the New World. Although Las Casas was, in part, responsible for the mass introduction of slaves into the New World, it was not long before he regretted his decision, realizing that one type of slavery was as bad as another. Las Casas even accused himself of ignorance and doubted if he would ever be excused in the eyes of God.[3]

The first American poem of literary merit in which Blacks appear is that of Alonso de Ercilla y Zuñiga's *La araucana* (1569–1594). This epic poem describes the Spanish campaigns against the Araucanian Indians of Chile. The executioner of the brave chief, Caupolicán, was a Black, a Wolof of Senegal. In the poem Caupolicán is so offended that his executioner is a Black that he aids in his own death by sitting on a sharpened stake.[4] The presence of the black slave in poetry is also as early as Silvestre de Balboa's 1608 poem "Espejo de paciencia," which narrates the capture of Bishop Juan de las Cabezas Altamirano by the French pirate Gilberto Girón. In the poem, the Ethiopian slave Salvador, a savior, rescues the bishop, defeats and decapitates the French pirate in Cuba and is rewarded with his freedom.

In the nineteenth century there was a dramatic increase in the number of works by and about Blacks in Latin America and the Caribbean. During this period, some Blacks learned to read and write, and liberal intellectuals used the black theme to combat the abuses of the slavery system. In the Spanish Caribbean this was also a period in which slaves outnumbered Whites and in which the tension between Whites and Blacks increased. For both slaves and slave owners the Haitian Revolution of 1804 was a recent event that could occur again. The British attempt to end the slave trade forced it to go underground; slavery and the slave trade became even more oppressive and ruthless. In the nineteenth century most African slaves were transported to Cuba and Brazil. By the mid-nineteenth century they were the only two countries in Latin America and the Caribbean still committed to the slave trade. The continuation of slavery during the development of narrative form allowed for it to be incorporated in the literature of Cuba and Brazil. Literature, in part, became a way of criticizing slavery. In Cuba the literary response to this turbulent phase in the history of slavery can be seen in Domingo del Monte's literary circle and the Cuban antislavery narrative of Anselmo Suárez y Romero's *Francisco* (1880), Félix Tanco y Bosmeniel's "Petrona y Rosalía" (1925), Gertrudis Gómez de Avellaneda's *Sab* (1841), Juan Francisco Manzano's "Life of a Negro Poet" (1840), Antonio Zambrana's *El negro Francisco* (1873) and Cirilo Villaverde's *Cecilia Valdés* (1882). Del Monte was indeed Cuba's most important literary promoter of the time. He encouraged his writer friends to write in a realistic manner that included portraying the theme of slavery.[5]

In South America the presence of Blacks in Brazilian literature increased after the 1850s due mainly to its abolitionist literature, which included the works of Joaquim Manuel de Macedo's *As Vítimas Algozes* (1869); Aluízio Azevedo's *O Mulato* (written 1879, 1881), *Casa de Pensão* (1884) and *O Cortiço* (1890); Júlio Ribeiro's *A Carne* (1888); and Adolfo Caminha's *Bom-Crioulo* (1895).[6] Although these and other works were influenced by European literary conventions, romanticism and realism in Cuba and naturalism in Brazil, they reflected the concern of the individual countries in which they emerged and denounced the slavery system through their tragic protagonists.

In the twentieth century the black theme took on a different form. The conspicuous presence of Blacks went beyond the geographic boundaries in which the literature was written. This period reflected the situations of Blacks in Latin America and the Caribbean but also became part of a European concern. Leo Frobenius's *The Black Decameron* (1910), Spengler's *Decline of the West* (1917) and Ortega y Gasset's *The Dehumanization of Art* (1925), among other works, signaled the change that was to occur.[7] Africa was seen as an exotic place, and Blacks became a theme of the avant-garde. Europe looked at Africa as a source of one alternative to Western culture. This process of simultaneous subversion and expansion of a dominant culture was captured by European art. For example, Apollinaire sculpted African statues and Picasso painted through black imagery and form his cubist "The Damsels from Avignon." Furthermore, the surrealists' emphasis on the subconscious made for an easier return to the primitive stage that Africa was assumed to represent. Europe's rediscovery of Africa also gave new meaning to the black theme in countries with black culture in Latin America and the Caribbean. Somewhat oddly, in spite of the European cultural rebellion, black writers living in Europe sometimes continued to look at themselves through European eyes. If poets like the Guadeloupean Gilbert de Chambertrand were still writing under the influence of the Parnassian movement, other more rebellious Francophone students, such as Etienne Léro, Jules Monnerot and René Ménil, sought to break with the past. They refused to assimilate into the dominant Western society and took pride in their racial and cultural differences. But these and other West Indian students lived in Paris and followed *la mode*; that is, their rebellion was a part of the avant-garde movements that attempted to undermine bourgeois realism. In 1932, Léro, Monnerot and Ménil founded *Légitime Défense*, a surrealist- and communist-inspired journal that opposed bourgeois culture.[8]

In an attempt to go beyond the concerns of *Légitime Défense*, Aimé Césaire, Léon Damas and Léopold Senghor created *L'Etudiant Noir* in 1934. The writers of the Negritude movement promoted black awareness and identity through poetry. Like other movements, Negritude formed part of a larger rebellion that was taking place in Europe. Ezekiel Mphalele's and Wole Soyinka's objections to Negritude are commonplace. Mphalele criticized the use of English or French to express African sentiments, while Soyinka questioned whether a "tiger has to express his tigritude."[9] Most of the poets of *L'Etudiant Noir* were from well-to-do families, lived in Paris and wrote "French French."[10]

By the same token, although the Negrismo movement of the 1920s and 1930s "deformed" the Spanish language to produce African sounds and rhythm, the more authentic social aspect of Negrismo as represented by Nicholás Guillén, Marcelino Arozarena and Regino Pedroso was inspired by their association with the Cuban Communist party. Other more innate movements began to influence the outcome of events of which Garvey's Universal Negro Improvement Association is an important part. But in spite of what may be perceived today as drawbacks to literary movements such as Negrismo and Negritude, writers like Guillén and Césaire played important roles in the dissemination of black identity throughout Latin America and the Caribbean.

Guillén and Césaire as representatives of the Spanish and French Caribbean, respectively, were not alone in the formulation of a black image. Their North American counterparts also helped to promote the black theme throughout Europe and the Americas. Writers like Claude McKay, Jean Toomer, Langston Hughes and Countee Cullen were in contact with African and West Indian writers living in Paris. Some of these writers even participated in Mademoiselle Nardal's literary salon and collaborated in her and Haitian Dr. Sajous's *La Revue du Monde Noir*, published in both French and English.[11] North American and Caribbean black writers were important for the literature of countries with a black population such as Uruguay. For example, the Uruguayan journal *Nuestra Raza* voiced the same concerns of other Blacks in the diaspora. Richard Jackson informs us that "in pursuit of its goal of fostering black consciousness and black pride, the journal devoted much of its space to commentary on black achievements outside the country."[12] Along with articles on Guillén, Antonio Maceo, Jesús Menéndez, René Maran and Machado de Assis, there are others, Jackson says, on Harrison Dillard, George Washington Carver, Booker T. Washington, Claude MacKay, Joe Louis, Jesse Owens, Langston Hughes, Marian Anderson, Paul Robeson, Ethel Waters and Duke Ellington. During this period there was an understanding of black issues on a global scale. In 1934, Guillén dedicated his poem "Sabá" to Langston Hughes, and the Scottsboro case of 1929, among other incidents concerning Blacks in the United States, was echoed in Regino Pedroso's "Hermano negro" in the pages of *Légitime Défense* and received wide support among the contributors of *Nuestra Raza*.[13]

The internal conditions of countries with black populations also affected the status of black literature in Latin America and the Caribbean. During the 1930s and 1940s the political and literary forces came together in the West Indies, resulting in an awakening national consciousness and the development of a national literature. As oppressed people, Blacks began to take hold of their destiny through their literature. The magazines published during the pre– and post–World War II periods reflected a sense of black self-awareness. For example, Jamaican writers Edna Manley, Philip Sherlock, Victor S. Reid and Roger Mais formed literary salons out of which emerged Manley's *Focus* in 1943. The importance of *Focus* for contemporary Jamaican literature is described as follows:

Focus signaled the beginning of a decidedly introspective and nationalistic approach to literature, marked by social protest and the growth of the People's National Party (PNP) headed by Norman Manley. Describing the Jamaican scene, authors began to portray the misery, poverty, and frustration they saw rather than to hide the real situation under an idyllic tropical camouflage. References to Africa and African culture increased as West Indian writers grappled with the question "Who am I?" A sense of embarrassment, ambivalence, and potential regarding their African heritage pervades literature and drama.[14]

Focus provided an outlet for literary expression previously not available. Out of the *Focus* group emerged the works of V. S. Reid—*New Day* (1949) and *Leopard* (1958)—and Roger Mais—*The Hills Were Joyful Together* (1953), *Brother Man* (1954), and *Black Lightning* (1955)—among others. Literature in other West Indian countries developed along the same lines as in Jamaica. In 1929, Alfred H. Mendes and C. L. R. James published *Trinidad*; in 1931, Albert Gomez edited *Beacon* in Trinidad; in 1942, Frank Colymore edited *Bim* in Barbados; and in 1945, A. J. Seymour published *Kyk-over-al* in what used to be known as British Guiana. In South America the second period of *Nuestra Raza* (1933–1948) and *Revista Uruguay* and Abdias do Nacimientos' *Quilombo* of the late 1940s in Brazil also reflected the concerns of Blacks for a literature in which they played an important part in their country's history.[15] These and other magazines provided an important outlet for writers in Latin America and the Caribbean.

The decade of the 1960s marked a significant stage in the development of black narrative, a period in literary history in which writers and critics became actively engaged in exploring and reevaluating the black image in Latin American and Caribbean literatures. This latest stage in black literature has allowed many to rethink the history of Blacks and analyze its past and present from another point of departure. If European writing created an interest in Blacks and Africa in the early part of the twentieth century, America in the second part of the century would be looking at Blacks and black culture not as an imported concept but as an integral part of the New World. It is from the perspective of Blacks and black culture as both an inherent part of and an alternative to a dominant Western literature and history that the black image is being explored by writers and critics alike. The present popularity of black literature is tied to the political and cultural events of the times. An overview of a sequence of events in literature and politics, mainly in the decade of the 1960s, helps to explain the growing interest in this literature.

In the 1960s, Cuba and the United States played important roles in the development of black narrative in Latin America and the Caribbean. The Castro revolution of 1959, the Bay of Pigs invasion of 1961 and the Cuban Missile Crisis of 1962 brought Cuba, in specific, and Latin America and the Caribbean, in general, to the attention of the world. A new confrontation between East and West in which world peace was threatened reached its most critical phase in the Caribbean. To some, this was no surprise. In a letter to Federico Henríquez y Carvajal dated March 25, 1895, José Martí already foresaw that the balance of the world would depend on a stable Caribbean.[16]

Cuba's economic, political and social policies and its potential influence on neighboring countries became the concern of the United States and Europe. The Cuban presence awoke a renewed interest on the part of the United States in the nations south of its border. But unlike in the past, where policy was geared toward individual countries, now the entire region became important. If Berlin occupied world attention during the 1950s, Cuba and its foreign policies would set the stage for the Cold War scenario in the decade of the 1960s and beyond. In 1960 the United States and other Western countries broke relations with Cuba. However, in spite of this political isolation and possibly because of it, Cuba, and consequently Latin America and the Caribbean, continued to be the focus of world attention.

Still, the tension existing between the United States and Cuba is not new and can be understood as the most recent stage in the two countries' historical relationship. Barry M. Blechman and William J. Durch outline the process involved in the following manner:

Cuba has figured prominently in U.S. security for 200 years, at times as an asset—as a base for U.S. warships in the Revolutionary War and for training U.S. forces in World War II. More often, however, Cuba has been seen as a threat—as a springboard for military forces directed against the U.S. heartland: British troops in 1812 and Soviet missiles in 1962.

Cuba also has figured as a political threat, the source of potential political contagion. Whether it was slave revolts in the nineteenth century or communism in the twentieth, the United States has worried constantly about the influence of Cuba on political developments in the United States and elsewhere in the Western Hemisphere.[17]

The possibility of a spread of communism throughout Latin America and the Caribbean forced the United States to become concerned with social progress in that area of the world. In 1961 the United States challenged Cuba's influence with Kennedy's Alliance for Progress, a ten-year economic and social program designed for development and reform in countries south of its border. This economic aid helped to expand important social structures that furthered interest in

Latin American politics, literature and culture, areas that contributed to the birth of the Latin American novel of the Boom period.

The Cuban presence affected the outcome of events in nearby countries. It certainly helped to promote Latin American and Caribbean culture in the United States and indeed influenced studies in U.S. institutions. Roberto González Echevarría explains the United States' response to Cuba as follows: "Only after 1959 did the United States begin to invest aggressively in the area of Latin American culture. The creation of many Latin American studies centers in U.S. universities came as a response to Cuban cultural activity, and large-scale projects—including the financing of literary journals—channeled resources into the cultural area in a way that had a crucial bearing on the creation of the new Latin American literature of the sixties." [18]

The study and promotion of Cuban and Latin American and Caribbean cultures aided the study of the Latin American novel, in general, and the black narrative, in specific. There is, however, another important event associated with the emergence of a black narrative in Latin America and the Caribbean. This event is primarily related to an awakening black consciousness and response to Blacks and black culture in the United States.

A new black awareness emerged from the civil rights movement of the 1950s and 1960s and the black power movement of the 1960s and spread rapidly to black communities in the United States and to other countries with a black population, including Australia. These movements underscored the importance of black culture that had already existed in the United States, as represented, for example, by the Harlem Renaissance. But, most importantly, they helped to broaden its popular appeal in a way that had been seen before perhaps only in the Garvey phenomenon of the 1920s. Just as the Cuban threat stimulated interest in and formation of Latin American Studies programs, the civil rights and black power movements paved the way for the creation of Black Studies programs in U.S. universities. The enrollment of black students in U.S. universities increased; and the number of black and white university students interested in black culture also increased during the 1960s. This pluralistic attempt at broadening the base of education facilitated an interest in all black culture, whether in the United States, Africa, Latin America, the Caribbean or the Pacific areas. Moreover, the number of black scholars and scholars interested in researching the various dimensions of the black experience also multiplied. In relative terms, national and foreign black intellectuals moved to positions of prominence including teaching and lecturing in U.S. universities. The concept of black pride provided a different way of looking at Blacks and black culture. Many analyzed and evaluated the black man's history in the United States, Latin America and the Caribbean from a different perspective: Instead of considering the Black as an outsider looking in, the black experience was perceived as an important center of American culture and society. Black and white writers, scholars and students alike, seized the black American experience as a means of evaluating and reevaluating the study of Blacks in the United States and in Latin America and the Caribbean.

The 1960s were also important years for the political destiny of West Indian countries. The struggle for independence of Anglophone countries would later become interrelated with the political events in these countries as well as the overall Caribbean political strategy of the 1960s. Political and economic problems both in England and its West Indian colonies during the 1930s led to social protest in its possessions: Trinidad in 1934 and 1937, Saint Kitts in 1935, Saint Vincent, Barbados and British Guiana in 1936 and Jamaica in 1935 and 1938. Anticolonialist sentiment in the British islands led to the independence of Jamaica and Trinidad and Tobago in 1962, Barbados and Guyana in 1966 and Grenada in 1974. However, the newly acquired independence of these countries occurred a few years after the triumph of the Cuban Revolution, a time in which Cuba and the United States were competing for hegemony in the Caribbean. The newly created nations were susceptible to special external pressures. For some countries Cuba represented a continuation of their own struggle against European and North American interests. For others the Castro government was an extension of Soviet influence in the Americas. Cuba and the United States each intended to bring these and other countries under its sphere of influence and gave their political and cultural systems recognition and unprecedented aid. For example, in 1972, Cuba established diplomatic relations with Guyana, Barbados, Trinidad and Tobago, and Jamaica. The political strategy continues with Reagan's Caribbean Basin Program of 1982 and with Cuban support of the recently defeated Manley government in Jamaica and of Grenada and Suriname until 1983. The tension in the Caribbean heightened most recently with a split in the Grenadian Central Committee of the New Jewel Party; that is, between the leftist policies of Maurice Bishop and the more pro-Cuban faction of generals Austin and Layne. The division resulted in the take-over of the Austin faction, the house arrest of Bishop, the protest by demonstrators who had gone to the Bishop residence to release him, and Bishop's subsequent death and that of Unison Whiteman, Minister of Foreign Affairs; Jacquelin Creft, Minister of Education; Vincent Noel, first Vice-President of the Grenada Trade Union Congress, and others. Under the guise of protecting American medical students, the U.S. intervened in the internal affairs of the small island and invaded Grenada on October 25, 1983, in order to put an end to its socialist government and Cuban influence and presence on the island. The U.S. government action served as a clear message regarding any initiative it would take to stop Cuban expansionism in the Caribbean and other regions. Moreover, the Reagan administration's actions attempted to reaffirm U.S. dominance in the Caribbean.

For some nations Cuba was something to be feared; for others Cuba was a symbol of their own struggles and a model to be followed. Additionally, these emerging nations represented votes in the United Nations to be sought after.

The desire for votes has been particularly true of the United States in its determination to isolate Cuba from all other Western countries and of Cuba's anticapitalistic and revolutionary policies. The political struggle, in part, resulted in the much-deserved publicity that West Indian writers have received in Cuba, the United States and other countries.

The recognition many black West Indian writers received during the 1960s is also tied to another historical event during this important decade. The recent popularity of black narrative in Latin America and the Caribbean is directly related to the literary and commercial enterprise of the Boom, a period in which the Latin American novel came to the foreground of Western literature. The birth of this novelistic movement can be traced to a combination of events in the late 1950s and early 1960s: to Jorge Luis Borges' joint acceptance with Samuel Beckett of the 1956 Formentor Prize for his *Ficciones*; to Jorge Amado's *Gabriela, cravo e canela*, which became the first Latin American best seller in the United States in 1959; and to St. John Perse's (Alexis Saint-Léger) Nobel Prize in 1960.[19] Writers like Julio Cortázar, Carlos Fuentes, José Donoso, Guillermo Cabrera Infante, Severo Sarduy and others received wide recognition, and their works were broadly circulated and translated into many languages, including English. Gabriel García Márquez' *One Hundred Years of Solitude* became an instant best seller. Cuba also participated in the promotion of the Boom novel. In 1960 Casa de las Américas was founded; its literary prizes, magazines and editorial house demonstrated Cuba's intention of breaking the cultural blockade against it and of establishing Havana as a major cultural center of Latin America and the Caribbean. It was mainly through Casa de las Américas and through the efforts of Carlos Franqui and his newspaper *Revolución* and its literary supplement, *Lunes de Revolución*, directed by Guillermo Cabrera Infante, that many liberal and left-wing intellectuals who identified with the revolution were invited to Cuba. The young Fuentes, Cortázar, García Márquez, René Depestre and others joined established Cuban writers like Alejo Carpentier and Nicolás Guillén in support of the initial aims of the revolutionary government. The Cuban government had a strong attraction for many writers. For them, as for emerging West Indian nations, Black Power and other groups, Cuba represented an alternative to the dominant Western capitalistic culture now represented by the United States. José Donoso describes the Cuban influence on the young Fuentes:

The most important thing that Carlos Fuentes told me during the trip to Concepcion was that after the Cuban Revolution he agreed to speak publicly only of politics, never of literature; that in Latin America the two were inseparable and that now Latin America could look only toward Cuba. His enthusiasm for the figure of Fidel Castro in that period and his faith in the revolution excited the entire Congress of Intellectuals, which was strongly politicized as a result of his presence. The large number of writers from all the countries on the continent almost unanimously demonstrated their support for the Cuban cause.[20]

Since his conversation with Donoso, Fuentes' position regarding Cuba has changed.

Although the political barriers between Cuba and the United States and the rest of Latin America were instrumental in promoting Latin American writers in general and the novel of the Boom period in specific, they also contributed to its demise and fragmentation. Cuban cultural policies became controversial for many intellectuals who supported the revolution. They objected to a lack of literary and cultural freedom. The most serious of these incidents surrounded the publication of Heberto Padilla's *Out of the Game* in 1968. His arrest in 1971 and the two *Le Monde* letters signaled an end to what might have been called a unity among Latin American and Caribbean intellectuals, dividing them into two groups—those who supported and those who opposed the Cuban Revolution.[21] If events in Cuba helped bring to an end the unity of the Boom, they also contributed to the promotion of black narrative. It is within the crevice of the Boom's rupture that a black narrative in Latin America and the Caribbean gained the attention of a wider audience already created by Cuba and the Boom novel. In this respect Cuba continued to play an important role in the promotion of black culture and literature.

The revolutionary government's interest in history as a way of interpreting its own success led to the rediscovery and official acceptance of Cuba's African heritage and its interest in other black countries. In his speech commemorating the fifteenth anniversary of the Bay of Pigs victory, Fidel Castro affirmed Cuban solidarity with African countries and acknowledged that Cubans are an ''Afro-Latin people.''[22] Many welcomed the elimination of structural inequalities associated with the Batista dictatorship that now brought black Cubans into the mainstream of economic and social activities. Cuba's black heritage and citizens became a means for establishing a bond with African and Caribbean nations. Cuba's revolutionary experience and indeed its black slave heritage has facilitated its interaction with other Third World countries with black populations and inspired it to rewrite its own history. For Cuba and for other countries with a similar slave history, the narrative of and about Blacks has become an important means for the reincorporation of Blacks not as a marginal and passive people but as an important element in the history of the country. César Leante's *Los guerrilleros negros* (1976) suggests that the events of 1959 are a part of a historical continuum that started with slave rebellions in the nineteenth century.

Cuba's interests in Blacks was reflected in the field of culture. Cuban editorial houses made important contributions toward the promotion of the black image in Latin America and the Caribbean. Many works by and about blacks have been reprinted, including the nineteenth-century antislavery narrative and the important anthropological studies of Fernando Ortiz.[23] Casa de las Américas also provided an important outlet for contemporary Caribbean writers who identified with the revolutionary process. For example, the magazine *Casa de las Américas* has published articles on Caribbean themes. Some on the Anglophone are included in issues numbered 48 (1968), 56 (1969), and 87 (1974).

Some of its titles illustrate the important role Casa de las Américas has played in promoting a certain type of Caribbean literature. Its many published titles including a reprint of Cornelis Gerard Anton de Kom's *Nosotros, esclavos de Surinam* (1981), an edition of Luis Palés Matos' *Poesía* (1975), a Spanish translation of Jacques Romain's *Masters of the Dew* (1971), a bilingual edition of *Caribbean Stories: Barbados, Guyana, Jamaica, Trinidad-Tobago* (1977) and Miguel Acosta Saignes' *Vida de los esclavos negros en Venezuela* (1978), to name a few. Some recent Casa de las Américas prizewinners from non-Hispanic countries are Andrew Salkey of Jamaica, *In the Hills Where Her Dreams Live* (poetry, 1979); Shake Keane of St. Vincent, *One a Week with Water* (poetry, 1979); Angus Richmond of Guyana, *A Kind of Living* (novel, 1978); Austin Clarke of Barbados, *Growing Up Stupid Under the Union Jack* (novel, 1980); Paul Laraque of Haiti, *Les Armes Quotidiennes et Poésie Quotidienne* (poetry, 1978); Anthony Phelps of Haiti, *La bélière Caraïbe (poetry, 1980); and Gerard Pierre-Charles of Haiti, El Caribe a la hora de Cuba* (essay, 1980.)

II

Voices from Under reflects the growing interest in black narrative in Latin America and the Caribbean. It is an attempt to capture and portray a moment of development and transition in a recent stage of a Western literary process. Unlike other collections, this book favors a literature of and about Blacks regardless of the linguistic, cultural, political, geographic, religious or other differences that separate them. These differences within traditional disciplines would not allow us to consider Costa Rican prose alongside Haitian narrative and would force us to view them as two distinct literatures with separate origins. The intent of the collection is to break with a narrow view of academic studies that considers literature the private domain of a particular linguistic mode, that is, of either the French, Spanish, English, Portuguese or Dutch languages. We propose a different course of study in thus bringing together literary essays of different countries, periods and languages that pertain to the black theme in Latin America and the Caribbean. These countries belong to an area whose history has been neglected, distorted and even invented by European countries. The common ground of these otherwise diverse regions originates mainly with African slavery, a historical phenomenon perpetuated more ruthlessly against black people, and the forced migration and displacement of Blacks to what is generally known as Latin America and the Caribbean.

The first black slaves to arrive in the New World were Spanish-born domestic servants of the conquerors and colonizers. An immediate attempt was made to regulate slave migration to the New World. On September 3, 1501, the governor of Hispaniola, Nicholás Ovando, received instructions not to allow entrance to Jews, Moors or New Converts, thus favoring over them the transportation of black but enslaved Christians. However, by 1503, Ovando objected to their presence because many were escaping and teaching the Amerindians what was perceived to be "bad customs." On the other hand, the need for slave labor increased as the Indian population was decimated by ill-treatment and disease. Some scholars differ regarding the size of the Amerindian population before 1492. The estimates range from fewer than 60,000 to as many as 8 million. However, by 1510 there was already a noticeable decline of the population of Hispaniola. The census of 1570 indicated that of the 85,650 individuals settled in twenty-four towns (which did not include the Caribs of the Lesser Antilles), 22,150 (26 percent) were Amerindians. Franklin W. Knight and Margaret E. Crahan propose that the classification may have been cultural rather than biological, thus suggesting that the demise of the Amerindian population may have been less than previously believed.[24] Nevertheless, slaves were brought with such frequency that the Decree of July 22, 1513, imposed a two-ducat charge per slave arriving in America. Las Casas narrates the incipient slave trade in the following manner:

The council of the Indies determined, on the recommendation of the Sevillian officials . . . to send 4,000 of them to the four Islands of Hispaniola, San Juan, Cuba and Jamaica. A Spanish on leave from the Indies asked for such license from Governor Bresa [Laurent de Gouvenot], a Flemish gentleman of the King's most private circles. The license was granted and sold for 25,000 ducats to Genoese merchants on the condition— among many others—that no license for black trade would be issued within a period of eight years. The Genoese sold it at a rate of 8 ducats minimum for each Negro.[25]

Since the demand for black slaves was greater than the number available in Spain, Emperor Carlos V allowed non-Christian slaves to be taken from the Guinea Islands and transported directly to the Antilles.[26]

Blacks soon appeared on the mainland. Many came from the Antilles while others arrived from the Old World. The slaves accompanied conquerors and colonizers throughout the American continent. The first Blacks traveled with Cortés to Mexico in 1519 and with Francisco de Montejo to Yucatan in 1521. Pedro de Alvarado took Blacks first to Guatemala in 1524, and then two hundred accompanied him to Peru in 1534.[27]

Most African slaves were brought to replace the almost extinct Amerindian slaves in the mines and in agriculture. Black slaves were used in limited numbers with Amerindians in Mexican and Peruvian mines. The numbers, however, increased with the discovery of gold, diamonds and copper in Venezuela, Colombia and Brazil. From 1694 to 1762 there were more than 80,000–100,000 black slaves working in mines and in mine-related tasks.[28]

Mass enslavement began with the needs of the emerging agricultural industry and indeed the sugar industry, first in the British, French, Dutch and Danish Antilles and Northern Brazil and later in Cuba and the other Spanish-speaking islands. Las Casas' recollections are also important here as he documents the origin of sugar in the New World and points to its economic importance:

The abundance of sugar cane [sic] inspired the residents of Hispaniola to engage in another type of business. In Book II I have already mentioned that a certain Aguilon of La Vega was the first to make sugar in the Indies. He extracted the syrup with certain wooden contraptions which, though primitive, made good enough sugar. That was about 1505 or 1506. Later, a surgeon named Bellosa, of Santo Domingo but originally from Berlanga, improved the instruments and made whiter and better sugar, around the year 1516. He was the first to make an almond-flavored sugar paste from it and I saw it, and he applied himself to the business, designing a press drawn by horses to extract the sweet juice of the cane. When the Hieronymite fathers saw the sample Vellosa brought to gain support for his enterprise, they were convinced of the possible profit and arranged to lend him 500 gold pesos from the royal treasury for him to start a sugar mill. I believe they kept lending him money because building mills was expensive. A few residents offered to build horse-drawn presses as well as the more powerful water mills. Today, there are about forty sugar mills in the Indies but sugar is none the less expensive. Before, sugar was made only in Valencia; then seven or eight mills were built in the Canary Islands and the price of an *arroba* went up to a little over a ducat; but now, with sugar mills all over the Indies, an *arroba* costs 2 ducats and the price rises every day.[29]

The slave population grew rapidly and disproportionately to Whites. Barbados serves as an important example, having first started as an island that produced tobacco, which was harvested by British immigrants with the help of white slaves. It was later converted into a sugar-producing country in 1643 with cheap African slave labor. The slave population rose from 6,000 in 1643 to 20,000 in 1655, 40,000 in 1668 (double the white population), 64,330 in 1792 and 82,000 by the time slavery was abolished in 1835.[30] Records show that in the Spanish possessions alone, there were more than 700,000 slaves during the sixteenth century. In the Portuguese possessions, in Pernambuco and Bahia, slaves in 1585 outnumbered Whites. The 2,000 slaves in Pernambuco in 1588 increased to 5,000 by the end of the century. The same increase was reflected in the Francophone islands. More than 3,000 slaves were transported by French vessels every year between 1670 and 1672 to the French islands. In 1687 the French Antilles reported a total of 18,888 Whites, 27,000 slaves and 1,484 freed Blacks or Mulattoes.[31] By 1730 there were more than 400 plantations in Surinam, producing sugar, coffee, tobacco, cacao and other products. Anton de Kom tells us that in 1749 more than 30,000 pounds of tobacco were sent to Holland, and in one year one plantation could produce 20,000 pounds of cotton and 50,000 pounds of coffee.[32] Above all, however, sugar became an important commodity. Manuel Moreno Fraginals states that in the seventeenth century, sugar was the most important agricultural product in the world.[33]

The displacement of Africans from their homeland to the Americas to work in the sugarcane fields was devastating for the slave victims. Entire families were killed or separated, linguistic and cultural differences were suppressed and the common tribal name was replaced by the generic term *slave*. The mixing became desirable for the owners. Slaves were gathered from the numerous tribal feuds, many of which were instigated by slave factors and traders. The different languages and cultures hindered communication, lessening the possibility of planned rebellions throughout the different stages of the slave trade. It is still difficult to assess the number of Africans who died when we take into account those who perished resisting enslavement in Africa and those who died en route to America. Moreover, clandestine transportation of Blacks is as early as the laws regulating trade with the Spanish colonies. On the one hand, illegal slave traders did not have to pay licenses to transport slaves; on the other, abundant numbers of slaves were available from other countries such as Holland, France, England and Portugal.[34] The clandestine trafficking affected Spanish interests. On June 28, 1527, the emperor informed colonial authorities that unlicensed traffickers were secretly introducing Blacks into the islands. This information was the first in a series of orders governors, mayors and other colonial officials were to receive in order to impede the illegal transportation of slaves. In their own interest the traffickers influenced the decree of August 28, 1571, which ordered that the registry and payment of slaves be moved from Seville to the Indies, where payment would be collected only for living slaves.[35] When the Spanish slave trade became illegal north of the equator in 1817 and south of it in 1820, slave contraband increased. In many cases slave traffickers threw entire slave cargoes overboard to avoid capture by the British. Many of the slave traders' accounts, two of which are Nicholas Owens' eighteenth-century *Journal of a Slave-Dealer* and Captain Theophilus Conneau's nineteenth century *A Slaver's Log Book* document this horrible moment in Western history. Here and elsewhere, the fiction of and about Blacks parallels the course of history. For example, Lino Novas Calvo's novel *El negrero* (1933), describes vividly the slavery path, from the moment slaves were captured in Africa to their journey through the middle passage to their enslavement in America. It is estimated that from 5 or 6 million to 12 million black slaves died during this crucial period in history.[36]

Slave massacres also occurred once slaves arrived in the New World. For example, Gonzalo Aguirre Beltrán tells us that in 1537 Mexico had its first slave massacre, in which a few dozen slaves were dismembered by scared Whites who feared a rebellion by an increasing number of slaves. But it was the typhus epidemic of 1545 that killed most of the slaves in Mexico.[37]

Works of literature also help to document this important stage in history. A dialogue of the times summarizes the slave trade during the nineteenth century, when the narrator of *El negro Francisco* states:

There have been those who have written that slavery is not a disgrace for the Black. A Spanish newspaper which classified as hollow phrases the laments of the abolitionist, took the trouble of investigating the origin of the slave trade, and thought itself a winner, had thought it had won its cause, when it found out that the savage king of Dahomey sold to Whites its prisoners of wars who were destined to be sacrificed. Slavery came to be a type of redemption. The Black, who in the remote corner of his rustic country would have died by the knife of the shadow of barbarism was tied like a bundle, given in exchange for an iron knife or barrel of rum, submerged in the bottom of the hold of the ship, transported, not as one transports men, but as one transports merchandise. If he was fortunate enough not to run into the British cruiser, he was not thrown into the sea; if he had enough vital strength he would not starve or die from thirst nor choke during the trip. Having arrived in Cuba he could in turn die of neglect on the arid beach, while they waited for the buyers or they evaded the authorities, he then would live without a country, without a family, without dignity, without rest, without hope, and usually whipped to death: all this when they were enlightened enough so that they would understand it well. The Spanish reporter opted for the proceedings known as civilization, we prefer those of the savage Dahomey king.[38]

From its inception slavery met with resistance. The slave's constant quest for freedom underscored and dramatized his hopes of fleeing slavery. In his "Los cimarrones en las Antillas y América continental," José Luciano Franco notes that slave rebellions were widespread and were recorded as early as 1522. In Jamaica alone there were more than 250 slave revolts and conspiracies. Within the context of Caribbean slave population and history of slavery, Orlando Patterson says that "Jamaica's record is most impressive. . . . The scale of the average Jamaican revolt was far greater and more dangerous than that of the average American. The most serious revolt in the latter country—that of Nat Turner—involved only 70 slaves. The average number of slaves in the Jamaica revolts of the seventeenth and eighteenth centuries was approximately 400, and the three most serious revolts of the island—the first Maroon war; the 1760 rebellions; and the 1832 rebellion—each involved over a thousand slaves."[39]

There were other important rebellions. As early as 1677 the black workers of the copper mines of Santiago del Prado, in Cuba, revolted against the Spanish authorities, for generations resisted in the mountains and constituted one of the first successful insurrections, winning their freedom in 1800.[40] In Brazil the runaway slave community of Palmares, which lasted from 1630 to 1697, was composed of eleven confederated communities, with over 20,000 inhabitants, and spanned some 250 kilometers. Unlike the Cuban copper miners who won their freedom, Zumbi and many others were killed trying to break General Domingos Jorge Velho's twenty-two-day siege.[41]

Insurrection and rebellion is also an important theme in literature. Unlike many works of history, the point of view expressed in the works of literature favors the life of its black protagonist. In Cuban narrative, as early as 1835 Juan Francisco Manzano was not only documenting his life as a slave but his escape into freedom. Some years later, in another (auto)biography, the ex-slave Esteban Montejo would experience a similar fate as told to Miguel Barnet in the 1960s. But unlike Manzano, Montejo did not escape into the city but into the country away from civilization until the end of slavery in Cuba. If these works give the impression that escape from slavery was a singular act, César Leante's *Los guerrilleros negros* shows that for many the threat of death by escape was preferable to living in slavery. The idea and practice of rebellions is pervasive: The names of rebellious leaders such as Cudjoe in Jamaica, the Bush Negroes in

Surinam, Coba in Cuba, Mackandal in Haiti and Zumbi of Palmares in Brazil, for example, are legendary.

The most important single event in the Caribbean and in the black world of slavery is the Haitian Revolution of 1791–1804, whose leaders not only defeated Napoleon's armies but established the world's first black republic and the second republic in America to proclaim its independence. The Haitian Revolution served as an example for other slaves seeking their freedom and for the colonial rebellions against Spain in which slaves, freed Blacks and Mulattoes took part. It is no surprise that the new Haitian president, Alejandro Pétion, generously helped Simón Bolívar and that Haitian volunteers fought in Mexico[42] or that Haitians advised and traded with runaway slaves off the Cuban coast.[43] Eventually, the manumission of slaves spread throughout the Americas: to the Federation of Central America in 1824, Mexico in 1829, Bolivia in 1831, the British possessions in 1833, Uruguay, Colombia, Venezuela and the French colonies between 1842 and 1856, the remaining Spanish possessions in 1886 and Brazil in 1888.[44] Unfortunately, the conditions under which Blacks lived would then be imposed on other immigrants, such as Chinese, Indians, Indonesians and Canary Islanders, brought after 1834 to replace slave labor in Guadeloupe, Guyana, Cuba, Trinidad-Tobago and other islands.[45] This influx of immigrants was also felt in parts of South America. For example, Arthur Ramos states that "from 1864 to 1935, 4,172,438 immigrants entered Brazil.[46]

The tension that resulted from the struggle between the black slaves seeking their freedom and the colonial forces prolonging their enslavement contributed to the creation of a new culture throughout Latin America and the Caribbean. What used to be two distinct cultures from two remote parts of the world came together in America, where their differences were both preserved and fused. It is interesting to observe how Western culture came in contact with African culture and vice versa. The amalgamation occurred in many different ways and at many different levels. Certainly, the colonial countries forced slaves and immigrants to accept their languages and customs as their own. The models set by them became the norm for all to follow. In countries with a sizable European population the mixing took on still a different form in producing noticeable racial gradations.

The Haitian Revolution depicts the black expulsion of Whites from San Domingo to constitute the first black state in America. However, the governments that soon followed the ejection of the French were based not on African but on European models. Henri Christophe's fourteen-year reign over northern Haiti as a European monarch is an important example.

A similar situation developed in the West Indies. Unlike the situation in Haiti, there was no need to expel the British from the islands, since most ruled their lands and slaves from England. The British islands became a place for investment and quick acquisition of riches. Neither absenteeism nor emancipation of slaves lessened the impact British culture had on islands such as Jamaica, Trinidad and Barbados, nor did the consequent need to meld several racial histories into one. Jamaica's national motto continues to be, "Out of Many, One People." C. L. R. James describes the process in a similar manner: "The West Indies has never been a traditional colonial territory with clearly distinguished economic and social relations between two different cultures. Native culture there was none. The aboriginal Amerindian civilization had been destroyed. Every succeeding year, therefore, saw the laboring population, slaves or free, incorporating into itself more of the language, customs, aims, and outlook of its masters."[47] The colonial structure created an interdependency between the colony and the mother country. But for many, the mother country remained the only center of civilization.

Brazil represents the genetic fusion that resulted from the presence of Blacks and Whites living in the same country. In *The Master and the Slave*, Gilberto Freyre explains the coming together of the two races. "The majority of our countrymen are the near descendants either of masters or of slaves, and many of them have sprung from the union of slaveowners and slave women." Freyre explains the union in the following manner: "Conquerors, in the military and technical sense, of the indigenous populations, the absolute rulers of the Negroes imported from Africa for the hard labor of the bagaceira, the Europeans and their descendants meanwhile had to compromise with the Indians and the Africans in the matter of genetic and social relations. The scarcity of white women created zones of fraternalization between conquerors and conquered, between masters and slaves."[48]

Although the rape of one culture by the other is devastating, Freyre goes on to clarify that the sexual union reduced the social distance between the groups, to the extent that black women became influential in the social structure of the Brazilian society. Discord resulted, he claims, in a harmonious society: "Men, animals, houses, vegetables, techniques, values, symbols, some of remote derivation, others native—all of these today, now that the conflict between modes of life and the at times bitter clash of interests have subsided tend to form one of the most harmonious unions of culture with nature and of one culture with another that the lands of this hemisphere have ever known.[49] Although Freyre's claim of harmony is somewhat optimistic, one can certainly agree on the syncretism of Brazilian society.

Miguel Barnet arrives at a similar observation when analyzing the impact sugar and slavery had on Cuba: "The small cell of the primitive grinding-mill, which would later grow into the huge complex of the sugarmill plantation, was the ground where these complex and heterogeneous human masses come together. Blending with the white Spanish immigrant, or native-born Cuban, the African cultures received, first from one another and then from the white groups a changing impact which resulted in the creation in our country of a new form of culture, affecting the whites as well."[50]

The synthesis of Africans and Spaniards has had specific manifestations within Cuba that resemble what occurred in other countries:

Along with the creation of uniquely Afro-Cuban culture forms and the movement toward a *sui generis* national character, this process gave rise to a sense of national or island identity. Long stretches of unbroken flatlands, or great, nourishing rivers, fostered the travel and dissemination of linguistic and cultural elements. The land itself, favored by nature and climate that encouraged expansion and opening-up, became the essential sustenance for the development of a sense of "what we are." The Spaniard, affected by black culture, ended up assimilating it unconsciously, though he might deplore it and even ban it. As Nicholás Guillén says in his "Song of the Bongo": "Here even the finest gentleman must harken to my call."[51]

The African contributions to European culture are numerous and are still being studied. The influence of African languages in Latin America and indeed in the Caribbean is widely recognized. For example, between 1966 and 1972, Maureen Warner Lewis identified Yoruba, Hausa, Fon, Kilongo and Arabic speakers in Trinidad. In 1972, she located Yoruba, Kikongo and Mahi speakers in Jamaica.[52] In a more recent study, Lewis traces Yoruba influence in Trinidad Creole English. She provides the following examples:

> Yoruba: O ya!
> Literal translation: It is quick/alive.
> Trinidad English: O ya!
> Gloss: "Let's go!" Exclamation used up until the 1960s by bandleaders or singers whenever music or a calypso was about to begin.

> Yoruba: Mo je tan.
> Literal translation: I ate finish.
> Trinidad English: I done eat.

> Yoruba: Fi omi si igi.
> Literal translation: Put water to plant.
> Trinidad English: Put water to the plant.
> Gloss: Water the plant.[53]

It is also widely recognized that such Cuban speech words as *cafú*, as in *murió como Cafú* ("he died like Cafu"), can be traced to the Mandinga language. Many words with *ñ* in the initial position are of African origin, and words with the prefix *ña*, which originally meant "mother", can be traced to the Bantus.[54] Moreover, West African culinary plates, such as *fufú*, are still prepared in Cuba.

By now it is commonplace to talk about the influence of African rhythm, songs and instruments in past and present Latin American and Caribbean music.[55] Many also recognize that African-originated religions like *voodoo* in Haiti, *santería* in Cuba, *espiritismo* in Puerto Rico, Shango in Trinidad, Pocomania in Jamaica, *obeah* in Guyana and *candomblé* in Brazil are still practiced today. It has been said that in spite of Cuban policy to do away with Afro-Cuban religions, many revolutionary leaders practice *santería* and consult regularly with *santeros* and *babalaos*.[56]

The ex-slave Esteban Montejo's recollection of the nineteenth century documents the African presence in Spanish culture. Regarding religion, he states:

The game of *mayombe* [African word meaning evil spirit] was connected with religion. The overseers themselves used to get involved, hoping to benefit. They believed in the witches too, so no one today need be surprised that whites believe in such things. Drumming was part of the *mayombe*. A *nganga*, or large pot, was placed in the center of the patio. The powers were inside the pot: the saints. People started drumming and singing. They took offerings to the pot and asked for health for themselves and their brothers and peace among themselves. They also made *enkangues*, which were charms of earth from the cemetery; the earth was made into little heaps in four corners, representing the points of the universe. Inside the pot they put a plant called star-shake, together with corn straw to protect the men. When a master punished a slave, the others would collect a little earth and put it in the pot. With the help of this earth they could make the master fall sick or bring some harm upon his family, for so long as the earth was inside the pot the master was imprisoned there and the Devil himself couldn't get him out. This was how the Congolese revenged themselves upon their masters.[57]

But in spite of the linguistic and cultural fusion and the attempt to bring both African and European descendants closer, history by definition will always maintain their pasts apart. Unless there is a moment of modernity[58] or any other moment that denies the past, the history of Africans and Europeans is destined to separate them. Their future may bring them together, but not their past. Writing also reflects this division. In some cases ''history'' continues to be written from a Western perspective, for it is this ''history'' that has privileged a Western interpretation of events. However, it has become the responsibility of historical fiction of and about Blacks to imitate, question and undermine Western history's own premise.

III

The history of black people in Latin America and the Caribbean has been one of constant struggle. The narrative of and about Blacks best describes this history. These works are not innocent: they are based on the black man's past and present experience and their intention is to make political and social statements regarding the lives of Blacks. The works are not political in nature, for all they do is narrate another side of history; but they become political because the view they express clashes with the general understanding of the course of written events. Some document history while others go as far as to correct it, so that Western history may fit in with the lives of Blacks in Latin America and the Caribbean. In some respects, art has a moral obligation to restore to ''history'' what it might not have offered during a given past. In his nineteenth-century novel, Zambrana addresses the moral question when the narrator states: ''And why should art fill these needs? Because art has the privilege of warming the souls, of taking them out of their apathy, because only it, and not cold reasoning, is apt to cause the noble anger, ardent enthusiasm, effective compassion, inflexible and intransigent antipathy, tools necessary for moral progress.''[59]

Past and present, the lives of Blacks in Latin America and the Caribbean seem to defy the chronology of historical time and to resemble instead the structure of time in those Borges stories that propose the immortalization of the instant or the cyclicality of events.[60] Alejo Carpentier's ¡Ecue-Yamba-O! (1933) is most revealing regarding the fragmentation of historical time in the lives of its protagonist. The author shows that life for Blacks in twentieth-century Cuba is not significantly different from slavery. Slavery is central to the theme of the novel and, as one might expect, is located near the physical center of the novel. It is by way of the chapter entitled "Juan Mandinga" that a return to the past occurs, placing the origin of the novel's present within the perspective of Suárez y Romero's Francisco and Zambrana's El negro Francisco. The past and the present fuse in the pages of the novel, just as they do in history. With emancipation, the present society eradicates what used to be the primitive sugar mills and replaces them with bigger and more advanced machinery. Likewise, the individual governing families have been replaced by the stronger foreign (North American) economic interests. Even though there has been a shift from slave to wage earner, the physical conditions remain practically the same. The present, like the past, offers a large disparity between the bourgeoisie and foreign technicians, on the one hand, and native and foreign black immigrants, on the other. There has, in effect, been no substantial gain for Blacks. The overbearing presence of Afro-Cuban religion in the novel allows us to consider other factors that contribute to the arrest of historical time, to take into consideration a mythical order present in black culture before the arrival of African slaves to America. The religious time in the novel parallels and even coexists with historical time. For the slave, adherence to his religious beliefs was more than a means of communicating with the gods; it was a matter of survival in preserving African tradition. African religion, in this case, is thus at the service of a need that is antagonistic to the sequential ordering of Western society.

The nonlinear vision of history described in ¡Ecue-Yamba-O! is also present in Miguel Barnet's The Autobiography of a Runaway Slave. If Carpentier's novel is a fictional account about Blacks, Barnet's Autobiography is based on interviews with the ex-slave Esteban Montejo regarding his experiences before and after emancipation. In spite of these fundamental differences, the two historical times proceed in a similar direction. In fact, one seems to mirror the other. Before emancipation, Blacks worked in the sugarcane fields and sugar mills, were forced to work long hours by the slave master and his overseers and slept in slave quarters. After emancipation, Blacks still worked in sugarcane fields and sugar mills, worked for overseers and continued to live in barracones. In essence the autobiography is pessimistic; very little has changed in Montejo's life since emancipation. His demystifying narrative recalls a previous historical time:

The first plantation I worked on was called Purio. I turned up there one day in the rags I stood in and a hat I had collected on the way. I went in and asked the overseer if there was work for me. He said yes. I remember he was Spanish, with moustaches, and his name was Pepe. There were overseers in these parts until quite recently, the difference being that they didn't lay about them as they used to do under slavery. But they were men of the same breed, harsh, overbearing. There were still barracoons after Abolition, the same as before. Many of them were newly built of masonry, the old ones having collapsed under the rain and storms. The barracoon at Purio was strong and looked as if it had been recently completed. They told me to go and live there. I soon made myself at home, for it wasn't too bad. They had taken the bolts off the doors and the workers themselves had cut holes in the walls for ventilation. They no longer had to worry about escapes or anything like that, for the Negroes were free now, or so they said. But I could not help noticing that bad things still went on. There were bosses who still believed that the blacks were created for locks and bolts and whips, and treated them as before. It struck me that many Negroes did not know that things had changed, because they went on saying, "Give me your blessing, my master."[61]

In fact, one could argue that Montejo's life became worse after emancipation. As a result of it, Montejo gave up his freedom in the mountains and returned to a society not much different from the one he escaped. History for Blacks in Cuba and other parts of Latin America and the Caribbean appears to follow the narrative structure of Carpentier's and Barnet's novels. For example, the Aponte Conspiracy of 1812, in which freed Blacks who had knowledge of the Haitian Revolution attempted to liberate Cuban slaves, was mirrored by the Ladder Conspiracy of 1844, in which freed Blacks accused of plotting against the slavery system were tied to a ladder, whipped and made to confess. Similarly, on May 20, 1912, Blacks in Cuba who congregated around the Partido Independiente de Color, under Evaristo Estenoz, were murdered when they protested their unrewarded participation in the Spanish-Cuban-American war of 1895–1898. Hugh Thomas compares the current atmosphere on the part of Whites to that of the "great fear" during the French Revolution. The black protest was strongest in Oriente. General Monteagudo, who suspended constitutional rights in the province, defeated four thousand black insurgents and claimed to have killed three thousand himself.[62]

The events of one country seem to repeat themselves in the history of others. On October 7, 1865, Blacks in Jamaica under Paul Bogle, a preacher at the Nature Baptist Church at Stony Gut, went to the Morant Bay courthouse to protest injustices against them. On October 11, he and others marched to the same courthouse to defend the ownership of their lands, which the British authorities questioned. In this confrontation the protestors were victorious. Subsequently, Bogle and others suspected of participating in the Morant Bay Rebellion were captured and killed. As a result, Governor Eyre strengthened his government. In 1944 a modification of the colonial system was introduced in Jamaica. The modifications included the legislative council, which consisted of an upper house of a bicameral legislature and a lower house of elected representatives. In spite of these changes, real power was not transferred to Jamaicans but remained in the hands of the governor. The sequence of these historical events is the subject

of Vic Reid's novel *New Day* (1949). Like history, the novel narrates the events
of the Morant Bay Rebellion to the "new day" in 1944. And as in fiction, the
events are not linear but appear to repeat themselves. During the rebellion, Bogle recalled the past; their struggle reminded him of the maroon resistance of
1655 and the Jamaican participation in the United States' War of 1812. The
passage of time did not bring significant relief to Jamaicans; life before the rebellion was virtually the same as when the novel ends. As in *¡Ecue-Yamba-O!*
the slave master has become the owner and the slave is now the worker.

The cycles of oppression and liberation and the alternation between Blacks
and Mulattoes as outlined by Carpentier's *The Kingdom of This World* are, of
course, prefigured in Haitian history. What in Carpentier's second novel appears to be a historical document is neutralized by what is clearly the circularity
of history. The tyrant's presence and fall, like the rebel's presence and fall, are
inevitable; what becomes unquestionable is the mutual displacement of the one
by the other, the only difference being a change in historical time. White slave
masters are replaced by Leclerc, who in turn is replaced by Henri Christophe,
who is in turn replaced by the mulatto Republicans. Similarly, Mackandal is
replaced by Bouckman, who is later replaced by Ti Noel, who led the attack
on the Palace of Sans-Souci and who will transform himself to fight the new
enemy. Carpentier foresaw in the history of Haiti (and the Caribbean) the in-
terrelationship between oppression and rebellion. History and fiction are also
interrelated; history appears to narrate the continuation of *The Kingdom of This
World*. Ti Noel's reaction to the presence of the Mulattoes may also have had
its origins in Carpentier's experience with Lescot's administration (1941–1945),
when the novelist arrived on the island in 1943. After his election Lescot attempted to prolong his term in office in light of the dangers of World War II.
Moreover, he used his office to enrich himself, his family and the mulatto elite.
Lescot was finally forced out of office by a popular uprising on January 11,
1946, which involved the market-women's attack on the home of the much-
hated interior minister and student strikes. In some respects, history continues
to narrate the ending of Carpentier's novel. The few gains made by Dumarsais
Estime, who proclaimed himself as a leader of the working people and of Blacks,
would later be challenged by the ruthless Duvalier governments.[63]

Robert Brent Topin concludes his survey of Blacks in Brazilian history in a
similar manner:

In the twentieth century some Negroes and particularly, mulattoes found positions of
social and economic importance in Brazilian society. Notwithstanding some subtle forms
of discrimination, they never confronted institutions of racial prejudice as overt and harsh
as those that troubled blacks in the United States in the same period. Yet the glaring
reality remained that an extraordinary disproportionate number of Negroes in Brazil were
locked in the culture of poverty, and, to a great degree, this problem could be traced to
the heritage of slavery. Long after the servile institution was destroyed, its victims continued to suffer from the repercussions of the experience in bondage. Without land, de-
ficient in education and stigmatized in the eyes of much of the white population, the ex-

slaves and their descendants found their opportunities limited. Despite the potentiality of social ascendancy for people of color, other economic and social barriers were not easy to surmount. The legacy of the slave past cast a heavy shadow, hampering the efforts of Brazilian Negroes to challenge the obstacles.[64]

As in history and fiction, the present resembles the past. The similarities between the two allow us to read one in the other and vice versa. Michael Thelwell's *The Harder They Come*, a novel based on history, presents a contemporary vision of Blacks that must not be overlooked by present-day scholars: Blacks are sufferers, and the protagonist Ivan's physical and metaphoric descent from the mountains into the city (a type of hell) will set the stage for the events that will accelerate his death. However, it is this movement from the mountains, nature, to the city and back again that recalls Carpentier's *The Lost Steps* and the protagonist's search for a time before the European arrival in the New World. Carpentier's protagonist had discovered the origin of Latin America in Santa Mónica de los Venados, but his final return to that beginning of time—that is, to a time before the advent of European-imposed history of America—is not possible. Similarly, Ivan had come to know a moment outside of historical time. Ivan was brought up in the country which symbolizes origin, innocence and tradition, but the environment that once guarded him against evil has been denied to him. Nature, which protected him and protected fugitive slaves, has been consumed, altered and even destroyed by the city and will no longer provide refuge for him. As in many contemporary novels, the city has become the new battleground for survival. Like Carpentier's protagonist, Ivan must return to and remain in the city. However, the return to a place of origin, as in *The Lost Steps*, does provide Ivan with a greater awareness of the society in which he lives. Ivan sees pressures that oppress him and, like a modern slave, rebels against them. What is proposed in this novel is that Ivan's rebellion must take place in the city. The escape to Africa, as declared by the Garvey movement, or to the mountains, as represented by Palmares, is no longer an acceptable alternative. The city must be the place of confrontation for the modern slave. And if Caliban used the same language Prospero taught him against his own master, Ivan will use the same weapons used to exploit him, his music and violence, in order to gain his own freedom. Even though the past is closed off to him, he retains remembrances of a distant culture. If music and musical instruments were a means of communicating with tribal gods, reggae will not only continue to embody that sacred value, but will also serve as a means to demystify Western society and serve as a call for action.

How to come to terms with history and how to view the past from the present, are problems that confront today's writers and critics and are evident in their works. Should writers reconstruct the past as written history explains it? Or should the writer, as privileged interpreter of history, impose a contemporary perspective on the past? The fusion of the past and the present, of history and fiction, is a concern of César Leante's *Los guerrilleros negros* (1976), which describes rebellious slaves, their escape from bondage and their formation of *palenques*, runaway slave communities in the mountains. Within the contemporary context of the writing, the slave insurrections reported in the novel recall the tactics used by the Castro forces in overthrowing the Batista regime. The term *guerrilla* used by Leante to identify his characters is, on the other hand, not of recent usage. Montejo, Barnet's protagonist, uses the term in its historical context. For him, *guerrilleros* were Cuban peasants who were employed as infantry and cavalrymen by the Spaniards to fight against other Cubans.[65] Thus, Leante discloses as much about the nature of contemporary Cuban society as about the period of which he is writing. Ironically, this dialectical portrayal of history may prove to be more accurate than earlier fictional and historical accounts. Elapsed time allows for a contextual understanding of events. Similarly, Lino Novás Calvo's *El negrero* narrates the *vida novelada de Pedro Blanco Fernández de Trava*, as the subtitle clearly informs the reader. By situating the work in the nineteenth century, Novás Calvo describes the life of one of the most powerful slave traders of the nineteenth century who retired from the trade in 1879 with one million pounds sterling. From his factories in Gallinas, presently the Kerefe River area of Sierra Leone, Blanco alone shipped to the Caribbean more than five thousand slaves annually and killed hundreds and thousands of others. However, approximately one hundred years later the ruthless Machado dictatorship which governed Cuba from 1924 to 1933 recalled Blanco's dominion over Gallinas. Novás Calvo was in Spain during the latter part of the Machado reign, but remained informed of the political situation in Cuba through journals and letters from his friends. His sentiments resulted in the writing of "La noche de Ramón Yendía," a story about the last day of the Machado period, which he is said to have written in 1933, the year Machado fled Cuba and the year *El negrero* was published.[66] Novás Calvo's knowledge of and experience with the Machado dictatorship helped him, in part, to narrate the life of one of the most savage men of the nineteenth century. Leante and Novás Calvo put into history what written history did not offer in a given past.

The purpose of this collection of essays is to allow a voice from under to surface, speak and be heard. It is a voice that has been silenced first by the physical oppression of black slaves and later by the denial of economic and political means to Blacks as a people. This isolated cry has gone practically unnoticed by the mainstream of Western society and has therefore been reduced to the margins of its literature. It is the marginality of Blacks that concerns us here. Our intention is to restore the black narrative voice to its proper place in Western literature. Only recently critics have been paying attention to this voice, but mainly in isolation, that is, as emanating from one literary movement or another, such as Negritude or Negrismo, and not as representing a continuum of Latin American and Caribbean thought. *Voices from Under* is based on the black man's historical condition, one that began with his enslavement and has continued with his struggle for survival as, for example, his situation under the Duvalier governments has shown. Although the literature of and about Blacks narrates the concerns of individuals, it nevertheless reflects the experience of a people. Literature in these works is not altogether fantasized or invented, as a certain view of fiction might suggest. No matter how inconceivable it may appear, it is tied to the black man's historical reality, from his enslavement in Africa to his arrival on the American continent. Many accounts are so incredible that one cannot help but think at times that even history must be the product of someone's imagination.

The scope of the collection follows history and encompasses early slave narratives, postslavery narratives and narrations depicting the conditions of Blacks in contemporary society. The essays herein uncover aspects of the black experience in the Caribbean, Central America and South America. They can be read individually, thus constituting separate realities, but may be better understood synchronically. As a whole, they reveal the life of Blacks and their conditions as victims in Latin America and the Caribbean. In this sense, the essays are a palimpsest in which each work reveals a little more about the black man's condition in the New World. They are a testament of his position and therefore an expression of the numerous slave rebellions and cultural upheavals, silent and silenced, that accompanied his presence. These actions were translated later into European languages. However, the works that were written did not alter the situation of Blacks. Like his actions, his literature and the literature about him had to be suppressed. Even the mildest tone threatened the existence of his oppressor, as is evidenced by the Cuban antislavery works of Juan Francisco Manzano and Anselmo Suárez y Romero—they were censored, circulated in a clandestine manner and could be published only abroad.

Voices from Under attempts to bring black narrative to the foreground of Western literature. The collection also attempts to make black narrative problematical in order to understand the various components in society and literature responsible for its composition. It does not make any distinction between works written by Blacks and works on black themes written by Whites. Although there is no question regarding the insight of black authors into the black experience, there should be no doubt about the useful perspective white authors offer with respect to the same themes. It is the latter who often provide an understanding of a power structure of which they are a part. Their point of view is another piece of information needed for the total portrayal of our subject matter. It is Pedro José Morilla's "El ranchador," (1856), Francisco Estévez' "Diario del rancheador" (written 1837–1842) and Lino Novás Calvo's *El negrero: Vida novelada de Pedro Fernández de Trava (1933)*, for example, that present a point of view seldom narrated by black authors, that is, the perspective of the slave hunter and the slave trader. And even if slave narratives such as Manzano's autobiography and Ignatius Sancho's *Letters of the Late Ignatius Sancho, an African* (1782) give readers a personal view of slavery, one still would have to question the representative nature of the work. This may be so if we consider the concept of a privileged slave who, unlike other slaves, learned to read and write. Education may have implied an acceptance and internalization of Western values. His counterpart, the maroon slave, escaped into the mountains as a way of rejecting all European values, including the law. And yet, at the end of his autobiography, Manzano does not escape into the mountains but goes to the city with the hope of finding someone who could help him. The Royal Decree of November 14, 1693, had empowered the captain general to take action against masters who abused their slaves.[67] Many slaves and freed Blacks attempted to abandon their culture in order to better themselves. To do so, they followed the only model available to them. Ironically, the model was that of the white oppressor. The works of writers like the eighteenth-century Brazilian Manoel Ignacio de Silva Alvarenga reveal more about his academic education than his African origins. Finally, it is the critic's responsibility to unmask literary texts, whether they were written by white or black authors, and restore to literary history and criticism not an isolated but a contextual understanding of Blacks in Latin America and the Caribbean.

The essays presented here were requested exclusively for this collection in order to capture a continuum and a recent stage in Latin American and Caribbean literatures and criticism. However, the themes of the essays were chosen by the critics. In view of the subject matters, we have divided the anthology into geographic areas and linguistic modes: Spanish, French, and English Caribbean, Central America and Spanish and Portuguese South America. Roberto González Echevarría's "Socrates Among the Weeds: Blacks and History in Carpentier's *Explosion in a Cathedral*" goes beyond the analysis of this novel contained in his *Alejo Carpentier: The Pilgrim at Home* and demonstrates how neo-African culture in the Caribbean shapes history. Richard L. Jackson's "Slavery, Racism and Autobiography in Two Early Black Writers: Juan Francisco Manzano and Martín Morúa Delgado" emerges from concerns already expressed in his *Black Writers in Latin America*. In his essay Jackson speculates that the second part of Manzano's autobiography, which was lost, would have reflected the more active intention of Morúa Delgado's works. Julia Cuervo Hewitt's "Yoruba Presence: From Nigerian Oral Literature to Contemporary Cuban Narrative" explores the presence of African folklore in twentieth-century Cuban literature. Selwyn R. Cudjoe's "V. S. Naipaul and the Question of Identity" and O.R. Dathorne's "Toward Synthesis in the New World: Caribbean Literature in English" complement each other insofar as they both seek direction for the West Indies. Cudjoe finds it in Wilson Harris' poems, reggae and calypso, while Dathorne sees it in those songs and above all, in Derek Walcott's works. Juris Silenieks' "The Maroon Figure in Caribbean Francophone Prose" identifies a universal value in a past narrative time as seen in the works of Edouard Glissant. Joseph Ferdinand's "The New Political Statement in Haitian Fiction" explores the relationship between politics and literature in the works of writers living both in and out of Haiti and specifically in the works of Marie-Thérèse Colimon, René Depestre, Gérard Etienne and Anthony Phelps. Lisa E. Davis' "The World of the West Indian Black in Central America: The Recent Works of Quince Duncan" offers important but little-known accounts of black society in Costa Rica. Jonathan Tittler's "*Juyungo*/Reading Writing" and Carol Beane's "Black Character: Toward a Dialectical Presentation in Three South American Novels" provide both a literary and a thematic continuum into an image that culminates with Adalberto Ortiz' *Juyungo*. Finally, Ronald M. Rassner's "Palmares and the Freed Slave in Afro-Brazilian Literature" traces the legend of Palmares and Zumbi in pre- and post-abolition Afro-Brazilian narrative and theater. And Lemuel Johnson's "The *Romance Bárbaro* as an Agent of Disappearance: Henrique Coelho Netto's *Rei Negro* and Its Conventions" uncovers the black man's presence and absence in literature.

It is our intention not to provide a definitive statement regarding black narrative but to offer ideas for a meaningful discussion regarding this important subject. Nor is it our aim to include essays on every aspect of black narrative in Latin America and the Caribbean; instead, we provide samples of some important writers and works. A more complete study would have included the literatures of Puerto Rico, the Dominican Republic and the Dutch Antilles. With more space, we would have commissioned an entire essay on the theme of black women and the literature of the slave hunter.

Although *Voices from Under* pertains to the black experience, we have welcomed an essay on V. S. Naipaul because his works are very relevant for a certain understanding of Blacks and other ethnic and racial groups in Latin America and the Caribbean. Even though it has been our intention to limit the scope of the anthology to narrative works, we have also included analyses of other genres as represented by poetry, theater and songs. We foresee the publication of other works that explore the black theme in Latin America and the Caribbean in other literary genres. Furthermore, we expect still other anthologies that are interdisciplinary and will gather texts of history, literature, politics, music and art on Blacks in Latin America, the Caribbean, the United States and Africa.

NOTES

1. See Gabriel Coulthard's pioneering work, *Raza y color en la literatura antillana* (Seville, Spain: Escuela de Estudios Hispano-Americanos de Sevilla, 1958).

2. See, for example, Edmundo O'Gorman, *La invención de América* (Mexico: Fondo de Cultura Económica, 1968), and Henri Baudet, *Paradise on Earth: Some Thoughts on European Images of Non-European Man*, trans. Elizabeth Wentholt (New Haven: Yale University Press, 1965).

3. See Bartolomé de las Casas, *History of the Indies*, trans. and ed. Andrée M. Collard (New York: Harper and Row, 1971), pp. 256–59.

4. In his study of Blacks in Spanish-American literature John F. Matheus cites *La Araucana* as his earliest source. See his "African Footprints in Hispanic-American Literature," in *Blacks in Hispanic Literature*, ed. Miriam DeCosta (Port Washington, N.Y.: Kennikat Press, 1977), pp. 53–64.

5. For an analysis of the Cuban antislavery novel, see my "La novela antiesclavista: texto, contexto y escritura," *Cuadernos Americanos* 236, no. 3 (1981): 103–16.

6. See David T. Haberly, "Abolitionism in Brazil: Anti-Slavery and Anti-Slave," *Luso-Brazilian Review* 9, no. 2 (1972): 30–46.

7. Roberto González Echevarría explains the importance of these writers within the context of Latin American literature in his *Alejo Carpentier: The Pilgrim at Home* (Ithaca, N.Y.: Cornell University Press, 1977).

8. For a description of these and other literary currents in French literature, see Lilyan Kesteloot, *Black Writers in French*, trans. Ellen Conroy Kennedy (Philadelphia: Temple University Press, 1974).

9. Janheinz Jahn, *Neo-African Literature: A History of Black Writing*, trans. Oliver Coburn and Ursula Lehrburger (New York: Grove Press, 1969), pp. 262–66. Contrary to Jahn, we contend that Negritude in the 1930s did not offer the subversive alternative that Caliban represented.

10. In "Hoquet" ("Hiccups"), Damas listens to his mother's instructions: "Be quiet/Have I or have I not/told you to speak French/the French of France/the French that Frenchmen speak/French French." For a bilingual edition of the poem see Kesteloot, *Black Writers*, pp. 127–31.

11. See Kesteloot, *Black Writers*, pp. 56–74.

12. *Black Writers in Latin America* (Albuquerque: University of New Mexico Press, 1979), p. 197.

13. Ibid., p. 96.

14. *Area Handbook for Jamaica*, ed. Irving Kaplan et al. (Washington, D.C.: Foreign Area Studies of the American University, 1976), p. 177.

15. For an in-depth account of the Uruguayan magazines, see Jackson, *Black Writers*, pp. 93–111.

16. See *Obras escogidas* (Havana: Librería Económica, 1953), pp. 1170–73.

17. *Washington Quarterly* 4 (1981): 89. For a recent analysis of U.S. foreign policy toward Cuba, see Wayne S. Smith, "Dateline Havana: Myopic Diplomacy," *Foreign Policy*, no. 48 (1982): 157–74.

18. See his "Criticism and Literature in Revolutionary Cuba," *Cuban Studies/Estudios Cubanos* 11, no. 1 (1981): 2.

19. See Emir Rodríguez Monegal, *El boom de la novela latinoamericana* (Caracas: Editorial Tiempo Nuevo, 1972), and José Donoso, *The Boom in Spanish American Literature*, trans. Gregory Kolovakos (New York: Columbia University Press, 1977).

20. Donoso, *The Boom*, pp. 48–49.

21. For a transcript of the *Le Monde* letters and other documents pertaining to the Padilla incident, see *El caso Padilla*, ed. Lourdes Casal (Miami: Ediciones Universal, 1971).

22. See *Foreign Broadcast Information Service, Daily Report* 6, no. 77 (1976): Q1–8.

23. For a summary of Ortiz' life and works, see Julio Le Riverend, "Fernando Ortiz, 1881–1969," *América Indígena* 29, no. 3 (1969): 892–98.

24. *Africa and the Caribbean: The Legacies of a Link*, ed. Margaret E. Crahan and Franklin W. Knight (Baltimore: The Johns Hopkins University Press, 1979), pp. 7–8.

25. Las Casas, *History*, p. 257.

26. For an account of the presence of Blacks in America during the conquest, see Gonzalo Aguirre Beltrán's *La población negra en México*, 2d ed. (1946; reprint ed., Mexico: Fondo de Cultura Económica, 1972), pp. 15–32.

27. Ibid., pp. 19–20.

28. See a paper by the Instituto de Estudios Africanos de La Habana, "Facetas del esclavo africano en America Latina," *América Indígena* 29, no. 3 (1969): 677–81.

29. Las Casas, *History*, pp. 256–57.

30. See Ramiro Guerra, *Azúcar y población en las Antillas*, (1927; reprint ed., Havana: Cultural, 1935). Also cited by Instituto de Estudios Africanos de La Habana, p. 687.

31. See Gaston Martin, *Histoire de l'esclavage dans les colonies françaises* (Paris: Presses Universitaires de France, 1948), pp. 21, 25. Also cited in Remy Bastien, "Estructura de la adaptación del negro en América Latina y del afroamericano en Africa," trans. Juan Comas, *América Indígena* 29, no. 3 (1969): 596. Scholars continue to disagree regarding the number of slaves in the New World. For example, when interpreting Phillip Curtin's figures, Knight and Crahan get "approximately seventy-five thousand brought to all of Spanish America (including the Antilles), and an additional fifty thousand introduced to Brazil during the sixteenth century." See, Crahan and Knight, *Africa and the Caribbean*, p. 11.

32. See Anton de Kom, *Nosotros, los esclavos de Surinam* (1934; reprint ed., Havana: Casa de las Américas, 1981), p. 27.

33. See El ingenio, 3 vols. (Havana: Editorial de Ciencias Sociales, 1978.)

34. See Beltrán, *La población negra*, pp. 25–28.

35. Ibid., pp. 28–29.

36. See Argeliers León, "Música popular de origen africano en América Latina," *America Indígena* 29, no. 3 (1969): 634.

37. Beltrán, *La población negra*, p. 23. Beltran's figures seem to disagree with those provided by Phillip Curtin who calculates that the total number of Africans who were brought to the New World ranged between eight million and twelve million. Both Beltran's and Curtin's figures suggest that as many Africans died traveling to America as those who survived the journey. Although this seems to be on the high side, one must nevertheless stress the incomprehensible number of Blacks who died because of slavery and the impossibility of ascertaining the exact figure. See Curtin's *The Atlantic Slave Trade* (Madison: University of Wisconsin Press, 1969). Also see Crahan and Knight, *Africa and the Caribbean*, p. 5.

38. Antonio Zambrana, *El negro Francisco* (Havana: Fernández, 1953), pp. 152–53, my translation.

39. See "The General Causes of Jamaican Slave Revolts," in *Slavery in the New World*, ed. Laura Foner and Eugene D. Genovese (Englewood Cliffs, N.J.: Prentice-Hall, 1969), pp. 211–12.

40. For a historical analysis of this event, see José Luciano Franco, *Las minas de Santiago del Prado y la rebelión de los cobreros 1530–1800* (Havana: Editorial de Ciencias Sociales, 1975).

41. For an account of Palmares, see Ronald M. Rassner's article, "Palmares and the Freed Slave in Afro-Brazilian Literature," in this volume.

42. See Bastien, "Estructura," p. 616 and note 39.

43. For a novelistic account of Cuban slaves and Haitians, see César Leante's *Los guerrilleros negros* (Havana: UNEAC, 1976).

44. Bastien, "Estructura," pp. 616–17.

45. Ibid., p. 619. Also see Juan Pérez de la Riva's essays in *Contribución a la historia de la gente sin historia* (Havana: Editorial de Ciencias Sociales, 1974).

46. See Ramos, *Las poblaciones del Brasil* (Mexico: Fondo de Cultura Económica,

1944); cited by the Instituto de Estudios Africanos de La Habana in "Facetas," p. 695.

47. *The Black Jacobins: Toussaint L'Ouverture and the San Domingo Revolution* (New York: Vintage, 1963), p. 405.

48. *The Master and the Slave*, trans. Samuel Putnam (New York: Alfred A. Knopf, 1978), p. xxix.

49. Ibid., p. xii.

50. "The Culture that Cuba Created," trans. Naomi Lindstrom, *Latin American Literary Review* 8, no. 16 (1980): 38.

51. Ibid., p. 39.

52. For a brief summary of these works, see Lewis' "The African Impact on Language and Literature in the English-Speaking Caribbean," in *Africa and the Caribbean*, p. 101.

53. For these and other examples, see, ibid., pp. 105–106. Also see, Barbara Lalla, "Sources for a History of Jamaican Creole," *Carib*, no. 1 (1979), pp. 50–66.

54. These and other African-related words are listed in Fernando Ortiz, *Nuevo catauro de cubanismos* (Havana: Editorial de Ciencias Sociales, 1974).

55. For example, see Argeliers León, "Música popular," pp. 627–64.

56. This information is contained in an unpublished interview conducted by William Luis, Julia Hewitt and Luis Betancourt with the well-known *santero* Arcadio Gutiérrez in Cuba in the summer of 1980 and entitled "Conversaciones con Arcadio el santero."

57. Esteban Montejo, *The Autobiography of a Runaway Slave*, ed. Miguel Barnet, trans. Jocasta Innes (New York: Pantheon Books, 1968), p. 26.

58. See Paul de Man's "Literary History and Literary Modernity" in his *Blindness and Insight* (London and New York: Oxford University Press, 1971), pp. 142–65.

59. Zambrana, *El negro Francisco*, p. 152.

60. Hayden White has shown convincingly that historians submit themselves to literary strategies. See his *Metahistory* (Baltimore: Johns Hopkins University Press, 1973).

61. Montejo, *Autobiography*, pp. 63–64.

62. See Hugh Thomas, *Cuba: The Pursuit of Freedom* (New York: Harper and Row, 1971), p. 523.

63. For a history of Haiti, see Robert Debs Heinl, Jr., and Nancy Gordon Heinl, *Written in Blood* (Boston: Houghton Mifflin, 1978).

64. "From Slavery to Fettered Freedom: Attitudes Toward the Negro in Brazil," *Luso-Brazilian Review* 7, no. 1 (1970): 3–12. Also see Eric Williams *Capitalism and Slavery* (Chapel Hill: University of North Carolina Press, 1944).

65. Montejo, *Autobiography*, pp. 208–9.

66. See Julio Rodríguez Luis, "Lino Novás Calvo y la historia de Cuba," *Symposium*, 29, no. 4 (1975), pp. 282–83.

67. For a discussion of this and other laws, see Zoila Danger Roll, *Los cimarrones de el Frijol* (Santiago de Cuba: Empresa Editorial Oriente, 1979), pp. 15–22.

Spanish
Caribbean _____

2

Socrates Among the Weeds: Blacks and History in Carpentier's *Explosion in a Cathedral*

Roberto González Echevarría
(For Linda Garceau)

> I watched for the three V's one above the others, at the height of a man's breast if he were standing on the water.
>
> Carpentier, *The Lost Steps*

> Thus we observe here as elsewhere in human affairs, in which almost everything is paradoxical, a surprising and unexpected turn of events.
>
> Kant, "What Is Enlightenment?"

Latin American history has always been a competition among warring versions of history. The chroniclers of the discovery and conquest of America were the first to realize that the existence of the New World unsettled their notions of history. As they met the natives, they asked themselves who these people were and how their magnificent civilizations could have been left out of the Bible. From whom did they descend? How was their history linked to the biblical histories and to classical history? Why had the Fathers not spoken of them? The theological, philosophical and political dilemmas opened by the discovery and conquest of the New World violently shook the foundations of European thought. The first indigenous historians faced similar dilemmas, but from a different perspective. Garcilaso de la Vega, el Inca, born in Peru of a Spanish father and a noble Indian woman, wrote that Cuzco was "another Rome" in order to signify that Incaic civilization should take a place next to Greek and Roman cultures. In other words, while the Incas were heathens, they were civilized and quite prepared to receive Christianity, at least as prepared as the ancient world had been.[1] Felipe Guaman Poma de Ayala, a full-blooded Indian, was bolder. He maintained that the Incas had known Christianity before the arrival of the Spaniards, thereby removing the theological justification for the conquest and at the same time inserting the history of his people into the mainstream of world history.[2] In the New World, particularly in the part we today call Latin America, the ordering of history has never been an innocent activity.

By the time America was discovered, the history of Africa had been given a place in the overall scheme of world history. Africa had been known to Europeans since the most remote of times, and for them Africans had been part of the unfolding of human history. But it was not until large numbers of Africans were brought to the New World that their role in post-Christian history began to assume a larger significance. Once Africans had been transported to the New World, they too became part of the problem of how to narrate history. Like the Incas, the Mayas and other pre-Columbian cultures, Africans had their own version of history, a version that soon began to include their fate in the New World. Enough work has already been done to know that African versions of history incorporated a possible return to Africa after the ordeal of New World slavery. It is also known that neo-African cultures soon began to develop in the Americas, and they, of course, had their own accounts of African history in the New World. These versions further enriched the multiplicity of those versions of history already present in America, a multiplicity whose main feature is the shuffling of competing histories that attempt to find the master version of American history.

Garcilaso, Guaman Poma and other historians, including the Spaniard Bartolomé de las Casas, saw clearly and early the magnitude of the dilemma these differing versions of history raised. They also saw how the competition among them was linked to conflicts whose ultimate consequences would amount to radical changes in mankind's conception of religion, politics and art. Garcilaso's answer to this issue was to adopt what Juan Bautista Avalle Arce has called *uniformismo*, a term he derives from Lovejoy's unwieldy *uniformitarianism*.[3] In essence, Garcilaso—an early Lévi-Strauss, or perhaps a Toynbee or a Spengler—believed that all peoples were endowed with the same reason; therefore, their cultures were uniform in development and structure. For Garcilaso's cool and elegant mind, history consisted of a harmonious evolution that culminated with Christianity. Guaman Poma, who was of a more contentious spirit, argued for a restoration, maintaining that the conquest had been an illegal act. He advocated vehemently the superiority of his people over the Spaniards in a number of areas, not the least of which was morality. Las Casas, a medieval mind who fought against Hapsburg Renaissance imperialism, conceived of an orderly Christian community in which the asperity of differing cultures would be smoothed over by charity and the peaceful conversion of non-Christians. His view of history was thoroughly medieval and his conception of the roles various peoples should play in it so anachronistic that it appeared to his contemporaries as a form of far-fetched libertarianism, when it was in fact quite conservative. But history, for Las Casas, was Christian history. By the eighteenth century the unsettling of European thought brought about by the discovery and conquest of America and the importation of large numbers of Africans provoked a radical questioning of European beliefs, a process that has come to be known as the Enlightenment. America was a powerful agent in generating the questions asked by *philosophes*, as has been persuasively argued by Arthur P.

Whitaker.[4] Carpentier's *Explosion in a Cathedral*, called in the original *El siglo de las luces* (that is, *The Age of Enlightenment*), centers on that moment when the various versions of history are again pitted against each other in an attempt to reach a master version.

Published in 1962, *Explosion in a Cathedral* is important to the Latin American literary tradition because of the way in which it delves into the very core of the dilemma of what constitutes American history and how to narrate it. For Carpentier the core of that dilemma is how Blacks are part of the history of the New World, how their presence undermines mainstream political thought and, in so doing, reveals the very problematic nature of any understanding of American history. This process of undermining is accomplished not simply by showing the political impact of Blacks in the course of events during the eighteenth century and the beginnings of the nineteenth, but more ambitiously by making of the presence of Blacks in the New World a break in history—that is, the repetition of a large, archetypal split. In a sense, Carpentier is repeating Garcilaso's gesture by showing that there is a certain uniformity to history. His meditation in *Explosion in a Cathedral* is as wide-ranging as Garcilaso's, and it implies much more than the issue of how to narrate history. It is a proclamation of an American poetics whose energy is found in the relation of neo-African cultures in the New World to European notions of history. The subversion promoted by Blacks is not merely a repetition of that provoked earlier by Indians; it is a subversion whose very compulsion to repeat is the essence of American history and more broadly of American culture.

Prior to Carpentier's works, Blacks had appeared in the Latin American novel only as individual characters. The Cuban antislavery novel gives us fine portraits of rebellious slaves, and various other narrators include important black characters in their novels and stories. But it was Carpentier, with *¡Ecue-Yamba-O!* (1933) and particularly *The Kingdom of This World* (1949), who showed that the presence of Blacks in Latin America was an important historical difference, a force that had to be reckoned with in any writing or rewriting of Latin American history. In *Explosion in a Cathedral*, Carpentier goes further by incorporating the presence of Blacks into an historical paradigm that transcends the New World as historical event. One can see a progression in these novels from the role of Blacks in the unfolding of Cuban history in *¡Ecue-Yamba-O!* to the Haitian Revolution in *The Kingdom of This World* to the impact of the French and Haitian revolutions in the entire Caribbean and, indeed, on the entire American continent. The widening scope of the historical and geographical meditation leads, it seems to me, to the all-encompassing, almost abstract consideration of historical evolution in *Explosion in a Cathedral*.

In *The Kingdom of This World* the slave rebellions that led to the Haitian Revolution are seen as part of a skewing of history by forces alien to Europe. Mackandal, Bouckman and Toussaint ally themselves with natural powers that help them rout the colonists. Carpentier transforms those forces into hypostases of African deities who come to the aid of slaves, turning the tide of European domination. *The Kingdom of This World* already presents a clash of different versions of history: the European one, in which the central event is the French Revolution, and the Afro-American one, in which the central event is the Haitian Revolution. How are they related? Does the first cause or determine the latter? In *The Kingdom of This World* European history is not given priority; in fact, it appears inauthentic in relation to the New World. European history has as its highest representative Pauline Bonaparte, who surrenders to sloth and sensuality in the tropical heat, while Afro-American history is represented by the various *loas* who incarnate in the black revolutionaries. The Haitian Revolution appears as an echo of the French, yet at the same time the novel shows that the slave revolts had begun much earlier. If the latter are echoes of the former, they are distorted, false repetitions that in some way deny the causality of the apparent relationship. The series of repetitions and the numerological coherence of the text of *The Kingdom of this World* pretend to be in consonance with the African version of history, linked as they are to the cycles of nature and to a secret, encoded form of knowledge. The authorial presence in the novel, particularly in the famous prologue, offers a European perspective.[5] The text of the novel pretends to be a representation of the magical forces that make the slaves believe that Mackandal has been saved from the stake, that he has flown away, while the Europeans "know" that he was burned to death. In *The Kingdom of This World* the competition between the various versions of history is not resolved. At the end Ti Noel, senile yet lucid, speaks of the tasks man must accomplish while on this earth, but he is being brutalized by the Mulattoes, who have adopted the repressive policies of the former colonists. The Mulattoes do not simply repeat history. They become a poor copy of the white regime. There is irony in this repetition, a thwarting of the intention of the black revolutionaries that gives a satanic twist to the nature-bound repetitions and doublings that appear throughout. The oneiric world of Ti Noel at the end of *The Kingdom of This World*, which is an extension of African beliefs and desires and, therefore, of the activities of the black revolutionaries, clashes with the historical world of the Mulattoes, a world that is a distortion of both African and European history. There is an obvious gap between Ti Noel's grasp of history and the turn that events take in the novel. It is that gap which represents the divergence between a European and an African, or Afro-American, conception of history, a divergence that remains unresolved here.

Explosion in a Cathedral, a book in which Carpentier returns to the historical landscape covered in *The Kingdom of This World*, is an effort to find a common ground for the warring versions of history present in the earlier text. This is evident not only in the expansion of the fictional world to include most of the Caribbean as well as France, but more importantly in the way in which the Caribbean and European worlds are presented in relation to each other. *Explosion in a Cathedral* is a vast geographico-historical experiment whose goal is to discover who are the prime movers of universal history and also how history turns to text. The slave rebellions in *The Kingdom of This World* ushered in the

Haitian Revolution and were contrasted to the French Revolution. In *Explosion in a Cathedral* the slave revolts are paradigms of an overall unfolding of history that includes the French Revolution. *Explosion in a Cathedral* is a hermeneutical machine that attempts to interpret the master tropes of history, particularly but not exclusively, American history.

There is an overall theme in *Explosion in a Cathedral* that unifies European and Afro-American cultures through the demonstration that both have a similar approach to knowledge, even if European thought pretends that it is different and unique. This theme is present, above all, in Ogé, the doctor and philosopher who cures Esteban. Ogé's magical interpretation of medicine is successful in finding the cause of Esteban's respiratory difficulties where conventional doctors had failed. Ogé's cure is highly instructive in that it shows how Carpentier contrasts European and Afro-American beliefs. The cause of Esteban's malady is a garden kept by the black servant Remigio in a secret part of the backyard of the house:

The sight that now met their eyes was very surprising; parsley, nettles, mimosa and woodland grasses were growing in two long parallel beds around several very flourishing mignonette plants. A bust of Socrates, which Sofía remembered having once seen, as a child, in her father's office, was set in a niche, as if displayed on an altar, surrounded by curious offerings, such as magicians use for their spells: Cups full of grains of maize, sulphur stones, snails, iron fillings. "*C'est ça,*" said Ogé, contemplating the miniature garden as if it had great meaning for him (p. 44).[6]

In spite of Sofía's smug doubts, Esteban recovers quickly after Ogé pulls out the plants in the garden and burns them. For Remigio, who bitterly protests the destruction of his garden, Socrates was the Lord of the Forests (p. 45), while for Ogé the cure would be accomplished because "certain illnesses were mysteriously connected with the growth of a grass, a plant or a tree somewhere nearby. Every human being had a 'double' in the vegetable kingdom, and there were cases where this 'double,' to further its own growth, stole strength from the man with whom it was linked, condemning him to illness while it flowered or germinated" (p. 44). Whereas in *The Kingdom of This World* there was irony implicit in the imbalance between the beliefs and practices of Blacks and a given reality (Mackandal is burned), here the irony has been reversed, for we can easily discover the "scientific" foundation of Ogé's diagnosis—allergies are the cause of Esteban's asthma.

The presence of the bust of Socrates in the midst of the garden is, of course, full of implications. It is obvious that the whole garden can be taken as an emblem of the mixture of European philosophy with Afro-American beliefs and, more specifically, of the conjunction in America of neoclassical art and thought with nature. But there are further implications. Socrates, the Master of Reason, of discourse, of logos, has been turned by Remigio into the Lord of the Forest, presiding over the medicinal powers of plants. In a sense Remigio has restored to Socrates, or more specifically to logos, its ambiguous power as purveyor of both poison and medicine.[7] In the beginning, Socrates and Osain, Lord of the Forest, have a similar function. The codification of plants in Remigio's garden is flawlessly true to Afro-Cuban lore, and the deification of the Lord of the Forests, of *el monte*, is at the very center of Afro-Cuban beliefs.[8] In *The Kingdom of This World* the plants used by Mackandal poisoned only whites; here they both poison and cure. *Explosion in a Cathedral* seeks an American hermeneutics, one that will allow a reading of American history in all its variety and conflict. It is not without implication that the character cured is Esteban, who will be the translator of revolutionary texts from French and who is associated with the figure of the writer generally and with Carpentier specifically. Esteban shares with Carpentier not only his birthday on December 26, but also the very malady of which he is cured by Ogé: asthma.[9] Remigio's garden in *Explosion in a Cathedral* underscores the problem of writing from and about the New World, the complexity of the variegated codes within which meaning is encrypted. Ogé's action of pulling out the weeds is similar to the notion of an explosion in a cathedral, for the *monte* is a temple. Temples, however, are very resilient in the New World.

While Esteban and Víctor argue in favor of abolishing religion, Ogé advocates a sort of *imitatio Christi*, refusing to give up the interpretative energy and consolation afforded by belief. Ogé "often referred to the *Bible*—accepting some of the myths on which it was founded—just as he used terms taken from the Cabbala and from Platonism, frequently alluding to the Cathars, whose Princess Esclaramunda Sofía knew about from a charming novel she had read recently" (p. 79). Like Ogé's cure, events and descriptions in the novel tend to cast an ironic perspective not on the beliefs of the Mulatto, but on those of the Whites. The prime movers of European history as well as the political practice of Whites appear to be inspired by religion, not by reason. Caleb Dexter, the American captain, is a mason who surrounds himself with the symbolic paraphernalia of the cult, and so is Víctor. The images and rituals of organized religion have not really been smashed; they have been replaced. Executions appear in the novel as *autos-da-fé*, and the guillotine itself, with its combination of lines and triangles, is a huge emblem in which freedom and death are enigmatically intertwined. The world of Whites, like that of Blacks, is permeated by religion, by a sense of the mystery of things, by the presence of signs whose interpretation requires a special gnostic process. The cross, the basic emblem of European belief, is invested in the novel with all of its primitive symbolical meanings. Dexter's navigational skills are based on a secret knowledge handed down by tradition the way religious practices are, and even Víctor's abilities as a merchant are couched on a certain occult knowledge of trading. The occult is the real knowledge as opposed to reason, which posits an ideal order. The occult is both knowledge and desire, or knowledge de-formed, *warped* by desire. In this sense, both Whites and Blacks practice occultism as pragmatic interpretation of reality. This is, as we shall see, what unites them in American history and poetics. Reason is the *urtext*, whereas the occult is the *text*; the former, paradoxically, turns out to be a sort of heuristic device of the latter.

Against the ideal order of reason *Explosion in a Cathedral* pits the disorder of revolution or, perhaps better, the real order of revolution. The French Revolution, as viewed by Esteban and as lived by Víctor, consists of a series of movements and countermovements, rituals and counterrituals that bring to power or topple from power various leaders and groups. Symbols are exchanged for other symbols, but the symbolic nature of the social process is never really altered. As an event in the novel, the French Revolution appears not as the logical product of a historical progression, but as the expanded version of the domestic revolution that takes place in the house of the protagonists after the death of the father. Events are repeated, expanded, distorted, not inserted into a causal relationship. Things become intelligible in their various relationships to others on a symbolic level, not as objects of a real order or as events in a given teleology. Even the arrangement of characters in the novel obeys a secret kabbalistic code, not necessarily a mimetic representation of human relations.[10] Everything in *Explosion in a Cathedral* threatens to become significant, legible, if only the reader can find the proper code or, perhaps, the master code. Like Ogé, we stand before a complex text, traversed by various codes whose intersection we must find.

The persistent reversal of revolutionary ideals belies the European notion of history as the progression toward a perfect society. The liberators soon become oppressors, and the guillotine turns justice into inquisitorial *auto*. In Guadeloupe the recently freed slaves are forced to return to work with the same methods of coercion used earlier by the slave masters. In Cayenne, Víctor is the jailer of many former revolutionaries. Lives, careers, whole historical movements are turned upside down or run backwards. The intended purpose of revolutionary language is often betrayed, as when Billaud Varenne's languid mulatto mistress fans her breasts with an old copy of *La Décade philosophique*. History turns out to be the error, the errancy inherent in all action, as opposed to theory or intention. Just as gnosticism is knowledge twisted by the force of desire, so history is intention bent by reality. What *Explosion in a Cathedral* pretends to do is show the errancy of history as well as the latent analogy between history, viewed in this manner, and the writing of history.

If in *Explosion in a Cathedral* doors become magical thresholds, guillotines become enigmatic symbols and the bust of Socrates appears in the midst of medicinal herbs, historical events are linked through an associative method whose coherence is hardly the product of reason. Although there is no more telling historical event in the novel than the French Revolution, what Carpentier offers are mostly the echoes of the Revolution as its shock waves reach the Caribbean. But are they echoes? Do they signify or represent the Revolution? Can one understand the Revolution through a reading of these peripheral events? The fact is that even in Paris itself, all Esteban and Víctor can perceive are the marginal rituals, the liturgical manifestations of the new order. Action itself is never to be seen, save for what appear to be its *reactions*. In the Caribbean the echoes of the Revolution are presumably distortions, but distortions of what ideal model? The laws enacted by the revolutionary government suffer a fate similar to the Spanish laws directed to the New World during the colonial period—*se acatan, pero no se cumplen*; their authority is acknowledged, but they are not put into practice. Besides, by the time the laws reach the French possessions, the government that passed them has often already been toppled. They are emanations from a locus of power that has disappeared, texts whose only validity lies with themselves, for their source has vanished and their link to reality is tenuous at best. This gap between law and practice is made manifest once and again by the way in which Blacks are shown in relation to the Revolution.

Throughout *Explosion in a Cathedral* the Blacks upset the course of history and set off unexpected side effects. But are these side effects? On the side of what do they appear? Not only do the Blacks upset history; they question its central tenets or, better yet, the myths about its centrality. By burning down Víctor's store in Le Cap, the Blacks thrust him into political action; and by burning down the whole city, they force the metropolitan government into taking action against them. The very same government that frees the slaves and confers French citizenship upon them has to send troops to quell their rebellion. The freedom proclaimed in Europe does not translate into liberty for the slaves in the Caribbean, as if crossing the ocean meant entering a world where everything is inverted. In a discussion with Esteban, Billaud Varenne and Brottier, the Swiss colonist Sieger emphasizes the magnitude of the gap between revolutionary law and the actions of the slaves: " 'All the French Revolution has achieved in America is to legalise the Great Escape which has been going on since the sixteenth century. The blacks didn't wait for you, they proclaimed themselves free a countless number of times.' " (p. 231). In one of the most memorable passages in the novel Sieger goes on to enumerate the important slave revolts in the New World from the sixteenth century to the time when the action of the novel takes place. Freedom as taken by the rebellious slaves is quite different from the freedom magnanimously bestowed upon them by the white rulers. Historical action differs radically from the course the French revolutionaries try to give history: A chasm opens between the text of the law and the actions of Blacks. Within that chasm there lie the transformations, the tropes through which American history is made and written. Reading must take into account this opening, this discontinuity wherein inversion and perversion take place. That gap, that no-man's-land, is the ground on which meet the warring versions of history that make up American history.

There is an obvious political irony in the break between law and action, between the freedom the French intend to give the Blacks and the freedom they take. On this level Carpentier's novel shows that the oppressed need no help from their oppressors to desire freedom and to try to obtain it. But there is more. With their own revolutionary action the Blacks break the continuity Europeans intend to give history, but at the same time their actions repeat an act of foundation that is part of a larger historical pattern. This break is not necessarily an interruption, but an anticipation, an action *avant la lettre*, as it were. As Sieger says, the Blacks did not wait for the French revolutionaries to grant them freedom, but took it several times before. On the one hand, the slave rebellions appear to have been unleashed by the Revolution; on the other hand, however, it turns out that they also anticipated it. Even in my own formulation of the process there are inevitable traces of a *retruécano*, a rhetorical inversion, a baroque figure that here, as it nearly always does, resembles a specular movement in which it is impossible to tell what takes precedence over what, what is the reflection of what. The *retruécano* is an equivalency in the process of displaying itself both in its inherent repetition and difference, in its reiteration and desired simultaneity. The inversion can be read in either direction, both ways meeting somewhere in a virtual center where appearances are reversed; in most inversions that virtual fulcrum is precisely an ellipsis. American history, American writing and, therefore, the reading of American writing must allow for the manifestation of such inversions, must practice such inversions; it is its system. To understand this, the more abstract significance of the presence of Blacks in the novel, we must turn to a scene that apparently has little to do with our topic: the one in which Sofía and Caleb Dexter visit the tomb of the grandson of the last Byzantine emperor in Barbados.

On her way to meet Víctor in Cayenne, Sofía stops over in Barbados. In the island she takes a carriage ride with Caleb Dexter, all the way to

the little rocky bastion of St. John, where, behind the church she found a tombstone with an inscription that referred unexpectedly to the death on the island of a person whose name bore a crushing weight of historical association: *Here lie the remains of Ferdinand Paleologue, descendant of the last Emperors of Greece—Priest of this parish—1655–1656.*

The bottle of wine he had drained during the journey had made Caleb Dexter somewhat emotional, and he uncovered himself respectfully. In the dusk, whose light was turning the waves red as they broke in a great spray against the rocky monoliths of Bathsheba, Sofía decorated the grave with some bougainvillaea which she had cut in the garden of the presbytery. The first time he visited the house in Havana, Víctor Hugues had spoken at length about this tomb of the unknown grandson of the Ecumenical Patriarch who had been killed during the final resistance of Byzantium, having chosen to die rather than fall into the sacrilegious hands of the conquering Turks. And now she had found it, in the place he had indicated. Across the grey stone, marked with the Cross of Constantine, a hand now followed the course which another hand had followed years before, searching out the hollows of the letters with the tips of its fingers.

To cut short this unexpected ritual, which he felt had already lasted long enough, Caleb Dexter remarked: "And to think that the last rightful owner of the Basilica of Saint Sophia should have ended up on this island" (pp. 306–7).

During his first visit to the house in Havana, Víctor had indeed mentioned, amid a tirade about the marvels to be found in the Caribbean, that there was in "Barbados, the tomb of a nephew [*sic*] of Constantine XI, the last emperor of Byzantium, whose ghost appeared to solitary wayfarers on stormy nights'' (p. 33). The context in which Víctor mentions this is significant, for the theme of the Caribbean as generator of strange, odd shapes and forms is quite germane to the issue of the unfolding of history in the novel. The linking of these two moments in the novel is also relevant to our discussion, insofar as they both occur at breaking points in the plot: Víctor's first appearance and Sofía's voyage to return to him. One can add to all this that Carpentier himself visited Barbados and wrote a piece about the tomb of Constantine's grandson for *El Nacional* in Caracas, which undoubtedly had an impact on the genesis of *Explosion in a Cathedral*.[11] But there is a lot more to this scene.

The existence of this tomb in Barbados would be merely one of those instances of the marvelous that Carpentier liked to cite, were it not for the fact that throughout the novel there is a sense that what occurs in the Caribbean is a repetition (though a skewed one) of what took place earlier in the Mediterranean. Are not Víctor and the others replaying in the Caribbean the roles already performed by Robespierre and other revolutionaries in Paris? There is even a direct allusion to the Caribbean as a new Mediterranean that leaves little doubt about the importance of this theme in *Explosion in a Cathedral*. The passage is part of one of Esteban's meditations as he travels in the corsair ship under Captain Barthelemy. I shall have to quote the original Spanish here because the translation into English has erased important features of the way in which the Caribbean and the Mediterranean are paired. I will then quote the translation and, by way of a critique of its failings, underscore the relationship I have in mind: ''En Francia había aprendido Esteban a gustar del gran zumo solariego que por los pezones de sus vides había alimentado la turbulenta y soberbia civilización mediterránea—ahora prolongada en este Mediterráneo Caribe, donde proseguíase la Confusión de Rasgos iniciada, hacía muchos milenios, en el ámbito de los Pueblos del Mar'' (p. 157). The English version reads: ''Esteban had learned in France to appreciate the noble juice of the vine, which had nourished the proud and turbulent civilisation of the Mediterranean, now spread into this Caribbean Mediterranean, where the blending of characteristics had for many thousands of years been in progress within the ambit of the peoples of the sea'' (p. 183). Fortunately the binomial ''Mediterranean Caribbean'' has been retained in English without mediating elements, for this superimposition is the way in which the relationship must be viewed; the only thing separating the two is literally the gap between the two names. But ''blending'' does not translate ''Confusión,'' and the elimination of the capitals takes away the cosmic sense of what the text proposes: This Confusion of Features is a single event setting in motion a series of historical echoes that refer back to their own dynamic movement of joining and dispersing, of blending and separating. (Carpentier likes to capitalize these ''mastermoments,'' these Mastermotions of history, a practice that may be more offensive to English readers than to Spanish ones, though in the latter language such capitalization is not common either. Another vexing change introduced in the translation is the breaking up of the text into paragraphs, something that Carpentier did not do in Spanish, also contravening common practice). The superimposition of the Caribbean on the Mediterranean allows the reader to realize the significance of the tomb in Barbados and of Sofía's gesture. The superimposition reveals the larger design of history that unfolds behind the plot of *Explosion in a Cathedral*, for, if the Caribbean is like the Mediterranean, then the history of the former is a repetition of the latter, to wit: The Byzantine Empire is to the Roman Empire as Caribbean history is to European history. In brief, America is to Europe as Constantinople is to Rome. If the fissure in the Roman Empire was its contact with the Eastern World, in America the break occurs through the presence of Africa.

If we turn again to the scene in Barbados, we notice that the text refers specifically to the grandfather of the man buried as he "who had been killed during the final resistance of Byzantium," that is to say, in the event—the fall of Constantinople—that caused, albeit indirectly, the discovery and conquest of the New World. This suggestion assembles at once a structure of repeated breaks: the formation of the Eastern Empire, the fall of Constantinople, and the independence of America, the major break already prefigured by the slave rebellions. All of these breaks, which are in consonance with those in the plot of the novel that bring the characters to Barbados, repeat the Confusion of Features mentioned above. I would like to think of this Confusion of Features in terms of the *retruécano* discussed earlier in connection with how things are transformed by crossing the ocean.

Like the famous basilica of the same name, Sofía is the hinge between different worlds that are distorted mirror-images of each other, and it is, therefore, appropriate that she be the character to be placed in front of the tomb in Barbados. She also incarnates a secret form of knowledge, a mystical, gnostic understanding. Thus she mediates between the contemplative Esteban and the active Víctor. Given the meaning of these characteristics, we can now surmise what her running her fingers on the letters of the epitaph means—"a hand now followed the course which another hand had followed years before, searching out the hollows of the letters with the tips of its fingers." At least three hands have preceded Sofía's on the epitaph: Víctor's, the person who chiseled them on the tombstone, and probably also Carpentier's. There are three dots after "*dedos*" in the original, Carpentier's conventional winking of the eye when he is referring to himself. In all three cases Sofía is acting out the process of reading—she is following a contour already inscribed by another. But she overcomes the secondariness of this act by seeking the hollow of the letters, that is to say, by looking behind the writing. Through this act she is reading the inverted shape of the letters, their specular image, at the same time that she is delving into the gap, the fissure that precedes them. Sofía is reaching into the Confusion of Features, of marks, searching out in the back of the letters their secret meaning that is not apparent on the visible surface. What Sofía is looking for is the "de-forming" by which Roman art becomes Byzantine art, the "mis-shaping" of the core of the Latin American baroque.

This process of changing something into something else appears to Esteban as characteristic of the Caribbean. The proliferation of shapes changing constantly into something other forces the language to hyphenate words in order to be able to designate the continuous act of changing, of being transformed:

Carried into a world of symbiosis, standing up to his neck in pools whose water was kept perpetually foaming by cascading waves, and was broken, torn, shattered, by the hungry bite of jagged rocks, Esteban marvelled to realise how the language of these islands had made use of agglutination, verbal amalgams and metaphors to convey the formal ambiguity of things which participated in several essences at once. Just as certain trees were called "acacia-bracelets," "pineapple-porcelain," "wood-rib," "tisane-cloud," and "iguana-stick," many marine creatures had received names which established verbal equivocations in order to describe them accurately. Thus a fantastic bestiary had arisen of dog-fish, oxen-fish, tiger-fish, snorers, blowers, flying fish; of striped, tattooed and tawny fish, fish with their mouths on top of their heads, or their gills in the middle of their stomachs; whitebellies, swordfish and mackerel; a fish which bit off testicles—cases had been known—another that was herbivorous; the red-speckled sand-eel; a fish which became poisonous after eating manchineel apples—not forgetting the vieja-fish, the captain-fish, with its gleaming throat of golden scales; or the woman-fish—the mysterious and elusive manatees, glimpsed in the mouths of rivers where the salt water mingled with the fresh, with their feminine profiles and their siren's breasts, playing joyful nuptial pranks on one another in their watery meadows (pp. 177–78).

The shape of these fish, of these creatures, is given not by the second term in the hyphenated word, but by the very process of changing one into another, by the hyphen itself. This movement from one order to another, from model to distorted copy, is also evident in the painting that serves as emblem of the novel and gives its title to the English version: *Explosion in a Cathedral.*

Ramón García Castro has rightly noted that this painting—which he had not been able to see—has much in common "with other Romantic paintings. It reminds one, because of the flames, of Turner's (English, 1775–1851) 'Fire in the Parliament,' which dates from 1834, a date later than the canvas in the house of the protagonists. Also, because of its violent lights, it is related to another painting from after the end of the eighteenth century, 'Pandemonium,' by John Martin (English, 1789–1854). . . . Also, because of the sun rays and the houses about to be razed, the painting could be related to Carl Brullov's 'The Last Day of Pompey.' "[12] There is no doubt that there is a romantic conception of art at the core of Carpentier's works, and one can feel a certain *Sturm und Drang* in the catastrophe depicted by Monsu Desiderio. But there is more than destruction in this painting, which, thanks to my colleague Verity Smith, I am able to include with this essay.

The painting is called not "Explosion in a Cathedral," but "King Asa of

Judah Destroying the Temple.'' While in the first description (pp. 18–19) of the painting the emphasis is on the row of columns breaking down, in the second the existence of an unbroken row of columns is also mentioned. It is easy to think only of the destruction of the church, particularly when we think that the novel deals with revolution, but the painting is in fact more complex than that. The second description of the painting reads:

Esteban suddenly stopped, stirred to the very depths, in front of the "Explosion in a Cathedral" by the anonymous Neapolitan master. In it were prefigured, so to speak, so many of the events he had experienced that he felt bewildered by the multiplicity of interpretations to which this prophetic, anti-plastic, un-painterly canvas, brought to the house by some mysterious chance, lent itself. If, in accordance with the doctrines he had once been taught, the cathedral was a symbol—the ark and the tabernacle—for his own being, then an explosion had certainly occurred there, which, although tardy and slow, had destroyed altars, images, and objects of veneration. If the cathedral was the Age, then a formidable explosion had indeed overthrown its most solid walls, and perhaps buried the very men who had built the infernal machine beneath an avalanche of debris. If the cathedral was the Christian Church, then Esteban noticed that a row of sturdy pillars remained intact, opposite those which were shattering and falling in this apocalyptic painting, as if to prophesy resilience, endurance and a reconstruction, after the days of destruction and of stars foretelling disasters had passed (p. 253).

While the interpretations suggested by Esteban are correct, looking at the picture we cannot fail to be struck by the broken symmetry, by the fact that the collapsing row of columns on the right is/was the specular image of the unbroken one on the left. In other words, the row of columns on the right is a *deformation* of the row on the left. What the painting suspends is not so much a catastrophe as the very process of transformation, of troping, by which one thing becomes another. American history, culture and poetics are not the ''de-formed'' right row of columns but *both* rows.

A similar, even more telling, example of transformation is found in the scene at Jorge's country estate on Christmas Eve, 1799. The date is important because the shift from December 1799 to January 1800 is the chronological center of the novel, the hinge, as it were, between its two larger halves. From a chronological point of view, this time segment is to the temporal sequence of the novel what Constantinople is to history, what Sofía is to the characters, what the central nave is to the two rows of columns in the painting ''Explosion in a Cathedral''—it is the crease, the break where repetition and distortion begin, the specular locus of transformation. It is characteristic of Carpentier's texts that this hinge scene should evoke a number of other breaks: the end of the year and beginning of the next, the end of the eighteenth century and beginning of the nineteenth, and, of course, Christmas itself, the paradigmatic revolution in the West. At the level of the fiction the death of Jorge marks a break and a repetition: His death, as the center of the chronological span of the novel is like the father's death, which opened the action. In terms of Cuban history and Latin

Monsu Desiderio, "King Asa of Judah Destroying the Temple." Copyright of the Fitz-william Museum, Cambridge (England). Official Photograph No. S3731.

American history in general, the scene denotes the transition from neoclassicism to romanticism, a transition made visible through the transformation of Jorge's house from a Roman palace to a burning palace, from neoclassical symmetry to romantic conflagration: "Set in the midst of palm trees and coffee plantations, Jorge's relative's house was a sort of Roman palace, with tall, smooth, Doric columns set at intervals along the external galleries" (p. 268); and later: "Behind the clumps of bougainvillaea, the house was a blaze of candelabra, lamps and Venetian lustres" (p. 271).[13] But the most significant shift is the one signaled by the swift swirl of rituals within the period of Advent. As I pointed out a number of years ago, there is a leap from the rituals of Christmas Eve to those of New Year's Eve. The evening of Christmas Eve begins: "On the evening of the 24th of December whilst some of the party were eagerly completing the arrangements for Christmas Day" (p. 269); but it ends: "Now they would have to wait for midnight, surrounded by trays of punch. Twelve strokes would ring out from the tower, and everyone would have to gulp down the traditional twelve grapes" (p. 271). This jump over the twenty-fifth of December, over the quintessential break in Western history, toward the end of the century, conceals a longer crossing into a ritual whose celebrants are the slaves in Jorge's plantation, a crossing that I had not seen in my previous commentary of this scene and one that is of primary importance to our topic.[14]

The shift in the rituals is announced by the sudden appearance of Blacks, who sing and dance disguised in various costumes: "The rain had stopped; the undergrowth was full of lights and fancy-dresses. Shepherds appeared, and millers with floury faces, negroes who were not negroes, old women aged twelve, men with beards, and men with cardboard crowns, all shaking maracas, cow-bells, tambourines and timbrels" (p. 271). It seems clear to me now that what the Blacks are celebrating is not Christmas Eve, nor New Year's Eve, but the Epiphany—January 6, not December 24 or 31. In a memorable study Fernando Ortiz demonstrated the importance of the Día de Reyes as a ritual during slavery in Cuba.[15] On January 6 the slaves, often divided into their regional culture-groups, *cabildos,* would choose a king-for-a-day (the cardboard crown in the quotation) and march dancing to the governor's house in Havana, or to the master's house elsewhere, to ask for their *aguinaldo,* or Christmas bonus (the word appears in the song the Blacks sing following the lines of the novel quoted above). In general terms the Día de Reyes was, according to Ortiz, a carnivalesque inversion ritual, in which the slaves were free for the day and their chosen king had power for that given period; it was a day on which any White was liable to be asked for money, and Blacks acted out, in a sense, their desire to be free and to return to their ancestral land. Ortiz notes that, coming at the end of Advent, the ritual had its origin perhaps in the so-called twelfth night, in which the end of the Christmas period was celebrated. Given the presence of the costumes, particularly of the cardboard crown, and the song about the *aguinaldo,* there can be little, if any, doubt that what the slaves on Jorge's

From Fernando Ortiz, *La antigua fiesta afrocubana del "Día de Reyes,"* (1925; reprint ed., Havana: Ministerio de Relaciones Exteriores Departamento de Asuntos Culturales, División de Publicaciones, 1960).

plantation are celebrating is this ritual of the Epiphany, whose significance in relation to our discussion of Blacks and history in the novel is vast.

Ortiz suggests that the Día de Reyes was a syncretic ritual, for the Three Magi were often seen as representatives of the various cultures that make up Cuban culture—Melchior was, more often than not, depicted as black, though this changed on occasion. The ritual includes elements of both African and European rituals. Its force, its movement, is given by inversion, by a kind of *retruécano* in which Blacks assume power, even if only mock power, and freedom, even if only for a day, and a fake freedom at best. Neo-African culture in the Caribbean thus appears as a tropological process akin to the one seen as the language of the islands. African culture is the difference that generates, among many other modifications, the time warp, the whirl of dates and rituals, the new, "de-formed" shape of history. If one sets out the significant dates in the sequence, it is evident that their arrangement is analogous to what we have observed in the painting "Explosion in a Cathedral": a series of repetitions, each of which is a distortion of the preceding one. The resulting one, the slave's feast of Epiphany, is a ritual in which the previous ones have not been erased, but new shapes have been superimposed on them to create a sense of motion, of dynamic transformation. The best example of this kind of superimposition is the text of the novel itself. If we read hastily, following only the flow of the story, we are bound to miss the violent leaping of dates, a distortion that does not appear to upset the conventional chronology of the story. Again, if we simply read along, we are sure to miss the repetitions in the plot of the novel and the larger historical repetitions that are suggested. Like Byzantine art, *Explosion in a Cathedral* appears to have a conventional, classical shape, only slightly askew, but if one looks closer, then larger, more significant distortions begin to appear. The novel demands that we, like Sofía running her fingers on the epitaph of Constantine's grandson, look beyond the surface shape of the letters to the hollow behind them, to the gap; that we, without losing sight of the contour of the signs, without ceasing to relish their very materiality, seek the hidden meaning.

In the end, what is most remarkable about *Explosion in a Cathedral* is that the text of the novel itself shares characteristics of Latin American culture and history as (mis)shapen by African culture. The text is not composed of letters that, like the French revolutionary law, presume to give history an ideal course. The text of the novel, like a ritualistic object, has its own value as a system of symbols, as access to an arcane gnosis wherein its complicated numerology and emblematic quality are more important than the ebb and flow of concepts. The text does not simply "side" with a neo-African American culture; it seeks to show that all symbolic activity, including literature, operates in this fashion. History, particularly written history, is not so much elucidation as cultural self-recognition and celebration. Enlightenment, *Aufklärung*, is a clearing, a demolition of local idols and an investiture of idols who will some day be meaningful to all mankind. By making Blacks the catalyst for this meditation on history, Carpentier is echoing Nicolás Guillén's renowned statement that Africans came to the New World to "give man his definitive profile"; but what is unchanging about that profile is that it is an agent for change.

Carpentier's wide-ranging meditation on history is, in effect, a manifesto of an American poetics. Only by taking into account the warping through repetition displayed in *Explosion in a Cathedral* and its suggested analogue in Byzantine art can we really begin to understand the nature of such American baroque artists as Wilfredo Lam and Aleijandinho. In fact, some of Lam's elongated figures and clearly Aleijandinho's angular and tortured prophets display a Byzantine "mis-shaping" that is the very essence of the Latin American baroque.

By reflecting on Carpentier's vast geographic-historical experiment, we can also understand that similar intellectual and artistic adventures by Garcilaso, Guaman Poma and others are not mere coincidences, but part and parcel of every American effort to narrate history; not an elimination of warring versions of history, but a superimposition: Cuzco on Rome, the Caribbean on the Mediterranean. Carpentier was perhaps the first to posit this self-consciously as a key to the narrative of America, a vision so powerful in its conception and execution that it has indelibly marked the works of other American writers, such as Carlos Fuentes in his *Terra Nostra*, Severo Sarduy in his *Maitreya*, and Gabriel García Márquez in his *One Hundred Years of Solitude*.

Explosion in a Cathedral also demonstrates that American narrative is never merely storytelling, or history retelling, but an activity that is akin to both philosophical meditation and religio-cultural ritual. It is a mutual recognition, sought through an understanding of symbolic exchange, of the process by which history as shared symbols of becoming and being are activated, rendered meaningful. Who knows how much this owes to Afro-American cultures specifically? What we do know is that it owes much to their integration into the larger process of American culture and certainly of American writing. Carpentier is urging us not to look beyond the symbols to the blank stare of Socrates' bust among the weeds of Remigio's garden, but to the forest of symbols that surrounds it.

NOTES

1. *Royal Commentaries of the Incas and General History of Peru*, trans. with an Introduction by Harold V. Livermore, Foreword by Arnold J. Toynbee, 2 vols. (Austin and London: University of Texas Press, 1966).

2. Felipe Guaman Poma de Ayala, *El primer nueva corónica y buen gobierno*, critical edition by John V. Murra and Rolena Adorno, 3 vols. (Mexico: Siglo XXI Editores, 1980).

3. *El Inca Garcilaso en sus Comentarios (antología vivida)* (Madrid: Gredos, 1970), p. 20.

4. "The Dual Rôle of Latin America in the Enlightenment," in his *Latin America and the Enlightenment* (1942; reprint ed., Ithaca, N.Y.: Cornell University Press, 1961), pp. 3–21.

5. I have analyzed this at length in my *Alejo Carpentier: The Pilgrim at Home* (Ithaca, N.Y.: Cornell University Press, 1977).

6. *Explosion in a Cathedral*, tr. John Sturrock (New York: Harper Colophon Books, 1979). All references in the body of this paper are to this edition of the translation. Among various other problems, this translation gives chapter number 27 to both chapters 26 and 27. For the original I am using the first edition: *El siglo de las luces* (Mexico: Compañía General de Ediciones, 1962).

7. My source here is, of course, Jacques Derrida's "Plato's Pharmacy," in *Dissemination*, tr. Barbara Johnson (Chicago: University of Chicago Press, 1981).

8. Lydia Cabrera, *El monte. Igbo. Finda; Ewe Orisha. Vititi Nfinda* (Miami: Ediciones Universal, 1975 [1st ed., 1954]). The description of the powers of the various medicinal herbs are taken, it seems, from Cabrera's work.

9. *Carpentier: afirmación literaria americanista* (Caracas: Ediciones de la Facultad de Humanidades y Educación—Universidad Central de Venezuela, 1978), p. 15. This is a kind of public interview with Carpentier, in which he gives details about the relationship between his life and the origin of his books.

10. In *Alejo Carpentier* I have given the pertinent details concerning the correspondences between various aspects of the novel and the Kabbalah. There are many, beginning with the title, since the *Zohar* ("Book of Splendors") is a "Book of Lights" ("*de las luces*"). The three main characters correspond to the sephiroth of the first tryad.

11. "Los fantasmas de Barbados," *El Nacional* (Caracas), September 17, 1958, p. 16. This article is now collected in *Letra y Solfa*, ed. Alexis Márquez Rodríguez (Caracas: Síntesis Dosmil, 1975), pp. 281–82.

12. "La pintura en Alejo Carpentier," *Tláloc* (New York), no. 7 (1974), pp. 8–9.

13. To understand this period of Cuban history one may consult Manuel Moreno Fraginals' *The Sugarmill: The Socioeconomic Complex of Sugar in Cuba*, trans. Cedric Belfrage (New York: Monthly Review Press, 1976). Moreno Fraginals proves beyond doubt the strength of Enlightenment ideas among the Cuban sugar barons. These scenes of *Explosion in a Cathedral* appear to be a rewriting of parts of *Cecilia Valdés*.

14. Echevarría, *Alejo Carpentier*.

15. Fernando Ortiz, *La antigua fiesta afrocubana del "Día de Reyes"* (1925; reprint ed., Havana: Ministerio de Relaciones Exteriores Departamento de Asuntos Culturales, División de Publicaciones, 1960).

3

Slavery, Racism and Autobiography in Two Early Black Writers: Juan Francisco Manzano and Martín Morúa Delgado

Richard L. Jackson

Slavery was living hell for Blacks. One can imagine the problems slaves faced, especially the slave man of letters, particularly if he dared to write about his plight. Juan Francisco Manzano (1797?–1854) was the best known of the slave poets; he was also the first Black to publish a book of poetry in Cuba, *Poesías líricas (Cantos a Lesbia)* in 1821. This work was a considerable achievement, whatever its literary value, when we realize that the author had begun to teach himself to read and write just three years before. His second book of poetry, *Flores pasajeras*, of which there are no extant copies, was published in 1830. These two books, some poems such as his much anthologized "Mis treinta años," his letters, his *Autobiografía* (1840) and his play *Zafira* (1842) represent the corpus of Manzano's work that has come down to us.

The year 1836 was perhaps Manzano's best: He gained his freedom as well as a wider forum for his literature. In that year he was allowed to appear before the prestigious Del Monte literary *tertulia* ("group") to read his poem "Mis treinta años," which continues to enjoy success even today. This sonnet, which speaks of his "thirty unhappy years,"[1] does not mention slavery directly nor does it need to, as oblique references leave little doubt what his thirty years spent as a slave have been like. We marvel at Manzano's restraint in suppressing direct reference to external circumstances of which he, a Black and a slave writing in a slave society, had to be acutely aware. Even his *Autobiografía* is underplayed.

Domingo del Monte, the "liberal" responsible for Manzano's freedom, "commissioned" the slave author to write his *Autobiografía*. This Autobiografía[2] is perhaps Manzano's greatest claim to fame: It is the only slave autobiography that we know of that was written during that long period in Cuban history, and perhaps it is Latin America's first and only slave narrative. In the United States and Africa black autobiographies, some of them classics, abound. The slave narrative itself was a prominent literary genre in the United States, and black autobiographies and autobiographical books continued to pour forth following the Civil War. To date, an estimated four hundred of these books have been published in the United States.[3] In Latin America, however, the black auto-biography is not a primary form, although autobiographical books by Afro-Latin Americans do exist, including Candelario Obeso's *La lucha de la vida* (1882), Manuel Zapata Olivella's *Pasión vagabunda* (1949) and *He visto la noche* (1959) in Colombia, Martín Morúa Delgado's *La familia Unzúazu* (1901) and Miguel Barnet's *The Autobiography of a Runaway Slave* (1966) in Cuba."[4]

Were it not for Del Monte's insistence, we would not have Manzano's *Autobiografía*. The circumstances of its creation, therefore, are illuminating and warrant some attention if we are to appreciate this slave narrative. The work's view from below offers perspective partly shaped by Del Monte's view from above. Del Monte who has been called "the first great patriarch of Cuban belles-lettres,"[5] was, in a sense, the Carl Van Vechten of his time. Del Monte's relation to black Cubans like Manzano was similar to the position Carl Van Vechten, who published his own *Nigger Heaven* in 1926, had in relation to black Americans like Langston Hughes, and indeed, to the Harlem Renaissance in early twentieth-century America. Both men were wealthy, white critic-patrons who sponsored black art. It must be remembered that in Manzano's time, as in the early days of Langston Hughes, Blacks, and some Whites too when dealing with black themes, wrote what influential Whites wanted and expected them to write, a fact of great significance in the history of antislavery literature in Cuba.

Both Manzano's *Autobiografía* and Anselmo Suárez y Romero's *Francisco*, the Cuban antislavery novel that has the distinction of preceding *Uncle Tom's Cabin* by several years, were written at the request of Del Monte, who had them produced largely for foreign readers. Both works were in fact first published out of the country: *Francisco* in New York in 1880 and Manzano's *Autobiografía* in English in London in 1840. Both works, however, did circulate in Cuba in manuscript form. Although Manzano's text circulated in Spanish, the original version was not published until 1937. Foreign exposure for these two works was to be gained through Richard Madden, the English author and friend of Del Monte who was entrusted with an antislavery portfolio containing them. Madden chose to publish Manzano's *Autobiografía* rather than Suárez y Romero's *Francisco*.

These two works were partly designed to reveal to the world outside Cuba the progressive and humanitarian positions of the concerned citizens within the country or at least those represented by Del Monte's group. The major limitation, though, was that neither book was allowed to go "beyond what are the 'official' criteria of the group."[6] The standard imposed by the Del Monte group, which was more reformist than abolitionist, called for "moderation and restraint"[7] in the depiction of the black slave. For this reason Manzano's own *Autobiografía*, controlled from above by Del Monte and resembling other antislavery works written around the same time, had to play down the threatening image of the rebellious slave while playing up the image of the docile and submissive slave. According to Ivan Schulman, the restraint served "to call forth a sympathetic reaction to slavery's abuses from the more enlightened members of the community, who would probably have been offended by a rebellious protagonist."[8]

Del Monte achieved something of a literary coup by having Manzano, an authentic black slave and an "admirable example of meekness and resignation,"[9] conform to these guidelines. Conforming was the only way Manzano could hope for continued support and protection. Since Del Monte knew he had a showpiece Black with a good image and intellectual capacity, why not display him? His talent made him one of the excellent exceptions: a slave who was not vile, stupid, and immoral, defects that Del Monte felt people born and raised as slaves inevitably had.[10] Further, and perhaps even more important, his display would prove that such exceptions could be produced under slavery, providing, of course, they had good masters.

Francisco Calcagno's phrase, "being a slave owner is no crime, but abusing that privilege is,"[11] is of enormous importance both in understanding the meaning of Manzano's *Autobiografía* and in clarifying Del Monte's reasons for supporting it. Manzano recounts numerous cruelties and punishments suffered for much of his life at the hands of the Marquesa de Prado Ameno, a sadistic, warped owner. Now, if Manzano represented one of the excellent exceptions to the mass of undesirable slaves, so too, it is inferred, was the marquesa an exception to other *amitos*, some of whom Manzano served under, who were paragons of kindness and goodness.

Manzano readers take note of his mistreatment at the hands of that cruel lady, and Calcagno asks the telling question in his *Poetas de color*, "Why could not the fate that made Manzano a slave at least have made him always a slave of Cárdenas? He would not have suffered the horrible treatment of which he often lamented with such humility and good reason; perhaps we would not today be reading this autobiography of his written with such bitterness."[12] It was during the period Manzano served with this *amito*, who was "correct, benevolent and magnanimous,"[13] that he taught himself to read and write, patterning his behavior on the good example set by his master. But the implications of the question Calcagno raises are clear, namely, that slavery, when not poisoned by bad masters or mistresses who abuse the system, is not really evil. This was a message even the censors would take kindly to, especially if the system could produce a man like Manzano.

Del Monte's reasons for wanting the book written and Manzano's concern about his personal safety meant the work essentially misrepresented slavery. Were it not written under control, its publication would have been "the biggest anathema of all"[14] against slavery. But as it turned out, Manzano had very little to fear since his *Autobiografía* is really an indictment not of slavery but only of abuses by some misguided owners. Further, perhaps Manzano had Del Monte's assurances that no harm would come to him in any event, as his book was destined largely for a foreign audience. We should remember that when Manzano dared publish his first book of poems approximately twenty years earlier, it was done "under guarantee," Calcagno tells us, "since slaves were not allowed to publish anything."[15]

Manzano's insistence on assurances or guarantees could perhaps account for his reluctance to get on with the writing of his *Autobiografía*. We know that he made four attempts before getting the manuscript under way. We know too, from his letter to Del Monte dated June 4, 1835, that once Manzano reconciled himself to the undertaking, he practiced the selective censorship required to bring his story in line with his benefactor's guidelines. In the same letter he writes, "I have prepared myself to account to Your Grace for a *part* of the story of my life, *reserving its most interesting events* for some day when, seated in some corner of my homeland, tranquil, *certain of my destiny* and my means of livelihood, I could write a truly Cuban novel."[16]

This letter, I believe, tells us more about Manzano than his entire *Autobiografía*, which, by the way, he labeled part 1. Part 2, as we shall discuss shortly, was mysteriously "lost." This letter suggests more than just intention to comply with the acceptable image, for the italicized parts are the keys to a fuller reading of Manzano's intentions. He is well aware that he is narrating only "a part" of his life story, that he is "reserving its most interesting events" for another time when "certain of [his] destiny" he could write what he calls "a truly Cuban novel." Manzano knew very well, in short, that it would take more assurances than those Del Monte guaranteed to get him to reveal more of his life story. But two questions linger: Did he dare elaborate on other aspects of his life in part 2, and is that why that volume was so quickly "lost"?

The fate of part 2 of Manzano's *Autobiografía* is problematic, and its disappearance "shortly after having been written and copied"[17] has not been satisfactorily explained. Madden suspects foul play. Writing in the prologue to his translation of the first part, he says: "The work was written in two parts; the second one fell in the hands of persons connected with the former master, and I fear it is not likely to be restored to the person to whom I am indebted for the first portion of this manuscript [Del Monte]."[18] Del Monte reports that the second part "was lost in the care of [Ramón de] Palma and was never seen again."[19]

When we recall that Manzano at the end of part 1 of his *Autobiografía* was finally beginning to come out from under the lamblike image he had so carefully constructed in that volume, we can assume that part 2 could well have been franker than part 1. Perhaps Manzano in part 2 forgot the original guidelines and expressed some views that, for all concerned including Manzano, were better left unsaid. Perhaps Manzano had tired of being circumspect and wanted to go faster and farther than his liberal white friends were prepared to go. At any rate it is unfortunate that part 2 was lost, or destroyed, particularly as it could well have come as close as he ever got to writing the book he tells us he was saving up for. Certainly the purge in 1844 seems to have silenced him— and many other Blacks. It is not surprising, therefore, that we have nothing from Manzano during the last ten years of his life. As it turns out, we are left only with part 1. Since it is written by a black slave who could tell us much, his autobiography is, perhaps, the most tragically controlled piece of literature coming out of that period of Cuban and Latin American literary history, certainly more so than Anselmo Suárez y Romero's *Francisco*, even though Suárez y Romero's novel did have the *subversivo* excised from it by the Del Monte group to make it conform to their requirement of presenting Blacks as submissive.[20]

Even tragically controlled, the first part of Manzano's *Autobiografía* does stand as an early example of black writing in Latin America, and as such it does bequeath something to following generations in terms of its faithfulness to themes and traditions relevant to black history in the New World. The theme of liberty, for example, that runs throughout the history of Afro-Latin American literature does exist in a very basic form in the *Autobiografía*. Manzano's search for identity (the development of which was interrupted by the division of his work into two parts) within the confines of his New World environment is also evident. With part 2 missing we can only guess whether his motivation in that second part derived from some radical change in his life that might have led to an "internal transformation of the individual."[21] We can only wonder, in other words, whether Manzano "describes not only what has happened to him at a different time in his life, but above all how he became—out of what he was—what he presently is."[22] Self-formulation or the discovery of the present self that was just beginning to take over at the end of part 1 could well have formed the organizing principle for part 2 of Manzano's *Autobiografía*. "Black autobiographies, including the slave narratives, are unique statements about identity,"[23] and Manzano's, even though he concealed a great deal, is no exception.

This is so even though Manzano presents himself in part 1 not as an *engaged* activist but as a *disengaged* pacifist, a harmless victim of the system and no danger to it. These two categories that Saundra Towns has defined, black autobiographies of the engaged and of the disengaged, help us understand and categorize part 1 of Manzano's *Autobiografía*.[24] In Towns' first group are authors who make a personal commitment to black liberation. But the single-minded pursuit by these men—political activists, social reformers and public men—of their goals is absent in the other category, the autobiography of the disengaged, whose authors show little interest in their ancestry or at best are reluctant to acknowledge it.

Arriving at what I consider a key phrase in her characterization of the second group, Towns writes that black writers in this group find it far better to forget the past and to subsume one's blackness under one's Americanness. I find this phrase crucial because I believe that is precisely what Manzano did. If we substitute "Cubanness" for "Americanness," we have what is a fairly accurate assessment of Manzano's integrationist concept of the future he desired in his *patria*. Being the artist that he was with a sensitivity to match his inclination, Manzano could not help but hope for some tranquil moments to develop his art and his identity. These quiet moments for Manzano could come only with his emancipation from slavery. But again we must remember that the purge in 1844 epitomized the hostile white environment of his time and put a quick end to whatever peaceful moments he was able to have.

Manzano, then, wanted not only to be free but also to be left to blend quietly into the Cuban landscape, for he felt as Cuban as anyone else. This is the same desire for integration, as we shall see, that will be picked up later by Martín Morúa Delgado with a political zeal matched only by his political clout. But Morúa, writing in the late nineteenth century, when slavery and colonialism were on the wane, was in a much better position to bring to fruition his ideas of belonging for himself and for his people in Cuba. Part 1 of Manzano's *Autobiografía* largely covers his period as a child slave and rightly belongs to the category of the black autobiography of the disengaged. We do not know how Manzano took the loss or the destruction of part 2 of his *Autobiografía*, but we cannot help but wonder whether this part, which probably reflected more consciousness of being a man, would have belonged to the category of the engaged.

With his freedom Manzano joined the other colored segment of colonial society, the free Black. Ironically, Manzano's plight worsened after gaining his freedom, and he even served a prison term. Life for free Blacks, especially writers who were under constant supervision in slave societies, was difficult, as they faced obstacles and persecution, sometimes worse than those faced by slaves. These early second-class citizens "outnumbered their slave counterparts in Spanish America well before the struggles for political independence."[25] Although not slaves, they too had their problems and obstacles to overcome. Occupying "an ambiguous intermediate position between the fully free and the enslaved"[26] free Blacks like "Plácido," Gabriel de la Concepción Valdés (1804–1844), were more of a threat than the slave and as a result were more feared. We repeatedly read such statements as the following: "For the Government, the free black, who was more intelligent, was more dangerous than the slave,"[27] and "the dangers of Cuba come not so much from the slaves as from the multitude of free blacks and mulattoes."[28] Or, "Consciously and unconsciously, free blacks and free mulattoes offered the seeds of revolt or threatened revolt to the unfree blacks. The free colored were usually among the first to raise the issues of personal liberty and class discrimination in the societies."[29] Free Blacks, particularly in Cuba, had no choice but to react, since "by the nineteenth century, racism was a prominent feature of Cuba's white society, and its most hostile manifestation was toward the free colored community."[30] This society, paranoid from suspicion and "blinded by fear and racial prejudice,"[31] came down hardest on the free Black in 1844 and after, when the purge of that year practically decimated the free black community for its involvement in political and racial plotting designed to free the slaves and give independence to Cuba.

These two features, racism and racial prejudice, are the ones the black novelist and politician Martín Morúa Delgado (1856–1910) chose to criticize in post-abolitionist Cuba. Martín Morúa Delgado was also a journalist, but his most substantial and ambitious work was done in the novel genre. Morúa launched a series of novels that he entitled "Cosas de mi tierra," and he completed two in this series, *Sofía* (1891) and *La familia Unzúazu* (1901), before his death. His novels are quite often placed in the tradition of the antislavery novels, because they deal with the evils of slavery. But by striking primarily against the white Cuban's "imponderable pride of caste, of class, of race,"[32] Morúa moves beyond the simple condemnation of slavery as an evil institution to a larger future vision of the role and place of the soon-to-be-liberated black slave in post-abolitionist Cuban society. His novels really address the crippling psychological effects of racism, the holdover from slavery that prevented white Cubans from accepting black people without reference to their past. Franklin W. Knight wrote that "the slave society in the Americas was essentially a coercive and racist society."[33] Morúa, who knew this as well as anyone, hardly ascribed to the preconceived theory of social class and race held by other writers like Villaverde, whose antislavery novel *Cecilia Valdés* (1882) Morúa took to task for its narrow view of black people. Morúa saw Villaverde as a typical example of a White who still harbored prejudices against Blacks; it was precisely Villaverde's racist approach that Morúa opposed in his own antiracist view. Unlike *Cecilia Valdés* and other antislavery novels from the nineteenth century, *Sofía* and *La familia Unzúazu* were written by a Black whose mother had been an African slave.

Morúa's novels, unlike the antislavery works that preceded him, were published after slavery had been abolished. It is not surprising, therefore, that he chose to turn his attention to the pervasive effects of the system that even after abolition continued to shape public opinion toward Blacks. Racism, as an evil inherited from slavery, was much more difficult to regulate, for unlike slavery, "conscious and unconscious feelings of racial superiority"[34] could not simply be abolished. For this reason the challenges facing Morúa as a black writer were greater than those faced by earlier abolitionist writers. The institution of slavery had been a large, fixed target, easy to attack, but Morúa used that system as a point of departure in his efforts to get the ex-slave to claim his rights under the law, to feel as though he belonged, and to get the ex-slave owner to recognize these rights and to look beyond appearances to see the worth of the individual. These are the points that Morúa emphasizes, first in *Sofía* and later in *La familia Unzúazu*.

Fidelio, perhaps one of Morúa's most significant characters in *La familia Unzúazu*, takes on autobiographical significance. A free Black who has numerous similarities with the author, Fidelio was prepared, like Morúa, to work toward the realization of a new Cuba. He, therefore, made the decision to join the enslaved Black with the "natural revolutionary impulse"[35] that had to become the trademark of the new "Cuban ideal,"[36] an ideal that has no time for ethnic divisions. Morúa's concern, first raised in *Sofía*, was with "the future of his homeland and the destiny of the race" (p. 176). Fidelio decides, as Morúa had done, to be useful to his country "by helping the improvement of a race that has been held back" (p. 305). He would do this by opting for journalism as a career, as Morúa had done at a crucial point in his development. "In the mind of Fidelio that night was born with powerful force the goal to which from then on he subordinated his inclinations: The publication of a newspaper in which he, usually at a loss for words, would expose the world of ideas which had accumulated in his brain" (p. 306).

Fidelio does little in the novel aside from making that decision, but it was for him, as it had been for Morúa, perhaps the most important one in his life. Commitment to all the people, particularly to the underprivileged, which at that time were the enslaved Blacks, was a necessary first step for anyone who genuinely wanted to work for the greater goal of a free Cuba. Martín Morúa Delgado made that commitment, one we should not forget even though it, like the literary blackness expressed in his novels, was overshadowed by subsequent and more controversial events in his political life.

Morúa's *La familia Unzúazu*, though not an autobiography in the true sense, nevertheless like Manzano's *Autobiografía* is a unique statement about his identity. If we accept that Fidelio represents the author, the "internal transformation of the individual" that we spoke of earlier in the case of Manzano is also evident here. If our speculations are correct regarding Manzano's lost autobiography, Morúa, like Manzano, changes from a disengaged pacifist to an engaged activist, thus making a personal commitment to black liberation. His attack will be not on slavery but on racism and racial prejudice, and his weapons will be politics and the black press.

In a sense, then, we may say that Martín Morúa Delgado's desire for integration is reflected in Fidelio's determination to work for the incorporation of the Black into the future plans of his homeland. What we have is an excellent example of an autobiographical statement that uniquely does in one work what we may speculate Manzano tried to do in two, namely, the merging of the goals of the engaged activist and the disengaged pacifist, which are black liberation on the one hand and integration on the other.

NOTES

1. Juan Francisco Manzano, *Autobiografía, cartas y versos*, con un estudio preliminar por José L. Franco (Havana: Municipio de La Habana, 1937), p. 92.

2. This autobiography has just received new life in a modernized edition by Ivan Schulman. See Juan Francisco Manzano, *Autobiografía de un esclavo*, Introducción, notas y actualización del texto de Ivan Schulman (Madrid: Ediciones Guadarrama, 1975).

3. See Russell C. Brignano, *Black Americans in Autobiography: An Annotated Bibliography of Autobiographies and Autobiographical Books Written Since the Civil War* (Durham, N.C.: Duke University Press, 1974).

4. Jean Franco calls Miguel Barnet's *The Autobiography of a Runaway Slave*, put together from interviews with his ex-slave subject, "imaginative documentary writing," a documentary type, she says, that has already been given literary respectability by Norman Mailer, William Styron and Truman Capote. See Jean Franco, "Literature in the Revolution," *Twentieth Century*, nos. 1039/40 (1968–69): 64.

5. R. Anthony Castagnaro, *The Early Spanish American Novel* (New York: Las Américas Publishing, 1971), p. 158.

6. César Leante, "Dos obras antiesclavistas cubanas," *Cuadernos Americanos* 207, no. 4 (1976): 177.

7. Ivan Schulman, "The Portrait of the Slave: Ideology and Aesthetics in the Cuban Antislavery Novel," *Comparative Perspectives on Slavery in New World Societies*, ed. Vera Rubin and Arthur Tuden (New York: Academy of Sciences, 1977), p. 36.

8. Ibid.

9. Francisco Calcagno, *Poetas de color*, 4th ed. (Havana: Imprenta Mercantil de los Herederos de Santiago, 1887), p. 71.

10. Domingo del Monte, *Escritos* (Havana: Cultural, 1929), 1:44, reprinted in *Autobiografía de un esclavo*, pp. 37–38.

11. Francisco Calcagno, fragment of the nineteenth-century novel *Romualdo, uno de tantos*, in *Islas* (Cuba), no. 44 (1973), pp. 107–8, reprinted in Manzano, *Autobiografía de un esclavo*, p. 30.

12. Calcagno, *Poetas de color*, p. 60.

13. Ibid., p. 62.

14. Ibid., p. 52.

15. Ibid., p. 62.

16. Reproduced in Ibid., p. 82 (emphasis added).

17. Manzano, *Autobiografía de un esclavo*, p. 47.

18. Reprinted in Calcagno, *Poetas de color*, p. 76.

19. Manzano, *Autobiografía de un esclavo*, p. 47.

20. Leante, "Dos obras," p. 185.

21. Jean Starobinski, "The Style of Autobiography," in *Literary Style: A Symposium*, ed. Seymour Chatman (London: Oxford University Press, 1971), p. 289.

22. Ibid., p. 290.

23. Catharine R. Stimpson, "Black Culture/White Teacher," in *New Perspectives on Black Studies*, ed. John W. Blassingame (Urbana: University of Illinois Press, 1971), p. 181.

24. Saundra Towns, "Black Autobiography and the Dilemma of Western Artistic Tradition," *Black Books Bulletin*, (1975): 17–23.

25. Frederick P. Bowser, "Colonial Spanish America," in *Neither Slave nor Free: The Freedman of African Descent in the Slave Societies of the New World*, ed. David W. Cohen and Jack P. Greene (Baltimore: Johns Hopkins University Press, 1972), p. 19.

26. Franklin W. Knight, "Cuba," in *Neither Slave nor Free*, ed. Cohen and Greene, p. 281.

27. Leonardo Guinán Peralta, "La defensa de los esclavos," in his *Ensayos y conferencias* (Santiago de Cuba: Editora del Consejo Nacional de Universidades, 1964), p. 75.

28. José Antonio Saco, cited in Peralta, "La defensa," p. 78.

29. Cohen and Greene, *Neither Slave nor Free*, p. 16.

30. Knight, "Cuba," p. 282.

31. Ibid., p. 292.

32. Martín Morúa Delgado, *Sofía* (1891; reprint ed., Havana: Instituto Cubano del Libro, 1972), p. 22.

33. Knight, "Cuba," p. 281.

34. Charles Boxer, *Race Relations in the Portuguese Colonial Empire* (Oxford: Clarendon Press, 1963), p. 56.

35. Morúa, *Sofía*, p. 165.

36. Ibid., p. 168. All other references to this novel will be cited parenthetically in the text.

4

Yoruba Presence: From Nigerian Oral Literature to Contemporary Cuban Narrative

Julia Cuervo Hewitt

It should no longer be necessary to emphasize the influence that African cultures have had on the New World. What does become necessary to point out is that of the many African tribes that were forced to adhere to new sociopolitical values, the Yoruba tribes were the most successful in preserving an important element of their culture, that is, their oral tradition. Scholars like Roger Bastide and William Bascom have amply studied the presence of these and other tribes in America.[1] However, it was the Cuban writer Rogelio Martínez Furé who recently pointed out that Yoruba literature in Cuba is perfectly distinguishable from any other African or European tradition.[2] At the same time, its mythopoetic imagery is comparable to the universal archetypes of great world mythologies.

The term *Yoruba* has been used since the nineteenth century to comprise those tribes of a common culture and linguistic stock in the areas of Kwara, Lagos, and the western states of Nigeria and the Republics of Dahomey and Togo.[3] Most likely originating along the Middle Nile, the migrators brought with them to Yorubaland the artistic cosmology and techniques of the old Nok culture.[4] It has been discovered recently that by 1300 the mythological center of Yoruba cosmogony, the city of Ile-Ife in today's Nigeria, had some of the most highly sophisticated schools of art in the world.[5] However, at the time of the greatest influx of Yoruba slaves into Cuba, in the nineteenth century, a common bond was still unknown to the individual tribes. Yet, all of the regions were able to trace their mythological and political origin to Ile-Ife. Furthermore, the enormous political and religious power that the region of Oyo had acquired two centuries before served as a cultural homogenizing element in the development of one of the richest mythologies Africa has known. In so doing, Oyo imposed the cult of its deceased divine, King Shango, upon the conquered people.[6] Thus, it is with the name Shango that many of the Yoruban socioreligious groups reached America.[7]

The fall of Oyo and the ensuing Yoruba civil wars sent crowded slave ships to Brazil and to Cuba with Yoruba slaves.[8] In Cuba these West Africans of similar characteristics in origin, language and physique became known as *lucumí*. But these slaves had another aspect in common unknown then to the Spanish and Portuguese trader, that is, a rich mythopoetic world from which emanated a vast oral literature. With time, myths, legends, fables and, most important of all, recitations from the Yoruba oracle, the Ifa, were written down in notebooks that were handed down from elder to younger Cuban-African priests. In so doing, they preserved not only the literature but also the language. As Furé further pointed out, it is not unusual to find amid the literary body present in these notebooks of sacred literature (known in Cuba as the *patakín*) homemade translations from books published in London about African Yorubas.[9]

Literature, whether oral or written, is the deepest expression of the most vital fibers of a people. Thus, as we become aware of the almost innate necessity to grasp and hold on to cultural origins, we can also understand why Cuban contemporary literature is enriched with Yoruban legends, characters, themes and mythopoetic imagery rooted in the African experience.

Due to a constant flow of migrations, trading and political influences within African regions, a great number of variations on tribal narratives traveled to Cuban shores. In this sense Cuba served as an alchemy vessel in which a syncretic fusion of African and European beliefs took place. But it also served as a syncretic catalyst of different African regional cosmogonies. For example, we find that, away from their respective territorial boundaries, Olokún, the coastal Yoruba sea god, and Yemayá, the inland Yoruba sea goddess,[10] became Yemayá-Olokún in Cuba. We can also see that in the African transculturation to Cuba, *orishas* were merged with Catholic saints. The revered image of the *alafin* ("king") Shango, for example, was identified with Santa Bárbara, a Catholic saint. But this was, in effect, only an illusion. Beyond the facade, in its new geographical manifestation, the African *orisha* remained intact.[11] (An *orisha* is not a god nor a deity in the Western sense of the word. It is a personified natural force, which, as a manifestation of a cosmological unity, interacts with man. *Orishas* and human beings are possessed and possess; are fooled and fool; are violated and violate; are strong and weak.) With time the highly developed Yoruba mythology was able to encompass all African tribal variations and match, if not surpass, Christian cosmogony. The reason was the underlying core of universal archetypes that, through centuries, had slowly solidified in Yorubaland. It was from that core that Cuban contemporary narrative began to feed. Lydia Cabrera's Afro-Cuban short stories and Rómulo Lachatañeré's legends in *¡Oh, mío, Yemayá!* (1938) opened a new mythopoetic vision in Cuban literature. Miguel Barnet's *Akeké y la jutía* (1978) and Manuel Cofiño's *Cuando la sangre se parece al fuego* (1975) reveal the still present tendency toward a highly stylized poetic vision of an African pantheon, which is now more than ever, mostly Yoruba. In the postrevolutionary period there has been a tendency to minimize the *orishas'* importance in the cultural context. However, their appearance in literature has produced the most intensified mythopoetic beauty.

Due to the vastness of the subject we have chosen only a few texts and passages that clearly exemplify direct links that exist, as far as Yoruba literary imagery is concerned, between Cuban and Nigerian narrative. We propose that the two main sources of all Yoruban imagery in Cuban literature are Yoruba mythology and the recitations from the oracle, the Ifa. We also propose that there is, deriving from the above, a specific intertextual relationship between both countries' literatures in terms of a Yoruba concept of poetry and language, music, presence and importance of diviners or *babalawos*, character, themes and vision of the cosmos.

SOURCES

Presently, the two most important narrative texts of Yoruba mythology in Cuba are Lachatañeré's *¡Oh, mío, Yemayá!* and Manuel Cofiño's *Cuando la sangre se parece al fuego*. These, together with Lydia Cabrera's multiple legends and fables, reconstruct a world of personified natural forces that the Yorubans call *orishas*. In Nigeria it is said that there are 401 such deities, which is to say, in effect, that they exist in infinite numbers.[12] To Cuba, however, fewer arrived. Those that did arrive firmly encompassed all other cultural projections that, in any form or fashion, were similar to their manifestations. Their penetration of Cuban cultural imagery was such that when a character in Barnet's *Canción de Rachel* (1969) cries out "Santa Bárbara" upon hearing it thunder,[13] one can be sure that it is not the Catholic saint whom she invokes but Changó, the Yoruba god of thunder and lightning.

Only one being stands above all, creator and giver of life, Olodumare. As a cosmological replica of the sociopolitical structure of Oyo, the Supreme Being (known also as Olumare, Ol[i]orum, or Olofi in Cuba) acquires the same characteristics as those of the kingdom's *alafin*.[14] Both, earthly and heavenly kings, are all powerful but do not rule personally. In the cosmological realm the *orishas*, as Oyo's elders, carry out the governing duties. Otherwise, Olodumare follows the archetypal characteristics of all universal Sky Gods[15] equivalent to Zeus, Yaweh or Alá. Nigerian legends well reveal that his orders are met without question and that, due to his isolation from man, Olorum does not require sacrifices or a specific cast of followers. He is, in effect, as the cosmological unity, all of the *orishas*. However, it is interesting to note that in Cuban legends, Olofi becomes capricious and fickle, a characteristic common to all Yoruban deities. In "El moquenquen de Orumbila" in Lachatañeré's *¡Oh, mío, Yemayá!* this aspect becomes quite apparent. Olofi, who likes to eat the flesh of children, is not able to do so for four days. Out of desperation he eats the child of his own servant, Orumbila, but promises never to touch human flesh again.[16] Olofi's indifference toward his creation is present in different myths and legends. As we find in Barnet's *Akeké y la jutía*, he gives but does not forgive and punishes.[17] In Cofiño's *Cuando la sangre se parece al fuego* we find that he does not talk, because Truth is mute and he is Truth.[18]

On the other hand, Orunmila (Orumbila in Cuba) is the second most important *orisha* in the main trilogy of Nigerian Yoruba mythology. He was one of Olorum's (Olofi's) first creations and was sent to earth with various deities and responsibilities. Orunmila became the god of wisdom and received, from Olofi, the power of omniscience (Ifa) in all time and space.[19] He is, according to Biobaku, the most important deity for all Yoruban tribes[20] and is, at times, confused with and known as the Ifa itself.[21] Other interpretations of the Ifa[22] and Afro-Cuban legends explain how Orunmila acquired the secret of the Ifa and became a diviner. Contrary to one version, which explains how Olofi himself gave Orunmila the "knowledge" of the Ifa, in Lydia Cabrera's *El monte* (1954), we find that the original power had been given to Changó, and the divining board (on which divination takes place) to Obatalá.[23] Both, however, finally became Orumbila's.[24] This version coincides with Lachatañeré's "Olvido," in which Changó makes Orumbila his favorite assistant but, as a diviner, the latter does not pay Eleguá (friend of Changó and deity of road and fate) his dues.[25] A power struggle ensues and Orumbila is defeated.

The apparent inferiority with which Orumbila is treated in Afro-Cuban legends, coincides with a term still used today in Africa to describe this deity: "Akere-finusogbón," or the small one with a big mind.[26] In Lachatañeré's "Las trampas de Ogún Arere" he appears small and thin.[27] In "Las cotorras de Orumbila" he becomes an old man too weak to satisfy his wife Ochún,[28] but yet he is the right hand of Olofi in "El moquenquen de Orumbila" and is astute enough to gain wisdom and power over death in "Orumbila y la Icú" (Goddess of Death).

The third most important *orisha* in the trilogy of the Yoruban pantheon is also the most feared one: Eshú-Elegbá. In Cuba he is known as Echú, Echó, Eleguá, depending on the manifestation implied. In Del Valle's "Ella no creía en bilongos," for example, we find that Echó and Eleguá are seen as two different deities, the first one (evil) influencing the second.[29] In the Ifa, however, he is the divine trickster assigned by Olofi to bring to him the sacrifices offered by believers. He makes sure that those who offer him gifts and sacrifices receive their requests in return and those who do not are punished.[30] According to Cabrera's *El monte*, he is not only the most feared one, but he keeps the key to all roads, the woods and fate itself;[31] his tributes must always be paid first. Failure to do so, would bring consequences similar to Orumbila's in Lachatañeré's "Olivido" and "Codicia," where his failure to pay Eleguá brought upon him weakness and loss of divining powers and, thus, loss of clients, fame and riches.[32] He is, as we find in Cofiño's *Cuando la sangre se parece al fuego*, the beginning and the end, the spy and messenger of the gods, the one who either saves or kills in an instant. He is also twenty-one manifestations in one.[33]

Beyond this main trilogy we find a large number of other *orishas* with very specific duties and responsibilities. Some of these are more important due to their popularity (archetypes that fit the new environment) and constantly appear in Cuban literature. Obatalá, for example, is characterized in the Ifa as being the deity or king that wears white clothing.[34] Corroborating this characteristic, in Guillermo Cabrera Infante's "En el gran ecbó," during the ritual (egbó) held for Obatalá, the followers, as it is customary, were all dressed in white.[35] Again, in *Cuando la sangre se parece al fuego* we find that Obatalá dresses in white and is the god of purity, whiteness, equilibrium and peace. Furthermore, Obatalá does not have specific sons or daughters, for he is father and mother to all—if Olofi created the world, Obatalá created man. Obatalá governs all thoughts and ideas[36] and, even though he can punish harshly, he always ends up forgiving man for his actions.[37] One day, however, while drunk, Obatalá created men with handicaps.[38] This same legend, as seen in the Ifa, speaks further about the myth that gave birth to the battle for power and property between the two culture hero gods, Obatalá (humans) and Odudua (Earth): a manlike deity, Obatalá (with man's weakness), in constant battle with the earth, Odudua.[39]

It is interesting also to note that Obatalá appears in several texts—as in, for example, Del Valle's "¿Por qué escondes a tu abuela?"—as Odudua's husband[40] and also, corroborating its hermaphrodite characteristic pointed out in *Cuando la sangre se parece al fuego*, as a serene young girl in "Las trampas de Ogún Arere."[41]

But above all the main importance of Obatalá's literary presence can be found in Joel Adedeji's case study of this *orisha*'s annual festival in Ede, twenty miles from Ife, cradle of Yoruban culture.[42] Adedeji concludes that the cultural conception of Obatalá fits the theory of the archetype and becomes the embodiment of all Yoruba morals and ethics.[43]

Another *orisha* often found in literary texts is Osaín, the benefactor of all *lucumí* people (Yoruba in Cuba) even though he, himself, is not Yoruba.[44] He was not born out of anyone; he simply came forth from the earth[45] and is a hunter like Ochosi. His keenness and wits are seen in Cabrera's "Osaín de un Pie." However, in Barnet's Osaín y el venado," it becomes apparent that he, like all *orishas*, is, at times, capricious and has disobeyed Olofi. The latter, as a punishment, left him as he is seen today: "Made out of wood, limping and missing an eye and an arm."[46] As further evidence of these characteristics, we find in Cofiño's *Cuando la sangre se parece al fuego* that he can limp or run, hears every sound, owns all that is in the woods, because he is the woods itself.[47] Hence, his image, as in *Akeké y la jutía*, is being nature's natural doctor.

Ochún, the Yoruban Venus, is, on the other hand, a different cosmological force. She is seductively erotic, astute and sexually insatiable. For this reason she has received in Cuba the label of "prostitute goddess."[48] As we find in Cofiño's *Cuando la sangre se parece al fuego*, she is all-giving toward her sons and daughters as well as men, but unforgiving when angered. She belongs to all and none. She made the first lamp in the world out of a calabash and dances with it on her head. She also wears five handkerchiefs from her waist to dance, and like Cupid, she creates love and desire in human beings.[49] She is above

Changó, according to Del Valle's "No fallaba nunca la Mayunga de Guinea,"[50] and in Lachatañeré's "El escamoteo" is Yemayá's oldest sister (goddess of the ocean, one in seven manifestations and mother of sixteen *orishas*).[51]

Changó (Shango in Africa) is the god of fire, lightning and thunder. He is, above all, the universal archetype of the storm god. But he also likes to play the drum, to dance; he likes women, he is impetuous and he is in constant war with Ogún Arere, god of iron, war and the woods.[52] The legends that speak of Changó's birth are various and different. However, as it is found in Lachatañeré's *¡Oh, mío, Yemayá!* he is the son of Obatalá and Agallú Solá. Obatalá, tired of Changó's disobedience, threw him in the air, and he landed on the lap of Yemayá (the great mother), who proceeded to raise him as her son. Once an adult, Olofi gave Obá to Changó as his first wife. For reasons that vary from legend to legend, Obá, faithful and loyal to her husband, mutilated her beauty to satisfy his capriciousness, cutting off her ears to season Changó's food. In return she received only his rejection.[53] Years later, this beautiful legend was adapted for the stage in Pepe Carril's play *Shangó de Ima* (1969). Here, as in José Zorrilla's *Don Juan Tenorio*, all the women involved come together to accuse Changó. Olofi gives him punishment, and Obatalá makes it public; he is forever to keep fire, lightning and thunder, but they must be put out by night and relighted in the morning, thus giving birth to the cycles of light and shadow and the eternal battle between life and death. Both play and narrative end with a Yoruban tradition: Guemilere's rite (or *bembé* Yoruba).[54]

Changó is by far the most popular Yoruban deity in Cuba and, thus, the most often found in various forms and images in literature. He is, for Del Valle's "El Tata," the most powerful *orisha* after Olorum, since he controls everything in life and has the power to summon other deities.[55] He is a good friend of Eleguá[56] and Osaín[57] and is, above all, king of Oyo and king of kings.[58] The legend of his kingship, in Nigerian legends and Ifa, is brought out again in Cuban literature by Barnet's "Changó y la jicotea." Here he appears as the fourth king of Oyo who is marrying Ochún, goddess of rivers, and invites all the animals to their royal wedding. However, he still loves and fears his counterpart, according to Cofiño's *Cuando la sangre se parece al fuego*, the passionate goddess of the wind, storm and lightning: mother of fire, Oyá.[59] It is worth noting that, in Cuba, Changó and Ochún have embodied the archetype of the Cuban *mulato* and *mulata*. Thus, in Cuban legends Ochún appears as Changó's favorite wife, while in Africa it is Oyá, his counterpart storm goddess, who is his favorite. Oyá's loyalty toward Changó is quite apparent in the African legend that narrates the *alafin*'s death. In it, upon realizing that Changó had taken his life, she does the same.[60]

Even though the myths of creation and conquest are (and were) known to all Yorubans, they were thought to be exclusively part of the recitations of the Ifa (some of which can be found today in written form), source of all Yoruba literature. The Ifa can be understood by Westerners as a type of Bible basic to Yoruban tradition. This collection, of hundreds of verses memorized by the tribal diviner or *babalawo* (*babalao* in Cuba), or originally *baba-li-awo* or father of secrets,[61] has the answers to the questions and problems of each situation that arises. In Bascom's opinion, all of the folklore and mythology in Yoruban culture can be traced in one form or another to Ifa verses. As part of the Yoruba oracle, the recited verses are thought to penetrate and explain the mysteries of the cosmos. The recitations are seen as the voice of Orunmila who, through the *babalawo*, shows the path to take. Each verse, or *odu*, is divided into three parts: (1) the first few lines present the *babalawo* and mythological character that comes seeking help, their problem and whether or not an offering has been given. (2) What happened for having or not having met the offering is recounted. This is done through a simple mention or an extensive explanation that introduces a myth explaining the first part of the verse, a part that is usually obscure. (3) The clarification of the relationship between the above and the client comes last. It introduces the new gifts or sacrifices that the client must offer.[62] This general structure is made up of approximately 256 *odus*, which, in turn, are divided into the first most important 16, and the rest. Next to this main narrative nucleus, we also find a second nucleus of great importance: the *ese* or poetry.[63]

DERIVATIVES FROM SOURCES

Poetry and Language

The presence of the *ese* can be seen in many narratives in Cuban literature. However, the poetic characteristic or actual imagery, whether in narrative or verse, has gone through the process of transculturation and rebirth in Cuba and can be seen flourishing in the language employed in some texts. *Akeké y la jutía*, for example, departs from the elaborate sophisticated imagery of modern fiction to return to the simplicity of the myth. But, if we must choose an example of a text that creates poetry in the form of a narrative, it is Cabrera's "Walo-Wila," which captures the multidimensional characteristics of the *ese*. In it, Wooden Horse, Goat Man, Bull Man and others pass by Ayere Kende's house. Impressed by her beauty, they want to marry her. She refuses all the offers after giving them a golden cup from which to drink and suggests that they marry her invisible sister, Walo-Wila, who is much more beautiful than she. Deer accepts and does what is required of him. He goes in the ocean and brings out a calabash that is given to him by Ayere Kende and is full of Olokún's (goddess of the waters) water. Only then can he enter Walo-Wila's chamber to encounter the ultimate beauty.[64]

Poetry, in the form of songs, is often found in African and Cuban narrative. Examples of the latter are Cabrera's "Saudende" and "El caballo de Jicotea." However, in spite of the closeness in content and structure that Cuban texts have been able to maintain, there is one element lost in a poetic transculturation: the artistic magic of the language itself. One word alone, in Yoruba, may be both question and answer in the form of a riddle. For example, in the Ifa we find a woman who wants to conceive a son. The answer to this request is to boil green beans (*ole*). The implication is that by following the diviner's advice an embryo (*ole*) will be conceived.[65] In Yoruba, rhetorical elegance is seen as the ability to create riddles.[66] Language, then, goes a step beyond the concept of the existence of supernatural powers to create a tool for man's control of the universe through the magic power of the word.[67]

Music

Unfortunately, mounting stereotypes of Blacks have emerged in the Western world due to a constant misunderstanding of the functions of music. In Yoruban culture, music surpasses human limitations to acquire supernatural powers. Music is a channel and a tool used by man and deity.[68] The materials used to make musical instruments and their shapes and ways of playing them are highly specialized, and sometimes just the notes to one drum may be an art that takes several years to learn. Each *orisha* has a specific music and dance that must be played in order to summon him.[69] It is often through music that deities communicate to followers their capriciousness, expectations and will. In Del Valle's "Había cosa mala en la ceiba," in order to cleanse a revered tree from what was thought to be an evil spell placed on it and to find out from the gods what was wrong, a ritual with at least one drum was necessary. Tata Nicolás saw in his divining shells that such a ritual had to be done immediately. However, even though there was no time for formal preparations, the importance of the musician's preciseness was such that Cuco, a drum player who lived at a distance but who could play better than anyone else, was the one summoned to play. The drum chosen for the ceremony was the Yoruban *batá*, which an old African slave still kept, inherited from his African ancestors.[70]

Most of the songs found in narratives, as we can see in the African legends collected in Yoruba folklore, show a pattern that indicates a possible original form of collective storytelling, with antiphonal recitations and an interspersed choir—a characteristic explained in detail by Alejo Carpentier's *La música en Cuba*.[71] In a collection entitled *Our Folk Lore and Fables* (1960) we find only one song, but it is interesting to note the importance of this song in that it coincides with a petition. It is the magic of music that predisposes the fulfillment of the request: forgiveness.

Oh my husband the Hunter
Pray shoot not at me,
My silver coat have I donned
While you were away
My belongings have I shared
And given my son
Pray do not shoot me
My husband Ogunlola.[72]

Music, as the tool that opens the channels of communications between man and the supernatural, is in Cabrera's "Cheggue" the form by which the forest's animals (nature) announce to Cheggue's father their punishment (death) for having violated natural law. The father calls his son with a song, which is followed by the reply from the forest:

Cheggue, Oh, Cheggue
Tanike Cheggue nibe ún
Cheggue, one chono ire ló
Cheggue tá larroyo (Cheggue is by the creek). . . . [73]

The song does not indicate a celebration by the animals for the young man's death, nor are they making fun of the old man. It simply indicates nature's triumph over man's disruptions of it; it proclaims a cosmological natural order of things and the consequences brought about when this order is broken, comparable to the function of the just voice of the choir in Greek plays.

The magic power of song and dance can find a multiplicity of functions within narratives. Songs can serve, as Amadís de Gaula's ring, to identify relationships with lineages.[74] It serves to weaken the *orishas'* decisions and stubbornness. Changó, for example, teaches his children (the *ibeyes*) a song in order to change Yemayá's opinion of him.[75] It is important to point out that power comes not from the person who sings but from the song itself. In Lachatañeré's "El escamoteo" it is not Ochún's erotic beauty that seduces the god of iron and war, Ogún Arere, but, rather, her song and dance.

Music can be a tool to create or participate in a hypnotic state of reality. In "Taita Hicotea and Taita Tigre," Turtle is able to place her captors in a musical trance and then escape,[76] just as Chicken did in "La prodigiosa Gallina de Guinea."[77] In Carlos Montenegro's "El timbalero" the prisoners became excited because Baró, the drum player who was always quiet, serious and sad, was going to play. While playing, he seemed to overcome sadness as he hit the drums harder, and a picaresque smile grew on his face while singing: "Muiños plays to the son of my son."[78] It was found during the afternoon that Baró and Muiños had escaped the prison.

Music can alter natural forces that rule man as well as the mysterious forces that rule the forest. If the strong god of iron and war, Ogún,[79] is attracted by Yemayá's soft melody,[80] in the Nigerian Yoruba folklore it is the soft, tender song of a mother that saves her son from the hands of an ape: "Still the mother sang on, and still the ape danced, always approaching the ground, so charmed that it never noticed its descent, until it stood on the ground. Then the ape gave back the child to the mother. . . . "[81]

Music is not only a tool that can act upon forces controlling man, but it is a multidimensional channel to reach alternate states of realities, to surpass human limitations, to enter the plane of the *orishas*. Orumbila, exhausted while in the forest, hears faraway drums. The music was slowly able to rid him of his tiredness, and upon reaching the village he was revived enough to dance to the drums.[82] It is through this music that Orumbila meets Ochosi and can accomplish Olofi's orders. It is also through music that in Cabrera Infante's *Three Trapped Tigers* (1967), the black singer, Estrella, can surpass the mediocrity of her life and the monstrosity of her physical appearance. And it is through music that man is allowed to be attuned to the mysteries of the forest; hence, in Lino Novás Calvo's "El otro cayo" the slaves can foresee the avenging storm about to come. While the white man mis-interpreted the music as a stereotyped diversion linked to bestial and sexual passions "typical of Blacks,"[83] the language of the drums spoke of an approaching hurricane sent by the supreme diviner whose wind was already blowing over the waters[84] but could not be seen by any white man. The power of music, the mystery of the forest, the cruelty of the white man and the vengeance of nature are intermingled in the freeing power of death. It was ultimately the destruction of oppression that the drums had announced and that nature's actions accomplished. We must also remember that in Alejo Carpentier's *The Kingdom of This World* (1949), it is only after two hours of song and dance that the mandinga slave, Mackandal, who was blessed by the gods with the wisdom of power over nature and whose return had been awaited for four years, appears, finally, behind the main drum.[85] In this same novel the black revolution, which later came about, is incited and sanctified by the priestess of Rodá through her songs and praises to Ogún.[86] And, it is also through the beat of the drums in César Leante's *Los guerrilleros negros* (1976) that the future of a nation is announced. The runaway slave, Coba, was resuscitated to the permeating beat of the drums that rolled from the mountains, symbolically, on Christmas Eve.

The magnetic power of Filomeno's music (rhythm) creates in Carpentier's *Concierto Barroco* (1974) a strange ceremonial rite that, like the frenzied drums in "El otro cayo," may remind us of Congo (*bantú*) drums. However, the basic function and essence of the music created adhere to Yoruban cosmovisional rites in its religious and transcendental purpose.[87] Taking this into consideration, such a rite, the musical-historical syncretism that Filomeno brings about, is inspired by a serpent (visual syncretism of the African Damballah and the Judeo-Christian devil[88]) that he sees in a painting on a wall of a European church building.[89] In this novel, Filomeno incarnates the African rhythm, "a rhythm which lived through centuries so that," according to the narrator, "the Bible could become rhythm" and inhabit the kingdom of this world "in a new musical movement"[90] in which, in a new dialectical synthesis, African rhythm and European melodies would converge to be transmuted into a new creation, a new musical form: America.

Divination and Diviners

Probably the most common element in the Yoruban literature of both countries that can be traced directly to the Ifa is the presence and importance of the diviner or *babalawo*.[91] An African legend tells of how Olodumare (Olofi) gave

Orunmila wisdom. He then came to earth and settled in the region of Ife. According to the third *Odu* of the *Ifa*, one of his eight sons insulted him, and Orunmila returned to the sky. As a consequence, chaos reigned. Man pleaded with Orunmila's sons for the return of their father.[92] But Orunmila refused to do so and instead gave them sixteen palm nuts so that with these nuts or shells or bones, man could come to know his will.[93] Hence, the *babalawo* is the chosen person to possess the secrets of divination, and thus, communicate the will of Orunmila, the Ifa, to men.[94] Most of the legends about Orunmila, however, reinstate him to his original position of diviner. We see this in Lachatañeré's "Olvido" as well as in the latest collection of legends and folklore written in Cuba; in Barnet's *Akeké y la jutía*, we meet Orunmila as Orula, the omniscient owner of the divining board of Ifa.[95] The importance assigned to the *babalawo* is seen in cases as Papá Ifá (father Ifá),[96] whose patron saint is the actual Ifa, knower of all hidden things,[97] and in Papá Orugán in "¿Por qué escondes a tu abuela?," in "El Tata," or even in Cristino's grandmother in *Cuando la sangre se parece al fuego*. In the latter, a *babalosha* (the feminine *babalawo*) who discovers, by reading coconuts and shells over the board of Ifa, that Cristino's friend belonged to Ogún, Changó and Eleguá, (the three greatest warriors) and must carry protective charms during his revolutionary activities.[98]

The literary presence of these *babalawos* and *babaloshas* speaks of the sociopolitical importance these figures have had in Cuban history. It was thought that they could uncover, foresee and act upon the future. Even in postrevolutionary texts like *Cuando la sangre se parece al fuego* or Samuel Feijóo's *Tumbaga* (1964), we find that in spite of the didactic reproach against diviners, no longer functional in a new society,[99] their social and literary importance is reemphasized.

Through his shells, Papá Ifá finds out the secret that was hurting ña-Feliciana[100] the same way that Taita in José Antonio Ramos' *Caniquí* (1936) foresees Filomeno's future. Filomeno (the black slave Caniquí) runs to the solitary place where the old black Taita lived and tells him his problems; following the divination process, Taita tells him another story about another slave caught and hung. Taita gives Filomeno specific instructions to try to alter fate, but at the end Filomeno is killed fulfilling Taita's prophecy. In Cabrera's *Cuentos de jicotea* (1971) we find a *babalawo* and a *babalosha* that are able to discover what no one else was able to see: Inside the singing drum that Tortoise had used to fool people and acquire fame, there was a lost child that she had imprisoned for her own gain. The *babalawo* and *babalosha* demanded that Tortoise open the drum, release the child and face punishment, that is, public shame.[101]

The Ifa explicitly points out the consequences that would come about if a *babalawo* were to violate the truthfulness and integrity of his role as Ifa's messenger in favor of his own gain.[102] Corroborating this warning are the punishment Orumbila received from Changó and Eleguá in Lachatañeré's "Olvido" and the punishment that Tortoise received from a true *babalawo*. Papá Orugán would help and give advice to anyone whether he received anything for it or not; however, truthful to the Ifa, he would not use the powers and forces of the forest that he had brought from the old country (Africa) to cause any harm.[103] Evil doing, in Yoruba legends, is frequently seen as a boomerang that falls back upon the evil doer or that causes good when harm was meant, as exemplified over and over in the case of Tortoise, the Yoruban trickster.

Themes, Plots and Characters

Probably one of the most interesting aspects of Yoruban influence is the intertextual presence of themes, plots and characters that reappear in various forms and treatment in the literature of both countries. In a Nigerian legend, Ogumefu's "Tortoise and the Whip-Tree," Tortoise goes to the forest during a famine, looking for something to eat. He finds a tree unknown to him and asks what kind of tree it is; it answers that it is a Chop-tree. Tortoise asks what it can produce, and the tree answers: a great abundance of food. Still shocked, he goes to another much more beautiful tree and asks the same question. The tree answers that it is a Whip-tree; but when asked what it can produce, it proceeds to give Tortoise a beating. Tortoise's wife, jealous of him because he seemed to be able to remain fat and plump, follows him one day and discovers the secret. She immediately goes to town and tells everyone. Tortoise then invites them to the lusher tree, which whips them to death. When the king becomes aware of Tortoise's wife's absence, he demands an explanation. Tortoise invites King and Nobility to the tree, where they all receive the same treatment. For this, Tortoise has to hide for the rest of its life.[104] A very similar version of this story appears in Cabrera's "La loma de Mambiala." Here, the main character is not a tortoise but a man named Serapio, a bum who prefers to keep his family hungry rather than to work. One day he decides to go to Mambiala's hill to see if Mambiala will help him. Once there, Serapio finds a pot; he asks its name and the pot answers, "Cazuelita cocina bueno" ("good cooking pot"), and proceeds to supply him with a banquet. Thrilled, Serapio takes it with him and invites a large number of people to eat. A rich man offers him a million dollars for it, and Serapio sells it with such bad luck that the man slips and breaks the pot, leaving Serapio and his family as poor as ever. Serapio returns to the hill and finds a cane that calls itself Mr. Manatí ("good giver"), but what it gives is a beating. Serapio takes it with him, gathers all the neighbors and rich men that used to come and eat out of the pot and asks the cane to perform. Serapio thanks Mambiala and throws the cane down a well after having wandered about all night. The waters seemed to invite him in to rest, and he proceeds to throw himself in the well. According to Cabrera, this story is the Cuban legend of Yaguajay's Well.[105]

The same intertextual presence of themes and plots can be found in terms of characters. However, of all the characters, whether man, *orisha* or animal, Tortoise is the most complex and paradoxical figure. The proximity that still remains between Cabrera's *Cuentos de jicotea* and Barnet's *Akeké y la jutía* and, for example, Tortoise stories in *Yoruba Legends* (1929) shows the faithfulness of this character's imagery to the Ifa.

Tortoise, a paradoxical and multidimensional character, is the epitome of wits and astuteness.[106] It can be broken up into pieces, but it never dies. It can appear as male or female, old or young, tramp or priest. Its intelligence and wits surpass that of any other animal or even human character. Tortoise can decipher enigmas, can acquire powers to become an evil king, can maneuver others for its own gain; it triumphs over evil or is punished for evil doings. However, in spite of punishments, Tortoise lives on.

In recently translated Nigerian legends the influence and twists of Christian morals and values have become, at times, apparent. In Cuba, however, Tortoise is the *taita* that shows, through her flattery and deceit, the attitude of African slaves toward their white owners:[107] Tortoise is also, in keeping with European fairy stories, the mythological character that gives a sack of gold and later punishes selfishness, taking everything away;[108] or the Spanish stereotype of the matchmaker Celestina in "La excelente Doña Jicotea Concha" and in "La porfía de las comadres;" or cruelty incarnate in "La jicotea endemoniada" and "El ladrón del boniatal;" or the seducer and destroyer of a queen's purity and happiness in "Arere Mareken."[109] It is Tortoise that brings about death in "Vida o Muerte," that makes the Sun go farther away from Earth so that it would not burn her in "Jicotea le preguntó al sol." It is the witchman in "Irú Ayé" and "La rama del muro" that holds and wins a battle of magic powers (*bilongos*) with José Asunción. It is Tortoise in Barnet's *Akeké y la jutía* that saves the goat from the serpent and then punishes the latter for its behavior.[110]

A passage from "Osaín de un pie," reveals that Tortoise has been granted a certain cosmological equality or proximity with the world of *orishas*.[111] If Tortoise is found in Barnet's "Los carapachos de tortuga y jicotea" as the underdog that triumphs[112] or in "Venado, jicotea y toro" as the victim that sees good come out of evil,[113] it is because in Tortoise's weakness lies its power and, in that power, its cosmological sensitivity.

Tortoise represents human characteristics: In her converge good and evil. Tortoise, in Barnet's *Akeké y la jutía* is the only animal that saves Goat from the snake[114] and in Cabrera's "Jicotea era un buen hijo" appears as a responsible and exemplary son. In this latter story, during a famine Tortoise hides his own mother after he finds out that mothers were chosen to be served as food. The devil, however, discovers the hideout and kills her.[115] Tortoise goes then to Changó of Ima to ask for revenge, and a battle between natural and supernatural powers takes place. Tortoise returns with his mother's death avenged and with his relationship with Changó established—a relationship based on a common element, fire.[116] After several days of rain, nature's battle is followed by calm and earth's resurrection:

Tortoise, mystery of water and fire, food which increases Changó's strength, went back down to earth intact. It returned to live in the already calmed river, where Ochún keeps her corals and gold and where she has a crystal palace at the bottom, guarded by fire and five crocodiles.[117]

Tortoise, according to popular folklore, incorporated many of Changó's paradoxical qualities, but, as a trickster, she comes closer to meeting many of the manifestations assigned to the Yoruban *orisha* Eshú-Elegbá, due to his contradictory malice, astuteness, wits and, at times, superiority and even helping hand. Numerous legends tell of how both, *orisha* and Tortoise, won bets and battles by taking advantage of other characters. However, above it all, Tortoise represents the multiple dimensions of man's nature in his sociopolitical realm, as well as what he has always interpreted as the natural and supernatural forces of the cosmos and man's relationship with it.

COSMOVISION

The aspects of Yoruban cosmology that have survived in Cuban literature are present in Ramos' *Caniquí* and described as one side of two opposing religious world views: European Christianity and African mythocosmology. In this novel two worlds converge in the protagonist Filomeno/Caniquí: Filomeno, the black slave subject to social and ethnic prejudices and the cruelty of a plantation master who forced him to think and behave according to European values; and Caniquí, symbol of the African mythohistoric past upon whom converged the beliefs and values of a different world still ruled by the magnetic forces of the forest. The runaway slave, Caniquí, is presented in the narrative with the mythopoetic imagery proper of a semi-Yoruban god. In the collective beliefs of the African slaves, they saw him as a type of Carpentierian Mackandal able to escape and fool the white man. At the same time, Caniquí himself had an unquestioning certainty about the protection offered by his guardian *orisha*, Olokún, goddess of the water. Given the numerous occasions in which he had escaped through his swimming ability, he was assured that no wrong could befall him while immersed in Olokún's kingdom, the water. In that kingdom he found the ultimate expression of freedom in death, floating on his back in Olokún's blue waters while looking at Obatalá's white open space.[118]

What ultimately stands out in this novel is the positive African cosmological outlook on life contrasted with the negativeness of European Christian theology. It is Caniquí's martyrdom that brings about his own freedom (in death) and the freedom from his white owner, Mariceli. It is Obatalá's cleansing and freeing power that we also see at work in Cabrera Infante's "En el gran Ecbó," where a woman who has come with her lover to see an *egbó* leaves completely changed, ready to break an adulterous relationship and start a new life.

The basic positiveness found in these texts coincides with Yoruban cosmology: the absence of conflicting polarization of goodness and evil.[119] These are seen not as battling forces, as in Christianity, but as complementary and harmonious ones. Goodness and evil are relative cosmic forces of cause and effect resulting from irresponsibility, violations or revered obedience of natural and divine laws, as exemplified in Tortoise's adventures, nature's punishment of Cheggue and almost all mythofolkloric Yoruban tales. However, also as in

Christianity, references are made to a time, long ago, when things were differ-ent and life was harmonious, when animals, gods, and men coexisted in some form or fashion. Then, gods were men[120] or could communicate directly with man and animal; or animals were humans, as in Cabrera's "Los compadres" and "Bregantino Bregantín;" or animals and men could speak to each other; or even the *babalawos* were the rats.[121] Change for the Yorubans, as for most West Africans, was brought about by a rupture between sky and earth. However, such rupture is seen as an outcome not of sin, as in the Judeo-Christian tradition, but as the result of indifference. Ill fortune is brought about by man's irresponsi-bility and violation and, at times, by the *orishas'* faults and capriciousness. Ob-atalá, for example, god of reason and purity, gets drunk on the day of creation and makes defective human beings.[122] Yemayá seduces her own adoptive son Changó,[123] the chaste Orisaoco,[124] and the invincible Ogún Arere.[125] One of the characters in Cabrera's "Los compadres" says, "All of us are sons [and daughters] of saints [*orishas*] and from them we get our malice and desire to sin."[126] The concept of sin is not present in Yoruban cosmology, as it is in Western cultures. On the contrary, every pure and virtuous behavior can be broken by the weight of its own inflexibility; every virtuous person can find his down-fall, given the natural weakness present in human nature as well as in nature in general. Mariceli, Caniquí's white owner, in her negative perception of the cos-mos and herself sees bodily punishment as her only way to purify and redeem herself from sin; she thought she was impurity and evil incarnated. Caniquí, on the contrary, was exempt from personal guilt. It was Elegbá's supernatural ca-priciousness and malice, not his own nature, that was responsible for his wrongdoings.[127] But, even though present, his fear and uneasiness of Eleguá are neutralized by the security he finds in Olokún.[128]

If in Yoruban cosmology Eshú-Elegbá manifests uncertainty (created in the beginnings of time), then certainty is found (created) in the Ifa, as well as the entire divining system around it. Man is subject to capricious forces, but man can also find out what they are and how to act upon them as long as the guard-ing *orisha* is pleased and grants help.

Redemption, as in Christian theology, is absent from Yoruban cosmology. The supreme Olofi (Olorum), indifferent toward his own creation,[129] aban-doned man at the mercy of lesser deities and natural forces. Man was left with no other alternative than to play the game of life by *orisha* rules. And it is man's astuteness in his dealings with nature and deities that can keep stronger forces happy and satisfied, allowing him to live his own life harmoniously.

The great balancing power of paradoxical forces characteristic of Yoruban cosmology is ultimately found in its own multidimensionality. All entities have multiple forms and manifestations. Changó, for example, is mainly two, one that travels by horse and one by foot.[130] Hence, when the priestess of Rodá in *The Kingdom of This World* calls upon Ogún in a ritual of vengeance against the white man, she includes the various manifestations assigned to this *orisha*: "Ogoun of the Irons, Ogoun the Warrior, Ogoun of the Forges, Ogoun Marshal, Ogoun of the Lances, Ogoun-Chango, Ogoun-Kankanikan, Ogoun-Batala, Ogoun-Panama, Ogoun-Bakoulé."[131] Some *orishas*, together with the property of being many in one, can also be hermaphrodites.[132] These cosmological characteristics allowed for a syncretic process to take place in Cuba in which religious entities (saints) of the Roman Catholic Church were added, in names and manifestations, to the same *orishas* without having to alter the basic cosmovision already held.

The multiplicity of cosmological possibilities is widened into every aspect of nature; thus, a woman-animal,[133] a leopard-man,[134] the intelligence of the Iroko tree,[135] the speaking ability of sweet potatos, calabashes[136] and animals.[137] Every aspect of life is influenced by supernatural entities. The forest, however, is the true stage for the multiplicity of manifestations and possibilities to reality. According to elder black men in Cabrera's *El monte* (''the forest''):

The forest is like a temple. . . . In the forest, each tree, each plant, each weed has an owner, with a well defined sense of property. . . . one does not go in the forest without proper respect and behavior. And much more when one goes to ask for something. . . . Where one would least imagine, there is a spirit. They are everywhere. We can't see them, but we stand elbow to elbow with the dead and with deities at all times.[138]

Upon this belief, the slaves in ''El otro cayo'' knew that there was an invisible race of beings that lived in the trees.[139] Jiménez' death could be foreseen through signs in trees and animals,[140] and they could, ultimately, foresee the holocaust to come. By the same token, Mackandal, in *The Kingdom of This World*, had been integrated into nature:

At night in their quarters and cabins the Negroes communicated to one another with great rejoicing, the strangest news:. . . . They all knew that the green lizard, the night moth, the strange dog, the incredible gannet, were nothing but disguises. . . . One day he would give the sign for the great uprising, and the Lord of Back There [Africa], headed by Damballah [serpent god], the Master of the Roads [Eleguá] and Ogoun, Master of the Swords, would bring thunder and lightning [Changó] and unleash the cyclone that would round out the work of men's hands.[141]

Hence, what for the white man was indifference and apathy on the part of slaves toward their revered leader, Mackandal, or for Caniquí toward his own life was in fact, a different cosmovision. For the slaves the body that the white master saw as dead was no longer Mackandal's. He had escaped again, this time transformed into a mosquito.[142] Caniquí, on the other hand, saw himself being absorbed in the kingdom of Olokún and Obatalá.

Yoruban cosmovision sees man as an important part of the whole; it sees life as the art of living with the astuteness and the knowledge (based on experience) of the magic games of the cosmos and with a vision based, according to *babalawos*, upon the solid certainty not of myth or legend per se but of the historicity[143] of the Ifa. As an umbilical cord, the Ifa goes from Cuban contemporary literature to the very beginning of a myth that gave sociohistorical identity to a people. If at times African mythological and folkloric images give the impression of being a literary exotic device, many of these forms do coincide with a cultural reality and, even more, with a much older mythopoetic imagery that attempts to explain man's depth through actions that never were but always are. They also reveal a collective consciousness alive in Cuban literature that, as the reflection of basic cultural characteristics, can be said to be no longer just Yoruba but Cuban *lucumí*.

NOTES

1. Roger Bastide, *Las Américas Negras* (Madrid: Alianza Editorial, 1969), pp. 112–20. Also William Bascom, "The Yoruba in Cuba," *Nigeria Magazine*, no. 37 (1957). This article is a study of Yoruba transculturation from Africa and its presence in Cuba today.

2. Rogelio Martínez Furé, *Diálogos imaginarios* (Havana: Editorial Arte y Literatura, 1979), pp. 210–11.

3. Saburi Olademi Biobaku, *Sources of Yoruba History* (Oxford: Clarendon Press, 1973), p. 1.

4. J. D. Fage, *A History of West Africa* (Cambridge: Cambridge University Press, 1969), p. 42.

5. Basil Davidson, *A History of West Africa* (New York: Doubleday, 1966), p. 98.

6. Ibid., p. 184.

7. Bastide, *Las Américas*, p. 112.

8. Fage, *History*, p. 104.

9. Martínez Furé, *Diálogos*, p. 212.

10. Bernard I. Belasco, *The Entrepreneur as Culture Hero* (New York: J. F. Bergin, 1980), p. 97.

11. El Akoni, *La voz de Orunla: El Cordón de Orilé* (New York: Studium, 1975), pp. 150–51. The Akoni, or teacher in the *lucumí* religion, claims that it was necessary during slavery to use Catholic saints' names for African gods. However, the image never changed, and today the believers "must give to Caesar what is Caesar's and to God what is God's," meaning that Yoruba gods should be called by their names and the two religions set apart.

12. Ulli Beier, *The Return of the Gods* (London: Cambridge University Press, 1975), p. 33.

13. Miguel Barnet, *Canción de Rachel* (Buenos Aires: Editorial Galerna, 1969), p. 153.

14. Fernando Ortiz, *Los negros brujos* (1906; reprint ed., Miami: Ediciones Universal, 1973), p. 28. Here Ortiz refers to an observation that was made by the missionary Bowen on Yoruba political structure and that coincides with all recent studies. Because of the many variations in the Yoruba language and the difficulty of translating the dialects of Yoruba into Spanish and English, a Yoruba name may have different spellings. For example, Obàtálá in Yoruba is written as Obatalá in Spanish. We have attempted to simplify the Yoruba accents and have written them as required by the language of the text in question.

15. John Weir Perry, *Lord of the Four Quarters* (New York: Macmillan, 1966), p. 28.

16. Rómulo Lachatañeré, "El moquenquen de Orumbila," *¡Oh, mío, Yemayá!* (Manzanillo, Cuba: Editorial del Arte, 1938), p. 178. Also see his "Ochosi de Mata," in ibid., p. 168.

17. Miguel Barnet, "El cangrejo sin cabeza," *Akeké y la jutía* (Havana: Ediciones Unión, 1978), p. 108.

18. Manuel Cofiño, *Cuando la sangre se parece al fuego* (Havana: Editorial de Arte y Literatura, 1975), p. 25.

19. Wándé Abímbólá, "The Literature of the Ifa Cult," in Biobaku, *Sources*, p. 42.

20. Ibid., p. 43.

21. William Bascom, *Ifa Divination: Communication Between Gods and Men in West Africa* (Bloomington: Indiana University Press, 1969), p. 103.

22. Abímbólá "Literature," p. 42–43.

23. This is the divining board of Ekuelé but in Lydia Cabrera's *El monte* (1954; reprint ed., Miami: Ediciones Universal, 1975, p. 70) we find it as *okpó Ifá*.

24. Ibid. The African Orunmila is known in Cuba as Orumbila.

25. Lachatañeré, *¡Oh, mío, Yemayá!*, p. 64.

26. Abímbólá, "Literature," p. 41.

27. Lachatañeré, *¡Oh, mío, Yemayá!*, p. 131.

28. Ibid., p. 121.

29. Gerardo del Valle, "Ella no creía en bilongos," *Cuarto Fambá y 19 cuentos más* (Havana: Ediciones Unión, 1967), p. 11.

30. Bascom, *Ifa Divination*, p. 103.

31. Cabrera, *El monte*, p. 76.

32. Lachatañeré, *¡Oh, mío, Yemayá!*, pp. 64, 68.

33. Cofiño, *Cuando la sangre*, p. 133.

34. Bascom, *Ifa Divination*, p. 103.

35. Guillermo Cabrera Infante, "En el gran Ecbó," in *Antología del cuento cubano contemporáneo*, ed. Ambrosio Fornet (Mexico: Ediciones Era, 1970), p. 197.

36. Cofiño, *Cuando la sangre*, p. 38.

37. Ibid., p. 49.

38. Ibid., p. 48.

39. Joel Adedeji, "Folklore and Yoruba Drama: Obàtálá as a Case Study," in *African Folklore*, ed. Richard M. Dorson (New York: Doubleday, 1972), pp. 338–39.

40. Del Valle, "Ella no creía," p. 64.

41. Lachatañeré, *¡Oh, mío, Yemayá!*, p. 33.

42. Adedeji, "Folklore," p. 321.

43. Ibid., p. 336.

44. Cabrera, *El monte*, p. 230.

45. Cofiño, *Cuando la sangre*, p. 38.

46. Barnet, *Akeké y la jutía*, p. 56.

47. Cofiño, *Cuando la sangre*, p. 39.

48. Cabrera, *El monte*, p. 86.

49. Cofiño, *Cuando la sangre*, p. 79.

50. Del Valle, "Ella no creía," p. 92.

51. Cofiño, *Cuando la sangre*, p. 34.

52. Del Valle, "Ella no creía," p. 111.

53. Cabrera, *Cuando la sangre*, pp. 224–26.

54. Pepe Carril, *Shangó de Ima* (New York: Doubleday, 1969), p. 89. Also Lachatañeré, *¡Oh, mío, Yemayá!*, pp. 181–83.

55. Del Valle, "Ella no creía," p. 111.

56. Lachatañeré, "Olvido," *¡Oh, mío, Yemayá!*, p. 60.

57. Cofiño, *Cuandro la sangre*, p. 39.

58. Ibid., p. 100.

59. Ibid.

60. Judith Gleason, *Orisha: The Gods of Yorubaland* (New York: Atheneum, 1971), pp. 92, 110.

61. Bascom, *Ifa Divination*, p. 121.

62. Ibid., p. 122.

63. Abímbólá, "Literature," p. 45.

64. Lydia Cabrera, "Walo-Wila," *Cuentos negros de Cuba* (Madrid: Ramos Artes Gráficas, 1972), p. 38.

65. Bascom, *Ifa Divination*, p. 130.

66. Ayodele Ogundipe, "Yoruba Tongue Twisters," in Dorson, *African Folklore*, p. 214.

67. Adebayo Adesanya, "Yoruba Metaphysical Thinking," *Odu*, no. 5 (1958), p. 36. According to Adesanya, the difficulty of Yoruba language is the multi-interpretative dimensions that it can have due to its idiomatic expressions and technical phraseologies. It demands much from one's power of comprehension and quickness of understanding.

68. Father K. Carroll, "Yoruba Masks," *Odu* no. 3 (n.d.), p. 13.

69. Timi of Ede Laoye, "Yoruba Drums," *Odu* no. 7 (n.d.), p. 5.

70. Del Valle, "Ella no creía," p. 75.

71. Alejo Carpentier, *La música en Cuba* (Mexico: Fondo de Cultura Económica, 1946), pp. 294, 299, 304.

72. J. A. Danford, and S. A. Fuja, *Our Folk Lore and Fables* (Lagos: Crownbird Series, Ministry of Lagos, 1960), p. 5.

73. Cabrera, *Cuentos negros de Cuba*, p. 30.

74. Lachatañeré, *¡Oh, mío, Yemayá!*, p. 177.

75. Ibid., p. 95.

76. Cabrera, *Cuentos negros de Cuba*, pp. 64–65.

77. Ibid., pp. 160–63.

78. Carlos Montenegro, "El timbalero," in Fornet, *Antología del cuento cubano contemporáneo*, p. 76.

79. Del Valle, "Ella no creía," p. 111.

80. Lachatañeré, *¡Oh, mío, Yemayá!*, p. 137.

81. John Parkinson, "Yoruba Folklore," *African Affairs* 8 (1909): 171.

82. Lachatañeré, "Ochosi de Mata," *¡Oh, mío, Yemayá!*, pp. 164–65.

83. Lino Novás Calvo, "El otro cayo," *Cayo Canas* (Buenos Aires: Espasa Calpe, 1946), p. 64.

84. Ibid., p. 66.

85. Alejo Carpentier, *The Kingdom of This World*, trans. Harriet de Onís (New York: Collier Books, 1970), p. 50.

86. Ibid., p. 52.

87. Father Carroll, "Yoruba Masks," p. 14: "rhythm is strictly subordinate to liturgical reverence."

88. Carpentier, *La Música en Cuba*, pp. 291–92. Cuban *comparsas* had specific themes, as for example, the killing of a snake or a scorpion. European melodies together with African rhythm gave birth to Cuban music (p. 362).

89. Ibid., p. 64.

90. Alejo Carpentier, *Concierto Barroco* (Mexico: Siglo XXI Editores, 1974), p. 82.

91. Also known as Yaloche.

92. Abímbólá, "Literature," p. 42.

93. Ibid., p. 43.

94. Cabrera, *El monte*, p. 86.

95. Barnet, *Akeké y la jutía*, p. 17.

96. José Antonio Ramos, *Caniquí* (Havana: Cultural, 1936), p. 192.

97. Del Valle, "Ella no creía," p. 91.

98. Cofiño, *Cuando la sangre*, p. 197.

99. Samuel Feijóo, *Tumbaga* (Las Villas, Cuba: Editora del Consejo Nacional de Universidades, 1964). He depicts the diviner as a trickster, parasite of society, who is unable to cope with the new changes. Cofiño's novel also shows the alienation of a *babalosha* from the realities of a new society and the changes being brought about.

100. Del Valle, "Ella no creía," p. 92.

101. Lydia Cabrera, "Ilú Kekeré," *Cuentos de Jicotea* (Miami: Ediciones Universal, 1971), p. 176.

102. Bascom, *Ifa Divination*, p. 77. Also Cabrera, *El monte*, p. 47.

103. Del Valle, "Ella no creía," p. 59.

104. M. I. Ogumefu, *Yoruba Legends* (London: Sheldon Press, 1929), pp. 80–84.

105. Cabrera, *Cuentos negros de Cuba*, p. 102. Also compare Ogumefu, *Yoruba Legends*, pp. 43–45, and Cabrera's *Yemayá y Ochún* (Madrid: Forma Gráfica, 1974), pp. 102–3. The African Iroko tree is the Cuban Ceiba.

106. Cabrera, *Cuentos de Jicotea*, p. 9.

107. Ibid., pp. 131–38.

108. Ibid., pp. 139–70.

109. Cabrera, *Cuentos negros de Cuba*, pp. 124–26.

110. Barnet, Akeké y la jutía, p. 132.

111. Cabrera, *Cuentos negros de Cuba*, p. 155. See also Cabrera, *Yemayá y Ochún*, p. 37.

112. Barnet, *Akeké y la jutía*, p. 32.

113. Ibid., p. 120.

114. Ibid., p. 132.

115. This is an example of syncretic overlaying of Eshú-Elegbá and the Christian devil.

116. Cabrera, *Cuentos negros de Cuba*, p. 47.

117. Ibid., p. 48.

118. Ramos, *Caniquí*, p. 388.

119. H. U. Beier, "The Historical and Psychological Significance of Yoruba Myths," *Odu*, no. 1, (1955): 24.

120. Parkinson, "Yoruba Folklore," p. 174.

121. Ibid., p. 177.

122. Cofiño, *Cuando la sangre*, p. 48. Also Beier, "Historical Significance," p. 25.

123. Lachatañeré, *¡Oh, mío, Yemayá!*, pp. 53–54.

124. Ibid., p. 148.

125. Ibid., pp. 140–41.

126. Cabrera, *Cuentos negros de Cuba*, p. 67.

127. Ramos, *Caniquí*, p. 184.

128. Ibid., p. 188.

129. Cabrera, *El monte*, p. 77.

130. Ibid., p. 223.

131. Carpentier, *The Kingdom of This World*, p. 67.

132. Cabrera, *El monte*, p. 86. Western influence can be seen in that this flexibility within an already broad reality is interpreted in Cuba through terms as homosexual gods, *orishas maricas*.

133. Parkinson's section on "The Hunter and the Hind," in the article "Yoruba Folklore," p. 1.

134. Ogumefu, "The Leopard-Man," *Yoruba Legends*, pp. 18–21.

135. Ibid., p. 11.

136. Cabrera, *El monte*, pp. 354–62.

137. Wándé Abímbólá, "Yoruba Oral Literature," *African Notes* 2, no. 3, (1964): 2.

138. Cabrera, *El monte*, pp. 14, 15, 21.

139. Novás Calvo, "El otro cayo," p. 55.

140. Ibid., p. 59.

141. Carpentier, *The Kingdom of This World*, pp. 41–42.

142. Ibid., pp. 51–52.

143. Bascom, *Ifa Divination*, pp. 121, 123. Also Abímbólá, "Yoruba Oral Literature," p. 12.

English
Caribbean _____

5
V. S. Naipaul and the Question of Identity

Selwyn R. Cudjoe

> In this age and time, one's native land (and the other's) is always *crumbling*; crumbling within a capacity of vision which rediscovers the process to be not foul and destructive but actually the constructive secret of all creation wherever one happens to be.
>
> Wilson Harris, *The Eye of the Scarecrow*

It is correct to begin a discussion of V. S. Naipaul and the question of identity with the words of Bob Marley, the Masta-Rasta, if only because they testify to an alternative mode of seeing the nature of social reality in the Caribbean. In a song entitled "Babylon System," Bob Marley gives us an insightful perception into what he calls "Babylon System:"

> We refuse to be
> What you wanted us to be
> We are what we are
> That's the way it's going to be
> You can't educate us
> For no equal opportunity
> Talking 'bout my freedom
> People freedom and liberty
> Yeah, we've been trodding on the wine press much too long
> Rebel, Rebel
> Yeah, we've been trodding on the wine press much too long
> Rebel, Rebel
> Babylon system is the vampire
> Sucking the blood of the sufferers
> Building church and university

> Deceiving the people continually
> Me see them graduating thieves
> And murderers, look out now
> Sucking the blood of the sufferers
> Tell the children the truth
> Tell the children the truth right now.[1]

Such a perception of Caribbean reality is important when one realizes that from London to Boston, V. S. Naipaul is proclaimed the new oracle of colonial truth. Francis Wyndham, writing in *Okite* in 1972, called him "the finest living novelist writing in English,"[2] while Margaret Manning of the *Boston Globe* felt no less constrained in her praises. In her review of his last published work, *The Return of Eva Peron*, Manning complimented him in almost identical terms and called him "probably the best writer alive who writes in English."[3]

That V. S. Naipaul speaks "the truth" about colonial reality is a fact that few critics are wont to question. Whether he speaks about history or literature, culture or politics, V. S. Naipaul is seen as the new guru, dispensing the truth about colonial reality that will set colonial peoples free, if only they would but listen to his new gospel.[4]

But does he? Is there really any human subject, any social being who writes or speaks about human reality who is beyond the pale of an ideological perception of the world?[5] Or does the vision of the writer come pure and untainted from afar, having, like John Milton, only to call upon his "Celestial Patroness, who deigns/Her nightly visitation unimplor'd,/And dictates to me slumb'ring, or inspires/Easy my unpremeditated Verse."[6] One critic has gone as far as to suggest that Naipaul is without precedent or predecessor; that he is, to use the critic's words, "wholly original . . . maybe the only writer in whom there are no echoes of influences."[7]

These are strange words, particularly when it comes from an esteemed critic and writer. And perhaps one wonders whether or not Ralph Ellison's response to Irving Howe's article, "Black Boys and Native Sons" (Howe, of course, is another booster of the brilliance and originality of V. S. Naipaul),[8] was not really a comment about most white critics when Ellison questioned: "Why is it so often true that when critics confront the American as *Negro* they suddenly drop their advanced critical armament and revert with an air of confident superiority to quite primitive modes of analysis?"[9] These words were uttered in 1963. If we substitute "nonwhite" for "American as *Negro*," these words would be as true today as they were when they were written. Perhaps they become even more perceptive when they are applied to the noncriticism that attends the works of V. S. Naipaul.

That no writer, no matter how gifted, is without a tradition is obvious. That each writer reflects or signifies a specific social reality is equally as true and need not be subjected to any unnecessary or esoteric debate.[10] That Paul Theroux—like other European and American critics who banter their banalities without so much as recognizing the antihistorical nature of their methodology—continues to detract from the kind of serious literary criticism that the works of V. S. Naipaul deserve is also obvious.[11] Because these critics have unusual access to the vehicles that promulgate the word on V. S. Naipaul, a not too fortuitous coincidence, they become the most "authentic" interpreters of Naipaul's truth. The process they use distorts his truths and renders an injustice to the field of criticism. The West Indian critics who may have important things to say about Naipaul are generally denied access to the media of this country.

Born in Chaguanas, Trinidad, V. S. Naipaul is a colonial man of East Indian heritage. Like most Caribbean writers, V. S. Naipaul examines the realities of his specific group.[12] And like any other writer, he is wedded to a particular perception of the world, privileges certain truths and writes almost invariably to convince his readers of them. In this respect V. S. Naipaul is surely no different from any other writer.

It is, however, to his credit that while he has consolidated the terrain of West Indian and Caribbean literature, like Wilson Harris and Alejo Carpentier, he has used his experience in order to explore much larger universal themes. Therefore, no matter how universal his themes appear, he begins with the particular, knows only the particular and reverts back to the particular to expound the universality of his truths.

Like most West Indian writers, V. S. Naipaul is concerned most immediately with the central problem of Caribbean existence: Who or what am I in the alien world of the West Indies? Stolen, marooned or indentured, each group must articulate and make some sense of what it means to exist in the wilderness of the New World. At least, this is how the problem of being posed itself initially, and it is to this question that Naipaul's first short stories and novels addressed themselves.

Miguel Street (written 1955, published 1958), *The Mystic Masseur* (1957) and *The Suffrage of Elvira* (1958) are Naipaul's first apprentice novels. In many ways they establish some of the themes of his later novels. In these early works his major concerns pertain to the questions of internal East Indian conflicts, the absurdity of certain aspects of both East Indian and African life and the inability of the colonial society to grant its inhabitants a sense of well-being or of identity.

A House for Mr. Biswas (1961) follows and is by far Naipaul's most successful effort. In this work the major theme revolves around Mr. Biswas, a colonial subject who tries to define himself within the context of the colonial world. Caught up between the demise of the old feudal order and the rise of nascent capitalist relations, Mr. Biswas is forced to articulate a sense of self within the context of these two contradictory movements of social organization. Within the conflicting demands of a society in transformation Mr. Biswas is able to demonstrate through his life what it means to be a colonial subject in a world that is controlled by the other.

But if *A House for Mr. Biswas* examines the question of what it means to be a colonial subject in a colonial world, it is left to *The Middle Passage* (1962) and *An Area of Darkness* (1964) to examine the specific social environment that created that subject. In these two novels he explores the factors that were responsible for the shaping of colonial man. Both these works take the form of travelogues. While the former draws largely upon the ideological perceptions of the English travel writers of the nineteenth century (the era of England's rise as the chief imperialist power, 1840–1900), the latter records the horror with which V. S. Naipaul looked upon his motherland for the first time. For him India was naught but an "area of darkness," while the Caribbean islands that he visited turned out to be places where nothing could be "achieved" or "created."

The Mimic Men (1967), Naipaul's next major work, sought to understand *how* the colonial subject ought to function within the context of formal independence. For Naipaul, colonialism created only subjects who pretend "to be real, to be learning, to be preparing [them]selves for life."[13] Yet, as the narrator of the novel concludes, these subjects are nothing more than "mimic men of the New World, one unknown corner of it, with all its reminders of corruption that came so quickly to the new."[14]

Whether or not mimicry is characteristic of all colonial subjects during the early phase of formal independence is not a topic with which we shall now take issue. Yet, if one accepts Jacques Lacan's concept of the "mirror phase" of social development, a period in which the individual subject assumes its social identity, then much insight can be gained from an analysis that explores the nature of mimicry of the colonial subject, as the society goes from colonialism to formal independence. What is to be questioned, though, is the assumption that one's social identity must be seen only in terms of the subjects' relationship to the colonizer.

It is within the context of the latter assumption that certain epistemological and ontological questions persist in any analysis of V. S. Naipaul's work, for it would seem that at that point of his career (the period ending with *The Loss of El Dorado* [1969]), Naipaul had made certain decisions about the manner in which he would apprehend the world and what values he would privilege. Certainly, he had decided that European society (particularly English) represented the apogee of all human culture and knowledge, and thus it *is* the source of all standards and judgments. This manner of perceiving the world would generate a particular epistemological position that always and everywhere would privilege the culture of the colonizer (that is, the culture of the oppressor). *The Loss of El Dorado* is used exclusively to confirm this way of apprehending colonial reality (the specific society being Trinidad), and all judgments about any society are fashioned from this narrow point of view. Negro life is seen as nothing more than a "whole underground life of fantasy."[15]

The essays collected in *The Overcrowded Barracoon* (1976) serve only to update the judgments that were made earlier; thus, the fantasy of slavery takes on a "new touch of lunacy" in the contemporary era and is manifested in that strange aberration called Trinidad carnival. Yet what is unmistakable, by the time that we arrive at the end of the second phase of Naipaul's development (that is, with *The Loss of El Dorado*), is that all judgments about the colonized society must be seen against the backdrop of the ideology of the oppressor. Furthermore, life "means" only to the extent that it conforms with the dominant colonialist ideology. From this point on, there is little that is new that Naipaul could say about his and our societies. He has exhausted all his original insights and, therefore, can only repeat himself.

The publication of *Guerrillas* (1975) and *A Bend in the River* (1979) ushered in what might be called an apocalyptic period in Naipaul's fictional and non-fictional works. In this period of development (a period that began with *In a Free State* [1971]) Naipaul sees only gloom and helplessness in colonial societies, and nothing good can ever issue forth from the land of Egypt. *Guerrillas*, possibly Naipaul's worst work, is a grotesque, caricatured and fictive account of the life of Michael X (on whom he did two articles for the *Sunday New York Times Magazine* in May 1974). In this work (and certainly from the beginning of this period of his writing) Naipaul is unable to respond to the changing contours of Caribbean life and its process of revolutionary transformation. Nor was he equipped with the language or form to express these new realities. The "bad-John" talk of the Trinidadian society of the 1940s and the ironic gestures that were adequate to depict the colonial society were no longer adequate to reflect or to signify the realities of post-colonial societies of the 1970s. Jimmy Ahmed, the major protagonist of *Guerrillas*, is neither revolutionary nor leader. He is simply the caricatured bad-John of an earlier era, a rejuvenated "project" that does not really reflect or signify a contemporary Caribbean.

A Bend in the River takes the apocalyptic gloom of *Guerrillas* further. The colonizer comes to the bush, opens it up and brings the glad tidings of civilization. When independence comes, he leaves, and everything goes back to bush. Nothing is possible without the "white man." In the beginning of Naipaul's literary experiments, Hat, one of the major characters of *Miguel Street*, is wont to exclaim: "White people is God, you hear."[16] Therefore, when God goes (as he does in this last work), all goes back to bush and to blood, and the terror of the native is heard in Ferdinand's warning to Salim when he asks him to leave the country: "We are all going to hell, and every man knows this in his bones. We're being killed. *Nothing has any meaning.* That is why everyone is so frantic. Everyone wants to make his money and run away. But where? That is what is driving the people mad. They feel they're losing the place they can run back to."[17] This is the same sense of apocalyptic gloom that we encountered in *Guerrillas* when James Ahmed cried out in desperation: "Things are desperate Roy, when the leader himself begins to yield to despair, things are bad. The whole place is going to blow up, I cannot see how I can control the revolution now. When everybody wants to fight there's nothing to fight for. Everybody wants to fight his own little war, everybody is a guerrilla."[18]

Are we to believe that this is the general condition of the colonial world? Bush and blood; guerrillas and half-made people in these "half-made socie-

ties'' of the world?[19] And are we supposed to conclude from Naipaul's significations, presumably as the distinguished American writer and critic Elizabeth
Hardwick has suggested, that

now, he [Naipaul] has passed beyond India . . . to a universal ''darkness.'' Talking to
him, reading and re-reading his work, one cannot help but think of a literary yesterday
and today, of Idi Amin, the Ayatollah Khomeini, of the fate of Bhutto. These figures
of an improbable and deranging transition come to mind because Naipaul's work is a
creative reflection upon a devastating lack of historical preparation, upon the anguish of
whole countries and peoples unable to cope.[20]

Hardwick ends her discussion of Naipaul (and the article in question) by asking
him somewhat mystically and misty-eyed: '' 'What is the future, in Africa?'
His answer: 'Africa has no future.' '' [21] Are we supposed to accept the judgment
of V. S. Naipaul and the interpretations of the Hardwicks, the Therouxs, the
Mannings, et al. as the last and authentic word on our fate?

One can begin to respond to these judgments and interpretations in a literary
manner by suggesting, as Colin McCabe does, that each text depends on every
other text for its fullest possible explication. And, as he argued: ''Every text is
already articulated with other texts which determine its possible meaning and
no text can escape the discourses of literary criticism in which it is referred to,
named and identified.'' [22] Just as we began with the Masta-Rasta, Wilson Harris can help us determine another possible meaning of Naipaul's text.

In his *The Eye of the Scarecrow* (1965), Wilson Harris gives us an alternative vision of West Indian life, a vision that is different both in its form and in
its ''overstanding'' (to use the language of the Rastafarian brethren) of the content of colonial experience. His work is an examination of the psychical experiences of the people of Guyana from the 1920s to 1964, a period of constant
turmoil involving the movement toward formal independence, which was achieved
in 1965. The novel, however, concerns not the physical characteristics of those
experiences but the psychic trauma (or transformation) to which the people of
Guyana were subjected. As a result, the novel bores beneath the consciousness
in order to understand what this experience meant to the people of Guyana,
proceeding by paradox and indirection, displacement and condensation, into the
world of the unconscious.

But the unconscious by definition is not to be observed so much through the
process of *conscious discourse* as through the lacunae and gaps of the subject's
discourse. By situating the central thematic movement of the novel in those gaps
in the conscious discourse of the major characters of the novel, the narrator is
able to reconstitute in a rather convincing manner the psyche of colonized subjects. It is in this sense, therefore, that the narrator is able to argue that: ''Language is one's medium of the vision of consciousness. There are other ways—
shall I say—of arousing this vision. But language alone can express (in a way
which goes beyond any physical or vocal attempt) the sheer—the ultimate 'silent' and 'immaterial' complexity of arousal.'' [23]

Harris, then, does not emphasize unduly the nature of physical activity. While he recognizes the "grave conflicts between capital and labour, between parties and powers, between institutions and masses,"[24] it is "the convulsion in the psyche of ordinary men and women"[25] that these events cause that concerns him most. For Harris, therefore, it is the psychical world of imagination and memory, emotions and repressions, dreams and hallucinations and so on through which the unconscious world of the Caribbean subjects is revealed. When we speak of the unconscious, we do not speak of "some bestial nature that has suffered a necessary, if inadequate, censoring *but the inevitable result of the entry of the body into language.*"[26]

It is on this level of psychical reality, this level of unconscious unfolding of the Caribbean subject, that one can begin to understand the world of which both V. S. Naipaul and Wilson Harris speak. It is only from this level of "open surrender" that one can begin to make the journey toward true internal liberation. For as the narrator of *The Eye of the Scarecrow* concludes,

the true beginnings of possible dialogue, the breath of all obstructive physicality one receives standing upon a borderline (as silent words stand on their speaking page) between an Imagination capable of reconciling unequal forms present and past and an Imagination empty of self-determined forms to come, black frames, indwelling non-resemblance, freedom from past, present, future form and formlessness. *It is in this unpredictable and paradoxical light one begins to forgive and to be forgiven all.*

And I have much of whom and of which to ask reconciliation in the present and forgiveness in the future.[27]

Naipaul, in *The Mimic Men*, seemed to understand the necessity for some sort of internal transformation in the movement from colonialism to independence. It was Harris, however, who "overstood" and explored the psyche through the flickering signs of language, allowing the reader, as Terry Eagleton suggested, no "secure position of knowledge and dominance in relation to the text."[28] With Harris's *The Eye of the Scarecrow*, the reader participates actively in the text, and all "ideological certainties" with which the reader is confronted in a realistic text, such as Naipaul's, "are threatened by a great swell of language which knows no absolutes, gender roles ruptured by a kind of polymorphous perversity of the word."[29] Here, the elusiveness and problematic nature of the truth are counterposed to the vexedness and rigid ideological positions that V. S. Naipaul always seems to present as truth confirmed. No wonder the great realism and naturalistic details of V. S. Naipaul seem so inadequate for answering the complex problems with which the emerging colonial person and his/her consequent psyche are faced in the 1980s.

At the end of *A Bend in the River*, Salim seems to echo the solution to what can be called "the mechanics of transition" of colonial subjects by arguing that one needs to scuttle one's past. He explains:

There could be no going back; there was nothing to go back to. We had become what the world outside had made us; we had to live in the world as it existed. The younger Indar was wiser. *Use the airplane; trample on the past*, as Indar had said he had trampled on the past. *Get rid of that idea of the past*; make the dream-like scenes of loss ordinary.[30]

But could one really accept Salim's formula as the means of constructing a future for Caribbean and other colonial peoples? Could one truthfully ask colonized peoples to seek refuge in a culture that was "anti-them" and could one really construct a future through the denial of the past? To do so would be to succumb to what has been called in literature the "metaphysics of the text," a condition in which the literary text is abstracted from its history and its culture and made to serve ends that are antithetical to its value and function as text. Anthony Bennett has argued most persuasively that "it is not the text's origins or its purely formal properties which determines its literariness but its mode of functioning within a society's culture as determined by its contingent, and therefore, historical and changing relations with other forms."[31] The nature of the text's literariness makes a work a critical and important historical entity, capable of study and subject to the rigors of literary criticism.[32] As a consequence, the literariness of Naipaul's texts must be seen within the context of the society (or societies) of which it speaks and in which it is supposed to function. In light of the foregoing discussion, one can now begin a much more specific penetration into the value of the works of V. S. Naipaul.

In a recent interview Naipaul is reputed to have said of his society: "No, my books aren't read in Trinidad now—drumbeating is a higher activity, a more satisfying activity."[33] And this, presumably, was meant to be insulting, derisive and elegant. It was intended to reflect a certain kind of disdain for the vulgarity of a society that preferred "drumbeating" to the gems of wisdom that trickle down from his purloined prose. And paradoxically, he was correct when stating that the people of Trinidad do find drumbeating a higher and more satisfying activity, perhaps because it is the only original creation the island has ever given to the world. Novel writing, as Naipaul must know, is a borrowed form, and no matter how much he wallows in the accolades of "Babylon System," the novel will never be our own.

Perhaps the society does prefer drumbeating, reggae and calypso to the prose of V. S. Naipaul because these forms speak in a much more authentic register about the aspiration and sufferings of a people. And so the Masta-Rasta is by far more relevant when he sings about "redemption songs" or asks in much more relevant urgency, "And who's gonna stay at home/when the freedom fighters are fighting";[34] or as the calypsonian Lord Valentino, once announced,

Trinidad is nice, Trinidad is a paradise
[For] Amoco and Shell, business went swell
On your oil, dem foreign parasites dwell.
Trinidad is nice, Trinidad is a paradise

Yet the song I sing, like I hearing the
chorus sing God Save the King.
But ah hear ma brother talking revolution
day, fighting on de way[35]

It is not that Lord Valentino does not condemn what he calls the "carnival mentality" of Trinidadians; rather, it is only that he arrives at a different conclusion about the possibilities of the society.

The question then must be asked: For whom does Naipaul write? As early as 1958, Naipaul declared his intention:

The Americans do not want me because I am too British. The public here do not want me because I am too foreign. . . . I live in England and depend on an English audience. Yet I write about Trinidad, and more particularly about the Indian community there. . . . I write for England. . . . It is an odd, suspicious situation: An Indian [sic] writer writing in English for an English audience about non-English characters who talk their own sort of English. . . . The only way to overcome public indifference is to cease being a regional writer. . . . I would like nothing better. But . . . I feel I can never hope to know as much about people here as I do about Trinidadian Indians.[36]

Naipaul may now have fulfilled his highest ambition. He has become much more than a regional writer; he is now an international writer, speaking the truths that the oppressor class (be it English, French, American or Portuguese) dearly loves to hear, and so they have acclaimed him the "best" novelist writing in the English language today.

Yet what is most important is the fact that Naipaul's acclaim cannot be abstracted from its class content. Terry Eagleton, writing in *Social Text*, has argued that "texts are practices; all literary texts are in some sense ideological—that is to say, aligned somewhere on a spectrum of significations which contribute either to securing or transforming the conditions of existence of the dominant social relations of production. It follows that to read is to be engaged in the class struggle."[37]

To write is also to be engaged in the class struggle, and Naipaul has clearly aligned himself on the side of the dominant class. The intellectual world will continue to praise him. But to the brethren and sisters in Kingston, Port of Spain or Georgetown, the Masta-Rasta, the steel bandman and the calypsonian would always be more important than V. S. Naipaul. For they know that these brothers always signify for them in terms that are clear, uncompromising, unrelenting, and affirmative. The terms fit within the context of "the constructive secret of all creation wherever one happens to be." As the Masta-Rasta says in such lucid terms:

We no know how we and dem
A go work this out
We no know how we and dem
A go work this out

> But someone would have to pay
> For the innocent blood
> That they shed everyday [Oh children mark my word]
> It's what the *Bible* say, Yeah! Yeah!
>   We no know how we an dem [A go work this out]
> We no know how we an dem [A go work this out].[38]

The quest of identity in Caribbean people can be found not in the texts of Naipaul but in the songs that express the anguish of its people. And so, in the final analysis, what really matters to the oppressed and the downtrodden is what signifies for us as opposed to what signifies for the oppressor. Obfuscation to the contrary, V. S. Naipaul has long since ceased to signify for us.

NOTES

1. Bob Marley and the Wailers, *Survival* (Island Records, ILPS 9542, 1979).
2. *Okite* 1, no. 3 (1972): 52.
3. *Boston Globe*, March 31, 1980, p. 27.
4. In Christian theology the invocation of the gospels implies the bringing of good news or glad tidings. Edward Schillebeck points out that inherent in the bringing of those glad tidings is the "spreading" of those glad tidings which are central to any teaching of the gospels. See his *Jesus: An Experiment in Christology*, trans. Hurbert Hoskins (New York: Seabury Press, 1979).
5. We understand the term *ideology* to mean a series of discourses and practices through which a subject apprehends his/her world.
6. *Paradise Lost*, "Book 9," in *Complete Poems and Major Prose*, ed. Merritt Y. Hughes (New York: Odyssey Press, 1957), p. 379.
7. Paul Theroux, *V. S. Naipaul: An Introduction to His Work* (New York: Africana Publishing, 1972), p. 7.
8. See his review of *A Bend in the River* in the *New York Times Book Review*, May 13, 1979. He says: "For sheer abundance of talent there can hardly be a writer alive who surpasses V. S. Naipaul" (p. 1).
9. *Shadow and Act* (New York: Random House, 1974), p. 107.
10. We use the terms *reflect* and *signify* in order to make a concession to those literary theorists who believe in the reflection theory of literature (the Hegelians) and those who see literature as a signifying practice (the Russian formalists). For the former the crucial question revolves around the degree to which the works of literature correspond to social reality, while the critical question for the latter has to do with the degree to which works of literature signify aspects of reality. For a discussion of this point see Tony Bennett, *Formalism and Marxism* (London: Methuen, 1979).
11. We do not mean to suggest that critics of European or American origin do not write perceptively and well about V. S. Naipaul. Helen Tiffin's Queen's College doctoral dissertation is perhaps one of the finest studies on the works of V. S. Naipaul. Tiffin is an Australian, and one presumes that she is of European origins. See her "The Lost Ones: A Study of the Novels of V. S. Naipaul" (Kingston, Ontario, 1972).
12. V. S. Naipaul was not the first West Indian writer to examine the problem of the East Indian in the West Indies. A.R.F. Webber, *Those That Be in Bondage* (George-

town: Daily Chronicle, 1917), Edgar Mittelholzer, *Corentyne Thunder* (London: Eyre & Spottiswoode, 1941), and Samuel Selvon, *A Brighter Sun* (Trinidad: Longman Caribbean, 1972) dealt with the question of the East Indian subject in the West Indies and, as such, preceded V. S. Naipaul in his examination of that reality.

13. V. S. Naipaul, *The Mimic Men* (Harmondsworth: Penguin, 1969), p. 146.

14. Ibid.

15. V. S. Naipaul, *The Loss of El Dorado* (London: André Deutsch, 1969), p. 251.

16. V. S. Naipaul, *Miguel Street* (London: Heinemann, 1959), p. 155.

17. V. S. Naipaul, *A Bend in the River* (New York: Vintage, 1980), p. 272 (emphasis added).

18. V. S. Naipaul, *Guerrilla* (London: André Deutsch, 1975), p. 87.

19. V. S. Naipaul, *The Return of Eva Peron* (New York: Alfred A. Knopf, 1979), p. 216.

20. Elizebeth Hardwick, "Meeting V. S. Naipaul," *New York Times Book Review*, May 13, 1979, p. 3.

21. Ibid., p. 36.

22. Colin MacCabe, *James Joyce and the Revolution of the Word* (New York: Harper and Row, 1979), p. 3.

23. Wilson Harris, *The Eye of the Scarecrow* (London: Faber and Faber, 1974), p. 95.

24. Ibid., p. 8.

25. Ibid.

26. MacCabe, *James Joyce*, p. 5 (emphasis added).

27. Harris, *Eye of the Scarecrow*, p. 98.

28. "Molly's Piano," *New Statesman*, September 19, 1980, p. 21.

29. Ibid.

30. Naipaul, *A Bend in the River*, p. 244 (emphasis added).

31. *Formalism and Marxism* (London: Methuen, 1979), p. 60.

32. By *literariness* I mean the properties of a text that define it as a work of literature. As such, it cannot be reduced to an adjunct of economic, social or historical phenomenon but exists as a primary mode of knowing in its own right.

33. Michiko Kakutani, "Naipaul Reviews His Past from Afar," *New York Times*, December 1, 1980. In his interview with Elizebeth Hardwick, Naipaul gave the same information: "My work is only possible in a liberal, civilized Western country. It is not possible in primitive societies" ("Meeting V. S. Naipaul," p. 3).

34. Bob Marley and the Wailers, "Natty Dread," *Natty Dread* (Island Records, 790037–1, 1974).

35. Lord Valentino, "Dis Place Nice," (Straker Records, 1974).

36. "The Regional Barrier," *Times Literary Supplement*, August 15, 1958, p. xxxvii.

37. "Ideology, Fiction, Narrative," *Social Text*, no. 2 (1980), p. 31.

38. Bob Marley and the Wailers, "We and Dem," *Uprising* (Island Records, ILPS 9596, 1980).

6

Toward Synthesis in the New World: Caribbean Literature in English

O. R. Dathorne

Many of the statements made about Caribbean literature in English would equally apply to the literature in French, Spanish, Dutch or the various Creole languages. The reasons are obvious: the area shares a common history of early Indian presence that is, for all practical purposes, destroyed. But the myth of the Indian past remains a part of the present. In addition, there is an interesting phenomenon that goes into the making of New World man. First come persons of diverse ethnic backgrounds from the old worlds of Europe, India, Africa and China. Only in the New World do they affirm a new identity. Within their former habitats they were constrained by ethnicity; hence they were English, Scots, Dutch, Ibo, Yoruba or Hausa. Within the context of the New World they assume a new posture. They undergo a form of primary transculturation, and for the first time the European and the African are born. This is perhaps one of the most unique and profound ironies of history: Only within the vacant spaces left by the Indians are these newcomers from the old worlds able to assert a definite novelty; they become a new possibility that, within the context of Old World heritage, was an impossible one. Primary transculturation is, therefore, the manner in which narrow ethnic confines give way to broader areas. The European, the victor, and the African, the victim, are the new players in the social milieu.

In order to embark on a course that would bring New World persons closer to the possibility of contact, they have to seek ways of compromise. This is the beginning of a secondary transculturation, where Europe and Africa begin to interact with each other. They learn to speak a new language; they develop new ways of living together, adapting the old into a new format. Dance, religion, cooking, art, nonverbal communication, music and literature undergo a change. The result is a curious blend, where European and African elements come together into a powerful synthesis. The Mulatto typifies, at a physical level, the way in which this merging takes place, but the arts, particularly literature, manifest the manner in which the heritage of this historical union is best seen.

Within the folk tales that survive and the folk art, there appears the first element of this merging. The folk tales are told in English or in a dialect of English, but within them the ancient African tricksters and gods survive. Anancy the trickster does undergo some transformation. Within the Old World African context he is a spider whose cunning outsmarts the larger creatures of the animal world. In the New World context Anancy is not just an animal nor is he just a trickster. He takes on the role of the downtrodden victim in his efforts to survive. His ruse then is not just subterfuge but an attempt at compromise.

Elements of what may be termed "literature" are also present in the remnants of religion that persist. The Shango religion in Trinidad takes its name from the Yoruba god of lightning and thunder. He exhibits an excellent example of primary transculturation, for in him there are present not only Yoruba characteristics but the broader dimensions of African spiritual culture. Therefore, Shango in New World Trinidad is not only part of a pantheon of gods, but he is the godhead itself. In similar ways Pocomania (in Jamaica), *obeah* (in Guyana) and others incorporate in their liturgy aspects of the broader culture of Africa as a whole and fuse them with Indian and Chinese elements.

Another manner in which oral literature persists is in children's play songs. Because children teach children, there is a tendency to feel that what does survive is fairly pure. Side by side with "London Bridge," there are songs such as:

Lang lang, time
Janey gal
Awe na go backdam
Come leh we go backdam
Janey gal
Come leh we go backdam

The distinct manner in which "Janey gal" is obviously part of the choral interjection and the use that is made of repetition to aid memory suggest two conclusions. One is that this is a carryover in form from African lay and religious songs, and the other is that this has been modified to accommodate a New World experience. Other songs like "Missy lass she gold ring" and "Foreday Mahning cack a crow/Hear Anty Bess a holler" support this statement. The subjects are trivial and oftentimes amusing; these are perhaps the two main qualities that assured their survival.

Folk songs, calypso and reggae have continued this tradition. Use is made of a chorus, a refrain and humor. In addition, social comment very much like African masquerade songs are part of the genre. In calypso the social statement is not as sharp as in reggae, but earlier calypsoes of the 1940s and 1950s did stress some of this. For instance, the American presence in Trinidad during the war gave rise to songs berating runaway wives such as "My wife left me in November," culminating in the early classic by the Mighty Sparrow, "Jean and Dinah." Lord Kitchener meanwhile used the guise of female infidelity to launch attacks at the English overlord. His classics such as "Kitch," where a woman emplores the calypsonian to enjoy sexual bliss, and "Redhead," about English redheads and troublesome landladies, tried to place the colonial master in a perspective from which Afro-Caribbeans could see their frailty.

Reggae is the sound of protest and discontent. Reggae, like Dread, has its roots in the Jamaican jungle. The Rastas preach love and brotherhood and the necessity to return to Africa, away from the permissiveness of Babylon. Despite independence, the old colonial state persisted. The late Walter Rodney explained it in this manner:

Nationalization with an anti-democratic state structure and an increasing managerial bureaucracy under the control of the ruling party has put the political rulers in a position analogous to that of the former expatriate owners. Their use of state resources, privileges and facilities stamp them as a bourgeoisie of a new type, occupying with increased license the gap left by foreign business managers and their principals.[1]

Against the new colonialists the Rastafarians preach the goodness of Jah. Reggae constantly stresses his bountifulness in songs such as:

So Jah sah
Not one of my seeds
Shall sit in the sidewalk
And bake bread.[2]

Punctuated with a heavy rhythm and danced to the rhythm of a fight, reggae has become the statement of war.

Just as the folk literature had taken some time before it took up a definite social position, in the same manner the written literature goes through various cycles before it adopts a posture of social commitment. These stages, which compare with the social and historical reality, correspond to the literature of the colonized, the literature of insurrection, of freedom and of post-independent quest. The marked themes are those of identification, purpose and dedication and, finally, disillusionment and renewed identification. The literature has, therefore, undergone a cyclical path from an ancient disbelief to a renewed faith.

In the eighteenth century, Francis Williams (1700–1770), who was born in Jamaica and studied in England at a grammar school and at Cambridge University, wrote a ballad during his stay in England. Later he went on to compose a kind of pupil's literature—Latin poetry written to successive Jamaican governors. Edward Long, a contemporary Englishman, felt that his poetry was too derivative,[3] but the Abbé Grégoire, writing in 1808, held a different opinion.[4]

Other writers of the Caribbean were also published. Ignatius Sancho, who was born on a slave ship bound for Hispaniola and who went to England when he was two years old, had his *Letters of the Late Ignatius Sancho, an African* posthumously published in 1782. In all there were 157 personal letters and an additional 5 to the press. Dated between February 14, 1768, and December 7, 1780, they describe his family life, his personal problems and glimpses of his time. He is quite modest about them, saying in a letter addressed to a Mr. F, "As to the letters in question, you know Sir, they are not mine but the property of the parties they are addressed to—If you have had their permission and think that the simple effusions of a poor Negro's heart are worth mixing with better things, you have my free command to do as you please with them."[5]

Sancho unwittingly unleashed the debate about Caribbean literature in English that is still evident today. The paradox of Sancho was that he, like contemporary writers, was published in London and read by a European and American public. The question asked then as now is this: To what extent does this writer deal with concerns that are purely local? Accordingly, he was instantly contrasted with European writers. No less a person than Thomas Jefferson felt that "we are compelled to enroll him at the bottom of the column."[6] Francis Williams had fared equally badly with Edward Long.

Another writer of the eighteenth century is Ouladah Equiano, also known as Gustavus Vassa. His *Interesting Narrative* was published in 1789 and relates, in part, his experiences in the Caribbean. His proud and easy personality comes over very well in his account as he relates how he was the sole deliverer when a ship in which he was sailing was nearly wrecked near the Bahamas. He fancies himself as quite an accomplished seaman and tells the story of how, after he had successfully piloted a ship from Georgia to Antigua, everyone addressed him as "Captain." This, he readily admits, appealed to his vanity.

These are all works of identification—not with the Caribbean, but with Europe and Africa. The Caribbean is transitory for these writers, and indeed their attitudes are indicative of the nature of slavery itself. These men—Williams, Sancho, Equiano—cannot truly be dubbed "Caribbean" in any meaningful sense of that word. They may have been born there or may have written about it, but this does not surely constitute a literature.

This debate is not nearly as theoretical as it may seem. V. S. Naipaul, widely acclaimed as the best writer in English, has nevertheless described in *The Middle Passage* (1962) the "nightmare" of feeling that he was back in Trinidad. Therefore, from quite early, the writers compose for an alien reading public, are judged by the norms of that society and frequently lose contact with the realities of their own societies. In the eighteenth century the need was to seek freedom from serfdom in Mother England; in the twentieth century the perceived cause is not very different.

Another dimension to the artist's predicament within the context of intellectual colonization should be mentioned; it seemed easier to write not only *for* an English reading public but also *about* an English natural and social environment. After all, colonial education had fostered this type of self-denial, and the images of the mother country were native to the growing child. Therefore, not unexpectedly, English romanticism tortures Caribbean poetry in English during the nineteenth century. Egbert Martin (Leo), Tom Redcam, Constance Hollar and Lena Kent are all expatriates of the mind. The two anthologies of Caribbean verse in English that appeared in 1929 and 1931 are important mainly for historical reasons. The same point may be made for drama. Errol Hill, an important pioneer, has written: "Largely, however, the choice of plays, whether by expatriate societies or by native groups followed the pattern set by the West End of London."[7]

Yet drama existed in the Caribbean. Masqueraders came out at Christmastime and danced on stilts (as in Africa); *comfa* drummers played and danced as they had in the Old World of Africa. After 1833 the slaves in Trinidad began their own "mass," which has survived in somewhat commercialized form until today. In Jamaica and in the Bahamas, John Canoe (or Junkanoo) festivals were held and continue to take place. There was, therefore, a solid folk background for drama, as there was for poetry and prose in the myths, legends and folk tales. The fact that the transposition to a written form does not take place until the 1950s is a clear indictment against the failure of secondary transculturation. The non-majority but ruling culture imposed its norms and values on the subject culture. Anything that savored of the folk was considered vulgar and demeaning. If writing was to be a high and praiseworthy art, then its practitioners should compose with the culture of Englishmen.

From within this prison the new writers of the 1950s and 1960s attempted to break out. Many of them decided to use folk art in their work. Folk life gives breadth and validity to the written literature. The breadth of the literature is the scope—from the detailing of the banal to the ritualistic reordering of religion. Validity is what gives the literature its *locus* or its unique place, which distinguishes it from any other type of literature. Through folk expression, folk speech, folk art, folk mores, the literature is given a definite place in space and time— it belongs to a specific geography, a distinctive cultural environment.

If this seems to be limiting, as metropolitan scholars sometimes suggest, craftsmanship ably removes the action from any parochial strictures. For example, the folk presence in Wilson Harris' first four novels, the so-called Guyana quartet, may be said to give the books a local flavor. But Harris expands his space, distends his characters and subtly distances the artist from the creative process. Hence in *Palace of the Peacock* (1960) the entire book is a dream within a dream, witnessed by a protagonist who has one eye. The suggestion, therefore, is that New World history is no linear development of neatly ordered contrivances but a kind of lackluster happenstance. Here V. S. Naipaul, Edward Brathwaite and Harris possess more in common than is at first apparent. They all admit to a complex void that is seemingly the past. They cannot be sure that the heritage is lofty; hence Uncle Tom, the sycophant, the stereotype of the good nigger, becomes in Brathwaite's *Rights of Passage* (1967) a figure worthy of celebration. Poseidon, the bush African who is averse to European progress, takes on a similar perspective in Harris' *The Secret Ladder* (1963); and the would-be artists, poets, sign painters, newspaper columnists in Naipaul's *Miguel Street* (1959), *A House for Mr. Biswas* (1961) and so on depict the unrealized possibilities of this past.

No writer blithely suggests that the past is merely elusive and will manifest itself given a thorough investigation. After all, it has been complicated by the varied histories of ethnic presences. Edgar Mittelholzer's *A Morning at the Office* (1950) is perhaps the best example of the failure of the past; therefore, the office is a good example of the larger society in miniature, where color pigmentation mars any kind of real contact between persons. The characters, very much like Harris', bear witness to a kind of historical typecasting. They are trapped within appearances that have in turn bequeathed them certain functions; therefore, the office boy is black because his society has conscripted him in this role.

The burden of history or the absence of it, therefore, places a curious stricture on the characters of Caribbean literature in English. They assume certain proportions because they are unable to define their personal responsibility. Put differently, they have to be this way because they have been sculpted in this manner. They comprehend a force but also readily understand that they cannot control it. Lobo in Denis Williams' *Other Leopards* (1963) is not unlike Questus in my novel *The Scholar Man* (1964), not for the reasons that have frequently been given—that is, that they are in search of themselves in Africa (whatever that might mean)—but because they are both persons who represent an absence of the indwelling power of ancestry. Shaped by a world they do not understand, they are curious phantoms who lack the power to actively order their environment.

Since the environment manufactures and turns loose robots, the quest for authority must be found in the defining power of the environment. At times erratic, frequently dogmatic, but always assertive, the environment dictates the parameters of action. One does not in any way seek to imply that the environment is a part with which the characters may or may not comply. Michael Anthony's *The Year in San Fernando* (1965) and *Green Days by the River* (1967) show the authoritative nature of the local external environment. For Francis to live, experience and grow, he has to come to terms with its multiple manifestations, its class and color differentiation, its change of seasons, its apparently haphazard shift of emphasis from a matrifocal stability to fratricidal conflict.

The environment is not, however, only without; in George Lamming's *Season of Adventure* (1960), Fola realizes that it is beneath layers of an affected sophistication, which are released by the chants of the *houngan*. Selvon's characters like Tanty, who introduces credit to an English shopkeeper, or Bat, or the protagonist of "My Girl and the City," take the environment with them to the metropolis. There they find another quandary; the very people who were not at ease with their own world now use its remnants to shore up the cracking seams of European decadence. They bring a measure of true innocence, hearty laughter and common sense into a world that has forgotten these qualities. They are, in the final analysis, sad personae whose second failure to come to terms with the reality around them provides the occasion for ironic comment and indecisiveness. The bus scene in *The Housing Lark* (1965) is truly indicative of this, for the characters are ill at ease in their new environment, specifically because they have no link with a real and permanent past.

The literature, therefore, does not accord itself the luxury of wild inventiveness. Each reaction is not personal but group related, representing something that is part of the group life. This is perhaps why Edgar Mittelholzer achieved his best dimension as a writer in the Kaywana trilogy, since he is not simply a spinner of yarns, as he tended to be in some of his more lukewarm accounts. In the Kaywana books he wrestles, as Harris, Lamming, Jan Carew, Derek Walcott, John Hearne and other writers all do, with the strange psychology of victim and victor. Put simply, the books posit an interesting rhetoric: To what extent is the victim responsible for the victor? What common borderland of understanding exists between them? In attempting to answer this question, the writer frequently seeks to show the validity of paradox. We shall conclude by showing how Walcott's poetry reflects this. Specific attention will be paid to "Ruins of a Great House," two of the Crusoe poems and the extended poem "The Gulf," which appears in the volume of the same name.

"Ruins of a Great House" is a powerful poem.[8] Walcott uses the symbol of the so-called Great House (the big house where the slave master lived) as a paradoxical statement. This is a favorite Walcott device, and the "Great House" comes to stand for a heritage he has to accept and reject, one seemingly relevant and yet, in a larger sense, irrelevant.

At first the ruins of the house are all that the poet sees—stones, candle dust, stain. This is a poem of absences, of death, reinforced by the paradox of "A smell of dead limes quickens the nose." It is also a poem of adieu, of farewell to a way of life that Walcott associates not only with the British Empire but with Greece, southern American slavery, India. But there is a twist, for the empires were themselves part of an empire! He reminds us "that Albion too, was once/A colony like ours."

The emphasis is on the evil of imperialism; hence the dirt and grime are emphasized in the first stanza and recur throughout the poem. The "dead animal or human thing" further extends the range of the metaphor because the past seems to be not even worthy of a shoddy dignity.

There is a completeness in Walcott's metaphors. Here the "moth-like girls" are part of the "river's skirt" and "the imperious rakes" and "their bright girls gone." Similarly, images of death are linked up in the poem, combining to give an effect of totality.

The tone is one of despair; the theme is familiar, ably summed up at the end: "All in compassion ends/So differently from what the heart arranged." In fact, one may accuse Walcott rightly here of going back to his customary melancholy. There are reminders of Eliot, and this is reinforced with the actual mention of Kipling and Donne. Yet the poet wishes to distance himself from all that the British Empire represented.

In "Crusoe's Journal," Crusoe, carpenter and writer, is seen as symbol of New World man's desire to express himself in landscape.[9] The poem shows that the Caribbean poet cannot afford to be ornate; so "even the bare necessities/of style are turned to use." Art is not for art's sake, but it serves a purpose, a very specific one.

Crusoe merges in the poem into Christopher Columbus (as well as Saint Christopher, the patron saint of travelers) and is in turn associated with Adam. Adam is important, for he had to name things and the New World poet has this very same function. But the poet's purpose can become distorted. Our lands have known colonialism; the image of the missionary is apt for he baptizes our souls and

>alters us
>into good Fridays who recite His praise,
>   parroting our master's
>style and voice (p. 51).

Hence the New World poet in the Caribbean is colonized and has had a new language imposed on him. These are the models he follows to state his new freedom.

The realization comes that to be a parrot is not to be a poet. The symbol of the boy signaling to deaf ears is the young poet who would seek to break away from the imposition of tradition. He wishes to free himself from the consequences of colonialism in which he is entrapped, but "time that makes us objects, multiplies/our natural loneliness" (p. 52).

Hence, the boy, the lone voice, learns to make "something without use," to compose a poem that does not have to speak to the needs of a people. Crusoe had demonstrated the carpentry of words, but "we learn to shape from them, where nothing was/the language of a race" (p. 52).

The poet's task is more difficult in the Caribbean, as Walcott sees it. One has to move beyond the absence of forms, to the pressure of poetry as a practical skill, then beyond the myths with which foreign writers have embellished the Caribbean poet. With the recognition of the loneliness of being the outsider comes the startling revelation that the poet, like Crusoe, like God, like Adam, shares a common loneliness.

"Crusoe's Journal" is an intense, tightly packed piece of writing that ostensibly on certain levels might be about colonialism, the influence of the missionaries or even Crusoe himself. But on a far deeper level the poem explores the history of culture in the Caribbean and the place of the artist. Also the poem concerns itself with the nature of the New World art—how it must progress from the *utility* that both Crusoe and the missionaries recognized, through Adam's task of naming things and finally to the lonely but total response to an uncharted environment.

Throughout "Crusoe's Island," Walcott is concerned with the loss of faith, the loss of art and the loss of youth.[10] Images of the bell, the anvil, the castaway and "the rotting nut" emphasize the theme of the poem. The language is grave, melancholy at the beginning, but builds up into a tower of hope as it develops.

In the first part the poet/protagonist sees his island-house as the mere vestige of colonialism. In turn his art seems to be able to do little, for the poet admits to a loneliness; in this way the artist in the Caribbean, as Walcott sees him, is very much like Crusoe—alone.

The second section suggests the possibility of alteration. If one could become a creature, a thing of nature, the argument goes, this would be the essence of purity. The bell now seems less insidious; far from being the church bell that called the faithful to prayer, as cows follow one another, the bell can stand for hope. But there is no going back to the past, to youth or to the beliefs that were once held:

> I stand at my life's noon,
> On parched, delirious sand
> My shadow lengthens (p. 56).

The image of the lengthening shadow, apart from suggesting aging, takes the reader back to the castaway who was startled by his own shadow. The point here is that both castaway and poet had yearned for human compassion and yet had been startled by the possibility of its occurrence.

"Art is profane and pagan" begins Walcott's conclusion in the final section of this poem. It has to be, since it means the destruction of the myths of child-hood—the benign Christian God, the possibility of companionship, even the power to communicate:

> Craftsman and castaway
> All heaven in his head,
> He watched his shadow pray
> Not for God's love but human love instead (p. 55).

Hence the conclusion: If Art means the loss of faith and friendship, then Art is not a useful tool for life.

The most Art reveals is ultimate destruction, the poet argues. It gives the appearance of a shield, but it is "Achilles' shield," behind which is the very mortal Achilles. In the final analysis "that fabled, occupational/compassion" that is poetry consumes the poet.

Thus the poet reconciles himself to the world around him. The young girls going to church are true enough the descendants of slaves, "Friday's prog-eny," but their faith in what they do will save them. As Walcott notes:

> At dusk when they return
> for vespers, every dress
> Touched by the sun will burn
> A seraph's, an angel's (p. 57).

Poetry cannot make this magic transformation, only "the bell's/Transfiguring tongue" can. Therefore, the renunciation of Art is logical yet curiously para-doxical. "Crusoe's Island" is a bitter comment on poetry and particularly on the apparently utter uselessness of Art.[11] For "men fail/According to their creed." And poetry would seem to question too much and offer too few answers.

"The Gulf" is very important for a number of reasons.[12] It brings together many of the concerns of Caribbean literature in English, such as style, the search for home, the imminent hatred of the poor and the Black in search of satisfaction and the probability of ultimate destruction. Biblical references and language lend credence to the grim view the poet gives here. "The Gulf, your gulf, is daily widening" might well be the text of a sermon, for indeed the poem is about the Gulf of Mexico, which both connects and separates and which is seen here as a harbinger of the destruction the poet relates.

Beginning with a departure for the West Indies from Texas, the poem reflects on what America had meant to the poet. Going up in the jet liner, being "in the air," means that one cannot be sure any longer. The souvenirs the poet has—matches, a rose, a book—all take on different meanings. He then recalls the assassination of John F. Kennedy in Dallas, which in turn leads him to speculate on the mortality of the gifts he is bringing back with him, on the friends' and on his own deaths. Even the works of great men, he cynically adds, have no true permanence.

The second part of the poem returns us to the plane journey. The plane window through which he looks conjures up "the face of the loved object under glass," that is, of some dead person he once loved. But temporarily hope seems to return, and the landscape descriptions indicate this, as "some cratered valley heals itself with sage." The creeks that suggest siege and the water that hints at war drums return the poet's thoughts to the United States he has left behind. It is a place divided by the ravages of racial war, "smoke of bursting ghettos," as Walcott calls it. Here the Gulf now suggests not only the Gulf of Mexico, but Gulf Oil monopoly and tear gas fumes.

The reader is back in the southern United States in the third stanza. Old plantation houses and the drawl of southern speech are recalled, as well as the "heat heavy with oil." The previous mention of water and our association of "pouring oil on troubled waters" immediately remind us of the southern United States as a potential trouble spot. The poet is extremely personal here, a rare stance for Walcott. He remembers how he sounded and looked different in America, and he recalls his second-class status. The rose, given him by a child, takes on sinister proportions, as he is warned of the violence that is to come. A line from the hymn "Rock of Ages" reminds one of the absence of God in a land where Black Panthers and the Black Muslims seem bent on racial hatred, as the poet envisions it.

Finally in part four the poem concludes on a note of hopelessness. The Gulf "shines dull as lead" and America seems to obstruct the illuminating influences; the coast of Texas "glints like a metal rim." How can the poet have a home when the long, hot summers constantly bring about racial warfare? People do not learn; the deceased are "the uninstructing dead," for human beings repeat their mistakes time and time again.

Today one might find the poem a grim one. But it was written at a time when America seemed bent on racial warfare. Walcott is pessimistic of the outcome as he leaves America. True, he recalls an America that he both liked and disliked, but he realizes that his journey home is a pointless one, for he is intrinsically linked with the future of America. The Gulf is the symbol of both that link and the possibility it has for future chaos. The paradox that is always present rounds off the poem.

This use of paradox in Caribbean literature in English is most appropriate, for it attempts to conscript life into an art form. At the beginning of this discussion we showed how writers became a new force in the New World. Therefore, it was noted, African folklore was utilized for a different purpose, that of establishing a distinction between victim and agent. We noted that calypso and reggae had elements in them that embodied protest against Europe and sought a compromise with a half-remembered Africa. But equally we saw how early writers in English from the eighteenth century on were placed in a situation of paradox—objecting to the English overlord in the very language of the master.

The void, which was alluded to and which was noted in Mittelholzer, Harris, Lamming and others, was an attempt to restructure this broken past. We noted that in some of Walcott's verse the paradox reaches its ultimate point when the writer's art condemns art itself.

Caribbean literature in English, however, is seeking to come to terms with its mutilated legacy. Austin Clarke, Merle Hodge, Earl Lovelace, Orlando Patterson, John Stewart and the new Jamaican poets like Linton Kwesi Johnson have reversed this process. They do not seek to find answers in the Old World values of Europe or Africa, but instead they seek to construct a meaningful world on their own home front. We noted that Michael Anthony had pioneered this, and certainly some of Brathwaite's verse moves away from the crutches of Africa to the firm footsteps of indigenous New World art. This emerges best in the section of *Islands* entitled "Negus," where after the refrain "It is not/it is not/it is not enough," he concludes:

I
must be given words to shape my name
to the syllables of trees[13]

Of course, Martin Carter had done this in the 1950s, but his was then a lonely voice. Later, in Orlando Patterson's *Die the Long Day* (1972), Jason says, "I've always maintained that the blacks are the people I envy most in this place. For they alone can hope meaningfully."[14] He suggests that the synthesis will come about when a bloody revolution destroys the environment; or as John Stewart puts it, "the trick still remains to convince oneself that losing is winning";[15] or more positively, in Linton Kwesi Johnson's "Song of Rising":

dere'ill be peace
in da valley

forever
  dere'ill be love
dere'ill be love/in da valley/forever.[16]

The search has come full circle. The bitterness and the hostility are still there, but in the new writing authors are coming to terms with their world. None of them would seek to suggest that there is a void; their art proclaims the bountifulness of their world. In coming to terms with their environment, they have achieved a true synthesis.

NOTES

1. The Working People's Alliance, "Toward a Revolutionary Socialist Guyana," *Black Scholar*, no. 3 (1980): 46.

2. Bob Marley and the Wailers, "So Jah Sah," *Natty Dread*, Island Records, 7 90037–1, 1974.

3. Edward Long, *A History of Jamaica*, 3 vols. (London: Printed for T. Lowndes, 1774), 2:475–78. Francis Williams' poem to Governor George Holdane was erroneously translated by Edward Long, who attempted to place the black poet in a ridiculous light.

4. Abbé Henri Grégoire, *An Enquiry Concerning the Intellectual and Moral Faculties and Literature of Negroes, followed with an Account of the Life and Works of Fifteen Negroes and Mulattoes, distinguished in Science, Literature and Arts* (Paris: Maradan, 1808).

5. Ignatius Sancho, *Letters of the Late Ignatius Sancho: An African*, ed. Joseph Jekyll (London: Printed by J. Nichols, 1784), letter 83 dated January 1779, p. 225.

6. Thomas Jefferson, *Notes on the State of Virginia* (Philadelphia: Printed for Mathew Carey, 1794), p. 205.

7. Errol Hill, "Drama in the West Indies," *West India Gazette*, no. 9 (1961), p. 25.

8. Derek Walcott, "Ruins of A Great House," *In a Green Night* (London: Jonathan Cape, 1962), pp. 19–20.

9. Derek Walcott, "Crusoe's Journal", *The Castaway* (London: Jonathan Cape, 1965), pp. 51–53. All references to the poem will appear parenthetically in the text.

10. Ibid., pp. 54–57.

11. Ibid.

12. Derek Walcott, "The Gulf," *The Gulf* (London: Jonathan Cape, 1969), pp. 27–30.

13. Edward Brathwaite, *The Arrivants: A New World Trilogy* (London: Oxford University Press, 1978), p. 223.

14. Orlando Patterson, *Die the Long Day* (New York: William Morrow, 1972), p. 210.

15. John Stewart, *Last Cool Days* (London: André Deutsch, 1971), p. 190.

16. Linton Kwesi Johnson, "Song of Rising," *Dread Beat and Blood* (London: Bogle-L'Ouverture Publications, 1975), p. 60.

French
Caribbean _____

7

The Maroon Figure in Caribbean Francophone Prose

Juris Silenieks

Historical consciousness permeates the sensibilities of many contemporary writers. But the legacy of the past seems to haunt relentlessly the imagination of the Caribbean authors. V. S. Naipaul, a Trinidadian of East Indian descent, offers a view of Caribbean history that has elicited much comment and controversy: "The history of the islands can never be satisfactorily told. Brutality is not the only difficulty. History is built around achievement and creation; and nothing was created in the West Indies."[1] And truly enough, with the appearance and presence of the Europeans in the region, history seems to chronicle only death and destruction: the genocide of the Amerindians, the violent diasthasis of the black slave from Mother Africa, the agony of the Middle Passage, the brutal institution of slavery, the vehemence of slave revolts, the alienation of the indentured East Indian laborer, persistent economic exploitation, illness, unemployment, illiteracy and so on. The white historian and writer have frequently accorded a providential significance and a sense of mystique to the exploits of the white colonizer, soldier and priest. For the Afro-Caribbean this is a history imposed, determined by the white man, with the Black being reduced to a passive victim. Now, for those who share neither Naipaul's pessimism nor the white historian's bias, there is the task of the Afro-Caribbean's "historical reinsertion," to use Edouard Glissant's phrase, which is both an intellectual challenge and a poetic adventure.[2]

Jean Benoist concludes his study of the Caribbean region, significantly entitled, *L'Archipel inachevé* (1972) in these words: "The original Caribbean societies and cultures, which have incurred both the good luck and the misfortune of having a past so murky that their future must be invented, first must know themselves more thoroughly."[3] But in order to know oneself, one must know one's past, which for the Afro-Caribbean, as Aimé Césaire laments, is mute, not immediately accessible.[4] Folktales, fragments of old legends, chants and dances still echo the distant times of African freedom. Popular stories of defiant rebels and brave Maroons evoke the misery and the glory of the days of slavery. Folklore, however, represents, as Glissant puts it, the "collective unconscious." To raise the past to a higher level of conscious apprehension, to invest it with a new relevance of meaning, the poet and the historian must cooperate. The trauma of the past is to be transformed into a source of strength and future resolve, for the darkest days of mute collective suffering have also known defiant individuals who have asserted their refusal to submit to enslavement. In popular memory, the Maroon, the fugitive slave who fled to the mountains and forests, stands out as a figure much feared and admired. Thus, quite expectedly, marronage, as slave escape is often termed, has kindled the imagination of many writers. As a phenomenon quite unique to Caribbean history, it has also preoccupied the attention of historians and anthropologists.

Throughout history, slave revolts and marronage have been a concomitant of the plantation system. Historians of the period usually deplored revolts and marronage as acts of sheer savagery. Moreau de Saint Méry, the eighteenth-century chronicler of San Domingo, as Haiti was called until its independence, recounts the existence of runaway groups among whom were men of fifty years born in marronage.[5] "A thorn in the side of the colonial regime,"[6] maroon communities in Jamaica and Guyana, inaccessible by military expeditions, were granted freedom and autonomy in return for a pledge of allegiance to the colonial administration. Anthropologically, maroon communities presented unique aspects of reversal and progress, continuation of old African patterns of life and adaptation to new circumstances. Frequently, family and social life recalled African kinship models but also incorporated features of Euro-American civilization and Amerindian elements, creating new and varied complexes.[7] As in the case of Surinam and Jamaica, maroon communities where the geography was favorable to the formation of large-scale enclaves, the cultural gap between the Maroons and the slaves widened and the relationships often became strained.[8] The Maroons had only contempt for the passive masses and frequently descended from their mountain retreats to seize the slaves' women and supplies. Sometimes Maroons degenerated into wild desperadoes who preyed on anyone in their path. Their political allegiances were dictated by expediency. In San Domingo some of them sided with the Whites against Toussaint and gave support to Mulattoes against the Blacks. In Jamaica and Surinam the Maroons, in compliance with the treaties concluded with the authorities, helped track down new fugitives and sometimes enslaved their captives. But whatever accommodations the Maroons had to resort to in order to survive, their presence did benefit the cause of the Blacks and influence the white slaveholders to treat their slaves more humanely. More significantly, the Maroons served as a constant reminder that slaves could flee and even offer armed resistance to the master class: "They held out hope of escaping servitude, preventing the slave from becoming a prey to despair."[9] Furthermore, they exemplified the existence of "a slave consciousness that refused to be limited by the Whites' conception and manipulation of it."[10]

Indeed, the memory of the Maroon seems to be embedded in the Afro-Caribbean consciousness, at least among those who have not been subjected to European cultural assimilation. Melville Herskovits, in his studies of Haiti, notes the pride with which Haitian peasants recall their maroon ancestry.[11] One of the most famous Maroons in Haitian history is Mackandal. Mackandal had lost an arm while feeding sugar cane in the mill. Because of his handicap, he had become a shepherd. While roaming the hillsides with his cattle, he had learned the qualities of various plants, their healing properties and poisons. For his lore he was greatly respected and feared as a medicine man, a *quimboiseur*, fierce and courageous, vowing vengeance to all Whites and destruction of their property. According to some accounts, he had poisoned some six thousand persons. But the invincible sorcerer had a flaw: He loved drink and women. At a slave gathering he was betrayed and captured. Condemned to death, he was burnt at the stake. But popular memory perpetuated the belief that through his magic powers he had turned himself into a mosquito and thus again outwitted the Whites.

Alejo Carpentier in *The Kingdom of This World* (1949) devotes a good portion of the novel to the Mackandal story. To Carpentier, Mackandal is the true precursor of the struggle for independence, unlike the later leaders, such as Toussaint L'Ouverture, Dessalines, and Christophe, who as administrators betrayed the revolutionary zeal and, being assimilated Blacks, were too detached from the people. Mackandal embodies the ideal of liberty uncompromised and of Mother Africa untainted. His physical mutilation is the catalyst of his revolutionary consciousness, which he passed along to those who witnessed his execution. The slave preferred to believe that his "Mighty Powers of the Other Shore"[12] had rescued him from death. Mackandal, however, was a loner, without a revolutionary organization or following.

To René Depestre, one of the most militant writers of Haitian letters, marronage is a symbol of black resistance to colonialism and ideological brainwashing. In his ode dedicated to the memory of Mackandal, Depestre hails the famous Maroon as an atavistic revolutionary embodiment. Mackandal is the ancestral model of the violent destructive force that alone can liberate the Afro-Caribbean from external oppression as well as from the internalized sense of inferiority. The one-armed Maroon, with the unleashed forces of a tidal wave and an erupting volcano, runs rampant over the country, poisoning the wells of the Whites and burning their sugarcane fields. His strength is indigenous, coming from his intimacy with the land and his knowledge of the *voodoo* mysteries. He was the first to recognize the vulnerability of the Whites, to defy their idols of materialism and rationality. Descending "the slopes of Negritude" from his mountain hideout, he encountered violence with violence, and with his death he asserted his inalienable right to be free.[13] Like Carpentier, Depestre extols in Mackandal the real progenitor of black power for his uncompromising hatred for the white world and rejection of its false values.

The archetypal Maroon figure appears with many other Francophone Afro-Caribbean writers. The texts of Jeanne Hyvrard, from Martinique, suggest structures of the Caribbean consciousness. Her thematic constructs evolve from the specificity of the Afro-Caribbean experience toward a universality of meaning. Thus, for example, the Middle Passage evokes immediately modern analogues, as the Africans stacked in the holds of the slave ships become contemporary deportees piled up in boxcars sent to unknown destinations. Scattered throughout the texts are brief flashes of marronage, like the slave escaping to the mountains, joining the Indians and being resold to the slave owners who punish them brutally, sometimes immuring them alive—a practice, though, not commonly known in the Caribbean.[14] Like Hyvrard's other constructs, the primordial image of the original slave escapee always enlarges its scope to encompass all those who want to regain their freedom—the prisoner, the inmate of the insane asylum, the schoolchildren subjected to indoctrination by sadistic teachers, the dissidents challenging the usurpers of authority, like colonialists, assimilationists, imperialists, male chauvinists.[15] With Jeanne Hyvrard, too, the maroon figure, emerging from the Caribbean matrix, is ever renewed through successive periods of history and is present everywhere.

A similar timelessness of the Maroon is suggested by the Guyanese novelist Bertène Juminer, who in his second work, *Au Seuil d'un nouveau cri* (1963), probes the mentality of the rebel slave and his modern counterpart, the Marxist revolutionary fighting against colonialism and imperialism. For Juminer the Maroon's paramount exigency is to cease to be a fugitive: "To flee without stopping leads to nothing, and this nothingness is the fugitive himself . . . by the very fact that he has consented to be pursued without ever turning around and confronting the pursuer."[16] The Maroon's continuous flight signifies admission of his fault and the legality of the system he opposes. To challenge the pursuer, collective solidarity and leadership are essential. But organization and discipline circumscribe the rebel's intrinsic sense of freedom and preclude expression of his individual will. Modestin, the slave, is caught up in a rebellion whose leaders are pitiless Maroons. For disobeying the leader's order to kill his former benevolent master, he is condemned to death. And he will suffer his ultimate opprobrium by being executed together with despicable, cruel slave holders. Juminer argues that marronage cannot be an end in itself. The intransigence of the Maroon must be replaced by a commitment to the ideal of black/white solidarity. An episode recounts the rescues of a white girl, Véronica, by a black slave with whom she falls in love. The black revolutionary will find his ally in the white female, since between the two exist natural affinities that will eventually lead to a union of races. Juminer's liberalism has been impugned as that of a typical Caribbean intellectual who prefers to think revolution instead of making it and has internalized French racist attitudes.[17] Here, Juminer parts company with Depestre, who sees in the Maroon's violence the catalyst to help precipitate racial pride and solidarity. Similarly, Juminer's supraracism, as an evolvement of the Maroon's revolutionary dialectics, is negated by Simone Schwarz-Bart's *Ti Jean L'horizon* (1979), her latest novel, that, admixing elements of myth, legend and history, turns inward and toward the past.

Ti Jean, the central character in the novel, is a descendant of former Maroons, the people of the heights, "les gens d'En-haut," who live isolated in their mountain retreat, silent and in communion with nature. They have nothing but scorn for the people below them, "les gens d'En-bas," who comply with the order imposed by the Whites. The valley people imitate the Whites and send their children to school whence they return "docteurs," "whites of a new kind."[18] The indomitable people of the heights consider themselves of noble blood, true heirs of African traditions, imbued with the mysteries of life. Ti Jean, in his challenge to the beast who has devoured the sun, undertakes a long voyage back to his ancestral land, Dahomey, into the past and through the realm of the dead. The Africa of the past, however, is familiar to him, since his maroon ancestors have never lost touch with it. When he returns to Guadeloupe as an old man, after a series of adventures, successive deaths and resurrections, he finds that his lineage has almost totally disappeared, except for a former friend of his, a "jeune-homme-poursuivi-en-pure-perte" (p. 261), the young man who has never ceased to defy the white order. He is the eternally returning rebel: "I began to die and to be reborn, to die again and to be reborn" (p. 261). The others have integrated into modern times, accepting the humiliations and the hardships, the hypocrisies and the loss of identity that comes with assimilation. The Maroon, though, lives on as a poignant memory of an outcast whose fate is solitude and death.

These contemporary thematic preoccupations associated with marronage, like the dialectics of destructive violence and reconstruction, the import of the African heritage in the face of Western cultural aggressiveness, the Maroon as a paragon for the modern dissident and revolutionary, gain amplitude and depth with Edouard Glissant, a Martinican writer, civic leader and educator. Glissant's continuous inquiry into the meaning of the Caribbean past constitutes one of the salient features of his literary work and philosophic thought. Rejecting the main thrusts of Negritude, its nostalgia for Africa and its overreaction to white racism, as inadequate for the situation of the Afro-Caribbean, Glissant proffers the concept of Antillanité. Among other things, Antillanité encompasses a lucid apprehension of the Caribbean past experience and a projection of a future course toward the shaping of a distinct regional collective consciousness and destiny. The function of the Afro-Caribbean writer is to commit himself to the "decisive act, which, in the domain of literature, means to build a nation."[19] Nation building exacts a vision that can "perceive of the consciousness, the one and only operative, of our being" (p. 192). Furthermore, Glissant maintains that "for those whose allotted share of history is only darkness and despair, recovery of the near and distant past is imperative. To renew acquaintance with one's past is to relish fully the present."[20] A conscious collectivity is bound together by the heritage of a common past.

Collective memory is our urgency: Lack and need. Not the "historical" detail (not that alone), but the innermost is to resurge: The diastasis from the womb of Africa, the bifid man, the reshaped brain, the violent useless hand. An absurd manifestedness—where poverty and exploitation are wedded to something ineffably ridiculous—and where, noticeable to us alone, a drama without apparent import is being enacted which it is incumbent upon us to transform soon into a fecund Tragedy (p. 187).

Descriptive history, lacking raw data, is impossible. The historian must be seconded by the poet, since the task is not only to record and interpret events but to recreate the past in a new image. Thus, among other legacies of the past, marronage and its concomitant, violence, not just residual elements of primitive and savage Africa, need to be reevaluated in the total context of the Caribbean experience, past and present, with a view to a future destiny. The maroon figure, a deep construct of Glissant's imagination, undergoes elaboration and subtle transformations with each successive work.

In one of Glissant's early works, the play *Monsieur Toussaint* (1961), the celebrated Haitian Maroon, Mackandal, is among the six dead who surround Toussaint and signify a temptation, a potential, a conflicting loyalty Toussaint is faced with. Mackandal expects Toussaint to avenge him for his violent death with massacres of Whites and destruction of their property. But Toussaint, the nation builder who wants the new order in Haiti to be based on peace, justice and prosperity, refuses to yield to the temptation of requiting violence with violence. For the lawgiver, administrator and proprietor Toussaint, Mackandal's insistence on equal retribution can lead only to the impasse of self-perpetuating violence. On the other hand, Toussaint, imbued with the ideas of the Enlightenment and the French Revolution, remains estranged from the ethos of his people, and the Haitian Revolution, propelled by its own revolutionary dynamics, bypasses him and abandons him to his tragic solitude. The confrontation between the Maroon and the builder or the intellectual is further amplified in Glissant's novels.

The first novel, *La Lézarde* (1958), deals with the postwar scene in Martinique at the time of the first elections, when the island became a French overseas department. The plot of the novel revolves around a group of young radicals who plan the assassination of a turncoat in order to prevent the betrayal of Martinican aspirations to the metropolitan interests. To execute the plan and cover their tracks, the radicals inveigle a young shepherd, Thaël, who has been living up in the mountains like a latter-day Maroon, into drowning the traitor. In the course of their political pursuits the young activists visit Papa Longoué, a *quimboiseur* of Maroon lineage, who has refused to compromise with the modern times. He leads an isolated life on the mountain slopes, gathering his herbs, cultivating ancient African mysteries and wisdom. He is the last link with Africa, reliving in his memories passed from generation to generation the Middle Passage, the arrival of Africans in the New World, the days of marronage. As a final gesture of adamant refusal, on his deathbed Papa Longoué forbids his friends to take his corpse down to the cemetery for burial.

Papa Longoué embodies negation in its ultimate form. Thaël, however, signifies an evolution of the maroon prototype. Like Papa Longoué, Thaël leads a solitary life up in the mountains surrounded by legends and prophecies. But unlike Papa Longoué, he accedes to the request of his friends from the plain to descend from the heights and commit himself to political action in solidarity with the people. When Thaël returns to his mountain abode with his new bride, Valérie, following the elections won by the people's candidate, he assesses his adventure: "We left the mountains, we drank from the Source."[21] But the ultimate significance of his incursion into the life of the plains people remains ambiguous. Valérie is killed by his dogs, who had grown hungry and furious during his absence—in a way, a reminder of the punishment that slave owners inflicted upon runaway slaves. The final scene of the novel offers no resolution to the ambiguity of Thaël's adventure. As his faithful dogs are licking his hands, Thaël can only think of the ways he would kill them to avenge Valérie's death. The meeting of the mountain Maroon and the plainsman, the past and the present, the old traditions and modern mentalities signals the need for further rapprochement, but at the same time a kind of atavistic curse hangs over those who commit themselves to uncautious action. Glissant's second novel, *Le Quatrième Siècle* (1964), projects much further the trajectory of the Maroon's evolution in the face of the choices between the sterility of negation and the uncertainties of compromise.

Le Quatrième Siècle traces the destinies of two families, the Longoués and the Béluses, starting with the arrival of the progenitors in 1788, when two slaves fought a prodigious battle on the slave ship. Once on land, Longoué escapes to the mountains to lead the precarious life of a Maroon, free but constantly hunted by the pursuing Whites. Béluse, on the other hand, is branded and assigned to a plantation where, because of his good physique, he is singled out for stud service. The paths of "those who refused" and "those who accepted" often cross. Among their offspring there are marriages and murders, mutual hatred and attraction. The Longoué lineage ends with Papa Longoué, while the Béluses multiply and go along with the times. One of their descendants is Mathieu, a young intellectual, well educated and committed to action. He visits Papa Longoué in the latter's solitary hut, urging the old man to recount the past. In the presence of the old sage Mathieu, the educated and partially assimilated Black, senses a kind of shallowness and weightlessness of his being. Mathieu must find answers to the burning question: "What is the past? What is left us of the past?"[22] He wants dates, facts and motives. Papa Longoué insists that "we must not follow the facts logically, but guess, anticipate what has happened" (pp. 57–58). He cautions Mathieu: "The past is not what you know for sure" (p. 146).

For Papa Longoué the past is immobilized, prolonged in the sensations that are indelibly impressed onto his mind and body. The stench of the slave ship's hold is passed along from generation to generation like a precious heirloom. Papa tells the story how, before disembarking, in a kind of baptismal ceremony, the slaves were washed with sea water and scrubbed with brushes. "And yet . . . I feel it, this odor. My mother Stéphanie taught it to me, she held it from her man Apostrophe who held it from Melchior who held it from Longoué who was the first to board the ship" (pp. 23–24). Another legacy of the Middle Passage is a certain mutism born from ineffable suffering and hatred: "Mute was death. Mute was the drama hatched in the folly of the hold" (p. 61). Thus, when the Maroons descend from the heights to pillage the plantations, massacre the Whites and kidnap female slaves, their acts are perpetrated in a silence that contrasts sharply with their violence. The Maroon's world has "no end, no beginning" (p. 287). Papa Longoué lives in a continuous preterit state, incarcerated in his memories, unable to "attach the past to the future" (p. 19).

On the other hand, the plantation slave accepted submission quickly. The first defeat came with the learning of the master's language. "When they know the language, it's too late. They are brought to heel" (p. 61). For them, there is no going back, no "repetition of the first days when the familiar, maternal shore had disappeared without return" (p. 35). The plantation slave must cultivate oblivion and exorcise "le vertige de la mémoire" (p. 30) that obsesses the Maroon. And yet for all the scorn and condescension with which the proud highlanders regard their racial brethren of the plains, the Maroon must recognize the dependence of his *raison d'être* on the plantation slave: "The despised, the slaves, the enchained accepted to die in order to permit the haughty, the untamed, the spectacular gesture of arson and combat" (p. 147).

In spite of their incessant feuds and vendettas, an irresistible attraction develops between the Béluses and the Longoués: Stéphanie, a Béluse, lives with Apostrophe, a Longoué; Mathieu Béluse marries Mycéa, whose grandfather was Melchior, the son of the original Longoué. Melchior was the first to renounce hatred and vengeance as futile. He "unconsciously desired to confront, without arms or fight, the clear and ordered universe of the plain" (p. 162). And much later, when the two meet, Papa Longoué, the last of the maroon lineage, and Mathieu, the educated young man, symbiotically complement each other. As Mathieu articulates it: "We want to know by ourselves, you who know and yet would understand nothing . . . and I who know nothing and yet I can already understand you" (p. 58). The Afro-Caribbean must recognize the irreversibility of history and the futility of the nostalgia for Africa. "The infinite country over there beyond the waters was no longer this place of marvels . . . but . . . that part which, negated, in turn negated the new land, its peopling, its work" (p. 287). Papa Longoué's self-imposed reclusion in the past is a gratuitous exercise of the will to refuse. Mathieu, on his part, is to recognize the impasse of assimilation, the inauthenticity of his being immersed in the white world. The true meaning of Antillanité, as Glissant sees it, can be derived only from the relationship of the past to a future potential. Thus, the Maroon is dead and yet timelessly recurrent.

In Glissant's third novel, *Malemort* (1975), the maroon figure recurs under various complex forms. Reflecting the elaboration and ramifications of Glissant's thought during the recent years, which have seen also rapid changes in

the Martinican socioeconomic and cultural environment, *Malemort* is a discon-
certingly intricate mosaic of poetics and politics: a polymorphic style far removed from the French referential model; narrative techniques of varied an-
tecedence, ranging from the oral arts to the *nouveau roman*; a nonlinear,
nonchronological thematic scatter; a multitude of characters, some named and
easily identifiable as the assimilated Martinicans, others portrayed as vague human presences, anonymous and fraught with symbolism. More significantly
perhaps, the dialectical relationship between the Maroon and the plainspeople,
which in the previous novels appeared to evolve toward a syncretic resolution,
seems to be stunted in *Malemort*.

The primordial Maroon, the *négateur*, the naysayer, comes down from his
mountain to see the country and the people. Martinique appears like a sordid
caricature of what it should be: Elections are rigged; exploitation by metropolitan interests run rampant; unemployment has uprooted and demoralized the
masses; cultural assimilation and linguistic imitation of the French have rendered the Martinican an inauthentic being. For the contemporary Martinican the
naysayer "is but a vague discomfort in the stomach, a shoot without leaf or
root, a tear without eyes, a dead person without return."[23] A black policeman,
Tigamba, who was so sympathetic to the cause of the young radicals in *La Lézarde*, is now hunting down a fugitive from justice, Beautemps. Beautemps had
killed a rich proprietor from France who had abused Beautemp's wife. Like the
Jamaican Maroons who sold the new fugitives back to the authorities to protect
their own interests, in Martinique too, Glissant laments, "those who refused
and fled to the heights . . . became the police specialists, the memory of the
naysayer [is] diminished in Beautemps and abolished in Tigamba" (p. 183).
The distinction between those who refused and those who accepted is no longer
evident: "The one who refuses [imitates] the one who accepts and collabo-
rates" (p. 183). The original Maroon, living off the meager resources of his
mountain refuge, "became landscape and country" (p. 43). The modern Martinican, on the other hand, unemployed, disenfranchised, dispossessed of the
land that his ancestors drenched with sweat and blood, is a kind of spectral
being, uselessly wandering over the insular space.

Though most contemporary Martinicans live oblivious of their past, there is
in the collective makeup of the Martinican mentality an inarticulate memory of
some anonymous *ils*, the "they" who signify the ever-present strain of resistance and defiance. They are evoked in a vision of the *tombé levé*, the "fallen
risen" whose lineage extends back to the Maroon and continues in the rebel,
boycotter, union striker and nonconformist who throughout Martinican history
have defied the order of the slave owner, the colonizer, the oppressor, the ex-
ploiter. They have been persecuted and massacred, but they have always risen
from death and dust to continue their relentless struggle for dignity and justice.
In silent rage they wreak destruction as they rampage through the master's
mansion, the sugar factory, the modern department store. They are felled by
the bullets of the ancient *maréchaussée*, local militia, or modern gendarmes.

Dead, their bodies fade into the earth to arise from it later in a different historical setting convoked to "another rendez-vous" (p. 131). With their eternal return, "their fight without rest" (p. 132), they transcend history to become myth-like figures, voiceless, fatally driven by a mute urge to violence and an inarticulate sense of justice.

The silence of the anonymous collective "they" contrasts with what Glissant calls the "verbal delirium of the intellectuals." The Martinican intellectual evidences a predilection for logorrheic outpourings of clichés, speech mannerisms learned at school, a certain old-fashioned elegance of style and affectation of French culture. The verbal delirium is a symptom of the internal conflict that arises from the noncoincidence of the genius of the language spoken with the historical experience and the socioeconomic realities of the people on whom the language is imposed. The slavish respect for French has "sterilized the creative collective capacity."[24] The language of the people, Creole, was the slave's code of communication as well as his expression of protest and refusal. But Creole, the language of the uneducated and the poor, is being berated as barbarous by the Martinican intellectuals. In a way, as Glissant points out, Martinicans are a people without a voice. *Malemort* illustrates the verbal delirium as well as models for linguistic emancipation with usages of French and Creole that intimate "the future echo of speaking" (p. 151), "the material with which to build another language" (p. 158), "our language, impossible yet sought after" (p. 151). This language will have to come from the silences of the Maroon and the verbosity of the intellectual, if the language is to be the summation of the Martinican ethos, the expression of and the experience itself of the people. In the novel's glossary appendix, while offering explanations of certain Creole terms, Glissant admits that the indigenous reader is yet to be born. In *Malemort* the maroon figure loses its actuality and recedes toward the realm of timeless myth. The good tidings of Glissant's prophetic vision of the past are yet to be announced. Antillanité has not yet swept the minds and hearts of most Martinicans.

Nevertheless, Glissant and other Afro-Caribbean writers who constantly interrogate their mute past, to paraphrase Aimé Césaire, have conveyed through the archetypal maroon figure a Caribbean idiosyncrasy of paramount import for the understanding of the region that is still searching for its identity. But, in a way, the Maroon transcends history and regional bounds to become invested with universal values and their concomitant modern ambiguities that concern man's destinies everywhere.

NOTES

1. V. S. Naipaul, *The Middle Passage* (New York: Macmillan, 1962), p. 29.

2. Edouard Glissant, "Théâtre, conscience du peuple," *Acoma* 2 (1971): 57.

3. Jean Benoist, *L'Archipel inachevé* (Montreal: Les Presses de l'Université de Montréal, 1972), p. 343. Unless otherwise indicated, all translations of this and other works are mine.

4. Aimé Césaire, *Cadastre* (Paris: Editions du Seuil, 1961), p. 90.

5. Moreau de Saint Méry, *Description topographique, physique, civile, politique et historique de la partie française de l'île Saint Domingue*, ed. B. Mauel et E. Taillemite (Paris: Société de l'histoire des colonies françaises, 1958), 2: 309.

6. *Proceedings of the Governor and Assembly of Jamaica in Regard to the Maroon Negroes* (Westport, Conn.: Negro University Press, 1970), p. 2.

7. Eugene D. Genovese, *From Rebellion to Revolution* (Baton Rouge: Louisiana State University Press, 1979), p. 53.

8. Ibid., pp. 54–55.

9. Ibid., p. 80.

10. Richard Price, *The Guiana Maroons* (Baltimore: Johns Hopkins University Press, 1976), p. 2.

11. Melville J. Herskovits, *Life in a Haitian Village* (New York: Alfred A. Knopf, 1937), p. 61.

12. Alejo Carpentier, *The Kingdom of This World*, trans. Harriet de Onís (New York: Collier Books, 1970), p. 52.

13. René Depestre, *Un Arc-en-ciel pour l'occident chrétien* (Paris: Présence Africaine, 1967), p. 98.

14. Jeanne Hyvrard, *Les Prunes de Cythère* (Paris: Editions de Minuit, 1975), pp. 173–74.

15. Jeanne Hyvrard, *Mère la mort* (Paris: Editions de Minuit, 1976), pp. 73–74.

16. Bertène Juminer, *Au Seuil d'un nouveau cri* (Paris: Présence Africaine, 1963), p. 16.

17. See Merle Hodge, "Novels on the Caribbean Intellectual in France," *Revista/Review Interamericana* 6 (1976): 211–31.

18. Simone Schwarz-Bart, *Ti Jean L'horizon* (Paris: Editions du Seuil, 1979), p. 76. References to this novel will be cited parenthetically within the text.

19. Edouard Glissant, *L'Intention poétique* (Paris: Editions du Seuil, 1969), p. 36. References to this novel will be cited parenthetically within the text.

20. Edouard Glissant, *Monsieur Toussaint* (Paris: Editions du Seuil, 1961), pp. 7–8.

21. Edouard Glissant, *La Lézarde* (Paris: Editions du Seuil, 1958), p. 241.

22. Edouard Glissant, *Le Quatrième Siècle* (Paris: Editions du Seuil, 1964), p. 15. References to this novel will appear parenthetically within the text.

23. Edouard Glissant, *Malemort* (Paris: Editions du Seuil, 1975), p. 61. References to this novel will appear parenthetically within the text.

24. Glissant, *L'Intention Poétique*, p. 50.

8

The New Political Statement in Haitian Fiction

Joseph Ferdinand (For Alan J. Clayton)

PERMANENCE OF THE POLITICAL BACKDROP

The narrative discourse in Haiti traditionally limits itself to the geographic and cultural space of the country. This practice was even elevated to a literary dogma when Jean Price-Mars expressed a defiant nationalism to denounce Démesvar Delorme's tendency to produce exotic novels that show indifference "to Haitian things and life."[1] For Haitians, to talk about one's "things" also means to situate oneself politically in relation to them. This is obvious especially in today's literature. Since the overwhelming majority of the writers are actively committed in the political arena, their fictional production reads like an attempt at transposing their partisan convictions into the language of art. They could thus claim the following statement of a character: "It is maybe a twist within me, but the most trivial tale takes on political proportions" (*Mémoire*, p. 18).

This attitude is not without positive effects. In a genre where invention remains foremost, fidelity to traditional Haitian themes, like *voodoo*, could lead to an impoverishing of narrative resources. The political element, however, assures the constant renewal of the fictional context. By giving free rein to his passions, the author resituates the cultural phenomena with respect to his own

The English translation of the original French version of this study was done mainly with the help of Peter Aberger. Following is a list of the works used for this study. The abbreviations to identify these works and the corresponding pages will appear parenthetically within the text. Marie-Thérèse Colimon: *Fils de misère* [Fils] (Port-au-Prince: Editions Caraïbes, 1974); *Le Chant des sirènes* (Port-au-Prince: Editions du Soleil, 1979). René Depestre: *Le Mât de cocagne* [Mât] (Paris: Gallimard, 1979); *Alléluia pour une femme-jardin* (Ottawa: Editions Leméac, 1973). Gérard Etienne: *Le Nègre crucifié* [Nègre] (Montréal: Editions francophones & Nouvelle Optique, 1974). Anthony Phelps: *Moins l'Infini* [Moins] (Paris: Editeurs Français Réunis, 1972); *Mémoire en Colin-Maillard* [Mémoire] (Montréal: Editions Nouvelle Optique, 1976); and "Hier, hier encore . . ." ["Hier"] *Nouvelle Optique* 5 (January-March 1972): 5–28.

value system and within the historical frame of his generation; and by so doing, he endows them with a constantly new meaning.

After the shock[2] of the American occupation (1915–1934) and after the tremors produced by the riots of 1946, indigenism and socialism were proclaimed the progressive way of thinking, and questions concerning national identity, exploitation of underprivileged classes, betrayal through the political elite that was allied with American imperialism became important. These issues form the basis for the narrative discourse of Jacques Roumain, Jacques S. Alexis and Edriss Saint-Amand, among others.

THE PRESENT TURNING POINT

François Duvalier's election as president on September 22, 1957, created the conditions for a new formulation of the political discourse in Haitian fiction. The dark side of this regime was what brought it to the world's attention.[3] Elected for a six-year term, and forbidden by the constitution to seek reelection, Duvalier named himself president for life in 1963. Duvalier governed Haiti with an iron hand until his death in April 1971, when his absolute power was inherited by his nineteen-year-old son, Jean-Claude Duvalier. Since then, the situation has remained practically unchanged.

The Haitians rightly or wrongly are convinced that they are experiencing a uniquely atrocious period of their history during which totalitarian regimes have been rampant. René Depestre remarks: "In the present context of general crisis of the system, this latent, permanent *papadocquism* [after Papa Doc Duvalier], which is clearly distinguishable in the agitated course of our history, had to break out into horrors yet unseen in Haiti."[4] The experience will undoubtedly leave indelible marks on the collective psyche.

It is, therefore, not by accident that fiction, which has traditionally been nourished in Haiti by the past, was now seeking to use the present, whose citizens seem like characters from a fantastic novel. Even foreign novelists like Graham Greene and Gérard de Villiers do not disdain looking for inspiration there.[5] The tragic drama of the past two decades, enlarged and transformed within the shell of the imagination, is passionately narrated in Haitian short stories and novels. We discover a well-delineated universe. On the one hand the victim; on the other, the executioner. Here, the reign of torture, crime, rape, pillage and corruption; there, a people in shock: splendid heroism of some, but also cowardice or defeatism of others; immeasurable despair changing into a psychosis of exile. Finally, above all, hope that refuses to die.

Manichean divisions of this sort never fail to seem simplistic. Far from being naive, however, this narrow perception of "things Haitian" is the product of highly politicized, partisan and militant minds that are united in the same goal of national liberation. The only difference lies in the way of sending the message, for it is clear that writers in exile feel less of a need to guard their speech than their brothers who remain in Haiti. Thus, to understand fully the vast network of metaphors that flow throughout the text, one needs to look beyond its decorative purpose.

Of the novelists chosen for this essay two live in Quebec: Gérard Etienne and Anthony Phelps; one in Paris, after spending two decades in Castro's Cuba: René Depestre; and one in Port-au-Prince: Marie-Thérèse Colimon. But all four use an approach that relies on synthesis. Through their literary quality as well as their vision of the national conjuncture, they prove to be representative of the new tendencies in Haitian fiction. Needless to say, each of them preserves a very distinct personality, but the organization of the discourse is set by all of them according to a dialectic articulation: The campaign of *zombification* unleashed by the *tonton macoute* power produces in the victim the need to dezombify himself.[6]

THE STAGE OF ZOMBIFICATION

In Depestre's *Le Mât de cocagne*, the president, having decided to inflict on his political adversary a punishment that goes beyond the routine "of our usual methods" (p. 12) of torture, rejoices over his ingenious invention: "Let us make him a zombi for the rest of his days!" This term evokes one of the most dreadful beliefs of the Haitian mythology. Indeed, what is a zombi? Specialists find it difficult to agree on a definition, as often happens in the case of cultural phenomenon when empirical research encounters the taboos of *voodoo* practice. In a lecture given March 23, 1980, at the University of Quebec in Montreal, Emerson Douyon called the zombi a victim of a "ritual crime." The audience received the statement with strong reservation.[7] There is, however, one point upon which both popular and academic agreement exists: The zombi should not be considered a mere product of collective imagination. It all starts when a person in good health suddenly falls ill and dies. Rumors of unnatural death are soon spread all around the neighborhood. It frequently happens that witnesses come forward later and swear having seen somebody who is believed to be dead working for someone else whose connection with magic is commonly known. There has recently been a proliferation of famous cases, of which the press of Haiti has given copious account. The review *Collectif Paroles* states:

Radio Inter even had the most "famous" *zombi* speak, a Clervéus Narcisse of Pont l'Estère, who "died" in May 1962 and "reappeared" in January 1980. The *Petit Samedi Soir* (no. 323, February 2–8, 1980) printed his story, written by Jean-Robert Hérard, and also cited a meeting with Dr. Lamarque Douyon. . . . It was learned then that apart from Narcisse, two other *zombis*, Natagète Joseph and Francina Iléus, were under observation at the psychiatric center of Dr. Douyon, who is undertaking their psychosocial rehabilitation.[8]

A double conclusion can be drawn. First, there has not been a real death, even if clinical examination discovers the normal symptoms in the victim. Among Haitian peasants, as in any primitive culture, there exists a secret pharmacological knowledge, based on the familiarity with the properties of certain plants, that provides the recipe for the *magic* poison. Second, the fact that death is only apparent implies the possibility of a return to a normal life. It remains to be seen if the recovery (initiated through the contact with salt) will be complete. Through the effect of either the poison or the subsequent antidote administered to him, the zombi will find himself stricken with severe mental atrophy. This, incidentally, explains his unconditional submission to the master.

Literary description of the zombi phenomenon follows the common pattern with one significant change regarding the recovery process, which is now shown in an optimistic light. It could not be otherwise if the ultimate goal assigned to the narrative discourse is to be attained—that is, to rekindle the flame of hope and create the condition for the decisive upheaval. But first of all, depicting the ugliness of the present situation in Haiti constitutes the most pressing task of the writers. Gérard Pierre-Charles' title "X-ray of a Dictatorship" is, indeed, an accurate expression to define their preoccupation at this stage.[9] Every possible reproach against the hateful regime appears in their works. Hence we learn nothing new in that respect, and without the inventive qualities of the narrators the stories would probably remain political pamphlets.

Human degradation takes place at every level. Depestre's Henri Postel, a former prestigious senator, has not stopped deteriorating like a shrinking hide since he was made a zombi: "The man had arrived at Tête-Boeuf with the build of an athlete. Now he had disgustingly fattened at the neck, the shoulders, the belly, and the thighs. The nape of his neck, the lower part of his face and his hands were deeply lined with wrinkles. Everything about him was sagging" (*Mât*, p. 14). The process of zombification, as we know, leads to a reduction if not to a pure and simple halt of cerebral functions. So the president had prepared for his enemy "a death which eats slowly away at his mind before attacking his body" (p. 12). However, despite the signs of his physical deterioration and the chronic "drunkenness" into which despair is driving him, Postel preserves enough intellectual lucidity to work out solid political projects, to conceive of and execute successfully the ingenious operation of the *mât suiffé* ("greased pole"). In Phelp's book the government will no longer play cat and mouse with its adversaries, preferring instead to rely fully on the traditional method of torture, which is based essentially on blind brutality. One of Phelp's characters complains: "This is the period of the great blackness" (*Moins*, p. 153). In this type of literature, hyperbole is, of course, the rule. No other language could communicate to the reader, in all its blackness, the orgiastic feeling of this world teetering on the brink of the absurd and possessed by the delirium of self-destruction. The relationship zombifier-zombi defines an exceptional, baroque mode of living that predates the novelist's enterprise and imposes upon him writing norms capable of assuring the fidelity of the text to a situation where exaggeration and improbability are the criteria of *normality*.

Etienne's *Le Nègre crucifié* makes us relive the shocking adventure of a prisoner (the transfigured double of Etienne himself) who is beaten up by the militia and then, while awaiting the next torture session, tries to dream of the world as it is and as he would like it. The same forceful language is used in Phelps' fantastic story "Hier, hier encore . . . " where we find the eternal figure of the hero-martyr, dehumanized by the unbridled violence of the tormentor. However, the author seems less insistent on the brutality of the mistreatment than its meaning. The act of violence, stripped of its purely physical content, undergoes a conceptual transformation that displays its mythical essence. It becomes Violence, the blind goddess whose pleasure it is to crush implacably all those who fall into her power because she exists for that function alone. If Etienne's prisoner can accuse himself of having participated in "a plot" against the government (*Nègre*, p. 141), Phelps' prisoner is the personification of innocence crushed under the boots of the beast. Arrested because of an error by the *tonton macoutes*, who were looking for a certain Doctor Marcel, he is forced to assume the other's identity to the very end. Under the pseudonym of Mr. X, the once penniless but happy store clerk becomes the Victim, the symbol of all anonymous victims who are zombified by the horrors of daily prison life.

The Mr. X and the I of the narrator in *Le Nègre crucifié* represent the two images of the prisoner in contemporary Haitian fiction, both of which usually cross paths in the same text. On the one hand, there are the militant revolutionaries engaged in an activist opposition; on the other hand, there are those who suffer the violence of the regime as a consequence of the fateful blindness of that violence. By metaphorical extrapolation we must add to this group all those who, for one reason or another, must worry about the situation of the country. As Colimon's *Le Chant des sirènes* shows, this group actually comprises the entire population, from the most underprivileged classes to the bourgeois such as the Labédoyères and the Damien-Deltours.

Thus not only emigré writers criticize the savagery of the *tonton macoutes*' tactics. Colimon's character Ferdinand Daguerrand, Miss Rézia Régulier's fiancé, is declared a "trouble maker" (*Fils*, p. 106) by the government when he tries to put into practice the "new ideas" (p. 105) he has brought back from France. One day, he is shot openly in the street. This episode, which happens before the Duvalier era, contains enough allusions to contemporary experiences to justify the reader's suspicion. Is this a question of strategy? Even though Colimon avoids any reference to names or actions that could be interpreted as a direct challenge to the regime (torture scenes, for example, are banished from her work), she also finds the right note in denouncing the conditions in her country with as much determination as tact. In an unforgettable scene, in which a brutal reprisal is carried out against Ti Tonton's high school, she ironically underlines the fact that in order to put down a trivial student riot, the government of Duvalier found it necessary to mobilize its best-equipped troops: "those soldiers who, with weapons at the ready, were undertaking the assault of a high school with great determination" (*Fils*, p. 196). Indeed, *Fils de misère* and *Le Chant des sirènes* show how Colimon, who, unlike her emigré colleagues, cannot abandon herself with impunity to the delirium of political writing, is able to manipulate the text so as to intersperse her narrative with practical observations of life in Haiti under the reign of the Duvaliers. The political problem is thus *a posteriori* inscribed in and reflected through a large context of references encompassing the totality of lived experiences. Economy, sociology, metaphysics—the entire realm of knowledge defines the singularity of the individual or the social class without failing to stress the tragic abnormality of the situation and, beyond describing effects, to denounce the real cause of the problem through allusive incrimination. It is no secret that the reference is to the government. Merleau-Ponty writes: "But if language expressed as much between words as with words? With what it does not 'say' as well as with what it 'says'?"[10] This is the case for authors living in Haiti.

By comparison, the novelists in exile usually do not give descriptive accounts of their characters nor do they usually show any emotion that could be seen as their neglecting the political ends of their narrative. Because of their physical absence, they approach reality by arranging the facts in a hierarchical order according to whether or not they see the opportunity to reach their objective, namely, the preaching of anti-Duvalierist revolution. No wonder they often give the impression of dealing with an abstract world, for (1) they neglect details and are more sensitive to an historical synthesis; (2) they are less attracted by the facts than by the idea; (3) they are interested in convincing rather than informing; (4) they are constantly trying to rejoin the people, but only through the introspective grasp of their own emotions. None of them, for example, addresses the question of the massive exodus of Haitians, a national tragedy of incalculable consequences, with as much insight as Colimon;[11] none of them shows as correctly the social, economic and even political implications of the phenomenon. Worse yet, apart from Karl Toulanmanche's *Epaves*, subtitled "true story," no text is known to contain allusion to the people's experience in a foreign land (mainly New York) as lively and colorful as in *Le Chant des sirènes* or Frankétienne's play *Pèlin Tèt*.[12]

The difference is not fundamental, but rather one of perspective and method. All these authors, whether they are in Haiti or abroad, are stimulated by the same need to produce testimony on the mother country through the medium of their works. They are all concerned with the repressive fury of the regime and with what constitutes an attack on human rights,[13] what degrades man and what zombifies him: the absence of political freedom, of freedom of speech, of any freedom. The litany of ills is well-known.

Nevertheless, it is not enough to decry the present regime, which, incidentally, is not an accident of history either. Since being led to independence from France in 1804 by Toussaint L'Ouverture and Jean-Jacques Dessalines, Haiti has lived almost endlessly under a succession of shortsighted, incompetent or cruel leaders. It is obvious that such a political system is a failure and deserves to be denounced. The writers also know that the populace is not made up of heroes, and they have no intention of passing it off as a paragon of virtue or as a body playing the noble role.

The zombi, as we already pointed out, leads a hellish existence. The text shows him as sliding progressively into decay until he is totally alienated from society. But the most degrading wounds that mark him are not the physical and mental scars inflicted during his time in prison. The escapees from government jails are like soldiers returning from war: Their wounds represent a harvest of laurels; they have gained the right to admiration and respect. There is another truly degrading form of alienation that implies the participation of the individual in the process of his own degradation, the acceptance of *playing the game*, being faithful to the expectation of the zombifier.

The highest level of zombification is what Barbotog, the leading henchman of the president, calls triumphantly "zombification by oneself" (*Mât*, p. 12). In general, the zombi is kept in sight and is deprived of lucidity for fear that he might rebel against his condition. Here the system has reached such a degree of perfection that it no longer feels compelled to waste its energy with suppressing consciousness. The state of fear and panic felt in the country under the Duvalier regime guarantees the docility of the zombified people.[14] Out of self-preservation, one becomes cowardly, base, low; one sells one's soul to the devil and tramples on civic virtues. The novelist relating these actions cannot contain his anger. Phelps exclaims through Claude's mouth: "Security! Security! What disgusts me is our passiveness in the face of the crimes, the injustices" (*Mémoire*, p. 15). A furious reprimand from the narrator in *Le Nègre crucifié* echoes that feeling: "Make a gesture, for goodness' sake, in order to finally see the light! Make a gesture" (p. 28), because "it is despicable, dad, to accept your bleeding without rebelling" (p. 30).

Armed rebellion is, of course, the most drastic solution suggested in the narrative discourse. Another way to express dissatisfaction with the regime is simply to leave Haiti. That is the gesture made by an estimated one million Haitians, one-fifth of the population.[15] Thus almost everyone in this country seems stricken with the psychosis of exile. Colimon writes: "We live in a time when . . . it is firmly believed that living outside of one's country is a form of resurrection" (*Chant*, p. 130). The question is no longer who emigrates, but why everybody is looking for salvation outside of the homeland. *Le Chant des sirènes* becomes in this respect an indispensable reference text. Through a mass of extremely varied and true pictures in which all classes of the Haitian people are represented, Colimon reveals the result of her observations and, by so doing, shows an ambivalent pleasure—her ever-present humor being, no doubt, a compromise between anger and surprise. She sees no sign of civic health in her people, whose dearest dream is to excape from hell (Haiti) and enter happily "the promised land" (p. 17), the "blessed country" (p. 139), namely, the United States of America.

The emigré writers, who are always more subjective in their manner of narrating Haitian reality, tend to illustrate their own inner voyages. The hero of *Le Mât de cocagne* rejects traveling as a solution, because he sees in the contest of the greased pole an opportunity *in extremis* "to recover the reputation of his country'' (p. 30) and to achieve his dezombification. Phelps accepts the journey as a break from which one returns stronger, more than ever determined to perform "the necessary deeds" (*Mémoire*, p. 153). The decision to leave results from an act of reflection, of rationalization. After having intelligently weighed the pros and cons of the decision, Benoît does not flee; he leaves. Now he can declare to his friends: "That's why I *must* leave, I *must* go" (p. 110, emphasis added). It is a strategic retreat.

Etienne's position is more difficult to assess: If Postel or Benoît can determine his fate, the character in *Le Nègre crucifié* is fixed between the four walls of his prison and can only dream of traveling. What does it matter? Circumstances impose on all of them the necessity to redefine their strategy as fighters with respect to the reassuring attraction of the faraway places. Whereas Postel and Benoît present their choice as an act of political farsightedness, as testimony of their immutable faithfulness to the cause of the opposition, the prisoner turns back upon himself, incapable of deciding if the gesture must satisfy his rancor or his instinct as a revolutionary. He knows that "in this country there is no room for honest people" (p. 58). What can be done? "He, too, will leave. If he does not leave, he will become a zombi negro for the zombi negroes" (p. 134). In the final analysis, the animal love for his country and the obscure sense of responsibility as a militant seem to make him change his mind: " 'I must not leave,' he said. 'The Whites build their country. I must also build my country' " (p. 135). But one should not take this statement too seriously, since we are dealing with a very unstable person. The only thing that remains constant in his "split brain" (p. 125) is his urgent desire to pierce the hellish wall of the reality so that he can escape to a mythical land of freedom and happiness. The act of traveling consequently possesses, in his case, an essentially therapeutic function. It is not enough to say that his condition as prisoner allows him only to dream about travel; we must also understand that he survives only through this dream where both his past and future parade in shining images. He says, "So many memories prevent me from dying" (p. 104). We are far from the altruistic declarations of the revolutionary writing: Through his dreaming for survival the hero begins to enjoy the delirium of his imagination, the fascination of creation through writing, in short, the sensuous pleasure of the poetic state, which he celebrates with such enthusiasm. At the end of the story, he is seen amazed over "Never having seen so many stars in his life" (p. 150). Sitting in his cell as if on Rimbaud's drunken ship, could he escape any longer the temptation to wish to live only to dream? In his "prison-country" (*Moins*, p. 176) he will always feel the need to reinvent his odyssey again and again, spending his time on "imagining situations one would like to live, states of consciousness one would like to experience" (*Nègre*, p. 125).

Phelps' heroes also adore the sensation of poetic drunkenness. They believe it is the best antidote against the poison of "a more and more brutal and more and more ferocious reality" (*Moins*, p. 78). But whereas Etienne's prisoner settles irreversibly into evasion, poetry remains for them a stop where they pleasantly kill time while waiting for the propitious moment for attack. Marco explains, "Action, Paula. And when the moment is not right for action, let's escape through poetic dreams!" (p. 78).

Whether one escapes with Etienne's hero or chooses exile or out of inability to act follows Marco's advice, the practical result is the same: The government wins at every strike. Its politics of imposing imbecility on the people, which is denounced indignantly in the fictional discourse, seems to triumph effortlessly as Barbotog had foreseen when he defined the principle of "zombification by oneself" (Mât, p. 12). We have reached the extreme limits of despair. If the stars sparkle with such brightness at the end of Etienne's story, it is because the night has never been so black. The voyage has led man to the last stage at the end of the night, and he welcomes death as deliverance.

For someone like Etienne, who does not hide the depth of his religious convictions ("I believe . . . in God, my universe, my poison," he writes in Dialogue avec mon ombre),[16] the temptation to exploit biblical imagery to describe the passion of the people is irresistible. "Crucified is what I am" (Nègre, p. 30), laments his hero. The story unfolds untiringly within the allegorical orbit marked out by the title The Crucified Negro. Colimon shows the same tendency of reaching for a religious symbol in order to dramatize better the condition of existence of her characters. In their horribly deteriorated state, the "hands of this mater dolorosa" (Chant, p. 75), that is, Madame Josaphat Numitor, "revealed a long march to some unknown Golgotha." Postel will have to climb the same hill, nailed on "this [cross-] post covered with black suffering [which] summarizes the calvary from Pont-Rouge [where Dessalines was assassinated on October 17, 1806] to Zoocrate Zacharie [Duvalier's nickname in the novel]" (Mât, pp. 62–63); and later on the same Postel will be addressed by the loa (voodoo god), "you who carry Christ's crown of thorns" (p. 112). These references are even more striking since Depestre, out of ideological conviction, is not easily moved to a mystical outpouring.

THE STAGE OF DEZOMBIFICATION

The function of the fictional discourse at this stage consists of unveiling the strategy to be followed for the final victory. But before a code of resistance can be formulated, it is necessary to point out the importance of individual responsibility. If zombification is a collective drama, dezombification will then put the individual in the foreground and praise his courage and devotion to the common cause, his vision; in short, it will seek out the exceptional person who is capable of arousing the people from their lethargy. It is true, to some degree, that contemporary Haitian novelists carry the imprint of the messianic mentality of the 1960s. Any revolutionary movement must first bring forth its Fidel Castro and Che Guevara before it can succeed. Does this mean these writers cannot see another solution apart from the Marxist-Leninist road taken by the Cuban revolution? While there is no doubt about the leftist ideological position of most of them, their socialism remains a matter of principle rather than a dogmatic belief. Furthermore, the Haitian opposition carefully avoids stirring up again those ideological quarrels that weakened it in the past and turned its attention away from getting rid of the Duvaliers. Unity is being proclaimed noisily. The revolutionary act seems to limit itself, for the time being, to its immediate goal of overthrowing the regime. What counts above all is action; through action you succeed in mobilizing the masses. Postel is convinced of it. He declares to a skeptic: "Who tells you that my action will not wake up this country!" (*Mât*, p. 35). Benoît of *Moins l'Infini* expresses a similar view to his revolutionary comrades: "For eight years you have been refusing to understand that the revolution does not mean only to politicize the masses. It means also and first of all to train a group that will go into action and strike the enemy in order to show the masses that we are not coming to them with words and phrases, but we fight effectively for them" (p. 109).

Without their names being mentioned, we feel the legendary shadow of the *Barbudos de la Sierra Maestra* hovering over these texts. Also implicitly evoked is the image of the great men of this generation whose lives and deaths, being devoted to the cause of their people, have gained a radiance that can be seen beyond their ideological borders. The heroes pride themselves on resembling them. They too are exceptional men. They have endured the worst physical and mental suffering at the hands of the torturers of the regime, and it is precisely by their degree of resistance that their leadership ability is measured. In *Mémoire en Colin-Maillard*, Claude talked under torture but only at the end, when the brutality of the torturers had altered his judgment to the point where he no longer knew what he was saying. Phelps' purism in this respect is so rigorous that it does not allow for any weakness of character. Claude, therefore, will not be the expected Messiah.

Even if the other novelists stay clear of such extremism, they are not any less demanding with respect to the constancy of their heroes. Postel's excessive ordeal only sharpened his desire to attack:

They tortured before my eyes the only woman I ever loved. They opened her belly and put a big, magnificently red cock in the place of the seven-month-old baby she was bearing. Later on Barbotog took pleasure in extinguishing his cigars on the naked breasts of my oldest daughter. Our other children had already been killed right at our doorstep with my attendant. (*Mât*, 63–64).

Etienne's crucified man has also seen a few things. While he was receiving a series of blows all over his body, scenes of a fantastic horror came to haunt his memory:

A soldier assassinates a woman with a baby in her belly. While killing the woman, the baby has time to come out of her belly. He runs before the soldier's gun. The soldier catches the baby by the ear, throws him up in the air and impales him on his fixed bayonet. The baby dies. A soldier assassinates an old man coming out of the church.

Another tramples on a corpse. Another digs a hole and pushes the old man into it. Even in the hole, the old man continues to breathe (p. 68).

The surrealist description does not detract from the ferocious realism of the passage. The narrator's hallucinatory state does not by itself explain the obvious exaggeration, which is really not that different from the device used earlier by the *lucid* Postel. Since the *macoute* torturers habitually indulge in unimaginable excesses, hyperbole becomes the only way of faithfully describing that reality. Although the anarchistic nature of his political projects will undoubtedly disqualify him as a valuable leader, Etienne's hero too shows incredible courage. He declares, "My resistance really frightens the Master's militia. I know ways which allow me to tolerate pain" (p. 105).

For the novelists the mission to bring about the triumph of the revolution is incumbent on a singular individual whom we shall not try to define, since the text itself keeps him a great mystery, admitting only that he possesses all necessary qualities and powers. A black Christ? Perhaps, though Etienne makes him end his career on Calvary, stripped of his halo as a redeemer. In Phelps' messianic perspective he is an alchemist. This man is gifted with the knowledge of Prometheus and the wisdom of Saturn; he represents the romantic dream of a perfect harmony between citizens who are united in the quest for worldly happiness. It would be, of course, tempting to reproach Phelps' inclination for abstraction. The truth is that nobody tried as hard as he to define the role of action, of the armed fight during the course of the revolution. Without compromising the powerful flow of imagination that crosses his fictional universe from beginning to end, we can argue, he has shaped the master of his proud militants as much through lived experiences as through the creative dream. Anguish and doubt appear behind a curtain of metaphors and mirror the present disarray of the Haitian opposition. The evocation of the transcendent being becomes invocation and reads like a desperate invitation to correct "the irremediably Cain-like nature of man" (*Mémoire*, p. 11), to resolve the internal quarrels of the small anti-Duvalier groups, to gather together the precious "stones" (p. 78) of the resistance under a unified and competent direction so as to achieve what has seemed unachievable until today—in short, to accomplish the indispensable miracle.

Although the Marxist Depestre tries to put some emphasis on collective participation in the revolutionary act, the hero in his novel, former Senator Postel, also bears the mark of uniqueness. He imposes the magic superiority of his character on everyone, friends as well as enemies. Horace, the intellectually alert shoemaker, calls him spontaneously "master" (*Mât*, p. 16). "A real man, a real man" (p. 166), thinks Elisa of him; "a Negro altogether" (p. 167). These are almost the same terms used by Phelps and certainly the same used by Jacques Roumain to describe the transcendence of Manuel, the hero of *Governors of the Dew*. Postel appears *mutatis mutandis* as a kind of educated Manuel with city manners.

The novelist living in Haiti finds himself in a clearly unfavorable position compared to his emigrant brother when it comes to treating taboos. To speak of the process of the dezombification of the people and its consequence, the fall of the regime, is regarded as highly criminal by the government. Any suggestions in that area can be made only in the form of allusions, even though the relaxation in the political atmosphere during the past luster was favorable to the budding of a militant literature whose language was not characterized by timidity. The wave of plays in the vernacular, which started with Frankétienne's *Pèlin Tèt*, was stemmed only with the reimposition of state censorship in May 1979 and finally with the adoption of the Press Law of September 28, 1979.[17] Again there was silence. *Le Chant des sirènes*, published in 1979, contains no subversive provocation, not even a statement that recalls the innocently equivocal attitudes of certain characters in *Fils de misère* nor anything like Rézia Régulier's famous monologue when she denounces the people's shameful cowardice (see *Fils*, pp. 194–95). The thwarted intention is then made clear through ironical smiles with which Colimon greets the irresponsible proposals of her heroes. These proposals, in which a dangerous perversion of the revolutionary messianism takes place, carry obvious political connotations. An atrocious caricature of the redeeming act born out of the psychosis of exile—any quest for salvation, for instance—fatally leads to a depreciation of civic virtues instead of reconciling the person with himself, that is, his national values and identity. He who manages to leave the cursed shores of the island is "the savior of the family" (*Chant*, p. 76): He can procure drink and food for it daily until the day when all the members, provided through his help with the "visa of deliverance" (p. 15), take off one by one toward redemption in "the promised land" (p. 17).

Once the question of leadership is settled and once the principle of the inevitable triumph over the forces of zombification is established, the fictional discourse tries to define in detail the context of the struggle on the basis of its rejections and affirmations. Above all, the government and its alienating politics are rejected. Nothing is spared to arrive at the goal. Etienne's hero declares, "The country must be saved not with prayers . . . but with crimes" (*Nègre*, p. 44). Phelps' militants dream only of hecatombs of the enemy. And we have seen how Postel uses the gun after he won it on the top of the greased pole (*Mât*, p. 167).

In this blind confrontation, where everything is at stake and the moral conscience rests subdued, the violence of the language befits the violence of the act. A veritable battalion of incisive words is hurled at the enemy. Nothing is easier to understand: It is the only recourse for the revolutionary until the action can be moved on a concrete plane. War-like talk is liberating. One can avenge (or absolve oneself for) one's impotence to "perform the necessary deeds" (*Mémoire*, p. 153). Postel's furious statement indicates the degree of his frustration: "I shit on these gunshots I have never fired, which nobody fired. Shit for all of us. Here we are: Stretched out on blocks of ice, our arms crossed and our hands empty, our minds softened by the rum of resignation'' (*Mât*, p. 64). The string of ridiculous as well as contemptuous nicknames that Phelps fixes at every turn on the head of the state seems quite an innocent game compared with the licentious—that is, excremental—irreverence flowing forth from Etienne's and Depestre's pens. After all, it would be anachronistic, now at the end of the twentieth century, to wish to create a world from shamelessly obscene vocabulary that does not shock anymore because of its overuse by writers, singers and movie makers. This does not prevent that certain expressions in Postel's mouth seem to do more harm to his halo as a former senator than to the recipient of the insult. And what should be said of the grotesque episode in which Depestre shows the archbishop of Port-au-Prince presiding over a *voodoo* ceremony at the National Palace?

A further rejection is of the picture-postcard mentality (also of tourists) promoted by popular songs like ''Haïti chérie'' in which Haiti is celebrated as the best country in the world. That mentality made certain writers hide the reality of Haitian misery under the lyrical warmth of landscape descriptions. Few are the passages where the hero is shown hesitating in the contemplation of the Haitian nature, which, in spite of everything, remains eternally beautiful, as Paula found out at the very beginning of *Moins l'Infini* when ''her head raised, she contemplated the December sky sowed with an infinite number of brilliant colors'' (p. 9). On the other hand, being obsessed with pressing problems to resolve, trying to find ways for dezombification, one is more inclined to imitate Madame Damien-Deltour, who is ''indifferent to these offerings of nature, indifferent to the beauty of these mountains with fog-shrouded peaks, to the jade green of the sleepy plain embracing its sparkling waters, indifferent to this intoxicating symphony of sounds, smells and colors'' (*Chant*, p. 87). No more human respect, no more complexes are left: One shows to the world what one is, using, if need be, the same hyperbolic devices already used in overevaluating the opulence of the ''Pearl of the Antilles'' (Haiti's pretentious nickname). Depestre dares to write in his *Alléluia pour une femme-jardin*: ''If the world is a valley of tears, Haiti is the best watered corner of the valley. . . . the worst possible misfortune in the Americas was to be born in Haiti'' (p. 10).

Hence the inclination to unveil the national wounds. These literary strip tease numbers are a true shock treatment and must be understood as the didactic intention of the fictional discourse: The reader, and through him all Haitians, must be exposed to the most brutal recognition possible of their ruin as a people in order to create in them an attitude favorable to a new consciousness. The need to instruct is still felt in the way certain cultural factors are approached. First of all, *voodoo*, of course, is one of the most redundant commonplaces in Haitian writing. On the one hand, it is derided by Etienne, who sees an evil attraction in it, a source of collective zombification, and despised by Rézia Régulier (a trustworthy spokeswoman for Colimon?) in the name of traditional bourgeois values. On the other hand, it receives from Depestre and Phelps the condescending sympathy that has been typical of progressive intellectuals since

Jacques Roumain. It is of interest to note that the hero in Frankétienne's *Dézafi*, on his way to liberation, renders the satanic powers of the *houngan* (*voodoo* priest) ineffective.

Whereas the émigré writers concentrate foremost on the political revolution, those living in Haiti usually choose to take up the battle in the area of social alienation. Colimon is convinced that things will not change unless a deep reform of the Haitian mentality is undertaken. She goes right to the root of the problem, the outdated educational system of the country. Since her main characters are almost always women, her suggestions, interspersed with feminist ideas, represent a passionate appeal against male chauvinism whose presence at all institutional levels contributes to Haiti's lagging behind the rest of the world, including its Caribbean neighbors.

Even though the revolution mainly remains the men's business according to the impression given by these novels, we cannot pass silently over the fact that some heroines need not envy their male counterparts when it comes to devotion and courage on the battlefield. Illustrious examples are Paula of *Moins l'Infini*, Zaza Valéry of *Le Mât de cocagne* and Maria Dalbaïcin, the passionate heroine of Roger Dorsinville's *Mourir pour Haïti ou les croisés d'Esther*. What really motivates Depestre and Phelps, more than the desire to celebrate the contribution of some women to the national liberation movement, seems to be the need for a reconciliation between revolution and sex. The revolutionary is not this insensible savage, this brute he is believed to be. He (or she) falls in love like everybody else, makes love and floats into seventh heaven; his energy is reinvigorated by that. Thus when lovers like Postel and Zaza Valéry or Marco and Paula, as well as Ferdinand Daguerrand, an inveterate skirt chaser "favoring the lower class neighborhoods, the easy women and lots of liquor" (*Fils*, p. 106), are caught in a lascivious posture, as so often happens, they do not expect to be blamed for exerting what Depestre calls their "right to the orgasm" in his "Evangile selon St. Eros." [18] Adhesion to this "gospel" is certainly not unanimous, but we shall not find many characters like Etienne's hero, a self-proclaimed misogynist whose conscience, haunted by visions of rape and homosexual traumas, stimulates contempt for the sexual act—not to mention the political overtone of his resentment. He explains, "It is because of that animal [woman] that Negroes become torturers and kill opponents in order to have that animal" (*Nègre*, p. 57).

Finally, how do those facts help us understand the society contained in the novels? We know for sure that not only the *tonton macoute* government will be destroyed but also the entire traditional political structure out of which the Duvalier regime came. No more exploitation. No more suffering. Haiti will be transformed into a paradise where all citizens will enjoy unlimited freedom and happiness. Is it not a marvelous dream? The writers are not at all interested in defining a program of reconstruction as politicians would be. Art has nothing to lose and everything to gain when it removes itself from the reality it pretends to encircle or, under the circumstances, to correct, that is, to transform. The fictional discourse is destined to propagate a predominantly political message; it avoids, however, bowing to the level of an electoral campaign and mixing its content and style with those of a harangue. In other words, the writers refuse to give up their rights to invention. Beginning with reality and linked to reality, they never stop reinventing that reality out of the sum of their good or bad individual experiences, their hopes and their failures and above all their illusions.

LITERARY BACKGROUND OF THE DISCOURSE

But can the political purpose of the discourse be truly fulfilled if its artistic aspect is neglected? For the Haitian writers of today, reinventing reality also means exercising the right to renew their writing resources through the use of modern literary technique. They are eager to find the most adequate form to convey the originality of their dreams.

Following Magloire Saint-Aude, Etienne does not hesitate to penetrate fully into the hallucinatory universe of surrealism. One cannot read *Le Nègre crucifié* without thinking of André Breton or even more of Henri Michaux. This relationship is more than an adopted attitude and defines an esthetic choice that is again confirmed in the author's latest two works: *Dialogue avec mon ombre* and *Un Ambassadeur macoute à Montréal*. The influence of surrealism on *Le Nègre crucifié*, however, could not be any more desirable or opportune. No other approach would have allowed one to establish such an equation between language and novelistic intention. The hallucinatory impressions of the narrator, tossed between sleep and wakefulness, the confusion in his "split brain" (p. 125), the calculated incoherence of his delivery—all of that seems specifically designed to imitate the condition of the zombi.

Phelps is a master of psychological nuances. Unlike others, he does not give in to the temptation to turn his novels into a forum of exhibitionism for professional heroes who win every battle, regardless of how desperate the situation may be, because right and justice are supposed to triumph under all circumstances. Indeed, both *Moins l'Infini* and *Mémoire en Colin-Maillard* end with the failure of the protagonists. The revolutionary project remains viable and valuable, though; despite themselves, Marco and Claude moved farther away from that project. No, this "Negro of capacity who will perform the indispensable deeds" (*Mémoire*, p. 128), whom they felt vibrate in themselves, no, it will be another, not they. In the course of action they realize that the road to revolution is staked out with labyrinthine passages and that they, too, "not [as] a piece of wood" but like "other men" (*Moins*, p. 25) are subject to the same existential ambivalence. As Claude's mother said, "It is not like mathematics, where one and one are always two" (*Mémoire*, p. 75).

The structural organization of the narration also follows political uncertainty. Phelps does not mind using some writing devices from the *nouveau roman*: The linear discourse is rejected and the narrative time dislocated; the hero evolves inside a complex, multidimensional world where past, present and future, dream and reality are superimposed, are juxtaposed and penetrate each other depending on the narrative situation. As in Etienne's *Le Nègre crucifié*, there exists an equalization between the substance and form of the discourse, which itself is in the image of the desperately ruined nation: "And the Building is fissured, crisscrossed with cracks, dislocated" (*Mémoire*, p. 71). There is the further image of the hero's impenetrable fate as it appears to Monsieur X in its almost Dedalean entanglement (see "Hier," p. 16).

From that perspective, Depestre and Colimon appear conservative. Their narratives contain neatly arranged facts, a straightforward action unfolding harmoniously step by step toward its conclusion. The eye of the omniscient narrator leaves nothing in obscurity.

The language itself remains faithful to a tradition dating back to the first generation of Haitian romantics (1835). In that tradition the literary language does not hesitate to Haitianize French by incorporating expressions and syntactical elements from Creole. Today's novelists surpass the audacity of Jacques Roumain's stylistic variants in *Governors of the Dew*. Less so Depestre, whose style seems to aim at Atticism. His taste for pure French leads him to turn into French almost all the Creole terms flowing into his pen from the search for local color. In the body of the text he designates them with italics in order to avoid any confusion. That apparently trivial purism could earn Depestre some embarrassment today, when the struggle for the cause of Creole against French becomes more and more radical and dons the colors of nationalism. Frankétienne's novel *Dézafi* is entirely in Creole, a sign of the times.

Altogether striking in the contemporary Haitian novel is the existence of a vast network of "obsessing metaphors," according to Charles Maurron's expression, through which these emotional texts depict the overexcitement of the minds. As soon as one has become familiar with those recurring signs, the most hermetic passages can easily be deciphered, and those hastily judged to be of lesser value produce sudden resonances that open new perspectives to interpretation.

It is even more remarkable to see how authors who are so different from each other by temperament and style, but who are moved by the degrading situation of their country, could arrive at almost identical semantic modulations.

Between the act of descending into hell where Satan-Duvalier reigns (Etienne) and climbing to the top of the mast to pick up the gun of freedom (Depestre), a multitude of antagonistic attitudes are represented in the dialectic currently characterizing fictional discourse. There are signs to express the horror of the condition of a zombi and the inhumanity of the zombifier; there are also signs that sing of the hope of dezombification and of reconquering the paradise of dreams.[19] On the one hand is death; on the other, life. Phelps states: "oppression *buries the city deeper and deeper in the ground*, transforms it into the ore and stone of a *common grave*" (*Mémoire*, p. 42, emphasis added). As the ultimate expression of the violence of the state-gravedigger, the act of burying evokes also the frightening vision of the cemetery, where the zombi's martyrdom begins; this act, therefore, constantly haunts the text either through an un-ending repetition of the terminology in our preceding quotation or through im-ages taken from the same realm. Here is an apocalyptic description of the "Building" (Haiti) after the ravages of the Duvalier shock: "The mortar is gone, the iron is melted, the beams are sagging, the roof and walls are collapsed in a blinding dust cloud. Down to the trenches which vomited up the foundations" (p. 71). Etienne's equivalent expression is: "The city shrunk" (*Nègre*, p. 91). Claude, on the other hand, is perched on his balcony and has the feeling of dominating the events. He abandons himself to his favorite occupation: dream-ing. In the dream he sees himself armed with the submachine gun of revenge, mowing down *macoute* after *macoute* and presiding at the liberation of the peo-ple "from subjugation" (*Mémoire*, p. 28), that is, from their zombi state. Paul refuses for the same reason "to leave his balcony. It is his kingdom, as he says, his control tower" (p. 27).

Among the negative images we find the hole, the symbol of a strangulated country. It is also, through its association with the paradigm of death, the com-mon grave of the cemetery, the place for burying. In the last scenes of *Moins l'Infini* it provides an allegorical effect. On the contrary, the predominant pres-ence of the tree in Phelps' narrative is a good omen for the opposition. Père Emile undertakes his antigovernment maneuvering without the fear of being caught because his house is well protected against intrusion by spies: "The climbing plants all over formed a protective shield" (*Moins*, p. 55). The branches of Claude's nutmeg tree will play the same role of "protective shield" in *Mém-oire en Colin-Maillard*.

However, the great reserve of images come above all from the vital elements of fire and water. If everything that burns and reduces things to ashes indicates a reference to Duvalier, the watery element applies to him as well as to his adversaries of the opposition, not indiscriminately, though. Water in the form of rain, clouds or a simple trickle announces Duvalier's deluge, while the true symbol of resistance, the source of liberating patriotism, is the sea. Only through contact with its salt, according to the belief of the people, can the dezombifi-cation process be initiated. Etienne describes a torture session in prison: "Rain is falling. . . . This rainy weather gives Port-au-Prince the appearance of death. . . . The rain is raging. . . . Like atomic bombs, these raindrops on my head, these balls of fire on my skin" (*Nègre*, pp. 11–13). Comparing the good old days with the bitterness of today, Phelps weeps over the fate of his "sand of marine cities. . . . City of the sands of childhood, ignominiously trapped by the September rains" (*Moins*, p. 176). (François Duvalier was elected on September 22, 1957.)

On many occasions we have seen how the recourse to metaphor can affect the meaning of a whole narrative sequence. At the end of *Moines l'Infini* the optimism of the militants, who have regrouped after the vicissitudes of battle, cannot be taken seriously, particularly since the text chooses precisely that mo-ment to announce Marco's death as if to show his friends the limits of a man's courage. The optimism is, however, firmly underscored by Père Emile's final act, the metaphorical equivalent of an act of exorcism: "He raised his arm over his greying head and his fingers touched a ray of the setting sun" (p. 127)—the opposite of the act of *descending* into the "common grave."

Finally, we must understand the contribution of those signs to the reading of works produced and published in Haiti. Is that not the most convenient way possible to defy the system without attracting the thundering revenge of the government? What could be taken for pure dilettantism in Phelps' or Etienne's case now turns into an appeal inasmuch as the author intends to deliver a seditious political message. Rézia Régulier's monologue, at the end of *Fils de misère* is very revealing. She refers to a "bloodthirsty Hydra furiously crossing the country from time to time . . . toppling everything in its way, sowing destruction and ruin, and not retreating until everything was trampled and sacked, carrying away some of the bravest men of the nation in its *inflamed* mouth" (p. 197, emphasis added). These are the same images with which Phelps describes the apocalyptic collapse of the "Building." Guessing who is the present reincarnation of that zombifying monster spewing fire and ashes is an easy task. Colimon, in order to translate the feelings of her heroine, uses the marine metaphor through which other authors already testified to the revolutionary determination of the opposition: "as if she were . . . the *rising tide*" (p. 196, emphasis added). Likewise, the way the author expresses the state of fear and panic gripping the country when the army savagely intervenes against the inoffensive high school students echoes the militant tone of Phelps' and Etienne's writing and is tantamount to a political statement: "This country, *tightened in a vice of fire*, wasn't it really a picture of those souls frightened by the announcement of some *cataclysm*!. . . . 'Merci!' cried the *stones, threaded by the sharpened darts of this equatorial noon*" (p. 190, emphasis added).

Depestre belongs to a different family because of the metaphorical thrust of his language. His use of the symbols of fire and water is generally associated with erotic motives. His style is more classical and, therefore, less personal. His images fall easily into Bachelard's universal categories of the femininity of "psychisme hydrant" and the sexual impulses of the pyromaniac.[20] Moreover, the image of the woman who "allows the marvelously erect flames to lick her naked body" (*Alléluia*, p. 14) does not spring from Depestre's poetry. The imagery was simply less provocative in *Minerai noir* and *Journal d'un animal marin*.[21]

The realm of contemporary Haitian fiction reaches well beyond the perspective offered here. A more elaborate study would certainly make room for powerful anti-Duvalier fictional texts like Dorsinville's *Mourir pour Haiti . . .* and Emile Ollivier's *Paysage de l'aveugle*.[22] We should also include Michel Georges Lescouflair, author of a collection of short stories, *Cinq minutes d'escale*,[23] and others who chose to flee from the political arena—their sacred right—and to exchange that game "marked by blood" (*Fils*, p. 196) for another whose calm recalls the times of happy innocence, the good old days.[24] The great majority of novelists and writers of short stories, in the diaspora as well as in Haiti, clearly prefer to face reality. The Haitian literature of this generation, as the product of a shocking and brutal period, intends to be shocking and brutal not by compromising esthetic qualities but by renewing them auspiciously instead. By acting that way, these authors pay tribute to man, in whom they believe obstinately, through all the vicissitudes of "the period of the great blackness" (*Moins*, p. 153). Etienne's crucified man discovers to his relief that, even among the torturers, "even in our hell, love can still exist" (*Nègre*, p. 104). All the voices unite in this challenge to civic and moral defeatism. Depestre: " 'Yes', said Postel, 'Hope still has doors in Port-au-Roi' [Port-au-Prince]" (*Mât*, p. 140). Or Phelps: "Because the time of Infinity will be born again, passing from the least to the most, through our hands clenched into fists, turned blue on the trigger, hands holding arms and hands of bullets" (*Moins*, p. 90).

Happiness is not a gift; it must be earned through a merciless struggle against the tremendous forces of zombification. The writers, who are—fortunately— idealists, have no doubt about the outcome. In a letter to his mother Etienne's hero predicts with absolute certainty his triumphant return to the homeland after the extermination of the enemy: "Dear mother, it is time to return to the home-land. I swear that you will see other faces after the massacre of the black rulers of Haiti, other sands from the sea and other shells, too" (*Nègre*, p. 42). Invin-cible forces of the sea!

If the dream took longer to become reality than the revolutionary patience could endure—after all, one should not forget that a quarter of a century has already been spent under the Duvaliers!—what changes may then occur in the political statement of the fictional discourse?

NOTES

1. Jean Price-Mars, *Ainsi parla l'Oncle* (1928; reprint ed., Ottawa: Editions Le-méac, 1973), p. 263.

2. Title of a novel by Léon Laleau, *Le Choc* (1932; reprint ed., Port-au-Prince: Edi-tions de l'An 2.000, Imprimerie Centrale, no date). In this novel Laleau analyzes the impact of the occupation on the Haitian elite.

3. See Robert Rotberg and Christophe Olague, *Haiti, the Politics of Squalor* (Bos-ton: Houghton Mifflin, 1971). Also Bernard Diederich and Al Burt, *Papa Doc: The Truth about Haiti Today* (New York: McGraw-Hill, 1969).

4. René Depestre, *Pour la révolution, pour la poésie* (Ottawa: Editions Leméac, 1974).

5. See Graham Green, *The Comedians* (New York: Viking Press, 1966), and Gérard de Villiers, *Requiem pour tonton macoutes* (Paris: Plon, 1971).

6. *Tonton macoute* is the nickname for the frightening militiamen officially called National Security Volunteers. Originally, the phrase *tonton macoute* referred to a folk scarecrow whose function was to punish bad children.

7. See Cary Hector and Charles Pierre-Jacques, "Des zombis à l'université," *Col-lectif Paroles* 5 (April-May 1980):23–25.

8. Ibid.

9. Gérard Pierre-Charles, *Radiographie d'une dictature: Haiti et Duvalier* (Montreal: Editions Nouvelle Optique, 1973).

10. Quoted by Jonathan Culler, *Structuralist Poetics* (Ithaca, N.Y.: Cornell University Press, 1975), p. 75.

11. We have not been able to locate Pierre Clitandre's *Cathédrale du mois d'août*. For Firmin Joseph, it is a novel "in which the drama of the exodus of the Haitian people is described in all its brutality," see *La Nouvelle Haïti Tribune* (New York) 3, no. 61 (1981):5. Until his recent expulsion from Haiti, Clitandre resided in Port-au-Prince. Among new works inspired by the ordeal of the Haitian refugees (like their brutal and well-published expulsion from Cayo Lobos, a Bahamian island, in November 1980; the incarceration and trial of thousands of them in Miami; the drowning of dozens of them near the Florida coast), we recommend Jean-Claude Charles' book, *De si jolies petites plages* (Paris: Stock, 1982).

12. Karl Toulanmanche, *Epaves* (Paris: Pierre J. Oswald, 1972). Pierre Carrié's novel *Bonjour, New York* (Montreal: Ville St. Laurent, 1972), should also be mentioned here. The void left by the works of fiction of emigrated Haitian writers will be filled efficiently by the popular theater, whose success is proven by the plays of René Audain in New York and Fritz Dossous in Boston.

13. See *Report on the Situation of Human Rights in Haiti* (Washington, D.C.: Organization of American States, 1979).

14. Concerning this attitude, one should read the first chapter of *Mourir pour Haiti ou les croisés d'Esther* (Paris: Editions L'Harmattan, 1980), in which Roger Dorsinville offers a brilliant depiction of "that panic of souls" (p. 9). This novel is an excellent testimony about the psychological wounds caused by the zombification process.

15. Georges Anglade, *Mon Pays d'Haïti* (Port-au-Prince: Editions de l'action sociale, 1977), p. 2.

16. Gérard Etienne, *Dialogue avec mon ombre* (Ottawa: Editions Francophones du Canada, 1972), p. 96.

17. See *Report on Haiti*, chap. 4, pp. 43–49.

18. René Depestre, *Poète à Cuba* (Paris: Jean P. Oswald, 1976), p. 94.

19. Gérard Etienne writes in his *Dialogue*: "So we will build lunar cities for the earth to be recreated according to the poet's predictions and the awakening of the people thirsty for light" (p. 135). This is clearly a metaphorical language. When certain novelists confuse the country's future with the (hypothetical!) happiness of the childhood paradise, their thought must not be interpreted in a narrowly positivistic manner.

20. See Gaston Bachelard, *L'Eau et les rêves* (Paris: José Corti, 1942), p. 8, and *La psychoanalyse du feu* (Paris: Gallimard, 1938), p. 89.

21. See René Depestre, *Minerai noir* (Paris: Présence Africaine, 1956) and *Journal d'un animal marin* (Paris: Seghers, 1964).

22. Emile Ollivier, *Paysage de l'aveugle* (Montréal: Editions Pierre Tisseyre, 1977).

23. Michel Georges Lescouflair, *Cinq minutes d'escale* (Port-au-Prince: Editions Caraïbes, 1977).

24. It may be useful to note that Depestre's *Alléluia* is a collection of erotic stories without any real political connotation.

Central America _____

9

The World of the West Indian Black in Central America: The Recent Works of Quince Duncan

Lisa E. Davis

In his most recent novel, *La paz del pueblo* (1978), the black Costa Rican author Quince Duncan uses a brief scene in a Puerto Limón bar, on the sultry Atlantic coast of his country, to distinguish the various racial groups that share the life of that province and the tensions to which they are all subject. When a local black woman defends the activities of Pedro Dull, a young Black of Jamaican descent who has taken up the cause of the striking workers on the banana plantations, another client replies:

"Shut up, Jamaica woman, or we'll throw you out of the country. Go on back to Jamaica, you trash."

"Please not to bother the customer," said the Chinaman, "here everyone comes to buy in peace."

"You shut up too, you filthy Chinaman. I don't know why there are so many foreigners here. And they come to put ideas into the heads of peaceable people. For God's sake!"

"The Black and the Chinaman know how to defend themselves without any help," Pérez said, "but you are insulting them and I don't want them to have the impression that all Costa Ricans are like you. So, either you shut up or I'll give you one to remember, you son of a bitch!"[1]

In a manner that recalls Duncan's earlier fiction *La paz del pueblo* explores the peculiar pressures that characterize the province of Limón in Costa Rica, an area on the Atlantic coast that has highlands and whose population is still overwhelmingly Black, of West Indian and principally Jamaican origin.[2] In fact, since he began his career as an author in 1968, Quince Duncan has given himself over to telling the story of the province of Limón, where he was raised, and of this important racial community that has remained for so many years, for a variety of reasons, isolated and marginal from the mainstream of the national life.

Duncan, himself a descendant of Jamaican workers who began arriving in the newly constructed city of Puerto Limón in 1872, is a writer with deep working-class roots in the provincial countryside. He has practiced a variety of professions from agriculture to commerce and received a fairly unconventional and late education.[3] Duncan has become the spokesman for an entire segment of the population whose history and culture are generally unknown both within the nation and to outsiders. Furthermore, the world of the West Indian Black transplanted onto the soil of Costa Rica, which serves as the basis for Duncan's fiction, is representative of a larger reality, of a linguistic and cultural zone that extends the whole length of the Atlantic coast of Central America: as Duncan puts it in *La paz del pueblo*, "from Kingston to Belize City, from Bluefields to downtown Puerto Limón,"[4] and the Panama, Bocas de Toro, Colón and the Canal. Specifically, the novelist is speaking of the descendants of those Blacks who began to emigrate in large numbers at the end of the nineteenth century from the bankrupt islands of the British Empire—principally from Jamaica, but also from Barbados, Saint Kitts and others—to the republics of Central America, an emigration that mushroomed in the first decade of the twentieth century with the construction of the Panama Canal. The work for which these laborers contracted varied—railroad construction, the Canal, the banana industry—along with their destination. There seems to be a cultural continuity along the Atlantic coast of Central America perceptible today and reflected in literary works by both Latin Whites and Mestizos and by Blacks of West Indian ancestry.

A few examples of how this basically Caribbean and English-speaking culture survives, changes and functions in literature include the polemic short stories of the Guatemalan Alfonso Enrique Barrientos, *Cuentos de Belice, Stories from Belize* (1961).[5] The animating spirit and tone of these narratives, which denounce British imperialism in the region while showing real human concern for the mostly black citizenry, are summed up in a letter from Nathaniel Brown of Orange Walk to the queen. In the story, "Nat Brown" the protagonist complains,

When we were taken prisoners in my native land, and before our trip to Belize, many promises were made to us, promises of enjoying things which we thought much superior to what we had in Jamaica. . . . The descendants of the original group from Jamaica never saw themselves free from the forced labor impossed [sic] nor were given the benefit of the burial ground. It is well for your Majesty to know that when we die our bodies are thrown to the sea, if we pass away in Belize, and into the rivers if it happens in other districts of this immense territory.[6]

Moving south to the Atlantic coast of Nicaragua, an area of prime importance in the plans for national development drawn up by the victorious Frente Sandinista, two black poets of great potential in our opinion, David Macfield and Carlos Rigby, share a common cultural heritage in the region around Bluefields, a region traditionally impoverished, largely English-speaking, Black in population, and isolated from the rest of the country. Several selections of their poetry can be read in the important volume *Poesía nicaragüense* (1973).[7] Nevertheless, it is another Nicaraguan poet, Iván Uriarte, also from the Bluefields area but Latin by birth, who defines most succinctly the black presence on the coast and the isolation of that area from the political and cultural life of the rest of the country. Verses from his poem "Bluefields" give voice to the problems of linguistic and psychological diversity:

In Bluefields the Blacks grow up
Beneath the signboards of hotels and saloons,
Hanging around on the fringes of the China Club,
Singing ballads on the dock
In an unconcerned English,
Perched upon mammoth sacks of beans.

Mr. Molly was a respectable Blackman,
The owner of a small line of barges.
We used to drink highballs in the afternoon,
And he told me of places so faraway,
Like Hong Kong, Manila, Java . . .
"But I'dont [sic] know the Segovias,"
He always concluded sadly.[8]

But perhaps the case that has historically proved most compelling and difficult of resolution has been that of the West Indian Blacks in Panama, a country that welcomed a massive immigrant labor force from the English-speaking Antilles—first from Jamaica and then from Barbados—for the construction of the railroad connecting the Atlantic and Pacific coasts and subsequently for the Canal. The fate of the vast majority of those who did not return to the islands remained in doubt for many years. Witness the early declarations of the distinguished Panamanian poet Demetrio Korsi, who used Blacks as a folkloric motif in numerous compositions, including the well-known "Incident from a Cumbia" ("An Indian's complaint and a Blackman's cry/from within the cantina of Pancha Manchá").[9] In conformity with the purists who jealously defended Panama's white, Latin and Spanish-speaking identity, Korsi joined forces with those elements in government who actively sought the mass deportation of West Indians. In 1926 he said: "Let us send to their islands the sixty or seventy thousand West Indians who infest our cities of Panama and Colón. . . . The edict to expulse these parasitic multitudes must be written, the same way the Moors were forcibly removed in the fifteenth century from the Iberian Peninsula by the Spanish."[10] By the same token, while certain Panamanian writers like Joaquín Beleño Cedeño (born in 1922), author of the novels *Luna verde* (1951), *Gamboa Road Gang* (1960), and *Curundú* (1963), have treated West Indian Blacks sympathetically, a recent study by Roberto de la Guardia, "Los negros del Istmo de Panama," prefers to see many Panamanian Blacks, descendants of workers who laid the railroad or dug the Canal generations ago, as foreigners: "There is an obvious limitation on this presentation. This study deals with the Blacks of the Isthmus of Panama, so the West Indians are excluded since they have only recently arrived and are still unassimilated."[11] On the other hand, it is obvious that to ignore the dynamic role of the West Indian Black in the contemporary Panamanian social framework would be unrealistic, as their cultural and economic inroads have been considerable. According to one very recent commentator, university professor, essayist and editor Nils Castro, speaking of the Panamanians of West Indian origin, they have left a profound imprint on Colón and on the capital, while "they still constitute the principal component of the industrial working class, those who operate the Canal."[12]

In fact, Panama has doubtless played a singular role in the fortunes of West Indians in Central America. In the case of the Costa Rican Blacks it has been a refuge that promised work and survival in the tragic years after the strike against United Fruit in 1934, which served as a background for Quince Duncan's *La paz del pueblo*. As one character who wants to leave Puerto Limón for San José, the capital, is warned by a companion:

"As long as León Cortés is President of the country, I don't advise you to do that. . . . Haven't you realized that all the Blacks are going to Panama?"

"Logical. There's no work. If United Fruit goes to the Pacific Coast, there's no work.

"And why don't you go to the Pacific? Why don't all you Blacks go to the Pacific? They're going to plant bananas there too, didn't you know? Want me to tell you why? Because there's a law that forbids it. León Cortés just got rid of all the Blacks who were working on the railroad to the Pacific. He only left one, because the man was a personal friend of his brother's. . . . You can't go to San José, black boy. You have only two routes to choose from: Panama or stay here."

"I could go to Jamaica. . . . "

"Don't be ridiculous."[13]

And later on in the novel Pedro Dull, in imminent danger of arrest for murder and subversive political activities, is advised: "The strike's over, Pedro. Everything's shot to hell. Go on down to Panama."[14]

Apparently, some knowledge of the history of the economic development of the Puerto Limón area and its black population in relation to the rest of Costa Rica is essential in order to appreciate the significance of references like these and many others throughout the novel. While basically a novel of passion revolving around Pedro Dull and the beautiful Sitaira, both descended from illicit unions between White and Black on the island of Jamaica, this work attempts to provide as complete and evocative a portrait as possible of what life is like among the people of Limón—their past, present (in terms of the late 1930s) and future. Economic issues loom large in the lives of the characters in view of the history from which they spring.

Briefly, as the story is told in Duncan's *El negro en Costa Rica* (1972), West Indian Blacks were contracted to build, at the end of the nineteenth century, the section of the proposed railroad that would run from San José to Limón, a section later leased to the United Fruit Company under the name of the Northern Railway Company. From that perilous section of track, which passed through the lowland jungles and swamps, all native Costa Rican laborers had been withdrawn "for health reasons."[15] While the stories of tragedy and death among the newly arrived West Indians, mostly Jamaicans, abound in Limón, the testimony of an impartial observer like John H. Melvill, historian of the United Fruit Company, is most poignant for its objectivity. He reports that "more than four thousand perished during the laying of the first twenty-five miles of track" and quotes "an old saying of the time: 'There's a dead man under each crosstie from the sea to the mountain.' "[16] When the railroad was finished, one of the American engineers, Minor Cooper Keith, using the newly constructed facilities, founded a company for the production and export of bananas, which soon merged with another similar company in the United States to form the United Fruit Company. From that point until the 1930s, the banana industry, with all that it represented in terms of U.S. economic imperialism and the exploitation of labor, was the basis for the economy in the province of Limón and practically the only source of employment available to the West Indian, who was still considered a foreigner and a British subject, even though he had been born into a second generation of immigrants on Costa Rican soil. It was also established policy that Blacks could not go into the interior of the country beyond the town of Turrialba, which lies about halfway between Puerto Limón and San José, and could not become Costa Rican citizens.[17] Following the gradual decline of the soil under banana cultivation, together with the disastrous waves of disease that came up from Panama and destroyed much of the crop, the year 1934 saw the explosion of decades of frustration in a lengthy strike, an unexpected defiance for United Fruit. As Duncan puts it ironically in *La paz del pueblo*: "United Fruit lost millions to that strike. The Company that has given so much to Costa Rica. And the worst part is the bad example."[18] As a result of that bad example given by the banana workers of Limón, United Fruit was prompted to move its entire operation from the Atlantic to the Pacific Coast, converting the area around Golfito into a new sphere of foreign capital domination. In line with its racist policies and as recompense for the Blacks' participation in the strike, United Fruit secured the active complicity of the Costa Rican government in passing a law (December 1934) by which "it is forbidden in the area of the Pacific coast to employ colored people in the aforementioned jobs [the production and development of the banana]."[19]

The literature of Costa Rica, particularly that authored by writers who are politically left of center has recalled on other occasions the circumstances that prompted and the events that grew out of the strike of 1934. The well-known novel *Mamita Yunai* (1941)—"Yunai" being a phonetic re-creation in Spanish of the "United" of United Fruit—by Carlos Luis Fallas (1911–1966), begins by explaining the exodus of Blacks toward the Panamanian border:

They are about to turn this property over to United Fruit and it is almost abandoned since all the "Spanish" have gone to the Pacific, and there are very few colored people; the same thing's happening all over this area. Almost all the Blacks you see in these carts are going to the other side, trying to get across the Panama. . . . The Whites have the chance to go to the Pacific, but us? Don't you see they even invent obstacles to the legalization of our citizenship. There's no work; we can't work the land, and they won't let us make a living on the Pacific Coast. . . . Do we have to die of hunger, then? There aren't just one or two of us, but thousands of Costa Rican Blacks who cannot just become thieves and bandits. That's why we have to get to Panama.[20]

Likewise, Joaquín Gutiérrez' *Puerto Limón* (1950) has as its background the strike, and it is also notable for its sympathetic portraits of the Blacks of Limón, especially the railroad man Tom Winkelman and Azucena "his only sister: Forty years ago they had arrived with their father from Jamaica to work on the railroad."[21] Moreover, with Joaquín Gutiérrez, himself born in Puerto Limón in 1918, we draw closer to an intimate and multidimensional portrayal of the black population in an area that the author knew much better than the average Costa Rican. Whereas Fallas, in *Mamita Yunai*, with the noblest of humanitarian motives, depicts the Blacks only as a suffering collectivity that he sees from the outside—"I was the only white man traveling in the railroad car, and since I don't understand English, I couldn't even entertain myself by eavesdropping on the animated conversation of a group of young black women"[22]— Gutiérrez tries to penetrate and re-create in Azucena and Tom something of their individual aspirations, joys, pains and frustrations. For example, when it is discovered that Azucena has been stricken with leprosy and will never return to her work and family, the author muses on her simplicity and the cruelty of fate in the tropical world of Puerto Limón:

This time we were dealing with a black woman as innocent as a child, who had tried all her life to be a good cook, to keep the floors shining like mirrors and to memorize all the hymns of the half dozen religions practiced in Puerto Limón so that she could go on Sunday from service to service, from little wooden church to little wooden church, singing them all. That was her joy, her greatest joy, almost as great as the one she felt when she was granted permission and went to her brother's house to mend her little nephews' clothes and to leave for Tom, with shyness and infinite tenderness, under his pillow, the envelope that contained her paycheck so that he could take care of the little ones, so alone and sad since the death of Ruby, Tom's wife.[23]

Although the depictions of Tom and Azucena still suffer under the weight of stereotypes and the limitations of a Latin writer viewing an essentially alien culture from a certain distance, Gutiérrez does give to each a well-defined personality, which manifests itself in several facets of their lives, and a tragic depth of character.

Nevertheless, the fiction of Quince Duncan opens a plethora of new possibilities, because he speaks eloquently and knowingly from within the world of the Black of West Indian ancestry still only partially integrated into the mainstream of Costa Rican life. From the point of view of the Latin outsider, Duncan provides, in the words of Joaquín Gutiérrez, "an unusual vision with which he observes us from within through a small opening, looks at us from an angle that is accessible only to Costa Rican Blacks."[24] Or, as Fabián Dobles explains in his prologue to *El negro en la literatura costarricense* (1975), "previous writers who took the Blacks of Limón as their subject matter belonged to the dominant Spanish-speaking culture, and their works are their own reflections at different moments as they see themselves in the black mirror of the province of Limón."[25] Duncan, on the other hand, "speaks and feels from within the mirror."[26] From the standpoint of the black minority in Costa Rica, Duncan provides a voice that did not exist before, given the general poverty and isolation of the province of Limón, to say nothing of the language problem on the Atlantic coast, where until recently the West Indian population clung fervently to English and some semblance of British culture as a bulwark against rejection or assimilation by the country's Latin majority.[27] Indeed, within the milieu a professional writer of Quince Duncan's talents, and especially in Spanish prose, is still something of a rarity. Along these lines he relates that when his first book of stories, *El pozo y una carta*, appeared in July 1969, he went to Limón to sell it personally. As he later confirmed, with typical irony, "the people with whom I spoke told me it was amazing that a black man should write anything."[28]

In the first place, Duncan's unique position in the literature of his country derives from his overriding concern with the destiny of his people, which—though he writes with intensity and skill on other topics—is never far from his mind. The task he has set for himself as a man of letters remains that of contributing "effectively to the social, economic, political and cultural integration of the Blacks of the province of Limón, on a precisely equal footing with all other citizens."[29] And toward that goal we feel he has advanced considerably in his latest publications. Whereas his early works conveyed consistently a realistic vision of the Black's historical struggles against economic and natural hardships, against alienation and official rejection as a foreigner and on behalf of some sense of pride and identity, his more mature works add clarity and depth to that vision.

In both the novel *La paz del pueblo* and in the short stories of *La rebelión Pocomía y otros relatos* (1976), Duncan explores the historical, mythical and spiritual roots of his people in their triumphs and defeats, returning on several occasions to memories of Africa and its magic, the dark passage, the agony of slavery and the world of corrupted institutions and hypocrisy shared by Whites and Blacks on the island of Jamaica before the emigration to Central America.

From the outset the author suggests the African roots of this society, an inheritance that manifests itself above all in religious rites of an ancient and marginal character. Together with the gods, beliefs and a particular vision of the world, which have been preserved through the centuries of slavery, these rites reappear on the Atlantic coast of Central America as a focal point for identification, affirmation and rebellion against the new oppressor. As the author relates in "La rebelión Pocomía," the religion of the ancestors can provide a force to unite Blacks—"those from Saint Lucia, those from Saint Kitts, the Jamaicans" [30]—in their uprising against "a railroad of blood where death cuts off a thousand lives in the first twenty-five miles." [31] Under the direction of Mamá Bull the dancers repeat the rites of the Pocomía or Pocomanía sect, which went under both names as a minority cult of famous practitioners of white and black magic with devotées in Jamaica and Limón:

They dance counterclockwise; grunt out their gloomy chant with its dark beauty, words that make the bravest of the Jamaicans tremble. Men's naked chests, women's breasts exposed. The agility in male and female legs. The beating of drums with a Caucasian flare. Phrases adopted from Africa. Cadences from the Caribbean. The dampness of sweat on bodies that fall into a cataleptic state for hours. [32]

All this ritual proceeds to the accompaniment of the Protestant hymn: "Let us go together to the River Jordan/where the joyous and holy Word sounds/that Word which brings down on us grace divine/Let us go together to the River Jordan." [33] The latter furnishes one key to the peculiar mixture in the British islands of African religion, particularly the concept of *obeah*—or power, and by extension, spiritual power that can be used to protect oneself or to attack and harm enemies—and the Protestantism of the masters. [34] It is the same Mamá Bull who conducts Pedro Dull through the rites of spirit possession in *La paz del pueblo*:

But an unexpected wave of spasms invaded Pedro's body and he began to balance himself like the others, sweating, his eyes lost in space, his hand shaking violently in the wind; . . . and Pedro was panting uncontrollably, between cold and heat, the pallor of Mrs. Mariot's face tormented him, and the echoes of Sitaira, and the shine of Mamá Bull's skin. The God [Cuminá] became one with him to dance beside His people. . . . Restored, the God Himself, Yoruba drums in the night, faraway mysteries that emanated from the spirits of the dead ancestors [Samamfo]. [35]

By the keeping of these rituals, Pedro seeks to be made strong and to be protected, as did the followers of Pocomía who rose up against their bosses, because "we did not make this law. . . . Our law stayed in Africa!" (p. 174).

While "La rebelión Pocomía" takes us back to the epoch of railroad construction, the story "La leyenda de José Gordon" from the same collection gives literary form to a local myth of a later era, enhancing the stature and dignity of the hero, who stood on principle, was dismissed and fought throughout his charmed life against the abuses of the "Compañía Bananer," United Fruit. Accompanied like other mythical figures of folklore by a supernatural heat, and possessed of inordinate physical strength and a great thirst, José Gordon demands of the enemy

that the common laborers, with their sweaty skins and the constant smell of green bananas on them, should live in the Zone [where the high officials of the company lived], which would have meant, according to Mr. Brutt, the "bankruptcy of the enterprise." And also, he said, it would have brought certain disaster to comply with Gordon's alternative proposal: that the bosses live like everybody else in humble huts and small caves, simply because all of them would have resigned, and in that case, the stockholders themselves would have had to come and direct the business, and in that case they would have done better to take their money out of Costa Rica altogether, since in the last analysis there are many other countries ready and eager to receive them.[36]

According to the legend, besides being driven by a revolutionary ideology, José Gordon was in truth a man called by God, evidently the Christian one, to right the wrongs perpetrated against his people:

He had that fever for many days while he traveled into the deep forest, living in defiance of the insects, biting into wild fruits and quenching his thirst with water from small mountain streams. On Sunday he returned to the town and went into the temple. Those who were present recounted afterwards how his face shone like a star and how his words, spoken haltingly, beyond rational comprehension, sounded.[37]

On the other hand, the myths, legends and ancient religious practices of the region go beyond the bounds of traditional Christianity, and the local church—possibly Methodist, Baptist or even Anglican[38]—appears too tied to reactionary social and economic values to satisfy popular needs. For example, "Mrs. Been Brown, with her light skin, and her money, even though her husband is very black" (p. 77), a pillar of the local Protestant Church, whose members consistently accuse Mrs. Mariot, her daughter Sitaira, and Pedro Dull of practicing *obeah*, attacks the strikers and the forces that stand behind them:

Last night I was listening to a speech by one of those followers of Garvey, those madmen who insist that we all go back to Africa, to barbarism, to paganism. They were talking about the strike, which, I understand, affects the interests of a prominent member of this Church, and I hoped to hear from them some indication of solidarity, some hint of justice. I said to myself that although they were wrong, they had good intentions. But no: All I heard was about great African empires that only exist in their minds, and about the right that people have to resist oppression, and above all, the right that Blacks have to resist oppression by any means they see fit. I ask all of you: Is that Christianity? The Spirit speaks for me. . . . Hallelujah! (pp. 149–50).

Mrs. Brown's attitude is understandable given her husband's position as a gentleman farmer and black capitalist, on two hundred acres "all of them rented from United Fruit at a minimum cost" (p. 88); the propertied Mr. Brown denounces Pedro Dull and even the ex-president of the Republic, Ricardo Jiménez Oreamuno (1932–1936), as "Communist" (pp. 88, 156) because of their sympathy for the workers. Once again, according to the church congregation, Pedro is not only an outside agitator who has come "with his poisoned ideas, to stain the peace of this town, to sully people's good names, to preach hatred and not love," (p. 149) but also another "of Garvey's followers who want a new country" (p. 159).

In fact, there are several references in the novel to Marcus Garvey, the Jamaican Black of pure African blood, descended from Maroons who founded the Universal Negro Improvement Association, an organization that preached black solidarity in the 1920s to an enthusiastic audience, including the Blacks of Limón and other parts of Spanish America. Garvey actually worked for a time on a banana plantation in the province, but returned in later years as a spokesman for his Black Star Line and other financial projects. In Limón, Garvey was unfailingly successful in the number of members pledged to the U.N.I.A. and in the quantity of contributions received.[39] Doubtless Garvey's message of black pride and solidarity threatened the hierarchical notions held by Mrs. Been Brown, who proposed that "all of us know each other; we know that we are black, that Blacks should not set themselves against other Blacks, that each knows his place and should stay in his place, and that we all should behave consistently as though we were the children of God" (p. 150).

Black solidarity appears a remote possibility when such divisions as we find in *La paz del pueblo* are drawn along economic, class and color lines. Witness the outcome of "La rebelión Pocomía," when the Jamaicans join the Latin authorities—"some Captain named Castro, or Pérez, or López"[40]—against the other Blacks after the uprising. Mamá Bull, with her dying breath, "cursed all the Jamaicans of the province of Limón. They will always be like crabs in a barrel; . . . no one will ever get out because another will push him down again."[41] And Jean Paul, a rebel leader from Saint Lucia, became another victim of the rout, dying "a forgotten death on the island of La Uvita, riddled by bullets. They say he was finished off by a black man."[42]

This brings us to a primary tenet of Duncan's fiction. Despite a lengthy history of alienation and exploitation, it generally encourages a movement toward understanding and integration on the part of both black minority and Latin majority in Costa Rica. While promoting a knowledge and appreciation of the black past and heritage, including figures like Garvey, Duncan has made his cause not black separatism and not emigration to the United States, but the achievement of a united country, with equal rights, respect and opportunity for all its citizens. Toward that purpose the local Latin population is depicted consistently in its relations with the Blacks of Limón in either a realistic or a favorable light. Solidarity across racial lines is a fairly common note. In *La paz del pueblo*, Pedro Dull takes up the cause of the workers, who have struck Mr. Brown's plantation, because López, who lived at one time with Pedro's mother and treated the boy with great kindness, has been dismissed for having tuberculosis. Brown, a black man, complains about "that young man Pedro. . . . I understand he's a relative or friend of López and he took it upon himself to talk with the workers . . . to poison them against me. They want me to pay for a doctor for López" (p. 155). Likewise, when Pedro is accused of the murder of Sitaira, who was really killed by Brown's half-crazed son Cató, it is another Latin, Pérez, who defends Sitaira and her family: "Foolishness . . . malicious gossip. I have known that black girl ever since I came here. I slept in their house while I was building my own, and they never charged me anything. The child Sitaira has been very fond of me ever since then, and so has her brother. I know what I'm saying: That woman would never sell herself" (p. 170). Among the working-class citizens a basis exists for cooperation and acceptance, especially if there is some mutual recognition of their common exploitation by authorities in the service of the foreign-based United Fruit. As Duncan says, it is to be hoped that Costa Rica will not remain "with arms crossed and lose Limón" but, on the contrary, will be able to incorporate the province and its multiracial population completely into itself, "transforming itself [Costa Rica] in the process."[43]

In the epigraph to one of the stories from *La rebelión Pocomía y otros relatos*—"Los mitos ancestrales"—in reality an allegorical re-creation of black-white relations throughout the history of colonialism, Duncan expresses an optimistic resolution to the unity of people when quoting Indian A. Sivanandan: "On the margin of European culture . . . the 'coloured' intellectual is an artifact of colonial history. . . . He is a creature of two worlds and of none" (p. 73). His works offer a vision of black society in Costa Rica that had not been available heretofore to the outsider, and through his eloquent voice the history, folklore and sensibility of the Blacks of West Indian ancestry who settled the province of Limón reach us for the first time. Particularly in his most recent publications, we feel that he has made a unique contribution to the understanding of the historical position of the Blacks in his country and has spoken consistently for their integration as equals into that world where they have long been regarded as aliens. As a black Costa Rican writer, Duncan has thrown in his lot with the fusion of two worlds in creating a more progressive open society in his own country and elsewhere, through his writings and through his personal example.

NOTES

1. Quince Duncan, *La paz del pueblo* (San José: Editorial Costa Rica, 1978), pp. 171–72. Unless otherwise indicated, this and other translations are mine.

2. In his own *El negro en Costa Rica* (San José: Editorial Costa Rica, 1972), Duncan gives statistics on the black population of Limón, which are consistently complicated by the Costa Rican government's tendency to categorize all Blacks in the province as foreigners and, therefore, not subject to the census. See especially pp. 74–77.

3. *El negro en Costa Rica* has biographies of numerous distinguished Costa Rican Blacks, including that of Duncan himself (p. 249). Duncan's early publications include several collections of short stories—*El pozo y una carta* (San José, Costa Rica: Cuadernos de Arte Popular, 1969), *Bronze* (San José, Costa Rica: Cuadernos de Arte Popular, 1970), *Una canción en la madrugada* (San José: Editorial Costa Rica, 1970)—and two novels—*Hombres curtidos* (Panamá: Cuadernos de Arte Popular, 1971) and *Los cuatro espejos* (San José: Editorial Costa Rica, 1973). For the purposes of this study, however, we have limited our analysis to his most recent works—the aforementioned novel *La paz de pueblo* (1978) and what we consider a very fine collection of short narratives, *La rebelión Pocomía y otros relatos* (San José: Editorial Costa Rica, 1976). We have done so, first, because they are more readily available and may possibly become increasingly so to a reading public outside of Costa Rica, where Duncan already enjoys a reputation for seriousness, excellence and dedication to the art of literature; and second, because these last works demonstrate, in our opinion, a great advance in stylistic maturity and in the author's command over narrative techniques in general. We shall also refer from time to time to two seminal works, which were initiated and brought to fruition under Duncan's aegis and which trace the history of the fortunes of West Indian blacks in their progress toward full integration into the national life of Costa Rica. These volumes are *El negro en Costa Rica*, prepared with the historian Carlos Meléndez Chaverri; and *El negro en la literatura costarricense* (San José: Editorial Costa Rica, 1975), which includes selections that show the changing, and ever more sympathetic, image of the Black as a character in the national literature. It also has a prologue by the leftist author Fabián Dobles. Dobles has written numerous novels and short stories that call for social and political change.

4. Duncan, *La paz del pueblo*, p. 24.

5. This collection of short stories was originally published in 1961, in a bilingual volume with the stories in Spanish followed by a full English translation, and was recently reedited (1978).

6. Alfonso Enrique Barrientos, *Cuentos de Belice*, trans. H. Reina Barios (Guatemala: Centro Editorial del Ministerio de Educación Pública, "José de Piñeda Ibarra," 1961), pp. 65–66.

7. *Poesía nicaraguense*, ed. Ernesto Cardenal (Havana: Casa de las Américas, 1973). The poems of David Macfield appear on pp. 395–406 and those of Carlos Rigby on pp. 547–60.

8. Ibid., p. 490.

9. For the entire poem, see "Incidente de cumbia," *Poesía negra de América*, ed. José Luis González and Mónica Mansour (Mexico: Ediciones Era, 1976), pp. 143–44.

10. Demetrio Korsi, ed., *Antología de Panamá* (Barcelona: Maucci, 1926), p. 8.

11. *Lotería*, no. 250 (1976): 69. This essay was awarded the national Premio Ensayo Ricardo Miró for 1976, a very prestigious prize. For this reason the text appeared in the literary review *Lotería* which is financed, as one might suppose, by funds taken in by the national lottery.

12. Nils Castro, "El Istmo entre los Caribes" ("The Isthmus Between the Caribbean Seas"), *Casa de las Américas* 20, no. 118 (1980): 83. For more about the troubled history of West Indian Blacks (Chumbos) in Panama, see Leslie B. Rout, Jr., *The African Experience in Spanish America* (New York and London: Cambridge University Press, 1976), pp. 273–78.

13. Duncan, *La paz del pueblo*, pp. 74–75. León Cortés Castro (1882–1946) was the president of Costa Rica from 1936 to 1940.

14. Ibid., p. 77.

15. Duncan, *El negro en Costa Rica*, p. 62.

16. John H. Melvill, *The Great White Fleet* (New York: Vantage Press, 1976), p. 259.

17. For details on these and other policies of the Costa Rican government, see Duncan, *El negro en Costa Rica*, pp. 205 ff.

18. Duncan, *La paz del pueblo*, p. 89.

19. Duncan, *El negro en Costa Rica*, p. 79. It is worthwhile to point out that no definitive change occurred in this policy of legal discrimination in Costa Rica until after 1949. Then, under the direction of José Figueres, the Partido Liberación Nacional granted to Blacks freedom of movement within the country and opened Costa Rican citizenship to them without restrictions and inordinate delays. For the role of Figueres, see Duncan, *El negro en Costa Rica*, p. 146, and John Patrick Bell, *Crisis in Costa Rica: The Revolution of 1948* (Austin: University of Texas Press, 1971).

20. Carlos Luis Fallas, *Mamita Yunai* (1941; reprint ed., Havana: Ediciones Huracán, Instituto Cubano del Libro, 1975), pp. 22–23.

21. Joaquín Gutiérrez, *Puerto Limón* (1950; reprint ed., Havana: Casa de las Américas, 1977), p. 153.

22. Fallas, *Mamita Yunai*, p. 21.

23. Gutiérrez, *Puerto Limón*, p. 132–33.

24. This comment appears on the back cover of the paperback edition of Duncan's *La paz del pueblo*: "una visión insólita con que nos mira desde adentro por un resquicio por donde sólo los negros costarricenses podrán mirarnos." In fact, very few critical remarks about Duncan's fiction have been published and almost none outside Costa Rica. The one English-speaking critic who has dealt extensively with Quince Duncan and his works before *La rebelión Pocomía y otros relatos* and *La paz del pueblo* has been Richard L. Jackson in his books *The Black Image in Latin American Literature* (Albuquerque: University of New Mexico Press, 1976) and *Black Writers in Latin America* (Albuquerque: University of New Mexico Press, 1979). The former provides an introduction to Duncan and his early writings, while the second book dedicates a chapter entitled "Return to the Origins: The Afro-Costa Rican Literature of Quince Duncan" (pp. 171–79) to the novel *Los cuatro espejos* (1973).

25. In Duncan, *El negro en la literatura costarricense*, p. 8.

26. Ibid., p. 8.

27. See Duncan's brief history of the establishment in Limón of a separate educational system staffed by teachers brought in from Jamaica, with textbooks and instruction in English, in his *El negro en la literatura costarricense*, p. 13.

28. Quoted on the back cover of Duncan's *El negro en Costa Rica*.

29. Duncan, *El negro en la literatura costarricense*, p. 27.

30. Duncan, *La rebelión Pocomía*, p. 9.

31. Ibid., p. 8.

32. Ibid., p. 10. Concerning the history and rituals of the Pocomía or Pocomanía sect, see Duncan in *El negro en Costa Rica*, pp. 104–6.

33. *La rebelión Pocomía*, p. 10.

34. For further information about religious practices among the slaves in Jamaica and

162   Lisa E. Davis

in the southern United States, see Horace Orlando Patterson, *The Sociology of Slavery* (Rutherford, N.J.: Fairleigh Dickinson University Press, 1975), and Albert J. Raboteau, *Slave Religion* (New York: Oxford University Press, 1978).

35. Duncan, *La paz del pueblo*, p. 173. Appended to the novel, we find a *glosario* ("glossary") that explains words peculiar to the culture of Limón that might prove unfamiliar to the general public. For example, "Chumico—deriva de Jamaica, de su pronunciación en inglés. Se aplica a ciudadanos de ese país y por extensión a todos los negros" (p. 191; " . . . derives from Jamaica, from its pronunciation in English. It is applied to citizens of that country and by extension to all Blacks."); "Dopí—aparición; espíritu de persona muerta" (p. 191; " . . . apparition; spirit of a dead person"); and the complete definition of "Samamfo—palabra de origen ashanti que significa lugar o estado en que se encuentran los muertos, o los espíritus de los antepasados" (p. 192; " . . . a word of Ashanti origin that means place or state in which the dead may appear, or generally speaking, the spirits of the ancestors"). Further reference to this work will appear parenthetically in the text.

36. Duncan, *La rebelión Pocomía*, pp. 67–68.

37. Ibid., p. 60.

38. See Duncan, *El negro en Costa Rica*, p. 104, for the various Protestant sects most popular in Limón.

39. See E. David Cronon, *Black Moses: The Story of Marcus Garvey* (Madison: University of Wisconsin Press, 1969), and Carlos Meléndez Chaverri, "El pensamiento de Marcus Garvey," in *El negro en Costa Rica*, pp. 183–203.

40. Duncan, *La rebelión Pocomía*, p. 11.

41. Ibid., p. 12.

42. Ibid.

43. Duncan, *El negro en Costa Rica*, p. 127.

Spanish South America

10

Juyungo/Reading Writing

Jonathan Tittler

> The concepts of *écriture* and *lecture* have been brought to the fore as to divert attention from the author as source and the work as object and focus it instead on two correlated networks of convention: Writing as an institution and reading as an activity.
>
> Jonathan Culler, *Structuralist Poetics*

The word *juyungo* is unfamiliar to the Western ear. It is a curse, an utterance motivated by fear of the other. The mere enunciation of *juyungo*, a paronym originating in the language of Ecuador's Cayapa Indians, signals racism. An echo of the *yungla* (the jungle), juyungo urges to action, to violence; as with prophecy, word precedes deed. Juyungo's inscription also urges to action, but the written word attains from its context new meaning and effects an inversion of its spoken form. Adalberto Ortiz' *Juyungo: Historia de un negro, una isla y otros negros* (1943) encourages not destruction but reconciliation, compenetration, the transcendence of differences.[1] The movement from orality (saying "juyungo") to literality (writing "juyungo" and *Juyungo*) is thus more than a change in mode of enunciation. It mandates a conceptual shift, one we find mirrored in the following passage: "But juyungo is the devil, juyungo is the monkey, juyungo is evil, juyungo is the Black" (p. 51). Just as juyungo's equivalent in the quotation evolves in a series of predicate nominatives from "devil" to "Black," that is, from a malediction to a neutral substantive, *Juyungo* abandons the notion of a hierarchy of race in favor of a dialectic of color.

Published in 1943 after being judged the best new Ecuadorian novel the year before, *Juyungo* has enjoyed a crescendo of international critical interest only in the past decade.[2] In the United States the growing movement dedicated to black consciousness has benefited *Juyungo* along with other works falling roughly under the rubric of "black literature." Uncannily advanced for its time, even to the extent of voicing ecological concerns, Ortiz' creation responded to many of the imperatives of contemporary black criticism even before their declaration. *Juyungo* provides the credible characterization demanded by Antonio Olliz Boyd and—in the elaboration of its human metaphors—avoids the caricaturesque buffoonery that Lemuel Johnson finds prevalent in Hispanic literature dealing with Blacks.[3] It does not completely satisfy the more exigent Richard L. Jackson, who recognizes its artistic worth and praises its presentation of a figure evocative of black pride; but he looks upon its solution of miscegenation as "ethnic lynching," a threat to black identity.[4] Although it is admittedly anachronistic to apply prescriptive notions of the 1960s to a work of the previous generation, *Juyungo*'s ability to measure up to most of those recently devised criteria attests to its conceptual modernity.

Rather than categorize *Juyungo* from the start as a "black novel" and judge it according to the standards imposed by contemporary readers, we suggest a broader interpretation, one that takes into consideration the text as a product of several sets of literary conventions. The major groupings, each of which provides a possible approach to *Juyungo*, are as follows: (1) *criollismo*, or Latin American rural realism; (2) Negritude, or an appreciation for the black experience (in literature, adherence to the "Black Aesthetic"); (3) Ecuadorian nationalism; and (4) modernism, or a perspective that considers language as an autonomous, self-referential universe.

Singling out just one, two, or even three of these aspects, as has been the case until now, will inevitably lead to a partial, distorted reading of the novel. An analysis of all four factors, on the other hand, circumvents the trap of isolating textual ideas from their mode of exposition. That separation is based upon an inadequate notion of the text as consisting in an inviolable, stable core of meaning wrapped in an ornamental and disposable style. A more accurate model of the way texts function is that of a body of writing whose arrangements of constituent elements (repertoire) determines any potential meaning it may embody and whose ultimate meaning resides in the reader's own experience.[5] That is to say, the configuration resulting from the particular disposition of criollista, Negristic, and nationalistic schemata constitutes a unique texture whose effect is inseparable from any conceptual structure that may also be elaborated. It is that literary texture in *Juyungo* that we hope to unveil in the remainder of this essay.

Some basic definitions are in order. Ricardo Latcham has defined criollismo as "a literature of rural or native character, in which the landscape and the focus on atmosphere and local color predominate. . . . It was believed that in the countryside the primitive customs were conserved better, without the contamination of the city, which was more cosmopolitan and whose types were more similar to the Europeans."[6] Criollismo tries to abstract a certain indigenous purity from the dynamic and variegated phenomena of lived experience. Largely ethical in its concerns, the criollista novel of the past century tended to be linear in its temporal development and essayistic in its style. As part of his documentary enterprise the writer of rural realism would attempt in the dialogue passages to reproduce the linguistic patterns peculiar to the region of the novel's setting. The middle-class urban reader thus came into vicarious contact with picturesque native customs, beliefs and rituals.[7] This description at once conveys the conservative nature of criollista literature, which preserves for posterity a faithful image of the past, and reveals how imperfectly that term fits *Juyungo*. *Juyungo* is not a nostalgic snapshot of a bygone era. It does not avoid transmitting local color, but it does so in passing, as the starting point of a motion picture about motion itself.

Negritude is the second body of norms that influences *Juyungo*. A term originating with the Martinican poet Aimé Césaire, Negritude has also been studied by other Francophone writers of the stature of Sartre and Fanon, whose contributions to the study of black culture have not gone unnoticed in the United States. Negritude designates an ethnoliterary perspective that implies an affirmation of the worth of being black and a pride in having one's origin in Africa. The black novel, as it preserves the principally rural black heritage in Latin America, has many points of contact with criollismo, which also includes the novels of the Indian and the Gaucho, or, if we group works geographically, the novels of the coast, the plains, the mountains and the jungle.[8] One obvious difference inherent in the black novel is that the Black is no more native to Latin America than the European, having been brought to the New World by force after the establishment of the surgarcane industry. But like the Indian and the Gaucho, the Black provides an alternative to the Western world view; the black vision bears the seal of authenticity of an oppressed people. In general—and this implies adopting the broad definition advanced by Stanley Cyrus in *El cuento negrista sudamericano* (1973)—black literature creates pathos for the injustices suffered, shows appreciation for the beauty of the black physiognomy, recognizes the hard-earned achievements of Blacks in society and, most recently, applauds an emerging hero: the black intellectual.[9] As a landmark work in the Negritude movement, *Juyungo* must be read partially through the grid of those generic constraints it adopts. It is suspended along the Negritude axis in an intertextual tension with other black novels that preceded it, and it contributes in turn to the context of those which follow it. The numerous allusions herein to other black Spanish-American novels constitute an attempt at beginning to sketch the network of which *Juyungo* forms a part.

A third influence is Ecuadorian nationalism, a force that plays a major role both in shaping the novel's perspective on the world and in bringing *Juyungo* to its conclusion. In regard to the latter, it is in one of the frequent border disputes with Peru (1939–1941) that Lastre loses his life. That loss is counteracted in part by what his action in the war represents: a placing of the question of race within parentheses and a corresponding recognition of more inclusive issues. Irrespective of the angle from which *Juyungo* is related, the novel is liberally sprinkled with allusions to concerns of the *patria chica*: Ecuadorian territorial skirmishes with Colombia, the Conchist (black separatist) rebellion and American cultural imperialism, to name a few. Every time one of these elements appears, we are reminded of the sundry regional conventions and attitudes to which the text adheres and which contribute appreciably to the novel's particular flavor.

Modernism is what preserves *Juyungo's* artistic integrity. Considered to be antithetical to criollismo, modernism seeks not to record the extraliterary world in words but rather to create an ideal linguistic domain of its own. Its "content" ultimately deals with how language works to inform our very conceptions and perceptions of consciousness, literature and the world. In modernism's shift in focus from the signified to the signifier there lies another key distinction from other literary tendencies. As all literature exists only through language, the writer's consideration of the linguistic vehicle as object locates his mental activity structurally anterior to that of writers who take for granted language's transparence. Criollismo, Negritude and Ecuadorian nationalism are thematic qualities, dwelling for the most part on the referential side of language. This should not be construed to mean that works emphasizing the role of the sign are necessarily esthetically superior to those concerned with matters of theme. It is certain, however, that modernism can articulate with the other three literary facets listed above, while the thematic qualities must either conceptually subsume or exclude each other. When we focus on the writing of the novel, then, we are not limiting our scope but rather expanding our horizons, for not only are we able to consider the medium by which the work of art exists but also everything conveyed through that medium. Most important, in recognizing Ortiz' affiliations with modernism, and thereby viewing all *Juyungo*'s textual features as literary phenomena, we open the possibility of understanding how the conveying process works upon us as readers. That is the ultimate justification for reading the writing of *Juyungo*.

That nationalism is a vital force in the Ecuadorian novel can be illustrated amply by comparing *Juyungo* with its archetype, Juan León Mera's *Cumandá, o un drama entre salvajes*, (1879).[10] Recognized as the first novel of the then fledgling nation, *Cumandá* celebrates the landscape, institutions and peoples of Ecuador, and *Juyungo* may be seen as carrying on in that tradition. Reading writing also entails discovering previous texts within the text under scrutiny, for those "model" texts are helpful in highlighting key qualities of the modern counterpart's texture.

Cumandá is a late romantic work, in many ways typical of the Spanish-American *novela de la tierra* that continued to flourish through the 1930s. Historically, *Juyungo*'s writing does not coincide with romanticism. But in spite of the many years and literary movements that separate Ortiz' novel from the romantic period, there are still remarkable parallels that may be drawn between *Juyungo* and *Cumandá*. The racial conflict in both, for example, stems from a parent figure: It is Juyungo's uncle, Commander Lastre, who symbolically dominates the white race. Thus we see the past's role in perpetuating the issue of race. When the younger characters reject the model of their seniors, the split manifests itself as a sort of generation gap, causing the protagonist to be alienated from his/her own racial group. Both novels, too, end in the death of their respective heroic titular figures. We may trace this outcome to what each work sees as an atavistic regression, the descent to a previous stage of cultural development. Cumandá is drowned by the Záparo Indians so that she may accompany her deceased husband, the tribal chief, on his eternal voyage. Within the romantic and Catholic framework of the novel, the conclusion represents a triumph of heathen savagery over the true faith practiced by civilized society. Juyungo in turn dies attempting with a machete to take a machine gun nest manned by more than a dozen Peruvians. Driven by hunger and by grief over the loss of his woman and child, he begs the Peruvians to assist him in his own suicide. Juyungo has to perish because it would appear he is unable to subject his basic, present-oriented drives, reminiscent of Freud's pleasure principle, to the tempering impulse of the reality principle. Eschewing the reasoned judgment he has exercised frequently in the novel, Juyungo reverts to a quasi-bestial condition and destroys himself.

Another quality common to both novels is the scenery. Even though *Cumandá* takes place in the eastern Amazon region and *Juyungo*'s stage is the littoral zone of Esmeraldas Province, the tellurian jungle's role in both works is virtually identical. What Lydia de León Hazera has described in *Cumandá* as "that sensation of fatalism and useless fight against nature," John Brushwood has found also to be present in *Juyungo*. With particular reference to the prose-poems "Eye and Ear of the Jungle," Brushwood states: "They tend to communicate a sense of determination—that there is something behind the actions of men that is more persistent than they."[11] As Ascensión Lastre moves to and fro across this backdrop, one has a haunting sensation of *déjà vu*, as if the ghost of Cumandá inhabited the muscular frame of Ascensión, who is caught up in a fatal series of tragic repetitions.

The novels part company when discussing religion. The entire tale of *Cumandá* develops within a Catholic framework that creates the possibility of tragedy and, once realized, attenuates that very tragedy. That the beautiful and virtuous Cumandá (née Julia Orozco, sister of her lover) should be put to death in accordance with the barbaric customs of the Záparos seems inexplicably unjust. Her only tragic flaws, we may note, are that she is too beautiful (making her the favorite of her Indian husband, who selects her to die with him) and too virtuous (she sacrifices her own life to save her beloved Carlos). Yet, as with the drama of Golden Age Spain, the full thrust of tragedy is averted by the certainty of salvation. Removed to a Christian burial place and given posthumous last rites, Cumandá-Julia is assured of finding in heaven the justice that was denied her on earth. *Juyungo* maintains, in contrast, that for any salvation to be meaningful it must occur within this present, terrestrial existence. The death of Ascensión Lastre, who is no less beautiful or virtuous than Cumandá, though according to a different set of standards, assures us of nothing. The fact that Nelson Díaz, the idealistic social agitator, survives Ascensión indicates that the fight will continue on an intellectual plane; but it offers no certainty that Díaz's fate will differ from Lastre's.

Juyungo is thus an oracular novel, which also means it has a pronounced oral component. *Juyungo*'s orality spills over into the space where criollismo and modernism conjoin—where music results from the faithful representation of external reality. Along another axis, Ortiz has captured the various dialects native to Esmeraldas Province in northwest Ecuador: those of the poor Black, the Indian, the White and finally the educated Ecuadorian of no determined race or class. It is through these respective groups' speech, the idiosyncrasies of which shape the novel's writing, that *Juyungo* offers entry into its most basic thematic concerns.

The protagonist Ascensión Lastre, Juyungo himself, provides the prime example of the black dialect. In several senses Lastre speaks for his entire group. When he delivers such lines as "Vos me habéis insultado y me habéis buscao, ahora me vas a encontrá. !Yo soy un Lastre! Ya sabés lo que te quiero decí, no?" ("You insulted me an' searched me out. Now you gonna find me. I'm a Lastre! You know what I'm gettin' at, right?") (p. 73), the distinguishing characteristics of his speech, in regard to pronunciation and usage, emerge.[12] More a man of action than of words, Lastre's locutions are most frequently of a line or two in length. Even at his most loquacious, as when he leads a worker's rally (where words *are* social action), all we hear from him is: "Nosotros no podemos dejá que estos desgraciados se abusen y hagan lo que se les antoje con uno. ¿Verdá, compañeros? . . . ¡Que pa' eso somos hombres! . . . Nos aumentan la paga, o si no. . . . ¡Aquí hay bastante fierro!" ("We can't let these wretches take advantage of us an' make us do whatever they want. Right, brothers? . . . 'Cause that's what we men fo'! . . . They raise our pay, or else. . . . There's plenty o' iron here!") (p. 106). His tendency toward the exclamatory, his manner of enunciation and the pointed message he emits set Lastre apart as the exploited but spirited Black.

Ascensión's woman, María de los Angeles Caicedo, illustrates the speech of a poor Ecuadorian white. In response to a friend's praise of the man she has found, she replies: "Umjú. Todo será, pero creo que no me quiere. Cuando andaba detrás mío, mis amigas me decían: 'No importa que sea negro; los negros saben querer y estimar mucho a las blancas' . . . Y ya ve usted" ("Uh-huh. That may be, but I think he doesn't love me. When he used to follow me 'round, my friends would say: 'It doesn't matter if he's black; Blacks know how to love and respect white women a lot. . . . ' And now you see") (p. 80). María's syntax is intact; only the presence of contractions in the English (a rough equivalent of the vernacular "detrás mío" in the original) indicates the colloquial nature of her language. Even though neither María nor Lastre has had formal language training, in general the lines she utters deviate less frequently than Lastre's from normative Spanish. The distinction, one supposes, is due to the separate groups to which each belongs.

It is the speech of the Indian, the only indigenous group portrayed in the novel, that is utterly different. Orations such as "Tú, compadre chiquito, gustándome. Tú, sabiendo números, ¿no? Yo, necesitándote, aquí" ("Me, little friend, liking you. You, knowing numbers, right? Me, needing you, here") (p. 32) reveal the single most salient quality of the Cayapa dialect, the exclusive use of the present participle of the verb. Such a formulation indicates a consciousness with only a synchronic program, a vision of an eternally present continuum where actions always occur now. Whereas this perspective may provide a refreshing alternative to Western ideology, it guarantees the Indian's position at the bottom of the socioeconomic register. Spoken language in *Juyungo* thus not only denotes conversation between individuals and re-creates a verbal experience for the reader but, through the representation of dialectal differences, also serves to designate separate collectivities and locate them on a scale of social status.

The divisions sketched here constitute the thesis of racial tension posited early in the novel. But almost as they are presented, these ethnic differences are put into question. If we look at the message the Indian transmits to Lastre in the quotation above, for example, we detect a wish to establish a friendship across racial boundaries. María's timid, hesitant rhetoric, moreover, is determined more by her status as an abandoned woman than by her racial origins. The principal distinguishing features of her speech, rendered as the barely articulated "Uh-huh" and numerous contractions in English, are in fact common to both Blacks and Whites in the novel. Another quality common to the speech of both races is the tendency to resort to proverbs and maxims. When Eulogia asks: "Are we perhaps guilty of our parents' deeds?" the very dark-skinned Eva answers proverbially: "Claro que no; pero hijo de tigre sale pintao, y el hijo de la culebra se arrastra" ("Of course not; but the tiger cub has stripes, and baby snakes crawl on their bellies") (p. 165). The white María de los Angeles then adds: "O como dicen, de tal palo tal astilla" ("Or as they say, chip off the old block"). There is thus evidence of a strong oral tradition that ignores racial distinctions. Differences melt into nondifferentiation as it becomes apparent that the three speakers—Ascensión, María and the unnamed Cayapa—all belong to the lower socioeconomic classes; they share a destiny of poverty and exploitation at the hands of the powerful.

In contrast to the foregoing, the Ecuadorian of the future is epitomized by the fair-skinned, mulatto Nelson Díaz. He incarnates hope in the form of education. It is Nelson who first pronounces the words that become *Juyungo*'s standard: "Ten siempre presente estas palabras, amigo mío: más que la raza, la clase" ("Always keep these words in mind, my friend: Rather than the race, the class") (p. 91). Nelson has no race other than the human race. His discourse transcends the disjunction enacted verbally by the others. Nelson portrays himself in statements such as: "La cultura de los blancos nos ha metido, por medio del cine especialmente, el arquetipo femenino de la beldad blanca. ¿Y qué le ocurre a uno? El choque brutal entre esa ficción y la realidad nos hace polvo el espíritu'' (''The white culture has inculcated in us, by means of the movies especially, the feminine archetype of white beauty. And what happens to us? The brutal clash between that fiction and reality pulverizes our spirit'') (p. 124); and ''Creo que despertar al sentimiento patriótico y combativo en los pueblos débiles contra los poderosos, puede también ser revolucionario'' (''I believe that awakening in the weak countries the patriotic and combative sentiments against the powerful can also be revolutionary'') (p. 254). Díaz is cut from the same progressive mold as Santos Luzardo in Rómulo Gallegos' *Doña Bárbara*. Not only is his voice most correct in the academic sense (identical, not coincidentally, to that of the narrator), but his vocabulary is extensive and replete with abstract notions normally beyond the ken of autodidacticism. Ortiz undeniably utilizes *Juyungo*'s orality to produce linguistic verisimilitude, a concern he shares with the criollista artists. Concurrently the characters establish their individuality through their different speech habits and create a varied acoustical texture for the reader. But the dialectal variations also conform to an overall strategy; they provide the author with a means of representing the Ecuadorian racial hierarchy of the early twentieth century. By later dismantling the linguistic edifice through the insertion of the cultivated voice of Nelson Díaz, the novel symbolically subverts that hierarchy, replacing the old system of narrow interests with a structure whose foundations are considerably broader.

In spite of his vision, though, Nelson does have his inevitable blind spot, and his discourse can be deconstructed. His reasoned rhetoric is that of the conqueror, the legacy of the Spaniard, the Roman and the Athenian before that. In essence, Nelson's message to his people is for them to mimic their overlords, albeit in hopes of erasing the distinction between master and slave. But barring the novel's most basic and thoroughly Occidental assumptions it only reinforces the exhortation that race consciousness cede importance to class awareness. The conflicts involved in establishing the great empires of history were not necessarily racially inspired but rather were fought to gain social, political and economic supremacy. Nelson Díaz is the end product of imperial expansion, a symbol of the historical process wherein language is imposed by ruler upon ruled. As it lays a grid that is so pervasive as to be invisible, of course, linguistic domination necessarily leads to conceptual domination. Even in its central theme— the search for freedom and justice—*Juyungo* reveals itself to be a book about the insidious power of language.

We would do well to bear in mind that the various types of speech we have been discussing do not come to us unmediated. In the novel, speech is represented by a graphic signifier. The oral element is deferred and made different from the written component. *Juyungo* is, therefore, not only oral/aural; there are moments when Ortiz uses language in its conventionally rhetorical and representational way, as in the following passage: ''Naked, muscular torsos, which the inconstant forest sun seared and basted in acrid sweat, bent and straightened, started and stopped along a dead-end highway, lined with enormous trees from whose branches there rose a racket of birds that, from one second to the next, took off as if fired by a slingshot" (p. 79). The poised and balanced narrative is typical of Ortiz' technique: He not only evokes images ("naked torsos," "a racket of birds") but also enlists figures of speech ("fired by a slingshot"), tropes that conjure up images of images. At other times, he wields words incisively. Passages abound like the following, reminiscent of the *tremendismo* in Camilo José Cela's *La familia de Pascual Duarte* (1942), published within a year of *Juyungo*:

> With vengeance and fury the policeman unleashed an accurate blow with his machete on the skull of the wounded man, splitting it as easily as one splits ripe squash to make them into gourds. . . . In the soft mud which the animals pounded, mixing it with their excrement, lay the much-mentioned Don Valerio Verduga Barberán, terror of the region; with his intestines exposed to the strong tropical sun and his eyes lost in his own blood, his own brains, and his own secrets (p. 76).

In both these samples, the impact is clear and strong. It is an irony of textuality that the more vivid the scene or experience conveyed, the more does writing pose as nothing but itself.

Striking imagery is but one patent use of novelistic conventions whereby *Juyungo* locates itself in the mainstream of literature. The omniscient, third-person narrator provides an unproblematical voice that carries out its established function as a guide through the text. The temporal development of the novel is linear, except for a few brief interruptions occasioned by the recollections of the characters or by their telling of tales. Overt symbolism, such as the birds of ill omen that prefigure the occurrence of tragedy (pp. 200, 225), are distinct vestiges of the romantic era. It is plain that this text is not an example of the cryptic, "dehumanized" art that Ortega y Gasset saw looming on the horizon in the 1920s.[13] The names of certain characters are clearly allegorical, assuring the reader that the rules of this novel are familiar and dependable. Don Valerio Verduga Barberán ("barbaric executioner") is lasciviousness incarnate, Ascensión Lastre ("rising ballast") climbs in consciousness while maintaining his aplomb and Nelson Díaz combines the Anglo-Saxon tradition in his given name with the Hispanic tradition in his surname, promising a new day (*día*) in the amalgamation.[14] The tendency of the text toward autoexegesis increases in the later pages. Rather than leave the reader to draw the inference that Lastre is an epic hero representing the black cause, the narrator suggests: "This man seemed to be a symbol of his race in motion, growing and growing (p. 186). As did the writers of *Negrismo* poetry in the Caribbean, Ortiz is blending in *Juyungo* the Western tradition with the African experience. He cannot, therefore, assume that the characteristics of one culture will be shared or even recognized by the other. Quite appropriately, then, he tends to be explicit in narrating the rise and fall of Ascensión Lastre. Such self-demystification, also found in the closing pages of Alejo Carpentier's *The Kingdom of This World* (1949), is proper for the committed writer.

The most formally innovative aspect of *Juyungo*, the episodic prose-poem "Eye and Ear of the Jungle" at the opening of each chapter, provides instances of intensely self-conscious writing. Chapter 8, titled "La bocana" ("The Bayou"), illustrates:

And we saw palm trees that wept their widowhood and their solitude. But we could never remember their names. Others, aggressive, resembled the sparklers on Christmas Eve. One strum and another strum over the face of the water. The strum of a marimba in the distance; drumming out: Tucu-tucu-tunn-tucu-tucu-tunn. Rumbling, sounding, it skated, lugubrious, over the wilted afternoon. At the longest bend only the great hat of a canoeist could be seen and the rhythmic movement of his arm. Long, very long, the whistle of a horn, the whistle of a snail. It was the profound call which his mate came whistling. Punishment of the morning. Melancholy of the flesh and the afternoon. The jungle's punishment of the river of genuine steel (p. 117).

Animism inhabits the entire novel: The jungle speaks ("we could"); a forest's rain translates into tears ("wept their widowhood") at its own impersonality ("we could never remember"). As befits the passage's name, the jungle transmits chiefly two senses, sight and hearing. The sights are the sparklers of the aggressive palm trees and the canoeist, reduced within the magnitude of the setting to a hat and an undulant arm. Sounds dominate the scene (in a previous entry the voice tells us, "And when it is dark, more than with our eyes, we will live the jungle with our ears" [p. 79]). First they are introduced in the percussive naming and repetition of the "strumming." Entry into the music provides an escape from the prosaic existence of the black peasant, a departure signaled by a parallel release from the shackles of grammatical convention. As syntax breaks down, the picture becomes static in the verb's momentary absence. Everything is poised motionless, listening to the onomatopoeic, anaphoric marimba ("tucu-tucu-tunn"), which generates its own kinesis ("it skated") through the gerunds ("rumbling," "sounding"). Superimposed on that constant rhythm is the long call of a snail, again introduced in a sentence fragment and activated by the verb "to whistle" (*churear*). This Spanish word, the equivalent of the more universal *pitar*, lends linguistic authenticity to the passage and closes the view of the microcosm where music fills every niche. The last three fragments restate the despair of the initial sentence and accentuate the sadness of the drumming ("lugubrious"), fusing the actors and their backdrop ("Melancholy of the flesh and the afternoon") in an eternal natural conflict ("The jungle's punishment of the river of genuine steel"). The entire passage is an epanaphora (reference) to the events narrated in the body of that chapter, which consists of little action (suggested here in the many static descriptions) and much discussion of the injustices faced by the peasants (the insistent rhythm of the marimba and the river). Like all the sections called "Eye and Ear of the Jungle," this is an incursion into an imaginary, oneiric reality. It illustrates writing not as a vehicle to anything outside itself but as a motor for the reader's reflection on the intensity of the reading experience.

From the foregoing one might gather that *Juyungo* is a novel consisting principally of natural description and dialogue. But the sonorous stasis of the descriptions and the meandering pace of the dialogue are counterposed to the swift motions of the central character. Juyungo is a man of action, of dynamism, of feats of physical prowess, of firm decision and poise under pressure. The novel maintains a constant and rapid beat, covering a span of some twenty-six years (1913–1939) in its trajectory.[15] Lastre journeys from his home in the coastal lowlands to various parts of the jungle, to Santo Domingo de los Colorados, to the provincial capital city of Esmeraldas and to the frontier where Ecuador borders Peru before he meets his violent death. Always mindful of his legendary uncle Commander Lastre, whose effigy is evoked periodically, Juyungo sees himself as an exemplary individual. As he fulfills the role of the hero, he acts more like a personage than a person. His foil is the neurotic, vacillating Antonio Angulo. Dubbed the Hummingbird (*Tenteenelaire*) because of his tendency to expend tremendous energy only to remain in the same place, Angulo appears to die because he cannot decide to live. Ascensión, the antithesis of a Hamlet figure, can be envisaged as a black Don Quixote ("I know who I am"), the embodiment of all that is noble in his people.[16] Not only does he combat social injustice; but literary stereotypes of the Black, such as the *bembosidad* portrayed by some Afrophile poets of the 1920s and 1930s also crumble under the force of his bare hands. When Lastre defends a scarcely pubescent maid against the concupiscent Cocambo's attempted rape (p. 94), he asserts Judeo-Christian virtue over (supposed) Afro-Latin machismo. Even in the scene of his death in chapter 16, naked and at one with the night, he moves with an ever-firm tread in a quest he never questions.

Lastre can act so surely because he makes tacit assumptions about manliness and equality, thus freeing his mind from further debate on such matters.[17] His only doubts are in regard to racial hatred, and it is his uncertain flight from racism that rescues him from being a cardboard figure. Early on, the novel looks as if it will enact a simple semiotic inversion (adynaton), opposing what has come to be known as the "White Aesthetic."[18] Within such an inverted mode, things white are coded negatively while the more somber tones carry an ameliorative charge. The white woman, María, is shown to be more insecure than the black Aphrodite Cuabú, and the red-faced gringo, Mr. Hans, exists only to exploit the innocent Ecuadorian nationals. Nelson, moreover, confesses that he wishes he were darker and more negroid in his features (p. 88). Lastre, in addition, prefers the night—when it is cool and propitious for drinking, dancing and lovemaking—to the day, when one must toil for the ruling class under the tropical sun. But, as occurs with the ethnolinguistic hierarchy posited earlier in this essay, the symbolic system called the Black Aesthetic is not permitted to endure in *Juyungo*. Under the influence of the mulatto Nelson Díaz, Lastre comes to see the racial issue as a blind alley, a false dichotomy and a barrier to class solidarity.[19] The narrative, too, abandons black as an image with an immediately positive charge. It favors instead the freedom of chromatic ambivalence, as when we read ''darkness is always near love and death,'' (p. 221) or when Lastre is denominated ''that stellar Black'' (p. 233). Color is eventually rendered insignificant of anything but itself, as in the costumbristic passage: '' 'Why you boilin' clothes with corn leaves?'/'T' make 'em whiter' '' (p. 234). As does G. R. Coulthard in the title of his study *Race and Colour in Caribbean Literature*, the novel enacts linguistically the contention that the transcendence of the hierarchy of race is achieved by distilling color from race.[20] It, thereby, neutralizes the color code and justifiably renders trivial the question of ethnic superiority.

The moment of entry into the neutral color mode coincides with the introduction of the aforementioned nationalistic theme (p. 195), when the color of one's skin yields in importance to the colors of one's flag. We may see this new motif as a ''supersignifier,'' a metanarrative unit that controls the valence of the other textual components. It is inevitable and laudable to seek to establish alternative structures to those of classical culture; but the Black Aesthetic, if enforced rigorously, can be every bit as shackling as the traditional panoply of Western images. In fact, it becomes an inverse that in its insistent rebellion against a given model, inadvertently calls attention to and reinforces that which it was designed to surmount or subvert. It is to Ortiz' artistic credit that he withstands the temptation to embrace melodramatically the symbolic system of one extreme or the other. In this instance Modernism and Nationalism combine to give the novel its particular shape. Once *Juyungo* abandons the hierarchy of race, the text finds itself free to explore a polychromatic spectrum, exhibiting especially the blue of the sky, the green of the jungle and the red of the spilled blood of Ecuadorian patriots.

The nationalistic stance with which the novel ends is, of course, potentially as limiting as a strictly racial posture. But the movement from race to nation defines a principle of structural transcendence or an abandonment of codes that prove to be restrictive and obsolete. *Juyungo* thus provides the mechanism necessary to go beyond its own parameters. The dispute between Ecuador and its neighbor is prescribed to be resolved internationally through an awareness of Andean commonality. Conceiving such a bridge, where before lay only a breach, represents a quantum jump in consciousness analogous to that of Ascensión Lastre. In the title of the last chapter, ''Black among Indians,'' we find the termination of the process of subverting difference and the assertion instead of the essential sameness among peoples. Every foe of class awareness is thus equal in the novel's scheme (Lastre will not, for example, strike an exclusively anti-American pose: ''If it wasn't for gringos, we'd be in bad shape'' [p. 183]). A Russian spy, a CIA agent and an Ecuadorian racist, like the character Martín López y Bueno, all would be barriers to the global fraternity proposed in *Juyungo*.

Reading the writing of a Spanish-American black novel is not to devalue the suffering of the Black, the Hispanic or any other minority. It is not to be apathetic about current social issues and does not preclude, for instance, urging

American corporate divestment from countries that follow discriminatory policies. It is, rather, to take into account the complexity of the literary mechanism, the medium by which these ideas and impressions reach us. Reading writing, for instance, allows us to apprehend *Juyungo* as an exploration into the metaphor's potential for inducing extraliterary action. Black literature must continue to provide a healthy image of and for the Black, who in Latin American literature finds a dearth of models worth emulating. But regarding the black identity advanced in those metaphors, smashing idols or merely inverting their image is a rather uncreative, short-term answer and may not be an answer at all. *Juyungo* offers Nelson Díaz, a gray (black and white) symbol, an intellectual hybrid to be remembered more for his complexity than for his complexion. He signifies circumspect reason, the neutralization of national interests in favor of a global perspective and the dismantling of the racial hierarchy to make way for the dialectic between reader and text. Only when we locate the interplay between the signs and the receiver of those signs do we become aware of how we are constantly decoding symbols of a surprisingly vast range of orders (not only television images, for example, but also television sets). In short, Nelson's reasoned discourse is an extended metaphor for its own metaphoricity, one that can attune our awareness to the fact that Western civilization is always reading writing.

Juyungo is not just a black novel with a racial message to broadcast but an economy of forces in suspension. Some of the novel's language is determined by and refers to historical actuality, that which lies outside itself. But we should not, therefore, assume that the referential function of language dominates, first, because that external reality too is mediated symbolically, and it is to those imperceptible and primal symbols that the novel points. In addition, much of *Juyungo*'s writing conforms to purely internal necessities of the textual universe. Ortiz' text is original and prophetic; the novel features newly arranged aspects of several literary and sociopolitical tendencies of the past and announces a humanitarian plan for dealing with the future. Ultimately, however, it is *Juyungo*'s affair with the sign, its appropriation of signifier and signified to constitute a unique textuality, that determines that long after the particular issues treated have ceased to be timely, the novel will continue to play an important role in that future.

NOTES

1. Page references to the novel correspond to the Spanish (1943; reprint ed., Barcelona: Seix Barral, 1976) and will appear parenthetically in the text. All English translations are from the manuscript of Susan F. Hill and Jonathan Tittler (Washington, D.C.: Three Continents Press, 1983).

2. Since Renaud Richard's definitive thematic article "*Juyungo*, de Adalberto Ortiz, ou de la haine raciale à la lutte contre l'injustice," *Bulletin Hispanique* 72, no. 2 (1970):152–70, the novel has been the concern of many, including Karl H. Heise, "So-

ciety and Artistic Techniques in the Novels of the 'Grupo de Guayaquil' '' (Ph.D. dissertation, Michigan State University, 1972); Antonio Olliz Boyd, "The Concept of Black Esthetics as Seen in Selected Works of Three Latin American Writers: Machado de Assis, Nicolás Guillén and Adalberto Ortiz" (Ph.D. dissertation, Stanford University, 1975); John S. Brushwood, *The Spanish American Novel: A Twentieth Century Survey* (Austin: University of Texas Press, 1975), pp. 146–50; and Richard L. Jackson, *The Black Image in Latin American Literature* (Albuquerque: University of New Mexico Press, 1976), pp. 101–5. The author is interviewed by Moraima Semprún in *Américas* 30, no. 3 (1978):49–51. The novel is available in translation in five languages, including a French version by Michel Reboux (Paris: Gallimard, 1955).

3. See Antonio Olliz Boyd, "The Concept of Black Awareness as a Thematic Approach in Latin American Literature," in Miriam DeCosta, ed., *Blacks in Hispanic Literature* (Port Washington, N.Y.: Kennikat Press, 1977), p. 72, and Lemuel Johnson, *The Devil, the Gargoyle, and the Buffoon: The Negro as Metaphor in Western Literature* (Port Washington, N.Y.: Kennikat Press, 1971).

4. Jackson follows Abdias do Nascimento in labeling racial mixing "ethnic lynching"; he sees it as the Caucasian's strategy for "bleaching out" Negroid racial features. In his introduction Jackson states: "Ethnic lynching . . . is, broadly speaking, characteristic of all Spanish and Portuguese-speaking societies in Latin America, where the problems of color, some hope, can be erased by erasing the black race" (Jackson, p. 2). He does not take into consideration Carter G. Woodson's words of reciprocity, first uttered in the 1930s: "If the negroes are a blot among the whites, the latter are a stain among the blacks" ("Attitudes of the Iberian Peninsula [in literature]," in DeCosta, *Blacks in Hispanic Literature*, p. 28). Miscegenation tends to erase the extreme elements of both races involved. Arguments implying conscious strategies on the part of either race appear to be based more on emotion than reason.

5. Wolfgang Iser, for example, adopts such a textual model in his study *The Act of Reading: A Theory of Aesthetic Response* (Baltimore: Johns Hopkins University Press, 1978), p. 85. It is a paradigm that enjoys wide acceptance among poststructuralist critics.

6. "La historia del criollismo," *El croillismo* (Santiago de Chile: Universitaria, 1956), p. 11; unless otherwise indicated, all translations are ours. *Criollismo* derives from *criollo*, which José Juan Arrom summarizes as "the national, the autochthonous, the distinctive and very own of each one of our countries"; see "Criollo: Definición y matices de un concepto," *Certidumbres de América* (Madrid: Gredos, 1971), p. 25.

7. A black novel containing almost all the characteristics of *criollismo* except for the work's mainly urban setting is Cirilo Villaverde, *Cecilia Valdés: Novela de costumbres cubanas* (1882; reprint ed., Mexico: Porrúa, 1972). In spite of the city-scape in which it is set, *Cecilia Valdés'* dominant focus on the lower class' efforts to join the white bourgeoisie locates it within the scope of *criollismo*.

8. An example of the ethnic-centered approach to Latin American literature is Concha Meléndez, *La novela indianista en Hispanoamérica* (Río Piedras, Puerto Rico: University de Puerto Rico, 1961). For a study whose organizing principle is regional, see Lydia de León Hazera, *La novela de la selva hispanoamericana* (Bogotá: Instituto Caro y Cuervo, 1971).

9. Stanley Cyrus, ed., *El cuento negrista sudamericana* (Quito: Casa de la Cultura Ecuatoriana, 1973). The heroic image of the black intellectual, though still a rarity in fiction, may be found in the narrator-protagonist Natividad in Ramón Díaz Sánchez,

Cumboto (Madrid: Guadarrama, 1960). As we shall see later, *Juyungo* projects such a positive image in the cerebral character of Nelson Díaz, who survives when the more physical Ascensión Lastre perishes. But nowhere does the image emerge more clearly than through the narrative voice of Richard Jackson's critical study, *The Black Image in Latin American Literature*.

10. See Juan León Mera, *Cumandá* (Madrid: Espasa-Calpe, 1973). Angel F. Rojas proposes a view of literary nationalism in *La novela ecuatoriana* (Mexico: Fondo de Cultura Económica, 1948). Other helpful manuals on the history of the Ecuadorian novel are Benjamín Carrión, *El nuevo relato ecuatoriano: Crítica y antología*, 2d ed. (Quito: Casa de la Cultura Ecuatoriana, 1958); and Edmundo Ribadeneira M., *La moderna novela ecuatoriana* (Quito: Casa de la Cultura Ecuatoriana, 1958).

11. See León Hazera, *La novela*, p. 48; and, Brushwood, *Spanish American Novel*, p. 147.

12. The verbs *habéis* and *sabés*, which correspond locally to the second person singular *vos* (used instead of *tú*), cannot be rendered in English. To compensate partially for this lack of sensitivity in English, the translation converts the omission of both the intervocalic *d* in some past participles and the final *r* in infinitives, other typically distinctive features, into parallel elliptical tendencies of Black English, namely the omission of the auxiliary verb in perfect tense formulations ("You insulted me an' searched me out") and of the final consonant in the coordinating conjunction and the gerund ("an' "; "gettin' ").

13. José Ortega y Gasset, *La deshumanización del arte* (1925; reprint ed., Madrid: Revista de Occidente, 1970).

14. The deciphering of Lastre's names comes from Renaud Richard: "We think that certain names of the characters in *Juyungo* are not gratuitous, but are chosen in function of the evocative power insofar as they characterize the psychology of each one: 'Lastre'— 'ballast,' evokes an idea of weight, of heaviness, which translates, it seems to us, the aplomb, the self-confidence of the character; inside the permanence thus evoked, the first name Ascensión translates the idea of evolution; of anabasis; the two—given name and surname—join together to express the idea of progress, which fully characterizes Juyungo and his internal itinerary" ("*Juyungo*," p. 168).

15. *Juyungo*'s rapid rhythm of action can best be appreciated in contrast with a novel like Enrique López Albújar's *Matalaché* (1928; reprint ed., Lima: Juan Mejía Baca, 1970), where action is minimized and subordinated to numerous scenes of parlor conversations.

16. It is rare to find a sense of black community in the fiction; the Black, if distinguishable from other Blacks, tends to operate alone. A tightly knit (verbally communicative) black community is portrayed, however, in Manuel Zapata Olivella's *Chambacú: Corral de negros* (Bogotá: Bedout, 1967).

17. An example of a black protagonist who vacillates neurotically throughout the work is Israel, in Arnoldo Palacios, *Las estrellas son negras* (Bogotá: Iqueima, 1949).

18. In her lucid article, "The Eye of the Other: Images of the Black in Spanish Literature," Sylvia Wynter says: "In literature, the topos by which the prevailing reality is criticized by turning its structure of symbols upside down is known as *adynaton*" (DeCosta, *Blacks in Hispanic Literature*, p. 11). Examples of this semiotic inversion are in Ramón Díaz Sánchez, *Cumboto*, where the white maid Berta is known only for her voracious sexual appetite, and Nelson Estupiñan Bass, *El último río* (Quito: Casa de la Cultura Ecuatoriana, 1966), a burlesque of the "White Aesthetic" when embraced too zealously by a Black. DeCosta states in her introduction, "Primary [in the 'Black

Aesthetic'] is the shared experience of the apocalyptic holocaust and the 'deliberate desecration and smashing of idols, the turning inside-out of symbols' '' (p. 6).

19. We may find a similar defusing of the racial question in Rómulo Gallegos' *Pobre negro* (Caracas: Guadarrama, 1937). In its portrayal of the strong and decisive white woman Luisana, *Pobre negro* speaks to sexual as well as racial equality.

20. The original version is *Raza y color en la literatura antillana* (Seville: Escuela de Estudios Hispano-Americanos de Sevilla, 1958).

11
Black Character: Toward a Dialectical Presentation in Three South American Novels

Carol Beane

Fiction in which Blacks and Mulattoes are main characters "deals not with eternal essences or ideal forms of life, but with life lived in particular conditions."[1] Black characters and black character—a way of being—in Hispanic-American fiction reflect traits drawn from a social reality. Any discussion of black characters in literature must bear in mind that literary creation results from a complex interplay between historical and socioeconomic factors and imagination. The latter is the source of "all sorts of images of non-Western peoples and worlds which have flourished in our culture . . . images derived not from observation, experience and perceptible reality but from a psychological urge . . . that creates its own realities which are fully different from political realities."[2]

As literary subjects, Blacks and Mulattoes are charged with extraliterary associations. Slavery and oppression in the eighteenth century created stereotyped images, many of which appear in fiction.[3] Early portrayals were ostensibly sympathetic; later ones are less so. Blacks and Mulattoes have become the Other in relation to the society, or society is the Other in relation to the Blacks.[4] It is important to understand the origins of the stereotypes. However, equally important are the ways in which some writers, in their characterization of Blacks, have used stereotypes as a point of departure, disfiguring when not abandoning them. Such efforts express commitment to a truer image of the Black and to the artistic potential contained in the historical and cultural experience of being black.

This study is concerned with the characterization of Blacks and Mulattoes, two groups traditionally perceived as marginal in Western culture, even in South America, where they are a demographic and cultural presence. This is especially true in Colombia, Venezuela, certain parts of Peru and Ecuador, not to mention Brazil. Situations and experiences arising from a marginal state—slave until late in the nineteenth century, frustrated and oppressed laborer in the twentieth—form the material with which authors work. They attempt to give artistic expression to this marginality and the society's reactions to it. Conflict between the larger society and those outside it—inclusion and exclusion—sets the tone of their writing. We shall analyze three novels from continental Hispanic America: *María* (1867) by the Colombian Jorge Isaacs, *Matalaché* (1927) by the Afro-Peruvian Enrique López Albújar, and *Juyungo* (1943) by the Afro-Ecuadorian writer Adalberto Ortiz. These novels define and validate certain concepts of black character that vary according to the historical circumstances and the novelist's relation to his society and to his subject matter.

Stanley E. Fish's *Self-Consuming Artifacts* categorizes literary presentations as being either rhetorical or dialectical. He defines a presentation as being rhetorical

if it satisfies the needs of the readers. The work "satisfies" is meant literally here; for it is characteristic of a rhetorical form to mirror and present for approval the opinions its readers already hold. It follows then the experience of such a form will be flattering, for it tells the reader that what he has always thought about the world is true and that the ways of this thinking are sufficient. . . . Whatever one is told can be placed and contained within the categories and assumptions of received systems of knowledge.[5]

To the rhetorical presentation Fish opposes the dialectical, which is

disturbing, for it requires of its readers a searching and vigorous scrutiny of everything they believe in and live by. It is didactic in a special sense; it does not preach the truth, but asks that its readers discover the truth themselves, and this discovery is often made at the expense not only of a reader's opinions and values, but of his self-esteem.[6]

Fish's classifications are useful as a critical approach to a general study of Afro-Hispanic literature. They are especially helpful in discussing the characterization of Blacks and Mulattoes and the ways in which authors establish the parameters of their identity. The issues are perception and presentation: complicated relationships between the author, his culture, the historical moment, the literary creation, its internal parts and the reader. When describing the rhetorical presentation, Fish speaks of the "needs of . . . readers." For the sake of this discussion, we shall postulate a reader who will react to either the rhetorical or the dialectical presentation. Such a reader will be a representative of the dominant society and committed to its prevailing attitudes and values.

The context in which a black character is defined may be exotic, picturesque, sociopolitical, psychological or some combination of these. For the most part, exotic and picturesque treatment of Blacks and Mulattoes to which the reader responds functions as part of what Fish calls the rhetorical presentation. Attention to the social, political and economic implications of the picturesque detail, however, obstructs a picturesque perception; such a presentation then becomes potentially dialectical.

The predominant social attitiude toward Blacks and Mulattoes, especially since the eighteenth century, has been one of hostility, distancing, amusement and disenfranchisement.[7] It developed particularly in slave societies. The social structure of the large plantations engendered certain fictions about the nature of Blacks and their relations with Whites. These views appeared in literary fiction as social norms.

Prior to the nineteenth century, Blacks and Mulattoes in Hispanic-American fiction, for the most part, were treated in a picturesque way.[8] At the same time, the rigid codification of racial attitudes and categories of the eighteenth century and the restricted possibilities available for Blacks and Mulattoes can be seen as attempts to impose order and control in societies that were extremely dependent on their labor and participation.[9] It was, perhaps, faith in authority and security in a particular world view that enabled writers at this time to maintain an ethnocentric position.

In the early nineteenth century, religion and humanitarian sentiment, combined with a convenient failure of slavery as a viable economic system, influenced attitudes in favor of Blacks and Mulattoes. Portrayals of Blacks in antislavery literature—regardless of whether truly sympathetic or not—were created in reaction to the denigrating beliefs about Blacks current in nineteenth-century Hispanic-American society.[10]

The decline of slavery with the political instability that was occasioned by the wars of independence and continued into the post-independence period shook the old social order. Facing the prospect of greater and more formalized participation in society by groups theretofore excluded, society reacted. Pseudoscientific concepts of race such as those in Comte de Gobineau's *Essay on the Inequality of the Races* (1852–1853) were elaborated to rationalize the oppression of Blacks and Mulattoes. These ideas did not initiate negative beliefs but merely gave authority to existing sentiments. However, the terms of these new arguments were harsher and more dehumanizing than the commercial and legal ones of previous centuries—they exacerbated the negative attitudes about Blacks.

In nineteenth-century Hispanic-American characterizations of Blacks and Mulattoes, for example, one finds a duality of character types that clearly suggests an underlying ambivalence of that society. It seems apparent that character types such as the loyal slave, the maternal black woman, the amusing child and others are the more socially acceptable. Their counterparts are the rebellious, the lascivious, the sly and shiftless slave. Both types are creative expressions produced in a society attempting to identify and isolate elements that disrupt its social order. The ''good'' counterparts indicate efforts to accommodate Blacks rather than exclude them. However, the basis of the accommodation is exploitation. It is the perspective of the dominant society, the Other in relation to the black characters, that defines the types.

The uprising in Haiti in 1791 provided all slave owners in Latin America and the Caribbean with an example, long remembered, of the consequences of the rage of oppressed Blacks. Attempts to portray Blacks favorably in much nineteenth-century fiction share certain assumptions. The qualities that many authors attribute to Blacks and Mulattoes imply characters that must be made acceptable before readers will view them in a serious and sympathetic manner.

Characterizations of Blacks and Mulattoes in this period are based on a series of neutralizations. Neutralization is a way of coming to terms with those characteristics of which society disapproves. The writer eliminates the offending traits and substitutes them with others more agreeable to society. Those features most frequently neutralized are physical and psychological. Others, equally important, originate in the relationship between master and slave. They form the basis of the black character's identity.

We are interested in the elements that create the fictional identity of black characters: preoccupation with physical appearance, the external signs of identity; the types of rational and emotional responses attributed; the kinds of experiences allowed, the access that a character has to space and time.[11] The narrative voice that describes the black or mulatto character is also important. If this voice is hostile toward Blacks, we identify it as the voice of the dominant society, that of the Other. If a narrative voice is favorable to Blacks, we see it at odds with the dominant society. Black characters may also be described from their own perspective.

To present a Black or Mulatto characterizing positive affective language is not necessarily to portray him in a truly sympathetic way. Such presentations do not inevitably lead to a redefinition of black character in terms other than those set up by society. Indeed, the conditions of neutralization are those of the dominant society, revealing the extent to which authors share in the convictions of their culture. Portrayals of this kind seem to show a "desire to . . . merely expose and fight against . . . abuses in order to prevent deeper revolutionary upheavals."[12] The authors' characterizations also reflect the inferiority and undesirability of the Black and the Mulatto.

MARIA, A RHETORICAL PRESENTATION: PROPAGATING THE STEREOTYPE

Jorge Isaacs' *María* (1867),[13] is an example of the limitations of the picturesque placed on black characters. The episode in which the Africans, Nay and Sinar, appear provides an exotic interlude in this romantic novel. Although most of the action occurs in Africa, key incidents that define the black characters are to be found equally in the African and the American context.

This intercalated tale is the story of Nay and Sinar. She is the daughter of a famous Ashanti warrior; he, the son of a slain enemy chief, is captured by Nay's father and made a slave in his house. It tells of Nay's and Sinar's life in Africa, their love affair, their eventual capture by the slave traders, their separation, Sinar's disappearance and Nay's passage to America. The account of her life in America as a member of the household of the novel's protagonist, Efraín, begins with his father buying Nay, freeing her and changing her name to Feliciana and concludes with her death.

Isaacs uses distance—geographic, historical, narrative, aesthetic—to create black characters the reader will accept. However, the conditions of acceptance are set by the larger society, limiting the extent to which new perceptions of these characters are possible. Given the nineteenth-century view held by Western culture about the inferiority of non-Western peoples in general, it is difficult to see how any new perceptions of Blacks and Mulattoes could occur. New perceptions arise from new understanding and reevaluation of historical and cultural material. Isaacs approached his black characters as one against the inhumanity of slavery who, in spite of himself, accepted the inferiority of Blacks.

The story of Nay and Sinar abounds in picturesque details. More than exotic paraphernalia, they delineate the cultural dislocation of the former slave, Feliciana, and establish a new cultural context for her by providing another identity: Nay is the African persona and Feliciana the American one. The new identity becomes the reference point for the retrogressive presentation of this character. As a dying woman, Feliciana first attracts the reader's attention; however, it is as Nay, her African manifestation, that she sustains this interest. Isaacs has carefully prepared this transference of identities and shift of the reader's focus by changing the narrator and the setting. The picturesque detail alerts the reader that certain black characters must be considered in a new social condition that antedates slavery.

Isaacs' choice of narrator for the Nay and Sinar episode reveals his intention to portray Blacks favorably. It reflects the possibilities that society and the prevailing literary mode—romanticism—offered. He substitutes Efraín, the first-person commentator of the novel, for Nay-Feliciana, who originally narrates the events in the story. In this way the author provides the reader with a familiar, sympathetic, "reliable" narrator for Nay's tale.[14] Changing the narrator also establishes a temporal distance that parallels the spatial distance created by the exotic setting. As narrator, Efraín tells Nay's story as he had heard it, as a bedtime tale.

As narrator of this episode, Efraín becomes the mediator between the Blacks and the white society. His sympathetic view of them intercedes with the reader on their behalf. The change of narrator, for example, affects the language with which the episode is presented. The reader will not learn of Nay's life in her language, which the author refers to as "clumsy and touching" ("rústico y patético lenguaje"). Instead Isaacs employs Efraín's language. His learned diction, Latinate lexicon and syntax are better able to rouse the reader's interest and stimulate his sympathy. Furthermore, Efraín's language is a linguistic manifestation of socially approved authority; it invests the story it tells with dignity. His rendition of Nay's story has an elevated tone, associated with noble characters, the heroic, the epic. By avoiding Nay's common speech, Isaacs identifies her as a serious element of the novel. By not placing his black characters in comic positions, he does not subject them to a reduction based on limited roles and nonstandard speech or behavior ignorant of decorum.

On the one hand, Isaac's handling of narrator and language in the episode can be seen challenging images of Blacks as comic and inarticulate—images by which the dominant society dissociates itself from Blacks. On the other hand, the context in which Nay tells her story to the white character is marginal. It is domestic and occurs in the space of the least important members of the household, the children's quarters. This reinforces an image of Nay as Feliciana, the contented mammy figure. Her life and its significance to her is nullified, reduced to entertainment for the master's family.

In order to dispose the reader favorably toward black characters, Isaacs eliminates physical differences, making Nay and Sinar types that Whites accept, that is, more like themselves. Although Nay is Ashanti, she lacks kinky hair, a flat nose and thick lips.[15] Sinar, though not Ashanti, is one of the most beautiful young slaves Nay's father possesses. In neutralizing black skin color and other traits, Isaacs tacitly acknowledges them as undesirable, thereby confirming the attitude held by the larger society.

There are other instances of neutralization in this episode. Isaacs, attempting to portray the Black sympathetically, consistently selects the positive stereotypes. He avoids depicting slave women as sexually promiscuous, insisting on a maternal or domestic role for them, both of which are socially more acceptable. Sinar, a potential authority figure for Blacks in the New World, disappears. This eliminates the black male as a possible threat in the dominant society; there will be no Toussaint L'Ouvertures. The favorable image that the reader retains of Sinar, "young and handsome" (p. 234), is associated, nevertheless, with a character who, not unlike the novel's protagonist, always acquiesces to authority.

An implicit belief in authority underlies *María*. Isaacs' black characters show great respect for the social sanctions of age, incest taboos, marital fidelity. Isaacs takes advantage of a possible cultural overlap—the importance of authority and social sanctions in African culture as well as in that of nineteenth-century Hispanic America. On the one hand, he validates the existence of this respect in black characters. However, he does not focus on it in a cultural context that is significant to them. Instead, Isaacs emphasizes respect for authority as a quality that the dominant society in the New World favors as a means of control in general and particularly for Blacks. Stressing the use of social sanctions and authority in maintaining order and defending legitimate social relationships, Isaacs tries to allay the negative reactions to fears about Blacks based on threats of insubordination. Loyalty, gratitude, obedience (based on respect and affection), passivity and acquiescence neutralize rebellion, mistrust and revenge.

Although neither white nor black characters challenge or reject authority in *María*, the relation of Blacks to authority is obviously more problematic for the society of that period than for Whites. Society felt that Blacks were subordinate and, therefore, had a "place" from which they were encouraged not to move. Isaacs allows his black characters to be rebellious only in situations in which isolation nullifies conventional social relations or in which rebellion can be easily pacified. For example, Sinar urges Nay to elope with him and return to his homeland. In pressing Nay to disobey, he encourages disloyalty, disregarding both her filial obligation and his own position as her father's slave. Nay, however, takes advantage of Sinar's love for her to persuade him to stay. By so doing, she overcomes his challenge to the patriarchal authority.

Defeats and failures are thematic motifs that link the Nay and Sinar episode to the main plot of Efraín and María. Losses that the black characters suffer parallel and anticipate those of the white protagonists. The most dramatic moment in Nay's story is when the slave traders capture her and Sinar. The episode's most memorable event becomes the one that represents their loss of freedom, their culture and each other. This image of their failure is then fixed in the reader's mind.

At the same time the black characters (in this episode and elsewhere) are the only ones who escape complete failure and psychological devastation. Unlike Efraín and his family, Blacks are compensated for their losses. Nay as Feliciana gains her freedom; her child by Sinar enjoys the ''privileges'' of a house slave. Isaacs leads the reader to feel more admiration for the adjustment the black characters have made than sympathy for their oppressed condition. He surrounds the incidents that expose the cruelties of slavery with idyllic situations: in Africa, Nay's privileged life; Sinar's position among the Ashantis as a favored slave; in the New World, the kindness of Efraín's father, who buys Nay and frees her; Nay's life on the estate so suggestively named ''El Paraíso.''

Circumstances such as these distract the reader's attention from the unpleasant implications of slavery. By depicting the patriarchal society as benevolent to Blacks and destructive to Whites—Efraín is wretched, María dies—Isaacs affirms the prevailing sympathetic vision of the Black. The Black is victim; the Black is ward. Both these designations imply inferiority. Society, regarding the Black ''sympathetically,'' does penance for the wrongs of slavery. More importantly, it justifies keeping the Black subservient in order to do so.

Isaacs' presentation of black characters is essentially rhetorical. The needs and preoccupations of the dominant society define his black characters. The reader has no other perspective on them. The positive stereotypes to which Isaacs turns as he tries to validate the worth of Blacks to society serve only to reassure the anxious reader that his perception of the Black as inferior is valid.

MATALACHE, A COMPOSITE PRESENTATION: DISFIGURING THE STEREOTYPE

In the second half of the nineteenth century the Comte de Gobineau and others developed the pseudoscientific concepts of race that defined Whites as superior, nonwhites as inferior. These ideas have had a great impact well into the twentieth century. Although the Black, as slave, had been the more popular figure in nineteenth-century literature, in the early decades of the twentieth century the Mulatto captures this attention.[16]

There were several reasons for this. In a period of formulating its own identity, Spanish America identified the Mulatto with the New World, the Black with the Old. The Mulatto was conceived of as the future; the Black was associated with slavery and the past. In addition, the scientific interest stimulated by positivist thinkers saw in the Mulatto a specimen of the biological phenomenon of race mixing. Miscegenation was a reality of Latin America that had to be faced. The problem was how to convert *mestizaje* into a constructive value and eliminate its detrimental connotations, how to accommodate this growing marginal group of the racially mixed into a society in transformation. Domingo Faustino Sarmiento's *Conflictos y armonías de las razas* (1883) was the first systematic treatment of race in Latin America. After its publication, race figured prominently in all discussions of national character.

Enrique López Albújar's *Matalaché* (1928) is the first twentieth-century Hispanic-American novel outside the Caribbean with a clearly identifiable mulatto protagonist.[17] It is also the first to address the issue of the Mulatto's place in society as a dilemma to be resolved. López Albújar's novel is particularly interesting because of the way in which he accepts certain premises about the nature of the Mulatto while rejecting others. Given that López Albújar was himself a Mulatto and his subject matter was miscegenation, one senses a strong personal involvement with his subject.[18]

The novel tells the story of the love affair between María Luz, daughter of an estate owner, and José Manuel, the mulatto foreman, famous for his sexual prowess and sought after by other estate owners as stud for their slave women. López Albújar describes at length how the passion between María Luz and José Manuel develops. He examines the consequences: enlightenment, fulfillment and punishment.

Matalaché is about the inevitability of miscegenation and the potential of the Mulatto. The novel may be seen as part of the movement in Latin America during the 1920s and 1930s that sought "to recover America and that which is American—whether its origin be European, Indian or African, or an entirely new creation of this continent—that sought equality with at least the European cultural values which until that moment had been accepted here as the true, not to say the 'only' center of culture, of Culture."[19]

However, vindication of the Mulatto occurs at the expense of the Black. In nearly all the novels of this period that treat Mulattoes favorably, we find it to be to the detriment of the black characters. The Mulatto is depicted as superior to the Black. The Mulatto will be more sympathetic, more productive, more industrious; he will be physically, mentally, emotionally and verbally more active than the black character. Passivity and acquiescence are the Blacks' primary traits. In the narration Blacks are of little importance except as foils to the Mulattoes.

Certainly, the terms of the rhetorical presentation of Blacks we find in *Matalaché* are more intense in comparison to those Isaacs uses in *María*. Isaacs depicts Blacks working at various tasks on the estate; the mulatto *mayordomo* is an independent man, esteemed as a friend. The reader sees Blacks in an African setting, which regardless of how exotic or romantic its presentation, the author does identify as their own. In *Matalaché* the Mulattoes and the Blacks, especially the women, exist solely for the benefit and pleasure of the master. Furthermore, one senses the urgency and desperation of crisis in the white characters' defense of racial purity and their violent need to identify the Mulatto as useful only in a marginal context. It is also present in the hostile reaction to Blacks, expressed in extreme and grotesque images and situations that result in highly charged episodes intended to provoke and reinforce feelings of disgust and repulsion.

López Albújar emphasizes the inferiority of the Black, associating this condition with evil: The novel's villain is a black character. Moreover, the Spanish spoken by the *negro bozal* is that of the newly arrived African slave, a broken language the inarticulateness of which intensifies the animal nature that the author attributes to him. The restricted possibilities that exist for the Black of being accepted by and participating in the dominant society are suggested by use of space. For example, the space accessible to Blacks is confined; their movements are limited. The *negro congo* drives a mule round and round a small corral. In contrast, José Manuel moves quite freely about the estate. The plot line emphasizes this freedom of movement since ultimately José Manuel gains access to those spaces the society defines as the most intimate: the bedroom and body of the white mistress.

Matalaché presents the Mulatto as a tragic figure. However, this tragedy, the life of José Manuel, is an example of how society controls those it wishes to exclude. The misfortune of the Mulatto lies not in any inability to participate in society as society would suggest. Rather, it lies in society's denial of the Mulatto's participation. The anguished Mulatto image is created by transferring the blame for failure from the society into the Mulatto, converting the sociological phenomenon to a biological one. The characteristics of the tragic Mulatto are those society uses to punish attempts of trespassing the prescribed limits of the social boundaries. These traits are misspent energies: self-hate, alienation, suffering, frustrated aspirations.

López Albújar seeks to discredit the unsympathetic images of the Mulatto that the Mulatto himself projects, as well as others projected on him. The stereotype—the Mulatto as alienated, as frustrated, as stud, as lascivious beast, as happy-go-lucky music man—becomes the point of departure in attempting a more complex characterization. In deforming the Mulatto's reductive image, López Albújar moves toward a more dialectical presentation of this figure. The reader acquires new information about the nature of the Mulatto, new sources of definition and recognition. These are meant to affect favorably how the reader perceives the Mulatto and his place in society.

Whereas the stereotype of the Mulatto defines him as a physical being, stressing skin color, features, sexuality, denying him other aspects, López Albújar and others writing during the 1930s and 1940s did not. Many of the new possibilities they presented for the Mulatto can be described in terms of activity. Humberto Palza defines activity as doing: ''To do is to arrive, to overcome; not to do is to be overcome. And just think of the value this simple truth has for building a nation.''[20] We must point out, nevertheless, that although this concept allows one group of Afro-Hispanics greater means of expression, insofar as it reinforces certain distinctions, Palza's statement lends itself to a rhetorical presentation of Blacks.

López Albújar seeks to define José Manuel in terms of a productivity that is more than biological, something that will be a means of expressing emotion and achieving spiritual fulfillment. José Manuel's love for María Luz allows this to happen; she is the catalyst for the Mulatto's potential. He makes an altarpiece and slippers for her, labors of love and devotion. José Manuel is skilled with his hands, a master smithy, carpenter and leather worker. Yet white society begrudges him definition in terms of these abilities. The Mulatto's talents are disregarded as unessential to the stereotype because they are signs of recognizable human activity. For most of the white characters José Manuel is a breeder of slaves, nothing more.

However, even though disproving the image of the Mulatto that denies him creative or intellectual ability, López Albújar somewhat undermines these achievements in deferring to European cultural superiority as their source. José Manuel himself attributes the beauty of his handiwork to his "white" intelligence, not the African. In addition, the author makes clear that the inspiration for these creations originates in a white woman.

Productivity, seen as part of a rhetorical presentation, is another means of dissociating the Black from the Mulatto, confirming a racial hierarchy. What José Manuel makes, López Albújar designates a *creation*; what the Blacks make, a *product*. The Mulatto's objects are beautiful; those produced by the black slaves, ugly and stinking.

Identity on the basis of color and appearance is an important aspect in characterization of the novel. In this area López Albújar least successfully challenges the conventional norms. His treatment of color and the characters' reaction to it is more intense than, for example, Isaacs' *María*. There is in the background of Isaacs' novel a stable patriarchal authority. When skin color is mentioned, Isaacs does so matter-of-factly, following the formula intended to be sympathetic—nigra *sed* formosa. In *Matalaché*, however, the reader sees a society in flux. The novel's historical backdrops are the wars of independence, national identity and a reevaluation of *mestizaje*. The external signs of identity are more crucial; they produce strong reactions in the characters: disgust, anguish, revulsion, fear. Despicable, grotesque qualities are associated with blackness. Therefore, the black characters become objects to be repulsed. For the Mulatto his physical appearance is a source of self-hate. Blackness signifies not so much slavery and loss of freedom here as exclusion, denial, rejection. Color in *Matalaché* is a means of isolation; it is the basis for dissociation between Mulatto and Black, which is even more important for the dominant society's image of the Mulatto than the separation between Black and White.

José Manuel feels himself superior to the slaves on the estate. Conscious that his color prevents him from the privileges of legitimacy, though he has few Negroid features—and, therefore, might be less offensive as a protagonist—Negroid features obsess him. He abhors the "exudations of the full-blooded African's skin," "the harsh, rebellious curliness of his forebears' kinky heads," "that horrid flattening of the nose of his maternal ancestors, who lived with their nose eternally on display like a sign of gross bestiality" (p. 69). José Manuel does not, however, reject other signs of difference. López Albújar directs the reader's attention to the Mulatto's clothing: a tiger skin and sandals. The Mulatto wears these primitive, exotic garments proudly and never abandons them.

The Mulatto's reaction to his color is the imposition of a society wishing to maintain its own importance. It makes itself the object of desire of those it oppresses. To be white is to be free and to share in society. Society punishes the Mulatto for daring to aspire to a fuller participation by inducing self-hate and suffering. This psychological dilemma becomes an essential element of a rhetorical presentation of the Mulatto. It affects characterization, plot action and imagery.

It is important that the Mulatto be kept subservient. A principal means of doing this is to depict him as dangerous to society. In *Matalaché* and other novels this danger is presented in terms of sexual rivalry. The Mulatto is described exclusively as a sexual being. This insistence becomes the basis for distancing between the Mulatto and society and also between the Mulatto and the Black. López Albújar restates the nature of the Mulatto's sexuality by creating extremely negative images of sexuality. Although sexuality in Blacks as in Mulattoes is considered an expression of animal nature, in black characters the author presents it in its extreme form, lust. Because lust is associated with the novel's villain, the *negro congo*, it becomes a manifestation of sexuality calculated to arouse only grotesque fears. It is destructive and has no other possible interpretation. In this way López Albújar confirms the dominant society's fears about the vileness of Blacks and the degradation inherent in racial mixing. The bestial nature of the *negro congo* manifests itself in the obscene ditty he constantly chants under his breath about José Manuel. The *negro congo* is the envious voice of white men who lust after black and mulatto women and the frustrated voice of black men who resent the Mulatto's sexual privileges.

In order to give it other meanings, López Albújar attempts to handle the sexuality of the Mulatto in a more complex manner. He shows new aspects of character when linking the Mulatto's sexuality to an animal nature, according to a stereotype meant to dehumanize. Furthermore, he goes on to show how such a reductive image of the Mulatto reveals base tendencies in white characters. The characterization of the Mulatto as stud is much more a projection of the sexual fantasies of Whites, of the Other, intended to satisfy their voyeurism. López Albújar uses animal imagery to establish José Manuel's sexuality. Although these figures contain many negative elements, they possess some positive ones as well. The animal nicknames given to José Manuel express hostility and also envy. The language is pejorative ("tiger," "shark"); it stresses the predatory nature of the Mulatto. These names connote uncontrolled force, potentially dangerous to the white society.[21] However, these same figures, together with others such as "stallion" also suggest tremendous energy and more admiration than fear. José Manuel is attractive to the reader (he is handsome, well-mannered, soft-spoken, noble, kind, sad and more), in spite of the names other characters give him. "Tiger," "shark" and "stallion" introduce new factors into a reader's consideration of the mulatto character.

Sexual appetite in the Mulatto has more possibilities for satisfaction and for escape from the strictly pejorative connotations of animality than in the case of the black characters. For example, the physical prowess of the Mulatto establishes a certain superiority over Whites that is expressed in terms of energy and productivity. Moreover, after José Manuel falls in love with María Luz, López Albújar associates sex with fulfillment that is more than sexual. He describes it as an enlightenment. In this way the author increases the range of emotions the Mulatto experiences as well as certain actions possible for him. Indeed, to conceive of the Mulatto only as stud is to imply that he has no emotional involvement with the women he services. Contrary to this lack of feeling, López Albújar shows the reader the Mulatto's dissatisfaction with such a life. He portrays José Manuel as being not only able to perceive the indignity and humiliation of such an image but actually capable of reacting against it. By not exalting his own sexual prowess, as do the voyeurs, José Manuel refutes their image of him. The Mulatto, given López Albújar's presentation, cannot fulfill his potential without the support of Whites; the Mulatto remains inferior to them, reinforcing part of a rhetorical presentation affecting both Mulattoes and Blacks. However, any innovation in character definition that allows the Mulatto to challenge the negative images imposed by the dominant society leads the reader away from these perceptions of the Mulatto formulated by a hostile Other.

López Albújar uses two narrative perspectives to create his mulatto character: one private, open to change; the other public, hostile and resistant to change. In this way he portrays the stereotype and provides the basis for a more complex view of the Mulatto. The hostile public image is the one the reader first encounters in the opening conversation between two plantation owners about interracial sex: The Mulatto is an exclusively sexual being. The private view, the more significant and profound, is that of María Luz and develops with her love for José Manuel. She participates in revising the most pervasive stereotype of the Mulatto, a sexual ogre.

In humanizing the Mulatto in order to reduce his marginality, López Albújar forces the reader to consider the new vision he proposes by making the public in the novel witness to other dimensions of the Mulatto's character. The musical competition between José Manuel and a black slave from a nearby estate is the setting for this reevaluation. Toward the end of the novel the white characters who view the Mulatto as sexual being acknowledge this to be a defective myth. On first seeing José Manuel, a white woman remarks: "That was not at all how they had imagined Matalaché the Terrible. That lengendary one was an

ogre—a horrible insatiable beast. . . . The one before them was quite different, the opposite of the false legend: Here was a black Don Juan . . . and how
this man must be able to love and possess! His profound and masterful look
proclaimed it'' (p. 169). Although the terms of the white women's perceptions
remain sexual, the phrase "profound . . . look" suggests that "love" here refers to more than lust. After the concert, white men acclaim José Manuel's music as original and deeply moving; it has become more than a mere amusement.
This public reconsideration confirms María Luz' private redefinition of José
Manuel. By the time of the competition she accepts him without wishing him
white. The tiger skin and sandals he wears no longer disturb her.

Ultimately, López Albújar, as the mulatto character himself, challenges the
stereotyped view the society would have of him. José Manuel comes to understand human worth—his worth—in terms other than race, color or sexuality.
The incipient dialectical presentation we find in *Matalaché* culminates in its final scenes.[22] Facing death at the hands of María Luz' father, José Manuel asks
him: "Which of us is the beast? You or I?" (p. 186). This question permits
the Mulatto to assert—though weakly—the new conditions of his identity: faith
in his perceptions of himself. López Albújar's characterization of the Mulatto,
given its limitations, is remarkable for the transformations within and beyond
the context of the stereotype.

JUYUNGO, A DIALECTICAL PRESENTATION: ABANDONING THE STEREOTYPE

The disparaging portraits of Blacks common to most of the novels that treat
the Mulatto favorably are not the only definitions of Blacks found during the
first half of the twentieth century. Beginning in the 1930s, many authors created black characters who are notable because they depart from the stereotypes
propagated by the nineteenth-century attitudes toward race.[23] This occurs partly
because of a reaction against European cultural values, particularly the negative
attitudes toward non-whites. The reevaluation of the Mulatto in López Albújar's *Matalaché* is one manifestation of this. Another possible reason is the
preoccupation with the sociopolitical realities of Latin America, which gives
rise to a literary tradition of social protest.

The presentation of black characters created with this new consciousness tends
to be more dialectical than rhetorical. The qualities attributed to Blacks are not
derived from the society's antipathy to the Black. Instead, authors draw on a
perception of the Black that acknowledges the validity of certain traits that society attempts to demean: physical appearance, assertive behavior, ability to *do*.
By establishing a different source for the attributes of Blacks, authors force the
reader to examine them from a new perspective, a process that ideally leads
away from affirmation of negative views toward a reevaluation of them. Authors who write about the Black see him as a victim. However, unlike earlier
portrayals, which defined the Black in terms of the overwhelming quality of his

victimization (*María*) or dwelt on his more or less passive response to it (*Matalaché*), inter-novelists focus on different aspects of this victimization. They seek the sources of the black man's active resistance to oppression.

Adalberto Ortiz initiates a redefinition of the black character in the literature of South America with his novel *Juyungo* (1943). Given the strong tradition of social protest literature in Ecuador, its appearance here, perhaps, is not surprising. One critic describes *Juyungo* as "combining the characteristics of a novel of social protest with the protagonist's search for individual identity."[24]

Ortiz sets the novel in contemporary Ecuador rather than in times of slavery. The novel narrates the story of Ascención Lastre. It recounts his life among the Cayapa Indians in the jungle, in settlements along the river, with a small group of Blacks on an island, and his death in the war between Ecuador and Peru. Ortiz' characterization of his black protagonist is an effort to eliminate the perception of the Other, the dominant society. He allows the black character himself to determine his own image. To do this, Ortiz constructs a plot that allows the black protagonist to demythicize the dominant society.

Ortiz, like López Albújar and others who try to create a new image of the Mulatto, also utilizes activity as a primary element of his characterization.[25] Ortiz, however, is not as concerned with productivity as are novelists who deal with the Mulatto. By minimizing the importance of productivity, Ortiz shows less concern for validating the worth of the Black to society. He stresses instead the need for the character to define and appreciate himself. Energy, assertion, aggression become ways of defining a new image of the Black. The source of this energy is the black character. No superior being, such as the white women in novels about the Mulatto—María Luz in *Matalaché*, for example—figures as catalyst or inspiration of this energy. It originates in and is sustained only by the protagonist Ascención Lastre, an indication of sufficiency and independence that none of the black or mulatto characters considered so far have had.

On one level, *Juyungo* deals with the radicalization of Ascención Lastre. On another, its episodic structure presents the reader with a variety of interracial and intercultural relationships between Blacks, Indians, Mulattoes and Whites that describe Ascención's journey of self-discovery. This is his primary means of understanding his place in the sociopolitical reality. Ascención unmasks the exploitive nature of family, religion, politics, capitalist enterprises and white women.

Ascención demythicizes society using gestures of rejection and dismissal. He slaps away a priest's hand, exposes a false healer and a fraudulent shaman; he turns his back on his father, who had abandoned him; he kills the men responsible for the death of his son and his wife's insanity. These acts are at the same time expressions of assertion and aggression. They dispel the view of the Black as docile, as gullible, as exploitable. The reader sees these actions from the point of view of the black protagonist. His actions are no longer threatening but are statements of protection of the black man's self.

Asserting a revised image of the Black challenges the rhetorical view of him. There is no respect for the racial hierarchy. Ascención is unlike the Blacks in *María*, who know their place and keep to it. He is unlike the Blacks in *Matalaché*, who more actively want another place but barely articulate their desires. In both these instances the presentations of Blacks depend on an imposed and enforced passivity. For Ortiz' character, however, respect is not linked to race. Most important for him is his Self. He is confident in his dealings with Whites or light-skinned persons. He takes the initiative in small matters (asking a stranger his name) and in major ones (beating up a white onlooker who smirkingly jokes about a wedding party made up of Blacks, one of whom is Ascención).[26]

Ascención insists on setting his own conditions for acceptance. Let us consider how Ortiz uses color as a means of definition for his protagonist. Conventionally skin color has been a means of establishing superiority or inferiority. The Mulatto's violent reaction against negroid features in *Matalaché* affirms society's opinion of blackness. Such a response belongs to a rhetorical presentation of Blacks. Even in *María*, where there is no negative reaction to black skin, Isaacs tacitly acknowledges its inferiority by attributing good qualities to them in spite of being black. In many novels about Blacks, authors try to neutralize their characters' dark skin in some way. Ortiz, however, uses Ascención's skin color to reinforce the aggressive identity he has created for his protagonist.

Throughout the novel the black protagonist strives to define himself: sometimes in terms of color, more frequently in terms of action. Even as a young boy, living with the Cayapa Indians, Ascención retains a sense of his difference from them. He assumes their way of life completely, except that he will not paint his body with annatto, a reddish vegetable pigment. This refusal to disguise his blackness can be seen as an assertion of identity. It is significant that the black character himself makes the decision.

Later in the novel Ascención again describes himself: "I am ebony, black without, black within" (p. 232). Ebony suggests not only blackness, but also resilience, strength, durability. This positive concordance of outer and inner being is unusual. Referring to an inner blackness in a positive way is a declaration of acceptance. It contrasts, for example, with the dilemma of the Mulatto in *Matalaché*, whose frustration is the result of his feeling black without, white within. Blackness is the degrading factor. In *María* black characters really have no inner being. It has been "whitened" to make them acceptable. Furthermore, Isaacs suggests that the Blacks are satisfied with white identity.

Ascención's identity with blackness allows Ortiz to oppose the usual pejorative connotation of Black so frequent in other novels.[27] In this work these unfavorable associations appear in Ascención's nickname, Juyungo, which in the language of the Cayapa Indians means "devil, black man, monkey, evil." Another black character is Ascención's negative counterpart, Cocambo, a cowardly, brutal, slavish and ignoble Black who hates other Blacks. In using *Ju-*

yungo as the title of a novel, Ortiz demythicizes the unfavorable meaning of the word with the characterization of the protagonist. The positive nature of the character with whom the reader associates the name *Juyungo* destroys the negative semantic base.

Toward the end of the novel Oritz gives blackness its most forceful expression. When Ascención strips in order to storm better the enemy Peruvian camp, his black skin becomes a magic cloak, rendering him invisible, enabling him to perform the most daring and heroic act of his life.

Ortiz has provided a beginning for a new definition of black character. It is, however, only a beginning. He suggests other factors for identity ("more than race, class"). To understand how authors have attempted to expand the reader's perception of Blacks, it is certainly necessary to admit other formative elements. Ortiz' protagonist is ignorant of his history; "Africa" and "slavery" are vague, unfamiliar words for him. More significantly, he is uninterested in them. Yet knowledge of the historical and cultural antecedents of the Afro-Hispanic experience remains a rich source still not fully exploited for a dialectical presentation of Blacks and Mulattoes, particularly in fiction from continental Hispanic America.

NOTES

1. David Craig, *The Real Foundations: Literature and Social Change* (London: Chatto and Windus, 1973), p. 245.

2. Henri Baudet, *Paradise on Earth: Some Thoughts on European Images of Non-European Man* (New Haven and London: Yale University Press, 1965), p. 6.

3. For an analysis and discussion of race contact in the New World, see Magnus Morner's study, *Race Mixture in the History of Latin America* (Boston: Little, Brown, 1967); also Harmannus Hoetink, *Slavery and Race Relations in the Americas* (New York: Harper and Row, 1973).

4. This point is well dealt with in Sylvia Wynter, "The Eye of the Other," in *Blacks in Hispanic Literature*, ed. Miriam DeCosta (Port Washington, N.Y.: Kennikat Press, 1977), pp. 27–39.

5. Stanley E. Fish, *Self-Consuming Artifacts* (Berkeley and Los Angeles: University of California Press, 1972), pp. 1–2.

6. Ibid.

7. See Lemuel Johnson, *The Devil, the Gargoyle, and the Buffoon: The Negro as Metaphor in Western Literature* (Port Washington, N.Y.: Kennikat Press, 1971).

8. Luis Monguió, "El negro en algunos poetas españoles y americanos anteriores a 1800," *Revista Iberoamericana* 22, no. 44 (1957): 245–59.

9. Miguel Acosta Saignes, *Vida de los esclavos negros en Venezuela* (Havana: Casa de las Américas, 1978). This detailed study documents the role black slaves played in Venezuelan society through the end of the eighteenth century. It can serve as a model for other countries in Latin America insofar as the importance of Blacks to the economy and social organization is concerned.

10. The principal antislavery novels were Anselmo Suárez y Romero's *Francisco*, written in 1839; Gertrudis Gómez de Avellaneda's *Sab* (1841); Antonio Zambrana's *El*

negro Francisco (1873); Martín Morúa Delgado's *Sofía* (1891) and *La familia Unzúaza* (1901).

11. In developing this point, Lemuel Johnson's analysis of space and time as significant indicators of attitudes toward black characters was particularly helpful. These ideas appeared in his paper read at the Medgar Evers Symposium on Afro-Hispanic Literature, New York, June 1980.

12. Arnold Hauser, *The Social History of Art* (New York: Alfred A. Knopf, 1951), 4:118–19.

13. Jorge Isaacs, *María*, ed. Donald McGrady (1867; reprint ed., Barcelona: Labor, 1970), p. 232. Further references will appear in the text.

14. For a discussion of the "reliable" narrator, see Wayne Booth, *The Rhetoric of Fiction* (Chicago and London: University of Chicago Press, 1961), p. 250.

15. Isaacs Cesar Cantú, author of an encyclopedia work, *Storia universale* (1838–1846), is an authority on African tribes. Isaacs appears, however, to have rearranged certain items—creative license—to reinforce a white aesthetic. These are details of physical appearance.

16. Cirilo Villaverde's *Cecilia Valdés* (1882) and Avellaneda's *Sab* (1841) are the two most notable nineteenth-century Hispanic-American works about the Mulatto. Their presence suggests an earlier awareness of the issue of race mixing in the Caribbean than does the later appearance of novels about the Mulatto on the continent. However, nineteenth-century fiction of South America turns more to the Black as subject matter. See Isaacs' *María*; Eustaquio Palacios' *El alférez real* (1884); Eduardo Blanco's "Manuelote" in *Tradiciones épicas y cuentos viejos* (1879); and Rafael Bolívar's "La negra," in *El Cojo Ilustrado* 6 (1897): 850.

17. Rómulo Gallego's protagonist in *La trepadora* (1925) is of mixed blood. However, his characterization is not as essential to the novel, nor as obvious as in López Albújar's *Matalaché* (Lima: Juan Mejía Baca y P. L. Villaneuva, 1953?).

18. López Albújar's personal involvement with the subject of *mestizaje* is evident in his correspondence about the novel, *Matalaché*, with Ramiro de Maeztu. The Peruvian author defends his treatment of interracial love, justifying it in part by saying that the protagonist is a Mulatto (acceptable), not a Black (unacceptable). See *Matalaché*, pp. 10–11.

19. Monguió, "El negro," p. 246.

20. Humberto Palza, "El hombre como método," in *Ensayos sobre literatura latinoamericana*, ed. Arturo Torres Ríoseco (Berkeley: University of California Press, 1953), p. 184.

21. Rómulo Gallegos, "Las tierras de Dios," *Una posición en la vida* (Mexico: Ediciones Humanismo, 1954), p. 175.

22. Even in the final scene the Mulatto bases his superiority on his European and not his African blood; this somewhat weakens the argument about José Manuel's degree of understanding his situation. While generally Mulattoes are presented as inferior to Whites, exceptions exist. Mulatto protagonists in Arturo Uslar Pietri's *Las lanzas coloradas* (1931; reprint ed., Buenos Aires: Losada, 1949) and Alfredo Pareja Diez-Canseco's *Baldomera* (Santiago de Chile: Ediciones Ercilla, 1938) assert the superiority of the racially mixed person over both Whites and Blacks; Uslar Pietri's novel is the primary example.

23. New presentations of Blacks first appear in Caribbean literature. Cuban novelists in the early 1930s reinterpret the black slave in history. See, for example, José Antonio Ramos' *Caniquí* (1936; reprint ed., Havana: Consejo Nacionalde Cultura, 1963) and Lino

Novás Calvo, *Pedro Blanco el negrero* (1933; reprint ed., Buenos Aires: Espasa Calpe, 1944). See also Pedro Barreda's critical work, *The Black Protagonist in the Cuban Novel* (Amherst: University of Massachusetts Press, 1979).

24. John Brushwood, *The Spanish American Novel* (Austin: University of Texas Press, 1975), pp. 145–46. See *Juyungo* (Buenos Aires: Editorial Americalee, 1943).

25. Other novels about Mulattoes are Rómulo Gallegos' *Pobre negro* (1937 reprint ed., Buenos Aires: Espasa Calpe, 1961) and Ramón Díaz Sánchez's *Cumboto* (1950; reprint ed., Santiago de Chile: Editorial Universitaria, 1967).

26. The wedding incident in *Juyungo* repeats the conditions Quevedo satirizes in his poem "Boda de negros." See Johnson, *The Devil, the Gargoyle, and the Buffoon*, p. 71. Ortiz, however, inverts the roles of subject and spectator. Ascención's attack on the white onlooker is literally an attack on the perspective of the dominant society as Other. It becomes an assertion of the black character, a defense of his Self.

27. Black is negative in Uslar Pietri's *Las lanzas coloradas*, in Alberto Insúa's *El negro que tenía el alma blanca* (1922; reprint ed., Madrid: Espasa Calpe, 1958), in Dionisio Trillo Pays' *Pompeyo Amargo* (Montevideo: Claudio García, 1942) and in Alberto Ordóñez Arguello's *Ebano* (San Salvador: Dirección de Bellas Artes, 1954). Antonio Olliz Boyd discusses the persistence of black as a negative attribute in recent fiction in "Latin American Literature and the Subject of Racism," *CLA Journal* 19, no. 3 (1976): 566–74.

Portuguese
South America _

12

Palmares and the Freed Slave in Afro-Brazilian Literature

Ronald M. Rassner (for Abdias do Nascimento)

The length of the conflict between this independent community [Palmares] and the colonial government was so protracted, lasting as it did for some seventy years, and so important were the expeditions against it, that the Negro peoples of Alagoas, especially in the Barriga mountains, and the Paraiba and Mandahu valleys, still retain a recollection of these events in their folklore and popular plays.

Arthur Ramos, *The Negro in Brazil*[1]

During the second watch of that night, between the fifth and sixth of February, suddenly and tumultuously [Zumbi] with all his people and the equipment which could follow him through that space, made an exit. The sentinels of that post did not perceive them almost until the end. In the rear guard Zumbi himself was leaving, and at that point he was shot twice. As it was dark, and all this was taking place at the edge of the cliff, many— a matter of about two hundred—fell down the cliff. As many others were killed. Of both sexes and all ages, five hundred and nineteen were taken prisoner.

Letter from Domingos Jorge Velho, or one of his captains, to the Portuguese Overseas Council, February 1694[2]

I

And so ended the reign of Zumbi Sueca,[3] the last king of Palmares, and its siege by the relentless *paulista*[4] General Domingos Jorge Velho. History will show that Zumbi had strengthened and garrisoned his rocky fortress, Macaco, so that it was virtually impregnable. He built three lines of defense, using pits and traps, caltrops and fencing. All previous attempts to storm or overrun the fortress by the Portuguese had failed; Zumbi had successfully insulated himself and his people from the white invaders. It is at this point that Domingos Jorge showed his years of *sertao* (backlands) experience. Rather than attack, he laid a siege that lasted twenty-two days; he essentially imprisoned the already isolated black community. Let us examine the imagery at this juncture: Domingos Jorge Velho lays siege to an already imprisoned people. Zumbi, the individual, and Palmares, his nation, are besieged, in a "state of siege." There is no conceivable escape. Freitas, the most recent Palmares historian writes: "One thing remains clear: Zumbi and his people decided to accept a confrontation of which the result would be either a victory or a complete defeat. [It was a] crucial decision that illustrates vividly the Hegelian dialect between master and slave."[5]

The most famous and successful *quilombo* (maroon community) in Brazilian history, Palmares existed throughout most of the seventeenth century (1630– 1697). This *quilombo* was in fact an empire of eleven confederated communities that stretched 250 kilometers from Maceió, Alagoas, to Recife, Pernambuco. With a population of over twenty thousand inhabitants, the history of Palmares is a history of an African nation in Brazil and the history of a courageous people who maintained their African traditions, revolting against a landed Portuguese aristocracy for almost a century.

Arthur Ramos tells us that Palmares has never been adequately treated by the historian and that there exists a very considerable gap in the "broad chronicle of Brazil."[6] It is known, however, that with the arrival of Africans in Brazil (1532–1534) a social and economic polarity was established. Africans either worked as slaves for Whites in the *engenhos* (sugar mills) and *canaviais* (cane fields), or they ran away to the foreboding forests and backlands, living in isolated freedom. Slavery or freedom, the *engenho* or *quilombo*, represented a polarity that existed throughout most of the seventeenth and eighteenth centuries in various parts of Brazil. But in examining the choice, one also notices an ambiguity: Either live as an oppressed slave or live as an oppressed freedman, warding off continual raids by Portuguese or Dutch armies, local militias and generally recalcitrant Amerindians.

Nonetheless, contact between the *palmarinos* and the *moradores* (Portuguese plantation owners, many of whom were descendants of *novos cristãos*) was maintained secretly. This kind of awkward, behind-the-scenes contact is a prelude to black-white relations in Brazil today. A trade existed between *palmarino* gold, silver and agricultural produce and the *moradores* firearms and manufactured goods. Spies operated on both sides. Even with this underground contact the Portuguese could not tolerate the existence of a Palmares and what it signified. Various peace treaties were negotiated, only to be used as strategic, military advantages by a succession of governors in Recife.

Zumbi assumed power in a 1676 coup against King Ganga-Zumba, who had negotiated too much away to the Portuguese. Freitas describes Zumbi as a "Negro of unique valor, great courage, and rare perseverance; this is his advantage, because his hard work, judgment, and strength embarrass us, but exemplify his people."[7] In what will become important in the analyses below, it was rumored that Zumbi had as his wife a white woman. In spite of this, Zumbi led the *palmarinos* for almost twenty years. He escaped Domingos Jorge's siege, only to be betrayed and killed by a mulatto lieutenant one year later. As in the case of Palmares itself, extremely little is known about him. Yet he has come to symbolize freedom for Afro-Brazilians. Rabassa writes:

In many cases, the first event that comes to mind is the somewhat successful revolt of slaves who established the Black Republic of Palmares under the command of Zumbi, an almost legendary figure. *Zumbi represents the hope of many Blacks who today find themselves in precarious positions*, even though he [Zumbi] attained so much under conditions, obviously, which were less favorable for Blacks than they are today.[8]

But what did Zumbi attain? Can we evaluate his freedom? The words of Emanuel, the black lawyer in Abdias do Nascimento's play, *Sortilegio* (1978), may have been the last words spoken by Zumbi:

Life . . . death . . . it's all the same. I don't think I'll last much longer. My end is near. I finish like a stranger. Foreigner that I was in the world which glistens there below. It seems to shine with happiness. Can it really be a happy city? I don't know. Nobody knows. I know in this world there wasn't any place for me. A corner where one might live without humiliations. A country that wasn't hostile. Everywhere it's the same. Them, the whites, on one side. On the side, no. On top. And the black . . . beaten . . . robbed . . . killed. . . . Oh I'm alone! And I've lost![9]

In the introductory quote Ramos noted that the history of Palmares had been retained in the oral traditions of the peoples of the northeastern state of Alagoas. Palmares was also the subject of two relatively weak novels, both of which incorrectly or inadequately treat the legend. Jaime de Altavilla's *O Quilombo dos Palmares* is historically accurate and well footnoted but mingles eroticism and melodrama with fact.[10] The Zumbi Sueca is betrayed by another *palmarino*, Bamboré, who abducts his wife during the final siege. Some *palmarinos* flee the *quilombo* because they desire white women and *cachaça* (cane brandy), both of which are available (the former for "sight" only!) in the *engenhos*. The coward Bamboré is pictured as a *maconha-* ("marijuana") smoking fiend. Leda Maria da Albuquerque's novel, *Zumbi dos Palmares* (1914), was written for a juvenile audience and simply dramatized Zumbi's "suicide."[11]

The Palmares legend, however, has had more literary power as a secondary, supplemental or even suggestive theme in Afro-Brazilian literature. The images of a besieged nation defending itself against repeated white assaults, or of an isolated hero who refuses to surrender, has been preserved directly or indirectly in Afro-Brazilian literature since 1845. Essentially, both theater and narrative have treated the Palmares imagery in the same manner. First, writers in both genres have had to base the Zumbi/Palmares imagery on similar sources; indeed, the only data available are the ethnocentric accounts of Portuguese, Dutch and Paulista soldiers or later reinterpretations of this data. Second, and most important, the literary and historic treatment of African descendants by Brazilians illustrates a single fact: Afro-Brazilians have led, and lead, a life of physical or symbolic slavery that is simultaneously "condensed" and forecast in the Palmares imagery.

Therefore, the accuracy in the portrayal of the legend itself (which varies considerably), the distinction in its treatment by the genres of theater and written narrative or the chronological sequence of works (either nineteenth- or twentieth-century) have had little impact on the strength of the prevalent imagery itself. Certainly, subtle shifts in the legend's emphasis and influence are attributable to the political, economic and social awareness of the times. But the bottom line, the mentality of the siege, remains. It is interesting to note that chronological distancing remedies the historical inaccuracies, so that, in the conceivable future, a more accurate portrayal of the legend will occur. But this is to be seen not as a diachronic development but rather as a return to synchrony, to the common denominator between Palmares and the "cosmetic myth of racial tolerance" in Brazil.[12]

II

Palmares, a "Troia negra,"[13] was an African confederation insulated from, yet maintaining relations with, white society, all the while enduring the tensions of repeated states of siege and wars. The life and death of Palmares, and Zumbi, foreshadow the black heroic figure as it has been developed in Brazilian theater from Martins Pena to the Teatro Experimental do Negro and modern Brazilian drama. Moreover, the omniscient Palmares imagery has forced Brazilian playwrights, both black and white, to search for a legitimate black hero— and it is the result of this search to which we shall now direct this essay.[14]

Often called the founder of a truly national theater, Martins Pena was the first Brazilian playwright to capture the quotidian life of Brazilians in Rio de Janeiro. It was said that his plays reflected the vices and intrigues of the Rio scene; however, none of his plays focused on Afro-Brazilians.[15] Rather, Afro-Brazilians appeared in his work as tertiary personages, folkloric pieces or, simply, chattel. Pena's *O Cigano* (1845) offers an interesting perspective.[16] The gypsy Simão runs a smuggling operation with Tomé, a peddler, and Gregório, a customs official. Their most lucrative business is the kidnapping of slaves, selling them to other slave owners for work in the mines of Minas Gerais.

But their method of kidnapping is unreal; they convince the slaves that after eight days of work in the mines, they will be enriched and given their freedom. The assumption, on their part and Pena's, is that all the slaves, being dimwitted and slow, will jump at any chance to escape their present plight. There is no possibility for any black heroism. Tomé admits to the gypsy that "these devilish Negroes have an intelligence for thievery that is hard to believe,"[17] but the overall perspective is that the Afro-Brazilian has no intelligence for anything else. (This perception of "talent for thievery" is one that continues with the twentieth-century *malandro* theme in Callado and Gianfrancesco). Indeed,

Gregório states later, "So stupid these Negroes; they allow themselves to be deceived with such an admirable ease." [18]

The conclusion to the play offers some justice. One Black, who has been supplying the smugglers with stolen goods, reveals their operations to the police. Knowing that their end is in sight, the three smugglers accidentally confront the three young men who are lovers of the gypsy's three daughters. There is a scuffle—the smugglers think them to be spies—and Pena includes stage directions in which "the Negro jumps about happily, clapping his hands, while the others fight." [19] In what was designed, no doubt, for purely comic relief, Pena's black character, Antonio, jumps for joy when he sees the white men fighting among themselves. This is Antonio's only spontaneous, emotional moment in the entire play, and for this reason alone it is significant. Although another critic could read this action to be a comic mime of simian antics, its place in Brazilian literary history points to something more important. To observe the fight, to remain outside the focus, Antonio becomes a momentary center. His objectivity becomes a separation from the chained stereotype of a Brazilian slave and symbolizes the first independent step by a black character on the Brazilian stage. [20]

What significance can the theme of Palmares and Zumbi have for Antonio, a nonhero? Where can he go? What can he do? Not central to the play, he has no control over his own life and must answer to others, that is, his white masters. Is slavery itself a "state of siege?" Certainly it is for those who want out. But in *O Cigano*, "out" of slavery is "into" slavery.

This state of siege, of isolation, is also maintained in *Calabar* (1850). Agrario de Meneses' play is based on the true story of Calabar, a Mulatto who betrayed the Portuguese army during the Dutch Wars (1630–1645). [21] *Calabar* was the first play written in Brazil to have as its protagonist a man of color. It is ironic, then, that the choice would fall to (1) a traitor to Brazil and (2) a rapist. But was not Zumbi a traitor and plunderer as well?

Calabar, because of his knowledge of the terrain in Pernambuco, his experience with the Indians, his fighting and organizational abilities and his personal magnetism, is made commander of the Portuguese forces fighting against the Dutch. The plot is complicated by Argentina, the "beautiful daughter of the indigenes," whom Calabar loves. But she loves Faro, a Portuguese lieutenant, and runs off with him. Jealousy blinds Calabar, and in order to strike back at the Portuguese, he joins the Dutch army. But all these events—that is, which side Calabar fights for—becomes irrelevant. During the preparations for one battle, Calabar lectures his troops:

The Portuguese! . . . false, vile, cowardly! . . .
Let fall on him the brand of vengeance.
                            (Wielding his sword)
See again the strength of my arm! . . .
Reborn, growing! . . . Bloody and wild

> Is the fight to be now! . . . Tremble all!
> Holland or Portugal, masters both,
> Both tyrants, stealing our fatherland from us!
> A slave here, there, this one or that one,
> Does it matter? . . . Slavery is always death!
> Follow me friends; off to battle then![22]

For Calabar there is no difference between Portuguese or Dutch—the European is in Brazil to maintain the status quo, a "slave here, there, this one or that one,/Does it matter?"

From the moment he enters the stage, the hero finds himself isolated from other Brazilians. His rank and his color work toward his isolation. When he reveals himself to the Dutch, he cries "It's the Mulatto!! . . . Yes, it's the Mulatto, horrid and sad, indomitable and ferocious like the tempest, that swells the ocean's waves!!!"[23]

At the end of the play Calabar has seduced Argentina; with his capture by the Portuguese, his isolation is emphasized. Calabar is isolated, lost and besieged before his capture. But this is a man who is accepted by his peers, who leads white soldiers into battle. Can he, like his contemporary Henrique Dias, blend into the fabric of Brazilian society? The answer is decidedly negative; for Calabar, as a Mulatto, comes to symbolize the dual-edged threat faced by Brazil of the 1630s: Holland and Palmares. For the Portuguese both groups were the enemy.

JAGUARARI

> I don't know. Listen to me now, Albuquerque.
> Each day, stronger and bolder
> The Dutch armies are becoming.
> Besides the Janduis other allied
> Natives have gone to their side.
> Behold, finally, in the middle of Palmares
> The fearful Negroes have revolted!
> Before them is Zumbi, freeing a cry,
> Impelling them against us with raised scythe! . . .
> Let us think in winning that which is lost. . . .
> Where does the enemy halt?[24]

With the Portuguese, or the Dutch, Calabar remains a man apart. Late in the play he echoes a futuristic Emanuel, an older Zumbi: "There's no place in the world for a Mulatto."[25] Raymond Sayers also focuses on Calabar's isolation. He writes: "Thus the whole play seems to have been a study of the inferiority complex of the mulatto, of that extreme sensitivity which members of that mixed racial group are supposed to have their difficult positions in society."[26] These "difficult positions in society" are related to all men and women of color in Brazil. The theme of entrapment and isolation, of isolation in freedom continues in other plays concerning Afro-Brazilians. José de Alencar presented another significant protagonist, Joana, in his play *Mãe* (1860).[27] A middle-aged *mulata*, Joana takes care of her young master, Jorge, who is finishing medical school. Jorge's slave, Joana is also Jorge's mother, but for reasons of her inferiority complex, and for fear of jeopardizing her son's economic and social future, she refuses to divulge her secret. So the secret remains; and to maintain it, Joana uses all her skills to manipulate the individuals around her. Ultimately, her secret is revealed. Joana cannot live with the truth and commits suicide. Alencar has presented a character who is noble, pure, rational and heroic. But Joana's fate is similar to Calabar's. She cannot continue as a slave, nor can she survive free (indeed, before the dénouement Jorge frees her, yet she refuses to recognize her freedom). What then is this *nonmovement* that characterizes the Afro-Brazilian? The only solution, for Zumbi, Calabar and Joana, is death.

A similar fate awaits Lourenço, the black protagonist in Arthur Azevedo's *O Escravocrata* (1884).[28] As another antislavery piece, Azevedo presented the first Brazilian play to focus on the sexual relationship between a white woman and her slave (Lourenço). Their son Gustavo is raised by the cruel slave master and trader, Salazar, who is married to the white woman Gabriela. Lourenço finally reveals the truth to his son in order to stop him from stealing from his supposed father; and Salazar discovers this. Lourenço runs away, only to be caught and returned. He hangs himself, his son dies at his side and Gabriela is institutionalized. The fear and the inability to speak, to act, to be become the primary themes in *O Escravocrata*. Like Joana, Lourenço cannot reveal the truth, for to do so will destroy his son. His isolation is awesome. But his death does bring about some change. Other slaves on the plantation revolt, forcing Salazar to repent his cruelty. But like all chronicles concerning Afro-Brazilians, the ending is pessimistic.

In another play, *O Liberato* (1881), Azevedo creates a comedy around an old black slave who never appears on stage.[29] Throughout its entirety the other white characters, all of whom represent the spectrum of Brazilian society, attempt to decide Liberato's fate. Before they can do so, they learn that he has died. The final words in the play summarize this section on nineteenth-century Brazilian drama treating Afro-Brazilians: "You said that Liberato symbolized slavery; do you see? Decidedly, death is the only certain plan for emancipation."[30] In this, then, the only role for the Afro-Brazilian hero: a virtual nonmovement from slavery to isolation to death? These deaths repeat Zumbi's death without mention of the Palmares legend per se. The preabolition dramas focused on socially relevant issues, refusing to draw upon the historical precedent established by the Palmares legend. Nonetheless, the concepts of isolation and siege remain as indirect references to the legend and Afro-Brazilian life. The literature closest chronologically to the Palmares incident ignored it; ironically, twentieth-century drama began to include more direct references.

III

The image of Zumbi and Palmares, of a people separated from, yet used and destroyed by Brazilian civilization, does not stop with the abolition of slavery in 1888. This becomes a most remarkable aspect of Afro-Brazilian theater: Isolation, imprisonment, death (read "imprisonment" instead of "slavery") and isolation in freedom continue into the twentieth century and the era of modern drama. These images are most vividly portrayed in the work of Abdias do Nascimento.

Nascimento, of course, has been the only Afro-Brazilian Negritude playwright. His outcries against the social and physical *embranquecimento*[31] (bleaching) of Brazilian Blacks and his support for maintaining and praising African traditions in Brazil have evolved into a philosophy he calls *quilombismo*, a thought system based on the African experience in Brazil.[32] Nascimento's choice of words, *quilombismo*, then, recalls Palmares, just as his only play, *Sortilégio*, recalls Zumbi. Indeed, his revised title to the second edition of *Sortilégio* includes the phrase, *Mistério Negro de Zumbi Redivivo.*[33]

Nascimento founded the Teatro Experimental do Negro (TEN) in Rio de Janeiro in 1944 as an active protest against a society that aspired to be Latin, white and European, a society that did not hesitate to ignore African cultural values and influences.[34] The TEN became an institutionalized Negritude movement that attempted to stimulate the creation of a literature based on the Afro-Brazilian experience and to expose the racial dilemma in Brazil. Nascimento founded the TEN for the following reasons: (1) to liberate the marginalized values of African culture from a merely folkloric, picturesque condition; (2) to attempt an education of the dominant, white class; (3) to terminate the practice of having black-faced white actors playing the roles of Blacks on the Brazilian stage; (4) to discontinue the custom of using black actors in purely stereotyped roles; and (5) to unmask as inauthentic the pseudoscientific literature that failed to honestly depict the Brazilian racial context.[35]

Sortilégio was the first play written by a Black to be performed by the TEN. Nascimento completed the one-act play in 1951, but because of problems with the government censors it was not produced until 1957.[36] Oscar Fernandez has written that "among the charges levelled against it were that it might worsen relations between Whites and Blacks, and that it contained language not suitable for a public performance."[37]

The dramatic plot is as follows: A black *assimilado*, the lawyer Emanuel, is fleeing from the police. He climbs a steep bank onto the stage, entering a clearing in the woods. Emanuel enters the stage dressed in his coat and tie. The clearing is a *terreiro*, a *candomblé* or *macumba* (*voodoo*) temple, hidden "underground" in the woods because of persistent persecution by authorities. His arrival at the *terreiro* is not unexpected but is prophesized in the introduction of the play by three *filhas de santo* (*macumba* priestesses), much like *Macbeth*'s three witches. Upon sighting the *terreiro* initially, he decides to leave, realizing that the police may easily discover him there, due to their periodical raids on *macumba* practices. But he cannot leave; he is not permitted by the Orixás (the African gods) and their sorcery to escape. Forced to remain, Emanuel disrespectfully drinks the sacrificial *marafo* ("sugarcane rum"), smokes the god Exu's *charutos* ("cigars") and, in general, mocks the Afro-Brazilian religious customs. He is subdued by the sorcery to review his past, his present, his future. He was at one time in love with a black woman, Efigenia, whom he left after failing to defend her adequately in a trial. She became a prostitute for white men. Emanuel then married a white woman, Margarida. He fled from the police after murdering her. (On their wedding night he discovered that she was not a virgin; later he suspected that she took white lovers.) His past and his present fuse into a terrifying glimpse of one black man's attempt to be accepted in Brazilian society. The play ends as he ritually disrobes, dons traditional Afro-Brazilian garments and commits suicide with Exu's ritual *zagaia* ("spear," "assegai").

Emanuel obviously represents isolation and imprisonment in freedom and therefore recalls the presence of Zumbi, Calabar, Joana and Lourenço. He is unjustly jailed for defending Efigenia, and he is jailed for being with Margarida.

Structurally speaking, Emanuel's plight is not dissimilar to that of Lourenço, Joana or Calabar, except that he is a free individual and an educated *assimilado*. But has his life been different from a Lourenço or a Joana? As Emanuel remembers his childhood, he recalled the voices of his classmates yelling "Nig . . . ger! Nig . . . ger! Nig . . . ger! Nig . . . ger!"[38] And his cry, noted earlier, "I know in this world there wasn't any place for me," echoes Calabar and the thematic message of Brazilian Blacks since Zumbi.

Emanuel's marriage to Margarida also continues the pattern of black-white involvement. These relationships all end without hope. Note the following:

Zumbi	Calabar	Joana	Lourenço	Emanuel
Married to white woman.	Loving an Amerindian woman. (Argentina symbolizes Brazil).	Mother of a white man's son.	Father of a white woman's son.	Married to a white woman, whom he murders.

It is the relationship with Whites (Amerindian for Calabar—but then Calabar's mixed ancestry immediately works against him, and Argentina, who could symbolize the "untamed" Brazil, does fall in love with a white man, precipitating the conflict) that becomes the fulcrum for action and/or death in all the above-mentioned Afro-Brazilian heroes (Zumbi is perhaps an exception, as we shall note later in *Pedro Mico*). Both Emanuel and Efigenia strive for acceptance in the white Brazilian world—the one, a lawyer, with a white woman and the other, a prostitute, with white men—but both fail. Emanuel, at least, discovers that the source of his isolation, his imprisonment, is that white world, that same world for which he strived. To survive, he must reverse his movement or, better, make a movement. His death becomes a thematic rebirth. Yet how does his death differ from the dismal ends of the others?

The only distinction that Nascimento adds to the retentive nexus of imagery is the *candomblé*. And it is the addition of this imagery that creates a justifiable equilibrium, or polarity, lacking in the nineteenth-century dramas. It is not simply abolition or erasing inferiority complexes but, rather, an obtainable goal—the African heritage, the heritage from Zumbi and Palmares—that becomes, for Nascimento, the answer to the Brazilian racial dilemma.[39] This idea, coupled with Margarida's murder, that is, the destruction of mobility through intermarriage,[40] brings Nascimento full circle to self-reliance and his sense of *quilombismo*.

IV

The image of Palmares, of a community isolated and imprisoned in its freedom, is developed further in the *malandro* plays of Antonio Callado and Gianfrancesco Guarnieri. Both playwrights attempted to capture the daily life in the *morros* (hills) of Rio de Janeiro, the poor black slums of *Pedro Mico* (1957)[41] and *Gimba* (1962).[42] The protagonist of each play, Pedro Mico and Gimba, is a *malandro*, roughly translated as loafer, bum, good-for-nothing, vagabond, one accustomed to taking advantage of others, who never works and lives from day to day. Both Gimba and Pedro Mico are locally famous; they are heroes to their people, the Afro-Brazilian slum-dwellers of Rio. Both are wanted and attacked by the police for having killed others.

Gimba returns to the *favela* home of Guiomar, a woman he loved. Once there, Gimba creates a conflict with a rival, Gabiro, who ultimately reveals his whereabouts to the police. Gimba also confronts Chica, an old *macumbeira*, who forecasts his doom and death. Like Emanuel (at first), Gimba scoffs at the old lady and her epithets. But unlike Emanuel, Gimba did it out of fear. Ultimately, he realizes the truth of her words. At the end of the play, cornered by the police in a *barraco* (shack), he listens to Guiomar, who pleads with him to give himself up. He assents and walks outside, only to be murdered by a crazed policeman.

Gimba portrays the Palmares image effectively. Gimba is a free man in modern Brazil, at a time when all free Afro-Brazilians are slaves to wages and the economy. Gimba moves outside these dynamics, as the *palmarinos* moved outside the *fazendeiro*-slave economy. Like Palmares, Gimba is always hunted, attacked; and like the life-death of Palmares, Gimba is constantly pursued, imprisoned, held in a state of siege. However, Gimba leaves his posterity to the sickly lad Tico, who kills Gabiro at the end for bringing the police and runs from the police to continue the life of a *malandro*.

Pedro Mico presents a more obvious comparison with Zumbi/Palmares. The *malandro* brings a white prostitute, Aparecida, to his *barraco* in the Morro da Catacumba. Although informed by his friends that the police are near, Pedro Mico relaxes with his new girlfriend. And she tells him the story of Zumbi:

APARECIDA: When you were just talking about the cops climbing the hill, I was reminded about the history of Zumbi.

PEDRO MICO: Who is the guy?

APARECIDA: Oh, he was a Black, a slave who lived a long time ago. I don't know why, but when you were talking I was thinking that Zumbi must have been a Black just like you, or perhaps like Mauro Guerra. And he didn't mess around. He jumped right into a real fight. He was a runaway slave, but he didn't run away alone. He took with him a good number of other slaves, and together they climbed to the top of a hill.[43]

Much like the real Zumbi, Pedro Mico is "making" history by re-creating it. Pedro Mico, importantly, is to repeat the Palmares imagery as only *he* can. Pedro is worldly wise, a man of the streets; but he knows little about slavery or history. Aparecida continues her story, about the many times Palmares was attacked, about how the *palmarinos* were forced to kill people and about the end of Palmares itself:

APARECIDA: But finally the government sent a full battalion there, with cannon and everything. They destroyed the walls of the city that the Black's had built there, and the troops climbed the hill, just like you said the police climbed Mangueira to catch Mauro Guerra.

PEDRO MICO: And this Zumbi guy, what about him?

APARECIDA: Oh, Zumbi fought like a wildcat, killing many soldiers. As long as he had a comrade near him, he didn't stop fighting. In the end, he saw that all was lost. . . .

PEDRO MICO: And they killed him?

APARECIDA: No. . . . He climbed to the top of Palmares hill there, right where a rock descended steeply like the end of the world, and he threw himself down from the very top.[44]

Pedro Mico, the *malandro*, is so impressed with the story that he uses a similar tactic to escape the police. Callado has brought the legend of Zumbi back to life in his play, as did Nascimento in an afterthought to his second edition of *Sortilégio*. Unlike Zumbi, Pedro Mico has no army, no followers. Other than his escape, he performs no real courageous or extraordinary acts, heroic or honorable deeds. The *malandro* moves toward heroism by accepting and using Zumbi's history; he moves toward heroism by repeating and varying Aparecida's rendition of the Palmares legend (we are assuming that Zumbi did not die in the Serra da Barriga, as noted earlier). Pedro Mico leaves the *morro* thinking, as Aparecida pressures him: "What do you think, Pedro, if all the people in the morros got together in order to go down [to the city] on the same day?"[45] Aparecida, like Carlão, the white factory worker in *Gimba*, acts as an information source for the *malandro*, for the hero-to-be. And as *Gimba* portrays the death of Palmares, *Pedro Mico* portrays its rebirth. There is hope in Callado's play that Pedro Mico may some day become the contemporary Zumbi. The glorification of the *malandro* as the potential Afro-Brazilian hero is a logical choice. Who else, divorced from society, can regain the movement and break the state of siege of Afro-Brazilians? Surely not those imprisoned in the system. But neither should it be those, like Pedro Mico and Gimba, who may be imprisoned outside that same system.[46]

V

Brazilian narrative reflects the Palmares imagery, that is, an imagery that simultaneously infuses a sense of freedom on the one hand, with isolation, impotence and a state of siege—seizure—on the other. A full-length study of Afro-Brazilian narrative must include novelists from both the nineteenth and twentieth centuries. For our purposes here, Afro-Brazilian narrative will be defined as (1) fiction written by Afro-Brazilians (for example, Machado de Assis, Mario de Andrade, Lima Barreto) and (2) fiction written about Afro-Brazilians (for example, Aluzio Azevedo, Jorge de Lima, Jose Lins do Rego, Coelho Neto, Antonio Olinto and Jorge Amado, among others).

The mulatto Machado de Assis, Brazil's most famous author, wrote nothing centering on Afro-Brazilians. The reasons for his disregard of slavery and racial problems have been contested for years but do not concern this essay. Two short stories, however, written fourteen years apart, reveal a similar theme of isolation and seizure. Both stories, "O Caso de Vara" (1891) and "Pai Contra Mae" (1905), include an Afro-Brazilian character who, while not central to the narrative structure, becomes the climactic point upon which the message is revealed. The narrative time of both stories occurs prior to the abolition of slavery. The story "O Caso de Vara" revolves around Damião, a young white man who decides to leave the seminary; the conflict centers around his attempt to ease out of his priestly and family obligations.[47] In the process he resorts to using Sinhá Rita, a middle-aged matron who runs an embroidery school for slave girls. One of her pupils is a *negrinha*, Lucrécia, who is sickly, thin and scarred. Damião feels pity for her and resolves to protect her someday. Later, when Damião's troubles have been solved, Rita becomes furious at Lucrécia for her slow work and moves to beat her. Damião is given the choice to bring the *vara* ("switch") or appeal for mercy; to help Rita or save the black girl. Machado de Assis ends his story as follows:

Sinhá Rita, her face on fire, her eyes starting from her head, kept calling for the rod, without letting go of the little black girl, who was now held in a fit of coughing. Damião was pricked by an uneasy sense of guilt, but he wanted so much to get out of the seminary! He reached the settee, picked up the rod, and handed it to Sinhá Rita.[48]

In "Pai Contra Mae," Candido Neves, a bounty hunter for runaway slaves is evicted from his home with his wife, infant son and aunt.[49] Penniless and starving, they decide to give the child up to a *Róda* (foundling asylum). Candido desperately hunts for fugitive slaves. On the day he is to take his son to the *Róda*, he spots a *mulata* runaway. He captures her, Arminda, and despite her pleas—she is pregnant—he returns her to her master for his reward. Candido saves his family, and Machado tells us wryly: "There, on the ground where she had fallen, driven by fear and pain, and after some struggle, she aborted."[50]

Both Damião and Candido, the white protagonists, are sure to survive the conflicts in which they are entwined. Damião will leave the seminary and Candido saves his infant son. But the opposite is true, in terms of movement/progress, for Lucrécia and Arminda. The two represent together the spectrum of Afro-Brazilians during slavery, the one who remains and the one who flees. Both are punished, and both are imprisoned and impotent in their respective "freedoms": Lucrécia is free if she finishes Rita's tasks; Arminda is free if she avoids the bounty hunter. Neither of these two characters have any movement in the two narratives. Lucrécia's laugh and Arminda's appearance before Candido are brief, ephemeral moments of freedom and individuality. Their lives are frozen in pre-abolition time, which is, of course, in direct contrast with the lives of their two assailants.

The irony of the two short stories lay in the pivotal importance of the two Afro-Brazilians, thematically crucial yet structurally disguised. Note how the lives of the two slaves pattern the lives of the two protagonists, respectively:

Damião	*Lucrécia*
Wishes to be freed from seminary, a figurative "enslavement." Will avoid father's wrath.	Wishes to avoid beating (that is, the life) that she usually receives. Will not escape Rita's wrath.

Candido	*Arminda*
Wishes to save and keep son.	Wishes to save and keep child.

Although their occurrence in the narrative is brief, their inclusion adds depth and perception to what is essentially the Brazilian racial dilemma: "Help yourself, or help others? No, use others."

The theories surrounding Machado de Assis's unwillingness to write more centrally about Afro-Brazilians range from psychological treatises to economic ones. But for our purposes in establishing a pre- and post-abolition Brazilian mentality dating from Palmares to the present, let us consider Sayers' rationale: "The Negro could not serve as a subject for the irony of Machado, for the Negro could never determine his own conduct or fix his own position in society; *he was not a free agent.*"[51] This is an understandable perspective for the writings of Machado de Assis that revolve around pre-abolition Brazil. As slaves, the Afro-Brazilians were not "free agents." But what of post-abolition Afro-Brazilian narrative? Surely a case against imprisonment in freedom can be justified.

A most logical choice would be the early novels of Jorge Amado. In particular, *Jubiabá*, with the black *malandro* Antonio Balduino, offers a full perspective of freedom, isolation, white women, the importance of Zumbi/Palmares and the *candomblé*.[52] Boxing champion, lover of many women, dock worker, strike leader, plantation laborer, indigent and composer of *sambas*, Antonio Balduino is the embodiment of the Brazilian *malandro/desordeiro*. Could Amado have been thinking of Palmares upon writing this novel? He begins with a boxing match between Baldo (Antonio) and the German, Ergin. The partisan crowd in Salvador da Baia shouts, "Smash him! Knock him flat!" A "metallic" voice from the crowd, shouts, "Where is the Negro Antonio Balduino who beats the Whites?" and "Where is the destroyer of the Whites?"[53] This echoes the only drama about Palmares existing today: "Rest Negro/The white man doesn't come here./If he comes/A beating is in order."[54]

But other, more direct references to Palmares are made by Amado. When his only blood relative, Tia Luisa, goes mad, Antonio is taken to a *comendador*'s house on Travessa ("cross street," "alley," "connecting passageway") Zumbi dos Palmares. It is here that Antonio meets Lindinalva, the freckled, saintly-faced daughter, who will have an abnormal influence on his life. (Their love-hate for each other is never consummated—Lindinalva later becomes pregnant out of wedlock, turns to prostitution and dies. Antonio rears her son.) The name of the street fascinates Antonio, and he asks Jubiabá, the *candomblé* priest, to tell him about Zumbi:

[H]e was a valiant Negro and he understood more than others. One day he fled, together with a band of Negroes, and remained free in a land of his own. Here more Negroes fled and joined with Zumbi. They created a great city of Negroes. And the Negroes began to seek revenge from the Whites. Then the Whites sent soldiers to kill the runaway Negroes. But the soldier couldn't handle the Negroes. They sent more soldiers, and the Negroes beat the soldiers.

Antonio Balduino was wide-eyed and trembled with enthusiasm.

Then they sent many soldiers, a thousand times more than the number of Negroes. But the Negroes didn't want to be slaves, and when he saw that they were losing, Zumbi, in order not to be beaten anymore by the white man, threw himself down from the hilltop. And all the Negroes threw themselves down also. . . . Zumbi of Palmares was a good and valiant Negro. If at that time there had been twenty like him, the Negro would never have been a slave.[55]

It was on the day that his aunt died that Antonio Balduino found a friend to substitute in his heart for the old Luisa: Zumbi of Palmares. He was from then on Antonio's chosen hero.[56]

Just as Lindinalva, the white woman, becomes a desirable but unobtainable goal, Zumbi dos Palmares becomes for Antonio an accessible symbol for freedom, for the struggle against the rich Whites. Does not Antonio tell Gordo to quit praying, "But what this Negro who is here wants is to kill all the Whites."? And Zumbi is the subject for an ABC, a song of one's life:

> Africa, where I was born
> I remember you.
> I lives free, hunting
> Eating fruit and *cuscus*.
>   Palmares where I fought,
> I fought against slavery
> A thousand soldiers came here
> And none of them returned.
>   Zumbi of Palmares then,
> From the hilltop he flung himself down,
> Saying: My people, goodbye, I'm going to die
> Because a slave I'll never be.[57]

But at the passageway, at Lindinalva's home, Antonio learns to accept three things: (1) that he may love but never possess Lindinalva; (2) that Zumbi become his hero; (3) that he live the life of a *malandro*. For Antonio the latter choice is the only road to freedom. For young Afro-Brazilians the choice was plain: either a life as *malandro*, or thief, or the slavery of the factories, the plantations, the petty jobs. Thus, accepting Zumbi as role model and the life of a *malandro* as an economic escape from Brazilian society, Antonio Balduino's adventures begin. He runs away from the *comendador*'s home, becomes a street urchin (*moleque*) and beggar, a boxing champion, a tobacco plantation hand, a circus performer and vagabond and finally, returning to Salvador, his home, a dock worker. Amado has told us that *Jubiabá* is the life of the Negro race in Brazil, a life of adventure and poetry.[58] But what does Antonio Balduino accomplish? Is he really free? Amado's intention is to make Antonio aware of the class structure, and Marxist struggle. When Antonio joins the dock workers, it is for Amado, at least, the positive development in his life. But stripping away the euphoria, camaraderie, the Marxist call to arms, what is Antonio ultimately left with (beyond the novel)? The slavery of the proletariat, the economic pinning down of what was once a truly free spirit. In other words, Amado transforms Antonio from a *malandro* to a dock worker. The author uses Zumbi as a symbol of freedom. Antonio joins the strike, and like Zumbi, he will fight against slavery and oppression when, ironically, he has entered unequivocally into the trap of slavery, regardless of ideology. The symbol of *Zumbi*, as we have maintained, prevails: Antonio Balduino will soon remain imprisoned in his freedom. History resides with this interpretation. (It is ironic that Antonio joins the docks because of Lindinalva's bastard son, the son of a rich, white lawyer. Antonio does not know the father, but so influenced is he by Lindinalva that he accepts her deathbed wish to care for Gustavinho. Indeed, when she dies, he "[throws] himself at the foot of her bed like a Negro slave." [59])

And Jubiabá, the holy priest? It is notable, vis-à-vis Nascimento's *Sortilégio*, that Jubiabá's influence dwindles as the Marxist rhetoric grows. Jubiabá understands nothing of strikes and class struggles. But he knows cures, spells, history and *his* people. In one sense Antonio Balduino mistakenly turns away from Jubiabá in his total acceptance of the strike movement. In his battles against the authorities, in his empathy for his people, Jubiabá is the fulcrum of Afro-Brazilian religious and social life. Perhaps Amado is calling for an end to this—it is not apparent. What is apparent, however, is that unlike Emanuel, who returns to the *macumba*, Antonio moves away from it as he learns "to love all the Mulattoes, all the Negroes, all the whites, that on earth . . . are all slaves who are breaking out of their chains." [60]

The legend of Palmares and the image of Zumbi, then, remain in post-abolition, modern Afro-Brazilian narrative and theater. Can it be that Antonio's future—as an "economic" slave—disproves the token response; that is, with abolition, all Afro-Brazilians were free? The answer must be affirmative. Writing eighty years after abolition, Nascimento incredulously asks, "Is there really a free man descended from the African slaves in Brazil?" [61] Valiant, tenacious, resourceful, heroic and unbound, Zumbi was never free. Like Chico Rei, Zumbi was imprisoned in time and space. And this image continues through to most Afro-Brazilian characters in Brazilian literature. Nothing, in history or literature, has changed since the Palmares incident. Haberly defined the pre-abolition Afro-Brazilians as the Pitiful Slave, the Violent Slave, or the Immoral Slave. [62] It is as though we might add one category to Haberly's catalogue of slaves in Brazilian literature. Post-abolition Afro-Brazilians are not necessarily called pitiful, violent, or immoral, but rather, some are actually called Freed Slaves.

NOTES

1. Arthur Ramos, *The Negro in Brazil*, (Washington, D.C.: Associated Publishers, 1939), p. 98; published in Portuguese as *O Negro na Civilização Brasileira* (Rio de Janeiro: Casa do Estudante do Brasil, no date).

2. Ernesto Ennes, "The Palmares 'Republic' of Pernambuco: Its Final Destruction, 1697," *Americas* 2 (1948): 209–10. Ennes notes that this document "which we have just transcribed in part, belongs to a process, unfortunately incomplete, which is preserved in the Arquivo Historico Colonial." The best account of Palmares for a non-Portuguese reader is R. K. Kent, "Palmares: An African State in Brazil," in *Maroon Societies*, ed. Richard Price (Baltimore: Johns Hopkins University Press, 1979), pp. 170–90. For those who read Portuguese, we suggest Edison Carneiro, *O Quilombo dos Palmares* (Rio de Janeiro: Civilização Brasileira, 1966); Decio Freitas, *Palmares: A Guerra dos Escravos* (Rio de Janeiro: Edições Graal, 1978); and M. de Freitas, *Reino Negro de Palmares* (Rio de Janeiro: Editora Americana, 1954).

3. *Zumbi* refers to the title, or position, of chief or king of the *palmarinos*. According to Jaime de Altavilla, *O Quilombo dos Palmares* (São Paulo: Melhoramento de São Paulo, 1931); and Correia de Oliveira, *Entre a Historia e a Lenda* (Rio de Janeiro: Pyrausta, 1917), the last Zumbi name was Sueca.

4. The term *paulista*, in the seventeenth century, referred not so much to a native of São Paulo as it did to the backlands *bandeiras*, or pioneers, who were usually of mixed Portuguese and Amerindian blood and had traversed the vast Brazilian wilderness.

5. Freitas, *Palmares*, p. 174.

6. Ramos, *Negro in Brazil*, p. 50.

7. Freitas, *Palmares*, p. 123. This, according to the author, is a "description with important news from the Pernambuco interior, etc.," no doubt contained in some of the hundreds of documents examined by him in the Arquivo Historico Ultramarino. All English translations are mine unless otherwise noted.

8. Gregory Rabassa, *O Negro na Ficção Brasileira* (Rio de Janeiro: Edições Tempo Brasileiro, 1965), p. 437, emphasis added. Originally written in English as "The Negro in Brazil Fiction" (Ph.D. dissertation, Columbia University, 1954).

9. Abdias do Nascimento, *Sortilégio* ("Black Mystery"), trans. Peter Lownds (Chicago: Third World Press, 1978), p. 43. The original play in Portuguese can be found in Nascimento, *Dramas Para Negros e Prólogo Para Brancos* (Rio de Janeiro: Teatro Experimental do Negro, 1969).

10. Altavilla, *O Quilombo*.

11. See Leda Maria da Albuquerque, *Zumbi dos Palmares* (Rio de Janeiro: Editora Leitura, 1914).

12. David T. Haberly, "Abolitionism in Brazil: Anti-Slavery and Anti-Slave," *Luso-Brazilian Review* 9, no. 2 (1972): 45.

13. Joaquim Pedro Oliveira Martins, *O Brasil e as colonias portuguezas*, 3d. ed. (Lisbon: no publisher, 1887), p. 64.

14. Freitas, *Palmares*, p. 189. He also notes that the study of the Palmares war permits a demystifying comprehension of Brazilian history, discerning clearly the classes and their interests.

15. For the purpose of this essay, the term *Afro-Brazilian* will refer to *preto, negro, mulato* and *pardo*. Brazilian Portuguese offers a plethora of terms for people of mixed ancestry. See Pierre L. Van den Berghe, *Race and Racism: A Comparative Perspective* (New York: John Wiley and Sons, 1967), p. 71.

16. Martins Pena, *O Cigano*, in *Teatro de Martins Pena*, ed. Darcy Damasceno (Rio de Janeiro: Ministerio de Educação e Cultura, 1956).

17. Ibid., p. 347.

18. Ibid., p. 352.

19. Ibid., p. 357.

20. Yet, we know that there was no *black* character on the Brazilian stage until the 1950s. All roles for Blacks were played by white actors in black-face. This essay, however, is concerned, for the moment, not with racism in the presentation of these plays but rather with the import of the characters and plays themselves.

21. The most available version I have found is in *Dionysos* (Orgão do Serviço Nacional de Teatro) 6 (1955): 43–163.

22. Ibid., p. 79.

23. Ibid., p. 97.

24. Ibid., p. 127.

25. Ibid., p. 146.

26. Raymond S. Sayers, *The Negro in Brazilian Fiction* (New York: Hispanic Institute, 1956), p. 141.

27. José de Alencar, *Teatro Completo* (Rio de Janeiro: Serviço Nacional de Teatro, 1977), 2:253–310.

28. Arthur Azevedo and Urbano Duarte, *O Escravocrata* (Rio de Janeiro: A Guimarares, 1884).

29. Azevedo, *O Liberato*, in *Revista Brasileira* 10 (1881): 199–227.

30. Ibid., p. 227.

31. Abdias do Nascimento, *O Genocídio do Negro Brasileiro: Processo de um Racismo Mascarado* (Rio de Janeiro: Editora Paz e Terra, 1978), pp. 93–100.

32. Abdias do Nascimento, *O Quilombismo* (Petropolis: Editora Vozes, 1980).

33. Abdias do Nascimento, *Sortilégio II* (Rio de Janeiro: Editora Paz e Terra, 1979).

34. Nascimento, *O Genocídio*, p. 163. This section of the article is based on a paper given to the Fifth Symposium on Afro-Hispanic Literature, Medgar Evers College, June 6, 1980, Brooklyn, N.Y.

35. Nascimento, *O Genocídio*, p. 129. As for the latter point, Nascimento was referring, in particular, to the works of scholars such as Nina Rodrigues, himself a Mulatto, who wrote: "this truth . . . that even today the Negroes could not be able to become civilized people" and "The Negro race in Brazil has to constitute always one of the factors toward our inferiority as a people." See his *Os Africanos no Brasil*, (São Paulo: Editora Nacional, 1945). More to the point, Nascimento criticized individuals like George Alakija, who treated aspects of the *candomblé* as a pathological thesis. In Alakija's "The Trance State in the Candomblé" (published under FESTAC: "Colloquium: Negro Civilization and Science and Technology," January 1977), Alakija referred to the trance as a pathological, rather than a sociological-religious, phenomenon. In this regard Nascimento supported Roger Bastide's study *Estudos Afro-Brasileiros* (São Paulo: Editora Perspectiva, 1973). Nascimento's own words concerning this fifth point are roughly translated as follows: "to unmask as inauthentic and absolutely useless the pseudoscientific literature that focalized the Negro, save rare exceptions, as an aesthetic or diversionary exercise: The essays were hardly academic, purely descriptive, treating history, ethnography, anthropology, sociology, psychiatry, etc., whose interests were very distant from the dynamic problems that were emerging from the racist context of our society" (*O Genocídio*, p. 129). In other words, Nascimento was insisting that most academic studies concerning Afro-Brazilians were so purist that they consistently failed to recognize the inherent socioeconomic dilemma in Brazil.

36. Oscar Fernandez, "Black Theater in Brazil," *Education Theater Journal* 39 (1977): 11.

37. Ibid., pp. 11–12.

38. Nascimento, *Sortilégio II*, pp. 14–15.

39. The polarity situated in *Sortilégio* (white world vs. *candomblé/macumba*) appears in the two other plays written by Afro-Brazilians, both of which are included in Nascimento's anthology, *Dramas Para Negros e Prólogo Para Brancos* (Rio de Janeiro: Teatro Experimental do Negro, 1961). In Romeu Crusóe's *Castigo de Oxalá* (1961) a þlack-white relationship is explored against the background of an ominous *macumba*, with *atabaques* and the singing of *pontos*. The drama takes place in the Bahian countryside. Raimundo, a Black who is a timber contractor, returns home one day with a white wife,

the ex-prostitute Leonor. Their love for one another is juxtaposed to the jealousies of Rita, a local *mulata* who loves Raimundo, and Isidro, a *mulato* who loves Rita. The plot continues with this triangularity of hatred until Ernesto arrives. Raimundo is ignorant of Leonor's past, and it turns out that Ernesto was Leonor's pimp; Ernesto threatens to reveal her past. Realizing that he cannot convince her to leave her husband, Ernesto and Isidro set a trap to kill Raimundo. In the final scene Raimundo escapes the trap, finds Ernesto trying to drag away Leonor and shoots and kills his wife by mistake. He then shoots and kills Ernesto. Raimundo, who throughout the play has scolded his wife and Rita for their involvement in the music of the *macumba*, is told by the black laborer Belarmino, "Raimundo, evil has befallen you. It was Oxalá's punishment." It is probable to assume that Oxalá's malediction for Raimundo concerns the acceptance of the *macumba* and the elimination of all Whites as a preliminary first step toward movement in his freedom. For "Oxalá is the greatest of the Orixás, an androgynous entity, of the oldest surviving religious tradition in Bahia"; see Luis Camara Cascudo, *Dicionario do Folclore Brasileiro* (Rio de Janeiro: Instituto Nacional do Livro, 1962), 2: 543–44. Serge Bramby defines Oxala as the "god of the sky and universe, associated with Jesus Christ" in *Macumba* (New York: St. Martin's Press, 1977), p. 213.

Rosario Fusco's *Auto da Noiva* is a one-act farce that mingles the life of a black mother with her *mulata* daughter. The play is constructed on the repetition of their two lives. The mother was loved by two men, one white, the other black; her daughter is a product of the interracial union. But little information is given concerning the two men. The daughter is also loved by two men, black and white. She becomes pregnant with the white man's child; and the white man is murdered by her black lover, who receives help from a *babalorixa* at a *macumba* ceremony. The play's outcome (the pregnant daughter marries the black *namorado*), regardless of its eerie confusions and lack of dramatic sequences, points toward the elimination of the Whites but with the continuation of their blood line. This position is the reverse of Nascimento's message in *Sortilégio* and Crusóe's in *Castigo* in that they both appear to be arguing for the appreciation of African culture without the continued mixing of the races. Also the inclusion of a chorus of violists and the singing of *aboios* (songs of *vaqueiros*) are in direct contrast to the chorus of *Teoria dos Omolus* and the *pontos da macumba*. But the white-black conflict remains, along with the terrible circularity of life (nonmovement-siege) in the play. Both the mother and daughter are trapped in their inescapable fate, and the strength of the *macumba* appears in the *namorado*'s success.

These three plays by Afro-Brazilians have several themes in common:

	Sortilégio	*Castigo de Oxalá*	*Auto da Noiva*
Hero:	Emanuel (black)	Raimundo (black)	*filha* (*mulata*)
Married to:	Margarida (white)	Leonor (white)	*namorado* (black)
Other lovers:	Efigenia (black)	Rita (*mulata*)	*branco* (white) Allows death of white man.
Movement of hero:	Murders wife; accepting *macumba*.	Kills wife by not accepting *macumba*.	Accepts man who is aided by *macumba*. Follows her mother's life

Other than the similarities in which the *macumba* plays a decisive role in each play, and all Whites are eliminated from their respective worlds, which of the three protagonists incurs movement, or progress? Raimundo and Filha, although alive at the end of their plays, have certainly not lifted the siege on their lives: the former, left with Rita and a life he does not accept; the latter, repeating the senseless life of her mother. Ironically, Emanuel, the one protagonist who does die, breaks the siege barriers by accepting his new faith, by reacculturating the Afro-Brazilian traditions. Emanuel, oddly enough, is one of the more positive Afro-Brazilian characters in Brazilian literature. Other plays, of course, could be brought into this discussion. Nelson Rodrigues' *Anjo Negro* (1946) is so fraught with violence, murder, rape, incest and cruelty that one wonders how the marriage between Ismael, a black doctor, and his white wife Virginia can endure. Rodrigues' addition to the seige imagery, or nonmovement, then, takes on a dual aspect. Not only is Ismael frozen in his sadistic relationship with Virginia, but she is masochistically frozen to him. At the end of the drama, after the successive murders of their infant sons, Elias the stepbrother, the aunt and daughters and Virginia's white daughter, Ismael and Virginia profess to each other their love. The hatred begun in the beginning of the drama is reborn into a latent hatred by play's end. Rodrigues' Ismael is a weak character, who, dressed immaculately in white, cannot accept his black life. *Anjo Negro* confirms the inability for movement of a black individual who attempts to create a life in the white world.

40. It is possible to conjecture, as suggested by William Luis of Dartmouth, that by killing Margarida, Emanuel varies the repetition begun with Zumbi and continued through the twentieth century. Zumbi was married to a white woman, and all the other protagonists revolve around black-white relationships. Emanuel's act puts a symbolic end to mobility through marriage in Brazilian society.

41. Antonio Callado, *Pedro Mico: Zumbi da Catacumba* (Rio de Janeiro: Dramas e Comedias, 1957).

42. Gianfresco Guarnieri, *Teatro de Gianfrancesco Guarnieri* (Rio de Janeiro: Editora Civilização Brasileira, 1978), vol. 1.

43. Callado, *Pedro Mico*, p. 52.

44. Ibid., p. 55.

45. Ibid., p. 76.

46. Walmir Ayala, *Chico Rei* (Rio de Janeiro: Editora Civilização Brasileira, 1965). Ayala bases his play on Ramos, *Negro in Brazil*, pp. 67–69. There have been several other plays concerning the Afro-Brazilians that repeat the theme of siege vis-à-vis the Palmares imagery. Walmir Ayala's *Chico Rei* focuses on the first Afro-Brazilian abolitionist. Chico Rei was brought to Brazil from Angola a slave and worked his way to freedom. After obtaining his freedom, he freed his son and others, buying mines, churches, and the like. But even in his wealth, even in his freedom, Chico Rei suffers. He cannot return to Africa, he cannot successfully defeat the Portuguese colonialists, he cannot leave Minas Gerais—he cannot fight, but he must live to die a natural death as an old man. Chico Rei's imprisonment, literally and figuratively, accurately summarizes the position of Afro-Brazilian heroes and characters in Brazilian literature. This position is relative to the Brazilian narrative as well.

47. Machado de Assis, *Contos*, ed. Massaud Moses (São Paulo: Editora Cultrix, no date), pp. 223–30. The English translations that follow are from Machado de Assis, *The Psychologist and Other Stories*, trans. William L. Grossman and Helen Caldwell (Berkeley and Los Angeles: University of California Press, 1965).

48. Machado de Assis, *The Psychologist*, p. 83.

49. Machado de Assis, *Reliquias da Casa Velha* (Rio de Janeiro: W. M. Jackson, 1946), 1:11–30.

50. Machado de Assis, *The Psychologist*, pp. 110–11.

51. Sayers, *Negro*, p. 204, emphasis added.

52. Jorge Amado, *Jubiabá* (Lisbon: Edição "Livros do Brasil," no date).

53. Ibid., p. 13.

54. Camara Cascudo, *Dicionario do Folclore Brasileiro*, 2:639.

55. Amado, *Jubiabá*, p. 57.

56. Ibid., p. 57.

57. Ibid., p. 250–51.

58. Jorge Amado, "Os Romances da Bahia," introduction to his *Capitaes da Areia* (São Paulo: Livraria Martins, 1945).

59. Ibid., p. 279.

60. Ibid., p. 328.

61. Abdias do Nascimento, "Testemunho," *80 Anos de Abolição* (Rio de Janeiro: Ed. Cadernos Brasileiros, 1968).

62. Haberly, "Abolitionism," pp. 30–46.

13

The *Romance Bárbaro* as an Agent of Disappearance: Henrique Coelho Netto's *Rei Negro* and Its Conventions

Lemuel A. Johnson

Any return to the *merely* heroic, any lay, however good, that tells merely of brave men fighting to save their lives or to get home or to avenge their kinsmen, will now be an anachronism. You cannot be young twice.
C. S. Lewis, *A Preface to "Paradise Lost"*

Stone within stone, and man, where was he?
Air within air, and man, where was he?
Time within time, and man, where was he?
Pablo Neruda, *The Heights of Macchu Picchu*

The word "disappeared," used in its new form in English as a transitive verb, is unfortunately a very accurate description of what happens. In this case, a person does not disappear accidentally but at the hand of an agent of disappearance.
Barry Fatland, " 'Disappeared': What Does It Mean?"

I

Neruda's "and man, where was he?" is a climactic moment of lyrical and startled wonder in one of the most significant of modern poems. *The Heights of Macchu Picchu* was, of course, inspired by Neruda's journey to the ruined Peruvian city, high up in the Andes, one of the most beautiful and astonishing archeological sites in the world. There the epic need—indeed, the compulsion—to "scrape the intestine until I touch mankind" is not at all surprising in the face of the remarkable organization of labor, mind and space that Macchu Picchu represented historically and represents in the poetic vision and the will at work. "A 'tall city of stepped stone', Macchu Picchu stands in a grandiose setting, clinging to its geometrically terraced slope above the swirling river, among enormous mountains—their lower reaches and the lesser peaks all densely forested. Except for the absence of its straw-thatched roofs, the unpeopled city is intact.''[1] A dialectics of material presence and human absence sustains the poem in a fine lyrical and thematic tension:

> Famine, coral of mankind,
> hunger, secret plant, root of the woodcutters,
> famine, did your jagged reef dart up
> to those high, side-slipping towers?
>   I question you, salt of the highways,
> show me the trowel; allow me, architecture,
> to fret stone stamens with a little stick,
> climb all the steps of air into the emptiness,
> scrape the intestine until I touch mankind.
> Macchu Picchu, did you lift
> stone above stone on a groundwork of rags?
> coal upon coal and, at the bottom, tears?
> fire-crested gold, and in that gold, the bloat
> dispenser of this blood?
>   Let me have back the slave you buried here![2]

In a remarkable synthesis of moral will and artistic empathy Neruda finally imposes the voice and the value of *carne y hueso*, of flesh and blood, upon the "hours, days and years,/blind ages, stellar centuries" of an "Ancient America" that rises "from the jungle's edges to the rare height of gods." The poet here is an agent not of disappearance but of reappearance and incarnation: "I come to speak for your dead mouths./Throughout the earth/let dead lips congregate. . . . And tell me everything, tell chain by chain,/and link by link, and step by step" (p. 69). This passion for human contact is climaxed in a dramatic invocation that soars toward transubstantiation and transfiguration:

> Give me the struggle, the iron, the volcanoes.
> Let bodies cling like magnets to my body.
> Come quickly to my veins and to my mouth.
> Speak through my speech, and through my blood (p. 71).

Because Neruda is not an agent of disappearance, because the investment in art and insight is powerful in its moral sympathy, "In this steep zone of flint and forest,/green stardust, jungle-clarified. . . . The fallen kingdom survives us all this while" (p. 43). Pring-Mill's summary is acutely relevant to the issues that we wish to underscore in this study:

The poem's last major turning point comes with the question opening its tenth section: "Stone within stone, and man, where was he?" Neruda begins to wonder whether the men who built up stone on stone, in long-past time, may not perhaps have been like urban man today, and whether the geometrical precision of the citadel might not in fact have been erected on a base of human suffering: "Stone above stone on a groundwork of rags." If built by slaves, in what conditions did these live? Was Ancient America—that not only "bore the rose in mind" but could translate it "into the radiant weave of matter"—based on starvation, hoarding "the eagle hunger" in its depths? (p. xviii).

Consider, incidentally, as an additional and modernist extension of our premise thus far, Mauler's monologue in Bertolt Brecht's *St. Joan of the Stockyards*. There, in what Michael Schneider thinks is a "most brilliant literary expression,"[3] Brecht illustratively responds, in the contemporary idiom, to the trivialization of human labor and space and, consequently, of their historical significance:

And as for the thing made of sweat and money which we have erected in these cities: Now it looks as if a man had made a building, the biggest in the world and the costliest and most practical, but by mistake and because it was cheap he used dog shit for material, so that it would be pretty hard to stay there and at last his only claim to fame was that he had made the biggest stink in the world.[4]

II

In the *romance bárbaro* of which Henrique Maximiliano Coelho Netto's slavery novel, *Rei Negro* (1914), is an example, human labor and its historical and archetypal spaces do not survive charged with quite the same resonance that we find in Neruda.[5] Such *romances bárbaros* have yet to show an acceptably insightful response to the terror and to the range of powerful presumptions that coerced and organized human labor, human passion and the challenging vastness of a new world into structures that come so readily, perhaps too readily, to them and to us: Casa-Grande e Senzala, Mansions and Shanties, Big House and Slave Quarters. In effect, unlike the heights of Macchu Picchu, the enormity of *as casas-grandes* and *as senzalas*, their coming into being and their ruination, these things do not easily escape the pathos of melodrama or the equally reductive pathos of exotic art and crude or ingenuous sympathy. This state of affairs has maintained a somewhat stubborn continuity—in, for example, the nature of a quite recent remembrance of things past by Gilberto Freyre. Recalling that slavery was not abolished in Brazil until 1889 [sic], eleven years before his birth, Freyre said, "I knew some of the children of slaves. That probably affected my view of it. I am accused of romanticizing slavery, but I had good reason to think that not all slaves were victims of cruel treatment. My main theme was that the typical slave in agrarian, patriarchal Brazil was happier in lots of ways than the working men in the first period of the industrial society in Europe and in Brazil."[6]

David T. Haberly, in the consistency of his interest in the literature of invisibility, takes us by an alternative route, and a different set of principles, to the heart of the matter. He does so in a contextual summary of Joaquim Manuel de Macedo's *As Vítimas Algozes*. Haberly's aim is to underscore the fusion of antislavery and *antislave* sentiments:

All of the anti-slave appeals of Brazilian antislavery literature were tied together by Joaquim Manuel de Macedo in *As Vítimas Algozes* (1869)—the most sordid, grotesque, and effective product of the movement. Slavery, Macedo declared in his preface to this collection of short novels, "first affected the slave of our homes and our plantations, the creature who was born a man but transformed, by captivity, into a plague, a wild beast;" the slave-beast then inevitably sought conscious or unconscious revenge. "If you consider these narratives carefully," Macedo warned his readers, "you must abolish slavery, lest they repeat themselves endlessly. For these stories are wholly true, and were and are and shall be forever—so long as you own slaves. Read, and you shall see!" And Brazilians read and believed these exaggerated tales—of the spoiled house-boy who massacres the master's family; of the witch-doctor who poisons the livestock, fires the cane, and convinces the cook to seduce the *senhor* and poison the *senhora* and her children; of the mulatto maid who teaches her innocent young charge unspeakable perversions and helps her own lover seduce the girl.[7]

Such a view of things constitutes, of course, one response to the question that is finally so significant in Neruda's response to Macchu Picchu, "and man, where was he?" In the case of our *romances bárbaros*, however, we cannot and do not scrape the intestine until we touch mankind. Mankind, especially as black slave labor, is not at all likely to be present in a literary convention so different from that compelled by the heights of Macchu Picchu. There, Neruda makes repeated use of the following:

A whole range of heightened meanings with which he endow(s) his major themes and images: Earth and sea, the air; the fecund cycle of the seasons and the renewal of nature; the tree as an image of mankind and man; grain and bread, sexual love; irresistible Death, and the humiliating petty deaths and diminutions of humdrum urban life; the transience of the individual seen against the expanse of time; life as a rushing torrent; the experience of chaos and the hunger to discern some principle of order; the pointless surface of existence and the search for meaning; isolation among one's fellows, and the longing to 'communicate' and thus discover some significant identity by a reciprocal relationship (p. xi).

By contrast, the suspicion persists that the conventions of the *romance bárbaro* coalesce into a genre whose view of the slave, the black slave, removes him from the cycle of possibilities open to "mankind." Certain *a priori* assumptions and their thematic and narrative consequences call, then, for a particularistic reading of what is implied in C. S. Lewis' epic dictum (?) or caveat (?) that "you cannot be young twice." In our genre, to appeal to that sinister, transitive form of the verb "disappear" that the violence of contemporary Latin American politics has forced into use,[8] mankind is disappeared by what seems to be a congenital and aesthetic hostility to or reduction of blackness in human form. The protagonists of the narratives that result make their appearances "aged" in certain ways. In Haberly's view, for example:

Antislavery writers in Brazil, after 1850, could not entirely avoid the influence of foreign models, of the humanitarian stereotypes—the Noble Slave, the Faithful Slave, the Pitiful Slave. . . . The Pitiful Slave, nonetheless, did achieve a certain importance in Brazil. . . . White Brazilians, after 1850, were especially preoccupied with female slaves;

there were relatively few women slaves in the senzalas, and their very low fertility was a major obstacle to the continuation of slavery. The Pitiful Slave, in Brazil, was almost always a woman, and her usual fate—suicide after immense suffering—could be interpreted by Abolitionists as a great moral tragedy; pro-slavery Brazilians, on the other hand, must have been moved by the immoral waste of good breeding stock.[9]

There is additionally, Haberly tells us, the most striking interest in "two homegrown figures": the Immoral Slave and the Violent Slave. "The very high proportion of immoral and violent Negro characters in Brazilian literature, before and after 1850, nonetheless serves to illustrate the emotions and attitudes of white authors and readers."[10]

Still, the failure in response, the trivialization of *casas-grandes* and of *senzalas* and the inability to ask, with proper intensity, "and man, where was he?" are sometimes tempered by the occasional artist who senses the need, and even the conceits, of phenomena that range from "the jungle's edges to the height of gods." I repeat "the raging metaphysics," for example, of Derek Walcott's retrospective "What the Twilight Says: An Overture" as it responds to "those slave-kings, Dessalines and Christophe, men who had structured their despair." For Walcott they once rose, monumentally, out of the human waste of slavery:

Their tragic bulk was as massive as a citadel at twilight. They were our only noble ruins. . . . Those first heroes of the Haitian Revolution, to me, their tragedy lay in their blackness. . . . There was only one noble ruin in the archipelago: Christophe's massive citadel at La Ferrière. It was a monument to egomania, more than a strategic castle; an effort to reach God's height. It was the summit of the slave's emergence from bondage. Even if the slave had surrendered one Egyptian darkness for another, that darkness was his will, that structure was image of the inaccessible achieved. To put it plainer, it was something we could look up to. It was all we had.[11]

Something of the same effort to translate that structure, "stone above stone on a groundwork of rags" (to borrow from Neruda), and to respond to it in the metaphors of an epic of wonder and historical judgment is present even in Alejo Carpentier's reduction of the Haitian Revolution to a *romance bárbaro*. At bottom, its magical realism notwithstanding, *The Kingdom of This World* (1949) is driven by an exotic but clichéd and foolish sexuality that, here and there, threatens to reduce the slave uprising to a penis erection. Still, Carpentier does succeed in that momentary coalescing of wonder, style and terror that reveals La Ferrière to Ti Noel in the "Sacrifice of the Bulls" chapter:

Above the summit of Le Bonnet de l'Evêque, dentelated with scaffolding, rose that second mountain—a mountain on a mountain—which was the Citadel La Ferrière. A lush growth of red fungi was mounting the flanks of the main tower with the terse smoothness of brocade, having already covered the foundations and buttresses, and was spreading polyp profiles over the ocher walls. That mass of fired brick, towering above the clouds in proportions whose perspective challenged visual habits, was honeycombed with tunnels, passageways, secret corridors, and chimneys all heavy with shadows. . . . To wagon axles mortised into the walls were attached the suspension bridges over which brick and stone were carried to the topmost terraces, stretching between inner and outer abysses that filled the stomachs of the builders with vertigo. Often a Negro disappeared into space, carrying with him a hod of mortar. Another immediately took his place, and nobody gave further thought to the one who had fallen.[12]

The intensity of what is thus invested in the perception of human labor, human passion and their organization of space prepares us for that kind of *supremo instante de lucidez* toward which Carpentier strains and which Neruda more effectively allows us to experience.

III

Unattended by the larger vision, or intensity, that concerns us here, *Rei Negro*'s spaces and Blacks suffer a more typical, and banal, *romance bárbaro* disappearance. The fact of the matter is that we are dealing with the dramatization by disappearance of a black humanity and its plight by a modern writer who has, to borrow the words of Clementine Christos Rabassa, maintained many of "the primeval characteristics" of the genre, *romance bárbaro*, which provides subtitle, sensibility and technique for his novel. Rabassa discusses retention of technique and sensibility under finer circumstances: in their transmutation into epic re-creation in Aguilera-Malta's *Infierno negro*.[13] Rabassa also observes elsewhere in her remarkably comprehensive *Demetrio Aguilera-Malta and Social Justice: The Tertiary Phase of Epic Tradition in Latin American Literature* that "stereotypification is itself a variant of bondage."[14] This "variant" explains *Rei Negro*: The stereotypes in Coelho Netto's novel are the products of a convention of unripe characterization and of the pseudoscience of a deterministic naturalism. What results, in the final analysis, is a 1914 *casa-grande e senzala* novel that does not stray too far from the types and topography of Macedo's *As Vítimas Algozes*. Coelho Netto's Blacks remain in the primeval bondage that makes them hell's perfect characters. The note is struck very early indeed in *Rei Negro*.

It is, therefore, fitting that when the first dawn breaks on "uma das fazendas mais ricas do vale do Paraíba" to open the novel, technique and sensibility fashion creatures who have more dark, libidinal urges than men and women who must, and did, deal with the extraordinary fact of their extraordinary transplantation into a *senzala* at the edge of a continent still resistant to domestication. Fred P. Ellison's introduction to his *Brazil's New Novel* offers a cursory but nonetheless quite suggestive sense of exploitation of and evolution in that space: "The Northeast, especially around Bahia and Recife, was the center of sugar-cane production. The crop is ideally suited to the fertile black or deep red soil called *massape*. . . . After the Indians had been subdued, Negro slaves were imported, and a single crop came to predominate, forming the economic basis for a rural and aristocratic society founded on large landholdings and slavery."[15] Eduardo Galeano's *Open Veins of Latin America: Five Centuries of the Pillage of a Continent* is, as may be guessed, more apocalyptically suggestive of the consequences: "The Brazilian Northeast is today the most underdeveloped area in the Western hemisphere." He continues:

Sugar had destroyed the Northeast. The humid coastal fringe, well watered by rains, and a soil of great fertility, [was] rich in humus and mineral salts and covered by forests from Bahia to Ceará. . . . Naturally fitted to produce food, it became a place of hunger. . . . Fire was used to clear land for canefields, devastating the fauna along with the flora: Deer, wild boar, tapir, rabbit, pacas, and armadillo disappeared.[16]

It is on this arrangement, or arranging, of labor, space and privilege that the dawn breaks to reveal the special focus in *Rei Negro* on *fazenda* and *senzala*. A panoramic sweep, beginning with the novel's first words, "A casa, antiga e vasta," soon descends in sexual focus on the *senzalas* where, "em promiscuidade sórdida, rolovam corpos seminus, lustrosos de suor, adultos e criancas": "On being opened, the shacks belched forth from a fiery and stifling interior a bitter stench and thick billows of smoke from the coals that smouldered all night creating an oppressive atmosphere in which, in sordid promiscuity, half-naked bodies rolled together, glistening with sweat, adults and children alike."[17]

Not unexpectedly, apart from the stereotypical exception of the novel's protagonist Macambira, who is described, as is usually the case, as "um belo tipo de raça," the rest of the *raça* is predictably defined at the edges, as it were, of mankind; for the most part, they are impelled or obsessed by urges located below rather than above the navel. It all makes for a pattern of behavior, and therefore a narrative, that is essentially phallocentric and fustian. Thus, in spite of the charitable view in Alfredo Bosi's *O Pre-Modernismo* that Coelho Netto "nesse trabalho é sensivel o desejo de construir uma obra semi-épica," the conventions at work and their attendant assumptions and aesthetic consequences coalesce in other than epic or "semi-epic" ways.[18]

There is, in this respect, a citation in Michael Schneider's *Neurosis and Civilization* that may profitably serve here as a summation of and a prelude to what is implicit and decisive in the world in which Coelho Netto's imagination is more at home. Schneider's "Marxist-Freudian synthesis" makes a reference to Freud's *The Future of an Illusion* to demonstrate more precisely how the "economic structure" of society also influences what remains of sexual freedom.

Human civilization. . . . presents as we know two aspects to the observer. It includes on the one hand all the knowledge and capacity that men have acquired in order to control the forces of nature and extract its wealth for the satisfaction of human needs, and, on the other hand, all the regulation necessary in order to adjust the relation of men to one another and especially the distribution of available wealth. . . . The two trends of civilization are not independent of each other; firstly because the mutual relations of men are profoundly influenced by the amount of instinctual satisfaction which the existing *wealth makes possible; secondly, because an individual man can himself come to function as wealth in relation to other men insofar as the other person makes use of his capacity for work, or chooses him as a sexual object.*[19]

Moreover, to borrow from Jean Duvignaud's *The Sociology of Art*'s reading of aesthetic forms and milieu, "As both Pierre Francastel and Pierre Charpentrat have suggested, one can define a movement as a social practice, a mode of behaviour, a living attitude closely connected with a particular milieu. . . . In Latin America it involved a sumptuous consummation, an exalted kind of debauchery inseparable from the discovery of gold and new lands, often to the terror of the aboriginal civilizations."[20] The debauchery is, of course, not always exalted, nor is the consummation invariably sumptuous.

Accordingly, in what soon amounts to thematic refrain and narrative control, it is *como animais* that the *raça* fashions Coelho Netto's *romance bárbaro*. The *raça* is *como animais* either as beast of burden or else as oversexed creatures congenitally trapped in a *promiscuidade sórdida*. As beasts of burden, the *raça* is engaged in a momentous expenditure of labor whose wresting of shape, culture, even chaos (Schneider, above) out of the primordial space of a new world is no less extraordinary than the heights to which the builders of Macchu Picchu ventured to restructure the hard and precarious spaces of the high Andes. Something of the significance of and the coercive insistence on that labor is very well served indeed by what Bosi identifies as a "paradigm of Coelho Netto's style that seemed to posterity the author's only expressive form: An accumulative, virtuoso language."[21] This labor for the greater glory and benefit of others, with its attendant loss or reification of human identity, is thus acknowledged in the incremental repetitions of Coelho Netto's style:

Earth, water, and sun were there, surrounding the roots in fecundity, and the Blacks assisted nature by clearing fields, setting wasteland afire, setting down brush so the land could be used for successful sowing, or, with a sad, wailing song, they would sweep clean the gleaming branches of the coffee trees, filling their sieves with red berries, dig up manioca, cut cane, grind corn; and the carts would go down with a sharp creaking sound and the courtyards would be covered with drying coffee beans or the storage bins would attest to the cane or the corn waiting to be ground, to be husked (p. 1074).

And man, in all this, where is he? Coelho Netto aims, presumably, at an answer when he describes the procession of slave labor that passes before Manuel Gandra, "senhor da 'Cachoeira,' uma das fazendas mais ricas do vale do Paraíba." The plantation owner emerges from his "vast and ancient manor house . . . in rough cloth, boots of raw leather, straw hat with a broad brim . . . with the look of the master, standing here, or there, examining a full-blossomed rose, listening, enraptured, to the twittering of a bird." He also gives orders, "sending Blacks to sweep up the alley ways, clip the bristly lawn, prune a shrub, drive a stake, string twine" (p. 1073). Significantly, he does all this, and more, in the novel with a kind of patriarchal and benignly indifferent exploitativeness that suggests a character illustration of the phrase "being a slave owner is no crime, but abusing that privilege is (which Francisco Calcagno introduced)."[22] Be that as it may, the *romance bárbaro* moves ineluctably toward excess: Manuel Gandra's lineage is impeccably human but most untidily heroic; he is "adventuresome like those of his race." In that spirit, "he threw himself into his managerial work, proving himself worthy by his audacity and vigor" (p. 1076). Besides that, he is, in this respect, an improvement upon the obese concupiscence of Camilo Feitosa, whose *cachoeira* (waterfall) he had inherited after a somewhat noisy deflowering of, and therefore marriage to, Feitosa's virgin but lustful daughter Clara. Feitosa "became aware of his daughter's perdition when, one night, in the silence of the house, Clara's cries piercingly resounded" (p. 1077).

The fact is that the "fazenda . . . prosperou desenvolvendo-se prodigiosamente" is linked, among other things, to black labor: "Entraram escravos novos" (p. 1078). The novel clearly, however, belongs to a genre whose imagistic response to the *escravo* and his race is a somewhat narrow one. It is not surprising then that the Blacks involved in all this "passed by, dragging their spongy, swollen feet"; that they are "urchins who came out to face him with an *idiotic* look, ragged and filthy, eyes dripping, holding out a skinny hand in a *monkey-like* gesture, their black bodies lined with scratches, like African *idols of basalt*, scarred by an engraver's chisel" (p. 1074, emphasis added). The racial lineage is, in effect, impeccably subhuman, hovering just outside, or inside, the species to which Manuel Gandra belongs. Thus, to Pablo Neruda's cry, "Let me have the slave you buried there!" with its implicit belief in that slave's human and epic potential, is counterpointed *Rei Negro*'s inarticulate *ar idiota, gesto simiesco* and *manipanços de basalto*. In sum, we have a *raça* "a colheita humilimos, submissos como animais" (p. 1073). It calls to mind, from the nineteenth century, José Bonifacio de Andrade e Silva's strategically ingenuous ignorance of what Haberly calls the "invisible and unwilling culprits" of such history and art. As Silva put it, "If Negroes are men like us, and do not constitute a separate race of irrational animals, . . . what a picture of sorrow and misery do they not exhibit to the feeling Christian mind."[23]

There are other possibilities, of course, for making the inarticulate articulate—other than Silva's tractarian pathos. Their use, however, would demand a genre and a perception that do not fit easily into the purpose or the sense of black speech in the tradition at work in Netto. For example, "the literary contests which, in Europe, had once set minstrels and troubadours in competition with one another . . . were kept up in Spanish and Portuguese America, under the name *desafio*. . . . Such contests brought together men with a remarkable gift for improvisation, who 'warmed up' their individual talents by shouting abuses at each other."[24] Roger Bastide, from whose *African Civilizations in the New World* this remark comes, then makes it clear that precisely because of their fate, Blacks were certainly more articulately conscious than the minimal speech patterns of the *romance bárbaro* allow them to be, even in Brazil:

The Negro, who had excellent reasons for wanting to release his pent-up fury against the white man, could now do so with impunity, since the whole thing was just a game. Consequently here, too, he plunged headlong into what had hitherto been a Europeans-only contest. In Brazil, resounding battles took place between white and Negro improvisers, the results of which were printed on broadsheets and made known throughout the *sertao*. Very often, thanks to his sense of humour, it would be the Negro who ended by triumphing over the more bad-tempered onslaughts of his white opponent.[25]

Through passing references to Paulo de Carvalho-Neto, Arthur Ramos, José Juan Arrom, and "El Negrito Poeta" José Vasconcelos, Richard Jackson also suggests the range of articulation with which an *escravada* could have provided a *loquor, ergo sum* ("I speak, therefore I am") answer to tractarian or *romance bárbaro* speculation.[26] In this regard, among the examples of *desafio*, which Jackson refers to as "forced poetics," "counter-poetics," or "contrapunteo," is Bastide's use of a couplet, from Argentina, thrown off by the Negro competing with Martín Fierro in José Hernández's poem: "I too have something white about me—/The whiteness of my teeth."[27]

It is, incidentally, altogether intriguing that when this *desafio* appears in *Rei Negro*, it does so in a marked inversion of role and repartee. This time Manuel Gandra uses it in a kind of tart, "egalitarian" *contrapunteo* to deal with the startled diffidence with which Macambira (even he, "um belo tipo de raça") reacts to Gandra's decision that it was time he married and that he marry the almost white Lúcia. I cite the passage in summary illustration of speech, character and identity in *Rei Negro*'s plantation culture and moral ambience. Thus, paternalistic and displaying an oddly benign blindness to deeper possibilities in Macambira, Manuel Gandra makes his proposition: "You've got a house, a decent field, some money. . . . Now find a girl, a good one, one who really suits you, and get married." The two men do not, however, share the same consciousness of the human condition:

'Me marry! What for, Master?'

'Hah, that's a good one! What for! To have a family, your own happy little nook, what else?

'A man lives well alone . . . wherever he goes, he takes everything that he's got; he doesn't leave his thoughts hanging round the house, nor go with jealousy to his heart. A slave is a slave. Marriage is for those who can, for those who rule themselves.'

'And you, aren't you free? What do you need?'

'I know, Master. . . . A slave doesn't marry. A White sees, seduces, takes what his heart asks for; a Black, no: He marries as he works—where the Master says he has to.' And, once again, he shook his head no, concluding in a low voice: 'I want to live a quiet life, like up to now.'

'Quiet,' burst out the owner, 'I know well enough what your quiet life is like!'

The climax to this *contrapunteo*-like dialogue comes when Manuel Gandra, "d'olhos fitos no escravo, affirmou com segurança":

'It's Lúcia! You'll marry her, O.K.? What do you say? Work it out, O.K.? With her it's a real deal, right?' and he smiled. 'Come on; there's no way you can do better.'

'It's . . . I must be mad, Master! For me to think of Lúcia, a girl who's almost white . . .'

'White! So what? Teeth are white and no one has whiter ones than you' (pp. 1094–95).

It is, all in all, a sort of *contrapunteo* whose principals are, this time, a Gilberto Freyre (?) *fazendeiro* patriarch and an equally predictable Noble *and* Pitiful Slave. But the principals involved, the arranged marriage, the promise of a suggestively permitted and yet forbidden sexual consummation in a Black and *quase branca* union—all combine to fashion a state of affairs that is calculated to bring a *romance bárbaro* like *Rei Negro* to an explosive dénouement.

IV

This *submissos como animais* in labor, speech and features, the *senzala* can always be counted upon to lose the near-catatonic inarticulacy of the beast of burden whenever it surrenders, as it must, to a manic sexuality. Thus, precisely because the *escravatura* is *como animais*, it has conventionally served as the inspiration, catalyst and victim of the *romance bárbaro*'s ready descent into erotomania, with its attendant melodrama of sexual incontinence and "unspeakable rites." After all, as an 1843 author cited in Raymond S. Sayers' *The Negro in Brazilian Literature* put it, in a remarkably circular appeal to convention, "the vehemence of Negro love is proverbial; its jealousy is said to be excessive; it is; of this there are undeniably proofs; the *Moor of Venice* would be sufficient."[28] It is, after all, in the *senzala* that one finds in concentrated form the origins of that "fatality of biological laws" that weighs Euclydes da Cunha's "degenerate" Mestizo "down to the less favored race." Ellison thus cites from Euclydes da Cunha's *Os Sertoes* (1902).[29] Such views fall victim to but are also narratively powered by certain ethnocentric exaggerations widely held in Brazil, for example, at the turn of the century and later; they are the effluvia of the pseudoscience of nineteenth-century investigators of race such as Gobineau. The novel that results, Bosi writes, "pode chamarse, quanto a materia, 'documental', e quanto a forma, 'ornamental.' " Its episodes and dramatic development are very much responsive to a "determinismo biológico," the purpose of which is "descrever e amplificar varios aspectos da degeneração e da loucura"; the art is much given to a "*barroco científico*."[30]

The same "fatality of biological laws" with its attendant racial and novelistic consequences is also present in *Rei Negro*: Julinho's incontinent copulation is linked, for example, to the contagious availability of oversexed *mulatinhas zabaneiras*. In effect, *Rei Negro* cannot avoid the fascination of black sexuality, even though Coelho Netto's novel is post-abolition and appeared ages after Brazilian literature's climactic exploitation of the theme in Macedo's *As Vítimas Algozes*. In somewhat of an illustration of a "determinismo biológico" Julinho is at once a novelistic and genetic throwback to this grandfather: "Camilo Feitosa, the landowner, obese and clumsy, of a granite obtuseness, spent his days nibbling tidbits. . . . At night he tumbled in lust in the bunks of his female slaves" (p. 1076). Indeed, the most melodramatic of libidinal regressions takes place in Julinho, who, in an incontinent frenzy well-suited to Coelho Netto's style, with its *linguagem virtuosística e acumulativa*, lusts his way through *fazenda* and *senzala*. A certain frenzied backwardness of thought in Coelho Netto is, however, more clearly manifested; the style necessarily substitutes melodrama for psychological realism:

The son, Julinho, grew up robust and free in that dissolute atmosphere, surrounded by shameless little mulattas, precociously licentious, and lazy urchins with whom he went to their hangouts or danced wildly in the narrow road and, the longer all this went on growing stronger, the more there rose up in his blood a swinish sensuality which led him to sniff out the mulattas, rubbing up against them with a rolling motion, grabbing at them, feeling them over wherever he met them, in a frenzy of burning lust (p. 1079).

In sum, "he degraded the old Blacks, assaulted women in front of their husbands, and daughters before their parents, mocking them with obscene remarks" (p. 1080). Some half a century after Macedo, Coelho Netto's style drives to a rococo climax in its statement of the contagious nature of the *casa grande e senzala*'s "meio disoluto" as some Mulattas "*mais depravadas*" give in to Julinho's pleas that all he wanted was just a peep, "*queria ver, so ver*": "And the little boy knocked them down, tore at them frantically, rooting into them, biting them, while they, laughing, at first protected themselves shyly, until suddenly, excited, they locked bodies with him, overwhelmed him, madly brutalized him" (p. 1079).

Rei Negro underscores the contagion thesis in all its racial, deterministic and novelistic drama in a more direct way. We get this in the psychological background that presumably explains Donna Clara's (Julinho's mother) rages and violence. Her son, she feels, has as much right over the lives and honor of the slaves as he had over the fruits of the trees and the game of the hunt. Such a view is directly linked to a precocious depravity engendered and sustained by contact with *negras*, who, pathetically speechless or just minimally articulate in other matters, are suddenly but predictably, graphic in their sexual urges. Clara grew up, "spending her days among such black women, getting her fill of curses and the beatings of the mammies, hearing obscene lovemaking, laughing at what they told her, with a crude shamelessness" (p. 1077).

The climactic statement of the thesis is, as may be expected, pure *estilo coel-honetano*: As a child, Clara had gotten used to seeing the dancing buttocks of slaves as they copulated like dogs. Whenever she bothered them, by laughing or throwing rocks at them, they simply moved off into other shrubbery where, grunting, scratching, panting, they shuddered their way to a lustful satiety. In sum, "they were like animals that have no sense of shame." The narration is remarkable, and disturbing, in the ambivalent blending of persona and authorial points of view:

For Donna Clara her son had as much right over the lives and honor of the slaves as over the fruit of the trees and the game in the woods. . . . From childhood she had been used to seeing the slaves copulate, gyrating in the grass, grunting, clawing each other in the frenzy of their rutting. She would laugh, throw stones at them, and scream out, driving them away, and they would flee like chastised dogs into the undergrowth where, once again, they would grapple together with added lust. They were like animals that know no shame and, smelling female scent, would track them down, ferret them out, grab them, bite them, overpower them, satiating themselves instinctively with the same nonchalant, natural simplicity with which they would tear apart their meat or slake their thirst in a puddle of water (p. 1081).

And yet, in all this, it is only the obvious investment and expenditure of Coelho Netto's energies in 1914 that is perhaps remarkable, not the dramatically ubiquitous convention that the Negro has a special and catalyst relationship with the demonic, especially in its libidinous manifestation. The link is made in high art and low, in the sublime and in the ridiculous; it can be made early and late, in Portuguese or in an Australian accent. The connection is there, for example, in the *daemon ex machina* role that the high art of Arthur Miller's *The Crucible* (1953) assigns to the Barbadian slave Tituba—and this in a play whose McCarthyite and Puritan inspiration and excesses have little to do with blackness. The connection is also there in the amusingly wretched excesses of a recent Australian television series, *Prisoner: Cell Block H*, which introduces, with a suitably *ex machina* logic, a black pimp in the continuing story of Australian white women in an Australian prison.[31] To repeat, the debauchery is not always exalted, nor is the consummation invariably sumptuous. They are merely predictable.

We are, therefore, more than fully prepared by biological laws, *senzala* obsessions and a baroque sense of drama for that moment when, "almost on the eve of the wedding, there by the fig tree, on the road to the dam" (p. 1206), Julinho accosts Lúcia. "Disdainful, full of loathing," in a verbal assault that precedes his raping her virtually on the day of her marriage to Macambira, he tells her " 'Aren't you ashamed? . . . A girl, practically white, marrying a black!' . . . 'What does that have to do with you?' 'With me! Plenty! I don't want it!' " (p. 1138). Julinho's response by rape is here a kind of "racial punishment" that is further powered by his being a creature of volatile urges.

That rape is the form of punishment meted to Lúcia, a woman so near and yet so far from whiteness, for her arranged marriage to Macambira is also, under the circumstances, a predictable even if odd form of masculine "justice." This violation of woman and the quirky sensuality of Coelho Netto's "orientalism" make the premise of Nawal el Saadawi's *The Hidden Face of Eve* apropos: "The oppression of women, the exploitation and social pressures to which they are exposed, are not characteristic of Arab or Middle Eastern societies, or countries of the 'Third World' alone. They constitute an integral part of the political, economic and cultural system, preponderant in most of the world—whether that system is backward and feudal in nature, or a modern industrial society that has been submitted to the far-reaching influence of a scientific and technological revolution."[32] As it is, gender chauvinism and other conventions of genre and race eventually coalesce in Netto's use of a rather *grand guignol* and *droit de seigneur* rape to climax the role of slave, of woman and of Macambira in *Rei Negro*.

It is in the character and fate of Lúcia, then, that certain forms of the literature of excess, which the *romance bárbaro* typifies, become more clearly manifest. The *barroco científico e documental* of Coelho Netto's style is also allied to a good measure of oriental, escapist romanticism. They are together the reason for Gregory Rabassa's hyphenated view of Coelho Netto as a "românticonaturalist."[33] Coelho Netto himself provides the following origins of his *imaginação* in *A Conquista*:

My essential faculty is the imagination. I live my dreams; ideas swarm in my brain. I feel that they are the ancient seed from which forests spring. I began my studies with oriental books. *A Thousand and One Nights* was the book that left the deepest impression on my spirit during my formative years, followed by stories told to me on peaceful evenings and finally by my own readings. I sought, by preference, descriptions of levantine life in the poets—in Byron *Don Juan*, *The Bride of Abydos*, *The Giaour*; in Gautier his vast fantastic world; in Flaubert *Salambo*.[34]

Coelho Netto's preference for "levantine life" is stereotypical. In *Rei Negro* it all thickens into a turgid, sensual orientalism. The approach is obviously escapist and, less obviously, culturally and racially dangerous, a fusion of factors that make Edward Said relevant: "In the depths of this Oriental stage stands a prodigious cultural repertoire whose individual items evoke a fabulously rich world: The Sphinx, Cleopatra, Eden, Troy, Sodom and Gomorrah, Astarte, Isis and Osiris, Sheba, Babylon, the Genii, the Magi, Nineveh, Prester John, Mahomet, and dozens more; settings, in some cases names only, half-imagined half-known; monsters, devils, heroes; terrors, pleasures, desires."[35] Still, in all this, Said writes, "the web of racism, cultural stereotypes that hold in the Arab or the Muslim is very strong indeed."[36] *Livros orientais* are thus "governed not simply by empirical reality but by a battery of desires, repressions, investments, and projections."[37]

Accordingly, the dimensions of our *romance bárbaro* now expand in imagery and narrative form. Said underscores the relevant thrust:

If we can point to great Orientalist works of genuine scholarship like Silvestre de Sacy's *Chrestomathie arabe* or Edward Lane's *Accounts of the Manners and Customs of the Modern Egyptians*, we need also to note that Renan's and Gobineau's racial ideas came out of the same impulse, as did a great many Victorian pornographic novels (see the analysis of Steven Marcus of "The Lustful Turk").[38]

Steven Marcus's *The Other Victorians* is a study of sexuality and pornography in mid-nineteenth-century England; its purpose is, in part, to underscore the psychosexual excitements involved in such traffickings into "levantine" and other lives.

We need not, therefore, be surprised when this oriental battery of genre expectations, racial fears and cultural projections provides *Rei Negro* with the first of its two major sexual climaxes, one in which the principal actors are a Mulatta *horrorizada* and, she fears, a lustful Black. To the oriental genre is now added the *romance bárbaro*'s other source of excess and erotomania: "Africa proper," as Hegel had earlier called it. It is of some significance for the genre and metaphor in which Coelho Netto writes that not even on the philosophy of the brightest and the best does "Africa proper" have a calming effect. Three drafts, 1822, 1818 and 1830, notwithstanding, Hegel continues to insist on the following:

In Africa proper, man has not progressed beyond a merely sensuous existence, and has found it absolutely impossible to develop further. Physically, he exhibits great muscular strength, which enables him to perform arduous labours; and his temperament is characterized by good-naturedness, which is coupled, however, with completely unfeeling cruelty. . . . [Africa proper] has no historical interest of its own, for we find its inhabitants living in barbarism and savagery in a land which has not furnished any integral ingredient of culture. From the earliest historical times, Africa has remained cut off from all contacts with the rest of the world; it is the land of gold for ever pressing in upon itself, and the land of childhood, removed from the light of self-conscious history and wrapped in the dark mantle of night.[39]

An effluvium of nineteenth-century thought and imagery and the titillation of a romantico-naturalist orientalism thus combine to give us Coelho Netto's Lúcia and her cannibal and sacrificial-victim fear of Macambira:

The Mulatta shuddered, tears burst from her eyes, a great fear seized her: She felt the presence of death and, weak, like a victim before her sacrificers, seeing furious cannibals all around, she recoiled and, falling into a chair, leaned over the table and burst into tears, certain that in a moment it would all end at the hands of the black man— horrified, she lifted her head and cast a frightened glance around as if in search of her own corpse" (p. 1136).

Descent into a kind of rococo sentimentalism produces the wedding night description of Lúcia, transfixed "entre o amor e a morte" in the arms of her black husband. The morning-after recollection of that "angustioso instante" leaves her "numa inércia de anestesiada": "She breathed deeply, gulping, as if returning to life, and remained for a moment with her head bowed over, mechanically unraveling the fringes of the blanket; finally she became still, with the fixed gaze and the inertia of one anesthetized" (p. 1137).

The rape is as it should be in an author and a persona-victim much given to *livros orientais*. ("Lúcia . . . read to the boys . . . her sweet voice recounting the adventures of romances or the marvellous events in oriental tales" [p. 1093]). As a consequence, an act that the novel settles upon as the climactic and consummate manifestation, presumably, of biological determinism and of *casa-grande* assault on *senzala*, becomes an act of violation that is captured with all the turgidity, and coyness, of a romantic melodrama of bites, wild beasts on the grass, knee on the belly—and a swoon.

She bent back as if she would break, struggled to free herself, tried to bite him. They fell locked together, and there was a frantic rolling about, a struggle of wild beasts in the high grass. Finally, furious, overpowering her, Julinho put his knee on her belly and clutched her throat with homicidal rage. Tears then flowed from her eyes; she fought tooth and nail to avoid his kisses, spitting in his face, threatening to bite him, but her vision clouded over, her heart grew huge in her breast, she felt a mortal anguish. . . . When she came to, she was alone. It was a black night (p. 1139).[40]

The rest is predictable: A child is born, a *filho branco*; the child dies, of course, as does Lúcia, all in Macambira's absence. He returns to find out about the "violencia infame de Julinho." In the meantime, it all results in public scandal because "the news of the 'white-child' spread rapidly, carried by the Blacks of Cachoeira and on through the little shops along the streets and through businesses, from Barra to Vassouras the affair was rumoured round." As Macambira notes when he seeks satisfaction from Manuel Gandra, "tôda a gente vai tomá pagode i um homem tem sangue." But this appeal to his dignity provokes Gandra to his own sense of propriety, succinctly put in the *fazendeiro*'s "Com quem estás falando?" ("Who do you think you are talking to?") Besides, he claims, no woman can be raped against her will: "Quando a mulher não quer não há homen que a vença. . . . Ninguem força mulheres. . . . Está e que é a verdade" (p. 1209). The novel nonetheless ends with Macambira killing Julinho; thereafter, in a blood-intoxicated apocalypse he celebrates devastation, the vengeance of idols and Negroes, of religion and race. Macambira's is, presumably, an epic or semi-epic madness and hallucination, as we move from the novel's opening words, "A casa, antiga e vasta," to its end in an "alucinação do excídio"—as ever in that *estilo coelhonetano*, now full of "Africa proper":[41] "And Macambira, vibrant with heroic passion, waved the dagger, which gleamed in the sun and quickly, as if carrying out an assault, rushed up the slopes of the hillside and disappeared into the brush, howling in the delirium of his blood, in an intoxication of destruction" (p. 1248).

CONCLUSION

I return, finally, to an earlier observation: Coelho Netto's *Rei Negro* clearly thrives on many of the primeval characteristics of an aesthetic, racial and moral orientation that coalesce in a genre that has served as an agent of disappearance, given the scope and intensity of that which the black experience in the New World merits. Moreover, in still somewhat of a surprise, the ubiquitous persistence of black stereotyping notwithstanding, Coelho Netto's work appeared in 1914. This was three years before the Anita Malfatti exhibition and eight years before the Week of Modern Art in São Paolo, which would serve as prelude and consummation respectively of a ferment in Brazilian arts that Wilson Martins discusses in *The Modernist Idea*:

More than a simple literary school, or even a period in our intellectual life, modernism in my opinion was a whole epoch of Brazilian life inscribed within a wide social and historical process, the source and results of transformations which far overflowed their esthetic frontiers. Here as elsewhere a new society necessarily required a new literature. From the very first moment the theoreticians and the artists never tired of repeating this statement. In Brazil, as well as outside Brazil, the new art and the new literature were clearly far in advance of society, which was transforming itself much more slowly.[42]

On the other hand, the evidence suggests that a kind of racial distillate is at work and that this distillate shows a remarkable capacity to resist some of the most enlightened and generous of -isms.[43] It is, therefore, especially disquieting that Gilberto Freyre's 1924 "Plantation Boy" should illustrate that premise. Freyre's poetic remembrance of things past is a moment of sentimental astigmatism that gives us, in effect, that distillate pattern of imagery and vision that we have in Coelho Netto's more uninhibited narrative:

No doubt about it: A plantation boy
lived a happier life
than a city-bred child;
lived a carefree life, and dressed as he pleased.
    With his little black comrades
he played carrousel
on the old well-sweep:
And the music box
for that merry-go-round
was the mule driver's song.
    He could ride a horse
and roam in the woods
with the pickaninnies,
and hunt *curios* ["songbirds"].
    When the cane was ripe
there was always a farm hand
who'd cut him a fine juicy joint to suck.

> He'd crouch by the millrace
> and set flies and crickets adrift in paper boats
> and pretend to himself they were pirate heroes
> in tales of adventure he'd read.
> And then one day came a naked black slave girl
> to launch the plantation boy
> on his first adventure in love.[44]

And yet the countervailing view of the complexities involved have never been more effectively proposed than in Freyre's work:

The Big House completed by the slave shed represents an entire economic, social, and political system: A system of production (a latifundiary monoculture); a system of labor (slavery); a system of transportation (the ox cart, the *banguê*, the hammock, the horse); a system of religion (a family Catholicism, with the chaplain subordinated to the paterfamilias, with a cult of the dead, etc.); a system of sexual and family life (polygamous patriarchalism); a system of bodily and household hygiene (the "tiger," the banana stalk, the river bath, the tub bath, the sitting bath, the foot bath); and a system of politics (*compradismo*).[45]

The distance between distillate and comprehensive responses underscores the value of what Martins detects in the sociology of the author of *Casa-Grande e Senzala*: "It is a longing for the past (*saudosismo*). Around this sociology of longing he constructed his entire social history, of which *Casa-Grande e Senzala* remains the high point of reference."[46] Haberly is immediately and more specifically relevant:

Even Freyre could not wholly overcome the pull of the past. His obsession with African sexuality ignored his own ground-rules, confusing character and situation as completely as the arguments of most Abolitionists, with but a single difference: The Immoral Slave-Girl, long a symbol of danger and destruction, once more became a precious national institution.[47]

The regressive persistence of such literary phenomena as *Rei Negro*, their roles as agents of disappearance and the nature of what they cause to disappear are all apparent in the studies of critics like Haberly and Jackson. Despite its apparent focus on the black experience, in or out of slavery, the literature that results is "Negroid literature ('literatura negroide') . . . esteemed by Spanish American critics as the happy result of biological and cultural miscegenation. Its preeminence, however, has often served to suffocate the legitimate and authentic self-expression of Black, Spanish American writers." The phenomenon of disappearance is thus addressed in Haberly's "The Literature of an Invisible Nation."[48] Florestan Fernandes' study of the Afro-Brazilian's experiences in Brazil's past and present history ends with a relevant concern over marginalization of black labor and what that labor creates:

We cannot continue without serious injustice to keep the Negro at the margin of the development of a civilization he helped to create. As long as we do not achieve racial equality, we will not have a racial democracy, nor will we have a democracy. Through a historical paradox, the Negro today has become the test for our capacity to erect in the tropics the foundation for a modern civilization.[49]

The value—indeed, the necessity—of a literature of the black experience that can approach the "supremo instante de lucidez" of Pablo Neruda's "and man, where was he?" is perhaps best underscored by the apocalyptic nature of the final solution, which, Haberly proposes, has been and continues to be at work in Brazil:

Stereotypes of Negro immorality and violence, appearing almost a century after Brazilian Abolitionists first found them useful and effective, strongly suggest that the loudly-trumpeted racial tolerance of Brazil is a cosmetic myth, designed to buy time until immigration, miscegenation, and the *laissez faire* genocide of sharply higher rates of poverty, malnutrition, disease, and infant mortality provide a final solution to the danger of white contact with Negroes.[50]

We thus, for our purposes, come full circle to this study's opening excerpt from Barry Fatland's " 'Disappeared': What does it mean?"—and so, in effect, to the disturbing sense of things that provoke an Abdias do Nascimento to the view that we get in *O Genocídio do Negro Brasileiro: Processo de um Racismo Mascarado*.[51] We refer to the fact that *Afro*-Latin narratives of the black experience in South America as a whole are graphically concerned with a disappearance that is dangerously genocidal. There is, for this reason, more than a suggestion of involuntary irony in the title of Leslie Rout's study *The African experience in Spanish America*. The record, from 1502 to the present day, assures that. Part 2 of Rout's study, "Since Independence," very quickly becomes a chronicle of Afro-Latin disappearance, which, as in Chile, can occur with "dizzying rapidity"; this situation is mirrored in Argentina, where, Paul Theroux had once read, "a quarter of the population had once been black."

Theroux's *The Old Patagonian Express* climaxes in the library of Argentina's brightest and best refracting mirror, Jorge Luis Borges, who, in a "self-amused, pitying way," fashions fictions and facts: " '*Huckleberry Finn* is a great book. . . . Tom Sawyer appears and it becomes bad. And There's Nigger Jim. . . . yes, we had a slave market here at Retiro. My family wasn't very wealthy. We only had five or six slaves. But some families had thirty or forty.' "[52] The disappearance of the Argentinian Black is, Borges responds to Theroux, a mystery.

"But I remember seeing many of them. . . . *They were cooks, gardeners, handymen. . . . I don't know what happened to them.* People say they died of TB. Why didn't they die of TB in Montevideo? It's just over there, eh? There is another story, equally silly, that they fought the Indians, and the Indians and the Negroes killed each other. That would have been in 1850 or so, but it isn't true. In 1914 there were still many Negroes in Buenos Aires—they were very common. Perhaps I should say 1910, to be sure." He laughed suddenly. *"They didn't work very hard.* It was considered wonderful to have Indian blood, but black blood is not so good a thing, eh? There are some prominent families in Buenos Aires that have it—a touch of the tar brush, eh? My uncle used to tell me, 'Jorge, you're as lazy as a nigger after lunch.' You see, they didn't do much work in the afternoon. I don't know why there are so few here, but in Uruguay or Brazil—in Brazil you might run into a white man now and then, eh? If you're lucky, eh? Ha!'' (p. 370, emphasis added).

True, as Rout had earlier recorded, Borges' Blacks were good soldiers: "They fought in the War of Independence. . . . Our blacks won the Battle of Cerrito." But, oddly, "they thought they were natives!" And there was a regiment—the sixth—made up of gaucho horsemen and "very good" Negro infantrymen: "They called it, not the regiment of Mulattos and Blacks, but in Spanish 'the Regiment of Brownies and Darkies.' So as not to offend them." And in the Argentinian epic *Martín Fierro* "they are called 'men of humble color.' . . . Well, enough, enough. Let's read *Arthur Gordon Pym*" (p. 370).

Nacimento's Afro-Brazilian anxiety cannot, as it turns out, be relieved by the state of affairs elsewhere in South America. In contemporary Afro-Hispanic narratives, from Cubena's Afro-Panamanian *tremendismo* short stories to the Afro-Colombian novels of Arnoldo Palacios, the settings are graphically inhospitable.[53] Indeed, when Palacios' *Las estrellas son negras* (1971) sets about to demonstrate our disappearance thesis in what Restrepo-Millan tells us, correctly, is "la expresión immediata del dolor y la lucha y las gentes y el paisaje y el ambiente del Chocó,''[54] the unsparing and unromantically fierce narrative that results is as explicit a genocidal document as we can expect. "So many hungers," to borrow the title of Bhabani Bhattacharya's 1947 novel, are at work in Chocó[55]—just as they are in the Afro-Venezuelan world of Juan Pablo Sojo's Barlovento in *Nochebuena negra* (1943); in the Ecuadorian *tierra de negros*, the Esmeralda backwaters and half-emergent towns, of Adalberto Ortiz's *Juyungo* (1943); and in Manuel Zapata Olivella's Afro-Colombian setting and novel *Chambacú, corral de negros* (1963).[56] The intensity of Palacios' use of Chocó to illustrate the racial, psychopathological and dramatic implications of Paul Verghese's observation that "food is the primary requisite of human dignity; hunger debases and dehumanizes man" may be deduced from the cry that it forces from Restrepo Millán's review article in the *Suplemento Literario* of Bogota's *El Tiempo*. He notes, among other things, a state of affairs that is even more graphic than Haberly's somber speculation; we are, after all, in a world "donde el hombre se siente menos que el perro" ("where men are less than dogs"):

What a deep cry the character of the novel lets loose from within himself: "Ah, a town so small and inhabited by people below misery!"

And so that the phenomenon be more incredible, so much poverty, so much disgrace, reside and rot slowly on layers of gold and platinum!

What are the rulers and functionaries doing in their offices that they don't do anything to remedy such an inhumane and absurd situation? What are they waiting for? *That the last of those unfortunate people finally perish, in order that the lazy bureaucratic eyes never see again the repugnant spectacle that they offer? . . .* Or that they all one day run out of patience at the same time and that the delirium of rage be converted into a bloody, collective reality.[57]

Still, to see such narratives as Palacios' as a Nicholás Guillén–like *canción de los hombres perdidos* is to also introduce a revolutionary process of redefinition. And Derek Walcott is relevant here when he underscores, even if partially and too optimistically, the nexus of articulation, identity and historical survival:

What would save the New World Negro from servitude was the forging of a language that went beyond mimicry, a dialect which had the force of revelation as it invented names for things, one which finally settled on its own mode of reflection. . . . This, not merely the debt of history was his proper claim to the New World.[58]

Even more relevant, given our concerns here, and out of Surinam—that middle of the three Guianas, which with Venezuela form the upper northern ridge of South America—is J. G. A. Koenders and the mode of reflection and praxis that his 1946 *Foetoe-boi* publication "Wi Kondre" ("Our Land") gives us. Koenders fashions out of Surinam Creole, a language created after 1651 to serve as the mother tongue of Surinam slaves and as a contact between polyglot masters and slaves, an expression that does indeed have the force of revelation—to which is wedded a sense of history and labor that is not cavalier. He does so to arrive finally at an epigrammatic assertion of presence in "Meki we poti anu makandra *fu wi no tron figi futu*" ("Let us join hands *so that we don't become doormats*"): "By 'our land' we mean the land which is founded on the blood, sweat, and tears of our forefathers, the negroes who were brought from Africa, trapped like cockroaches in the beak of a chicken."[59]

In the final analysis, then, the *romance bárbaro* that Henrique Coelho Netto's *Rei Negro* so dramatically represents is, in effect, engaged in a contest of presence and absence with such a reading of mankind in history that we find in a Robert Hayden's "Middle Passage." Tragic but visionary, Hayden's epic focus is on "The deep immortal human wish,/the timeless will" that affirms a "Voyage through death/to life upon these shores" of the New World.[60] The need for such an angle of ascent is impeccable; and, pace the thrust of our opening epigraph, the purpose of such an exercise is not to be *merely* heroic.

NOTES

1. Robert Pring-Mill, preface to Pablo Neruda, *The Heights of Macchu Picchu*, trans. Nathaniel Tarn (New York: Farrar, Straus and Giroux, 1976), p. x.

2. Neruda, *Macchu Picchu*, pp. 57–59. Reference to this work will appear parenthetically in the text.

3. Michael Schneider, *Neurosis and Civilization: A Marxist/Freudian Synthesis* (New York: Seabury Press, 1975), p. 141.

4. Ibid.

5. Herman Lima writes that Coelho Netto was part Indian and part Portuguese: "Era mameluco, filho duma índia civilizada, Ana Silvestre, e dum negociante português, de poucas posses e algumas letras, Antônio da Fonseca Coelho." See his "Coelho Netto: As Duas Faces do Espelho," introduction to Coelho Netto's *Obra Seleta*, vol. 1, *Romances* (Rio de Janeiro: José Aguilar, 1958). Coelho Netto was born in 1864 and, João Neves da Fontoura tells us, "o sangue materno escaldar-lhe-ia o cérebro, o paterno dar-lhe-ia o acento melancólico, o sol subequatorial incendiara os seus primeiros racionínios" ("Discurso de Recepção," *Discursos Académicos* [Rio de Janeiro: Getulio M. Costa, 1938], p. X). Fred P. Ellison is somewhat precious on the issue of *mamelucos*: "The Portuguese, who have long been noted for their racial mobility, entered swiftly into the process of intermarriage. . . . The Portuguese colonizer apparently had few prejudices against the copper-colored native woman, whose nudity was often enhanced by liberal applications of red paint. From the very start there was a mix-blood or mestizo population known as *mamelucos*" (*Brazil's New Novel* [Berkeley and Los Angeles: University of California Press, 1954], p. 7). Netto died in 1934.

6. Gilberto Freyre, celebrated author of *Casa-Grande e Senzala* (Rio de Janeiro: Maia and Schmidt, 1933) is thus cited in Warren Hoge's profile, "Brazilian Author, Cosmopolitan in Land of Tradition," *New York Times*, June 2, 1980, p. 2. Freyre thus responds to criticism that his book is intellectually wanting and based on unscientific research.

7. David T. Haberly, "Abolitionism in Brazil: Anti-Slavery and Anti-Slave," *Luso-Brazilian Review*, 9, no. 2 (1972): 38–39.

8. See, for example, Barry Fatland's article, which begins: " 'You mean they're in hiding?' asks an elderly man in the audience. 'You can't say that so-and-so was disappeared!' objects a young English major. 'That's simply not proper English!' " See Fatland's " 'Disappeared': What Does It Mean?" in *USLA Reporter* 8, nos. 2 and 3 (1978). The publication is an official organ of the U.S. Committee for Justice to Latin American Political Prisoners.

9. Haberly, "Abolitionism," p. 24.

10. Ibid.

11. Derek Walcott, *Dream on Monkey Mountain and Other Plays* (New York: Farrar, Straus and Giroux, 1970), pp. 12–14.

12. Alejo Carpentier, *The Kingdom of This World*, trans. Harriet de Onís (New York: Collier Books, 1970), pp. 119–20.

13. Clementine Christos Rabassa proposes, "What may be termed the 'tertiary phase' of epic tradition is, then, a return to the spirit of the great examples of epic literature which reveal the essential concern for man's destiny while he stands in the midst of death and misery," in her *Demetrio Aguilera-Malta and Social Justice* (Rutherford, N.J.: Fairleigh Dickinson University Press, 1980), p. 31.

14. Ibid., p. 171.

15. Ellison, *Brazil's New Novel*, pp. 6–7.

16. Eduardo Galeano, *Open Veins of Latin America*, trans. Cedric Belfrage (New York: Monthly Review Press, 1973), pp. 74–75.

17. Coelho Netto, *Obra Seleta*, 1:1073. *Rei Negro* is the sixth novel, of seven, in volume 1, *Romances*. A French version, *Macambira*, was published in 1920. Citations will be from *Obra Seleta*, vol. 1, and will appear parenthetically in the text. I am grateful to Alexis Levitin for his translations into English of selected quotations from Coelho Netto's works.

18. Alfredo Bosi, *O Pre-Modernismo* (São Paulo: Editora Cultrix, 1967), p. 82.

19. Schneider, *Neurosis*, p. 23, emphasis added.

20. Jean Duvignaud, *The Sociology of Art*, trans. Timothy Wilson (New York: Harper and Row, 1972), p. 81.

21. Bosi, *O Pre-Modernismo*, p. 23.

22. Richard L. Jackson, *Black Writers in Latin America* (Albuquerque: University of New Mexico Press, 1979), p. 29.

23. See Haberly, "Abolitionism," p. 32.

24. Roger Bastide, *African Civilizations in the New World*, trans. Peter Green (New York: Harper and Row, 1971), p. 186.

25. Ibid., p. 187.

26. Jackson, *Black Writers*, p. 29.

27. See *Martín Fierro* (1879; reprint ed., Buenos Aires: Librería de A. García Santos, 1926), p. 303. Also in Bastide, *African Civilizations*, p. 187.

28. Raymond S. Sayers, *The Negro in Brazilian Literature* (New York: Hispanic Institute, 1956), p. 81.

29. Ellison, *Brazil's New Novel*, p. 12.

30. Bosi, *O Pre-Modernismo*, pp. 75, 80, 123, respectively.

31. I mean structurally, but, of course, not attitudinally or historically *ex machina*, given the experience of Australia's black Aboriginals in what was once their land. See, in this connection, the voices in *Living black: blacks talk to Kevin Gilbert* (London: Allen Lane, 1977). Also Thomas Keneally's *The chant of Jimmie Blacksmith* (New York: Viking Press, 1972), a most powerful novelization of the death-in-life fate of black Australia.

32. Nawal el Saadawi, *The Hidden Face of Eve*, trans. and ed. Sherif Hetata (London: Zed Press, 1980), p. i.

33. Personal correspondence. Gregory Rabassa, a fine and prolific translator, is also the author of *O negro na ficção Brasileira* (Rio de Janeiro: Edições Tempo Brasileiro, 1965).

34. Henrique Coelho Netto, *A Conquista* (Pôrto, Portugal: Lello e Irmão, 1928), p. 396.

35. Edward Said, *Orientalism* (New York: Vintage, 1978), p. 63.

36. Ibid., p. 27.

37. Ibid., p. 8.

38. Ibid.

39. Georg Wilhelm Friedrich Hegel, *Lectures on the Philosophy of World History, Introduction: Reason in History*, ed. Johannes Hoffmeister, trans. H. B. Nisbet (London: Cambridge University Press, 1980), pp. 172–73.

40. See K. P. Bahadur's *Love in the East* (Bombay: Jaico Publishing House, 1971),

when, using Burton's translation, he cites an incident of lovemaking from *The Arabian Nights*, "which has all its characteristic oriental violence." The incident is one in which "she came to me and took me, she tumbled me beneath her and rubbed me with astonishing passion, until all my soul rushed into a part of me which you can divine, my lord. I set to the work required of me, the work under my hand; I reduced that which was to be reduced, I broke that which there was to break, and ravished that which was to be ravished. I took what I might, I gave what I ought, I rose, I stretched, I drove in, I broke up, I plunged, I forced, I stuffed, I primed, I sank, I teased, I ground, I fell, and I went on again" (p. 84).

41. A good measure of this "Africa proper," and gothic, hallucination had been sustained throughout the novel in the old slave, Balbina; her consciousness provides the usual gateway into a darkly occult world of palm trees, enormous anthills, buffaloes and camels, warriors in feather headgear, and a warrior-king, Munza, who is periodically metamorphosed into Macambira. See, for example, page 1177, where ferocity, barbarism and cannibal yells coalesce in Balbina's vision of Munza overcoming an "agigantado e ferocissimo" enemy chief: "Via-o cair às mãos de Munza, via-o amarrado ao tranco de de um coqueiro e, em tôrno, em tripúdio, a gente negra brandindo os fimbos, fazendo estrondar os escudos às pranchadas das azagaias. Via-o sangrar talhado pelo ferro real, ouvia-o bramir à injúria dum escarro, golfar sangue do flanco a um pontaço de lança, por fim desaparecer no tumulto acirrado, e um momento, fimbos, zargunchas, azagaias ouriçando-se alaharem-no, alancearem-no, atassalharem-no e a dança cada vez mais confusa e frenética ao estridor barbáro da grita canibalesca." Balbina has this version of her recurrent visions of a *vitoria da raça* soon after she serves as midwife at the birth of Lúcia's *filho branco*.

42. Wilson Martins, *The Modernist Idea: A Critical Survey of Brazilian Writing in the Twentieth Century*, trans. Jack E. Tomlins (New York: New York University Press, 1971), p. 7.

43. We have already taken note of Hegel and "Africa proper." Houston A. Baker, Jr., discusses and explains Thomas Jefferson's criticism of black creativity in a partly "distillate" manner. See *The Journey Back: Issues in Black Literature and Criticism* (Chicago: University of Chicago Press, 1980) pp. 145–47. Thus, "without Anglo-Saxon blood in his veins, Jefferson implies, Ignacio Sancho scarcely stands a chance. The case is finally proved 'upon the pulses' " (p. 147). In *Liberty and Language* (New York: Oxford, 1979), Geoffrey Sampson explains, ingenuously, the problem of the support that Locke, in particular, is "alleged" to have given to the enslavement of Negroes: "But it seems clear that Locke in fact took the enslavement of negroes completely for granted—it probably never occurred to him that it raised a moral problem. . . . To the Englishman of the late seventeenth century, the facts on which this judgment are based were simply not available. . . . To Locke, negroes must have been almost as unknown as life-forms revealed by the Mars probes might be to us, and it seems merely anachronistic to accuse Locke of failing to acknowledge their right to be counted as fellow-humans" (pp. 134–35).

44. Cited from *The Gilberto Freyre Reader*, trans. Barbara Shelby (New York: Alfred A. Knopf, 1974), pp. 193–94.

45. See the preface to the second English-language edition of *The Masters and the Slaves* (1956), in *Freyre Reader*, pp. 156–57: "In northeastern Brazil the *banguê* was a variety of litter with leather top and curtains. The *tigre* was a vessel for the depositing and carrying away of fecal matter. *Compradismo* was a system of oligarchic nepotism"

(Translator's note). Moral passion and retrograde racism are also paradoxical poles that Bosi notes in their perhaps fiercer manifestation in Euclydes da Cunha: "*Os Sertões* são um livro de ciencia e de paixao, de analíse e de protesto: eis o paradoxo que assitiu à gênese daquelas páginas em que se alternam a certeza do fim das 'racas retrógradas' e a denúncia do crime que a carnificina de Canudos representou" (*O Pre-Modernismo*, p. 122).

46. Martins, *Modernist Idea*, p. 205.

47. Haberly, "Abolitionism," p. 42.

48. In *Journal of Black Studies* 7, no. 2 (1976):149. See also, in this connection, Edward Said on usurpation and identity: "Orientalism is premised upon exteriority, that is, on the fact that the Orientalist, poet or scholar, makes the Orient speak, describes the Orient, renders its mysteries plain for and to the West. . . . What he says and writes . . . is meant to indicate that the Orientalist is outside the Orient, both as an existential and as a moral fact. . . . The exteriority of the representation is always governed by some version of the truism that if the Orient could represent itself, it would; since it cannot, the representation does the job, for the West, and *faute de mieux*, for the poor Orient" (*Orientalism*, pp. 20–21). *Orientalism* thus notes, and expands, the implications of Marx's words in *The Eighteenth Brumaire of Louis Bonaparte*: "Sie konnen such nicht vertreten, sie mussen vertreten werden" (Said, *Orientalism*, epigraph, p. 21).

49. Florestan Fernandes, *The Negro in Brazilian Society*, trans. Jacqueline D. Skiles, A. Brunel and Arthur Rothwell; ed. Phyllis B. Eveleth (New York: Atheneum, 1971), p. 447.

50. "Abolitionism" ends on this most somber note.

51. Originally titled "*Racial Democracy*" in Brazil: *Myth or Reality?*, *O Genocídio* was rejected by the International Committee at FESTAC (Nigeria, 1976) for a symposium on "Black Civilization and Education." The Nigerian paper, the *Daily Sketch*, subsequently serialized the entire manuscript before publishing it in book form in 1977, with an introduction by Wole Soyinka. See *O Genocídio* (Rio de Janeiro: Editora Paz e Terra, 1978).

52. Paul Theroux, *The Old Patagonian Express* (Boston: Houghton Mifflin, 1979), p. 369. Reference to this work will appear parenthetically in the text.

53. It is the nature of things, perhaps, that this sense of urgency should be transformed by a Freyre into a kind of *costumbrista* lament for or romance of a vanishing, primitivist pageant: "Once the reconquest of Brazil by Europe began, it did not stop. Even today it overwhelms us, with the European of Europe now being substituted for by the quasi-European of the United States. The blond martyrs have triumphed in part, at least, in the battle joined in Brazil between the Nordics and the tropics. It was the yellow fever that was vanquished. And this reconquest brought about a change in the Brazilian scene in all its aspects. The re-Europeanization began by dimming the African, Asiatic, or indigenous elements in our life, whose bright colorfulness was typical of our landscape, attire, and habits" (*Freyre Reader*, p. 6). The approach obviously contrasts with Nascimento's recent collection of essays, *Mixture or Massacre: Essays in the Genocide of a Black People*, trans. Eliza Larkin Nascimento (Buffalo, N.Y.: Afrodiaspora, 1979), and with Leslie B. Rout, Jr. (see note 56, below).

54. J. M. Restrepo Millán's review article serves as preface to Arnold Palacios, *Las estrellas son negras* 2d ed. (Bogota: Revista Colombiana, 1971).

55. *So Many Hungers!*, perhaps *the* novel of the Asian subcontinent on the hunger theme, is "the story of the teeming millions . . . who have to face periodic outbursts

of hunger and famine, and encounter all the evil consequences flowing from such calamities." Shiv K. Jumar's observation is cited in S. Z. H. Abidi, *Kamala Markandaya's Nectar in a Sieve* (Bareilly: Prakash Book Depot, 1977), pp. 35–36.

56. See Jackson's *Black Writers of Latin America* for an introductory and comprehensive perspective on these and other writers. Leslie B. Rout, Jr., *The African experience in Spanish America, 1502 to the present day* (London: Cambridge University Press, 1976), is, of course, relevant here, given the urgency and themes of the writers that Jackson treats. In Theroux's journey "by train through the Americas" Limón crystalizes the black experience of Costa Rica: "Limón looked like a dreadful place. It had just rained, and the town stank. The station was on muddy road near the harbor, and puddles reflected the decayed buildings and over-bright lights. The smell of dead barnacles and damp sand, flooded sewers, brine, oil, cockroaches, and tropical vegetation which, when soaked, gives off the hot moldy vapor you associate with compost heaps in summer, the stench of mulch and mildew. It was a noisy town, as well: Clanging music, shouts, car horns. That last sight of the palmy coast and the breakers had been misleading. And even Mr. Thornberry, who had been hopeful, was appalled. I could see his face; he was grimacing in disbelief. 'God,' he groaned. 'It's a piss hole in the snow' " (*Patagonian Express*, p. 183). An appropriate enough metaphor, one notes. Theroux recalls, *"It's a white country*, a man had told me in San José. But this was a black town, a beachhead of steaming trees and sea stinks" (ibid.).

57. Restrepo Millán's review article echoes the graphic anguish and threat that one finds in the first and last stanzas of Guillén's "Canción de los hombres perdidos." Arnoldo Palacios, *Las estrellas son negras*. Editor's translation, emphasis added.

58. Walcott, *Dream*, p. 17.

59. *Creole Drum: Anthology of Creole Literature in Surinam*, ed. Jan Voorhoeve and Ursy M. Lichtveld, with English translations by Vernie A. February (New Haven and London: Yale University Press, 1975), pp. 138–39. "Around 1943 some women of the organization Pohama (short for *Potie hanoe makandra*, literally 'Join hands together')" enlisted Koenders' cooperation. "This organization tried to raise the poor from their inhuman conditions and stimulate them to aspire to greater heights. . . . *Foetoe-boi* ("Servant") was ostensibly a periodical put out by Pohama. It was regarded as Koenders' brainchild. . . . It was written in Dutch and Sranan Tongo. . . . Koenders addressed himself mostly to Blacks and to the inhabitants of the backyards of Parimaribo. He taught them to be proud of their skin, their history, their language, and their culture. . . . His favorite proverb, cited many times in *Foetoe-boi*, was: *Yu kan kibri granmama, ma yu no kan tapu kosokoso* ('You may hide your grandmother, but you cannot prevent her from coughing')" (*Creole Drum*, pp. 135–37).

60. Robert Hayden, *Angle of Ascent* (New York: Liveright, 1975), pp. 118–25.

Bibliographical Essay

Voices from Under: Black Narrative in Latin America and the Caribbean grew out of a need to fill a void in literary criticism. Of the many anthologies on black literature, most are limited to a country, a linguistic mode or the Caribbean. Of notable importance among the last group are James T. Livingston's *Caribbean Rhythms* (New York: Washington Square Press, 1974) and Casa de las Américas' bilingual edition of *Caribbean Stories: Barbados, Guyana, Jamaica, Trinidad-Tobago* (Havana: Casa de las Americas, 1977), which provide the much deserved publicity to West Indian nations. The content of these collections goes beyond the literatures of the individual countries. Like others, Livingston's *Caribbean Rhythms* gathers short stories and poetry but also includes essays and drama. Of the Caribbean anthologies Barbara Howes' *From the Green Antilles* (London: Souvenir Press, 1967) offers a wide range of writers and includes selections from the Spanish, French, English and Dutch Caribbean, in poetry, short story and novel. With a similar broad scope is José Luis González's and Mónica Mansour's *Poesía negra de América* (Mexico: Ediciones Era, 1976), which covers the Spanish, English, French and Portuguese languages; as the title indicates, its focus is poetry.

Although there are a number of anthologies regarding Blacks in history in Latin America and the Caribbean, of which Richard Price's *Maroon Societies* (New York: Doubleday, 1973) and David W. Cohen and Jack P. Greene's *Neither Slave nor Free* (Baltimore: Johns Hopkins University Press, 1972) come to mind, there is little in literary criticism. From an interdisciplinary and multidisciplinary approach, *Africa and the Caribbean: The Legacies of a Link*, eds. Margaret E. Crahan and Franklin W. Knight (Baltimore: The Johns Hopkins University Press, 1979) and *Comparative Perspectives on Slavery in New World Plantation Societies*, eds. Vera Rubin and Arthur Tuden (New York: The New York Academy of Sciences, 1977) bring together essays of different disciplines such as history, sociology, economics, art history and literature. Although these anthologies provide a welcomed perspective, they emphasize strongly the social sciences over the humanities. Of the few works published in literary criticism, Roberto González Echevarría's special issue of the *Latin American Literary Review* (vol. 8, no. 16 [1980]) is dedicated to Hispanic Caribbean literature and includes works of fiction in translation and essays. Miriam DeCosta's *Blacks in Hispanic Literature* (Port Washington, N.Y.: Kennikat Press, 1977) is the only attempt to view the theme of Blacks in literature beyond the confines of a particular country or region. It gathers essays from Spanish and Latin American literatures in both narrative and poetry. However, DeCosta's in-depth study of the literature of Spanish-speaking countries suggests that other non Spanish-speaking countries with similar black populations and histories have been omitted. Nevertheless, *Blacks in Hispanic Literature* represents a first step in providing a unified view of and about Blacks in an anthology of literary criticism. With a similar perspective are the proceedings of the yearly Afro-Hispanic Literature Symposium, which first met in June 1976, but its first volume corresponded to the 1977 meeting (*Studies in Afro-Hispanic Literature*, vol. 1 [1977]). The papers are gathered and edited by Clementine Rabassa and Gladys Seda-Rodríguez and, at times, include essays on Brazilian literature.

There are full-length studies that go beyond geographic and linguistic boundaries that must be mentioned. Some refer to Caribbean themes while others gather authors of different countries. Of the first group, one needs to cite G. R. Coulthard's *Race and Colour in Caribbean Literature* (London and New York: Oxford University Press, 1962). Originally published as *Raza y color en la literatura antillana* [Seville: Escuela de Estudios Hispano-Americanos de Sevilla, 1958]), Selwyn R. Cudjoe's *Resistance and Caribbean Literature* (Athens: Ohio University Press, 1980) and O. R. Dathorne's *Dark Ancestor: The Literature of the Black Man in the Caribbean* (Baton Rouge: Louisiana State University Press, 1981). As their titles suggest, these works approach Caribbean literature as a unity. In the second group, of importance are Lemuel Johnson's *The Devil, the Gargoyle, and the Buffoon: The Negro as Metaphor in Western Literature* (Port Washington, N.Y.: Kennikat Press, 1969), in which he studies the works of Langston Hughes, Nicólas Guillén and Aimé Césaire; and Martha Cobb's *Harlem, Haiti and Havana* (Washington, D.C.: Three Continents Press, 1979), in which she concentrates on the same linguistic areas and authors studied by Johnson except for Césaire, which she substitutes for Jacques Roumain.

Of particular importance are the works of Janheinz Jahn, which offer an analysis of the black theme in both Old and New World literatures, including the United States, in his *Muntu* (trans. Marjorie Grene [New York: Grove Press, 1958]) and *A History of Neo-African Literature* (trans. Oliver Coburn and Ursala Lehrburger [London, Faber and Faber, Ltd., 1968]). In recent years Richard Jackson has made important contributions to the study of Blacks in his *The Black Image in Latin American Literature* (Albuquerque: University of New Mexico Press, 1976) and *Black Writers in Latin America* (Albuquerque: University of New Mexico Press, 1979). Jackson looks at both established writers and important but not so well-known authors. Furthermore, there seems to be an implicit dialogue between Jahn and Jackson insofar as both critics' analyses go beyond the Caribbean and both question the status of the author: Jahn supports a criticism free of author's color, while Jackson does not, as the title of his latest book suggests. *Voices from Under* is the first attempt in comparative literature and criticism to bring unity to Latin America and the Caribbean by offering a wider approach to the image of Blacks by collecting essays from the Spanish, English and French Caribbean; Central America; and Spanish and Portuguese South America. This book aspires to serve as a model for other anthologies of literary criticism.

Index

About the Contributors

CAROL BEANE obtained her Ph.D. from the University of California at Berkeley. Beane has taught at Dartmouth College and Bryn Mawr College where she was also a Mellon Fellow. Presently, she is an Assistant Professor in the Department of Hispanic and Italian Studies at Brown University. Beane has written several articles on the Afro-Hispanic literature of Venezuela, Colombia, Ecuador and Peru and is preparing a book on character and spectacle in Afro-Hispanic literature.

JULIA CUERVO HEWITT was born in Cuba and received her Ph.D. from Vanderbilt University where she is an Assistant Professor in the Department of Spanish and Portuguese. She has written on Brazilian and Spanish American literature. Her articles have appeared in *Actas do I Congresso Internacional de Estudos Pessoanos, Cuban Studies/Estudios Cubanos* and *Luso-Brazilian Review*. She is the author of *Yoruba Presence in Contemporary Cuban Narrative*.

SELWYN R. CUDJOE was born in Trinidad and earned his Ph.D. in English at Cornell University. He has taught at Harvard, Cornell, Ohio and Fordham universities. He is a Contributing Editor of *Freedomways* and is the author of *Resistance and Caribbean Literature* and *Movement of the People: Essays on Independence*.

O. R. DATHORNE is a critic and writer who was born in Guyana and obtained his Ph.D. from the University of Sheffield, England. He read English at the universities of Sheffield and London and is Professor of English and Director of the Program in Caribbean, African and Afro-American Studies and of American Studies at the University of Miami. Dathorne has written widely on African, Afro-American and Caribbean literatures and has published many scholarly articles, short stories and poems. He is the author of numerous books which include *Dumpling in the Soup, The Scholar Man, The Black Mind: A*

History of African Literature, Dark Ancestor: The Literature of the Black Man in the Caribbean and *African Literature in the Twentieth Century.* Dathorne is also the founder of the Association of Caribbean Studies and Editor of the *Journal of Caribbean Studies.* His most recent novel is *Dele's Child.*

LISA E. DAVIS earned her Ph.D. in Comparative Literature from the University of Georgia. She has taught at the State University of New York at Stony Brook and York College and is presently employed by the Centro de Estudios Puertorriqueños and Hunter College. Her articles are published in *Comparative Literature, Sin Nombre, Cuadernos Hispanoamericanos,* and *Casa de las Américas.* Davis has translated Nancy Morejón's *Cuaderno de Granada/Grenada Notebook.* She is also Contributing Editor of the "Central American Prose Section" of the *Handbook of Latin American Studies.*

JOSEPH FERDINAND was born in Haiti and obtained his Ph.D. from Tufts University. He has taught at Vassar and the University of Vermont and is Assistant Professor in the Department of Modern Languages at St. Michael's College. Ferdinand is completing a book entitled "Gionisme et Panthéisme: la recréation de l'homme par Gean Giono." He is also editing an anthology on the complete works of the Haitian Regnor C. Bernard.

ROBERTO GONZALEZ ECHEVARRIA was born in Cuba and received his Ph.D. at Yale University where he is chairman of the Department of Spanish and Portuguese. He is the author of *Alejo Carpentier: The Pilgrim at Home, Relecturas, Calderón y la crítica, Isla a su vuelo fugitiva* and other books. González Echevarría's *The Voice of the Master: Writing and Authority in Modern Latin American Literature* will soon be published. He is a Guggenheim Fellow and his articles on Spanish, Latin American and Comparative Literature have appeared in numerous journals in Europe and America. He is also on the editorial board of many publications and is a member of the Advisory Board as well as contributing editor of the *Handbook of Latin American Studies.*

RICHARD L. JACKSON received his Ph.D. from Ohio State University and is Professor of Spanish at Carleton University in Ottawa, Canada. He has published in numerous journals and is the author of *The Black Image in Latin American Literature, Black Writers in Latin America* and *The Afro-Hispanic Author: An Annotated Bibliography of Criticism.* Jackson is currently writing a book on Black literature and humanism in Latin America.

LEMUEL A. JOHNSON is a critic and poet who was born in Sierra Leone and earned his Ph.D. at the University of Michigan where he is currently a Professor of English. He has also taught at Fourah Bay College, University of Sierra Leone. Johnson has published numerous poems and articles and is the author of *The Devil, the Gargoyle, and the Buffoon: The Negro as Metaphor in Western Literature, Hand on the Navel, Highlife for Caliban* and other books. His *Carnival of the Old Coast* will be published soon.

WILLIAM LUIS received his Ph.D. from Cornell University and is Assistant Professor in the Department of Spanish and Portuguese at Dartmouth College. He is Contributing Editor of the "Hispanic Caribbean Section" of the *Handbook of Latin American Studies*. He has written on nineteenth- and twentieth-century Latin American literature and his articles have appeared in *Latin American Literary Review, Cuadernos Americanos, Journal of Caribbean Studies, Cuban Studies/Estudios Cubanos, Linden Lane, The Afro-Hispanic Review,* and other publications. His latest work is on nineteenth- and twentieth-century Cuban slavery literature.

RONALD M. RASSNER is Director of the World Affairs Center and Associate Professor in the Department of Modern Languages and Literature and Comparative Literature at Beloit College. He holds a Ph.D. from the University of Wisconsin-Madison in African Languages and Literature and has taught at Yale, Northern Illinois University and the University of Wisconsin-Madison. His articles have appeared in *Critical Perspectives in Lusophone African Literatures, Research in African Literatures* and *The Oral Performance in Africa.* He is currently writing a book on oral narrative traditions from Brazilian *povoados isolados* and has been selected as a 1985 Fulbright Lecturer at the Universidade Federal de Pernambuco in Brazil.

JURIS SILENIEKS is Professor of French and Director of the Program in Modern Languages at Carnegie-Mellon University. He was born in Latvia and holds a Ph.D. in Romance Languages from the University of Nebraska. Silenieks has published a book on Armand Salacrou and numerous articles and reviews on the contemporary French theatre, Francophone Caribbean, African and Latvian literature. He edited Edouard Glissant's play *Monsieur Toussaint* and an anthology on *Contemporary Latvian Poetry.* He is a regular reviewer for *World Literature Today.*

JONATHAN TITTLER who received his Ph.D. from Cornell University is Associate Professor in the Department of Romance Studies at Cornell University. His published articles have appeared in journals such as *Chasqui, Crítica Hispánica, Diacritics, Hispania, Modern Language Notes* and *World Literature Today.* Tittler is also the author of *Narrative Irony in the Contemporary Spanish American Novel* and is co-translator with his wife Susan F. Hill of Adalberto Ortiz's *Juyungo.*